GW00696751

MY GOD, MY LAND

Anthropology and Cultural History in Asia and the Indo-Pacific

Series Editors:
Pamela J. Stewart and Andrew Strathern
University of Pittsburgh, USA

This series offers a fresh perspective on Asian and Indo-Pacific Anthropology. Acknowledging the increasing impact of transnational flows of ideas and practices across borders, the series widens the established geographical remit of Asian studies to consider the entire Indo-Pacific region. In addition to focused ethnographic studies, the series incorporates thematic work on issues of cross-regional impact, including globalization, the spread of terrorism, and alternative medical practices.

The series further aims to be innovative in its disciplinary breadth, linking anthropological theory with studies in cultural history and religious studies, thus reflecting the current creative interactions between anthropology and historical scholarship that are enriching the study of Asia and the Indo-Pacific region. While the series covers classic themes within the anthropology of the region such as ritual, political and economic issues will also be tackled. Studies of adaptation, change and conflict in small-scale situations enmeshed in wider currents of change will have a significant place in this range of foci.

We publish scholarly texts, both single-authored and collaborative as well as collections of thematically organized essays. The series aims to reach a core audience of anthropologists and Asian Studies specialists, but also to be accessible to a broader multidisciplinary readership.

Recent titles in the series

Aboriginal Family and the State
Sally Babidge
ISBN 978 0 7546 7935 6

Islamic Spectrum in Java
Timothy Daniels
ISBN 978 0 7546 7626 3

Collective Creativity
Art and Society in the South Pacific
Katherine Giuffre
ISBN 978 0 7546 7664 5

My God, My Land

Interwoven Paths of Christianity and Tradition in Fiji

JACQUELINE RYLE
The National Council of Churches in Denmark, Denmark

ASHGATE

Published by
Ashgate Publishing Limited
Wey Court East
Union Road
Farnham
Surrey, GU9 7PT
England

Ashgate Publishing Company
Suite 420
101 Cherry Street
Burlington
VT 05401-4405
USA

www.ashgate.com

British Library Cataloguing in Publication Data
Ryle, Jacqueline.
My God, my land : interwoven paths of Christianity and tradition in Fiji. -- (Anthropology and cultural history in Asia and the Indo-Pacific)
1. Christianity--Fiji. 2. Christianity and culture--Fiji.
3. Christianity and other religions--Fiji. 4. Fiji--Religion. 5. Fiji--Church history. 6. Fiji--Social life and customs.
I. Title II. Series
261'.099611-dc22

Library of Congress Control Number: 2010924841

ISBN 9780754679882 (hbk)
ISBN 9780754699705 (ebk)

Mixed Sources
Product group from well-managed forests and other controlled sources
www.fsc.org Cert no. SA COC-1565
© 1996 Forest Stewardship Council

Printed and bound in Great Britain by
MPG Books Group, UK

Contents

List of Maps and Figures

Maps

Figures

Series Editors' Preface
Woven Histories and
Inter-Denominational Anthropology

Pamela J. Stewart and Andrew Strathern[1]

Jacqueline Ryle's complex and subtly interwoven account of Christian practices and the histories of Christian institutions in Fiji is indicative of the tremendous influence of religious change in the overall workings of change experienced by Fijians today and in the past. As scholars who are also extensively involved in this arena of research in the Pacific, and as Series Editors for Ashgate, we were pleased to have read and commented on successive drafts of this work, to have assisted with the peer review process, and to have worked with Dr. Ryle to achieve the final form of her manuscript. We were glad to have encouraged her book project from the beginning, seeing in it the many contributions Dr. Ryle brings to her themes.

Her ethnography deals with Methodist, Pentecostal, Catholic, Anglican, and Inter-Faith practices and dialogues, with classic questions of change and continuity, and illuminates the layering of these practices in space and time as well as their topical foci. Previously published work on Fiji by Martha Kaplan, John Kelly, Christina Toren, Matt Tomlinson, and Karen Brison (all referred to by Ryle) has convincingly shown the pervasive and diverse facets of Christian practices. Ryle has added to this existing corpus by plunging in depth into various fields of social relations among different denominations and relating her whole account to the

---

1   Dr. Pamela J. Stewart (Strathern) and Prof. Andrew Strathern are a husband and wife research team in the Department of Anthropology, University of Pittsburgh, and are, respectively, Visiting Research Fellow and Visiting Professor, Department of Anthropology, University of Durham, England. They are also Research Associates in the Research Institute of Irish and Scottish Studies, University of Aberdeen, Scotland, and have been Visiting Research Fellows at the Institute of Ethnology, Academia Sinica, Taipei, Taiwan during parts of 2002, 2003, 2004, 2005, 2006, 2007, 2008 and 2009. They have published over 38 books and over 200 articles on their research in the Pacific, Asia (mainly Taiwan), and Europe (primarily Scotland and Ireland). Their most recent co-authored books include *Witchcraft, Sorcery, Rumors, and Gossip* (Cambridge University Press, 2004); and Self and Group: Kinship in Action (in preparation with Prentice Hall). Their recent co-edited books include *Exchange and Sacrifice* (Carolina Academic Press, 2008) and *Religious and Ritual Change: Cosmologies and Histories* (Carolina Academic Press, 2009). Their most recent research and writing is on the topics of Cosmological Landscapes, farming and conservation practices, minority languages and identities, Religious Conversion, Ritual Studies, and Political Peace-making (their webpage is www.pitt.edu/~strather).

broader narratives of the nation and its regional and global entanglements. She is able to bring out how the members of the different Churches view one another and how they attempt to attain a unity of perspective; how also they seek to contribute to the problems of inter-community relations between the indigenous Fijians and the Indo-Fijian population. In general, her work is deeply informed by a dual recognition of the importance of history and the significance of contemporary, participant-observation based, ethnography.

Among the many notable ways in which Ryle's work deepens the study of Christianity in Fiji, and elsewhere, we pick out just a few here for comment. First, she has given us a careful review of much of the burgeoning literature on the problem of continuity and change in relation to Christianity and 'custom' in the Pacific. (This is an arena in which we have ourselves published widely, see, for example, Stewart and Strathern 1997, 1998, 2000a, 2000b, Strathern and Stewart 2000, 2004, and more recently our edited volume *Religious and Ritual Change*, Stewart and Strathern 2009, which includes a review of much of the literature on this topic in our Introduction, Strathern and Stewart 2009a). Dr. Ryle acknowledges, as others have done, the complexities and paradoxes involved here. One important clue is to consider the analytical problem itself in historical terms; not in terms of the anthropologist's project of analysis, but in terms of the people's own projects of self-realisation. Very striking in Ryle's discussion is her exposition of the ways in which the Methodist Church has come to base itself on the Fijian idea of *vanua*, the land. This is a rhetorical trend indicative of the Methodists' long historical engagement with, and experience of, indigenous Fijian society and its values: an effort to harness these values to a Christian way of life, and literally to ground that Christian way of life on an ideology of continuity. In the volume mentioned above that we have previously co-edited on a whole range of comparable topics handling evidence from the South-West Pacific and Taiwan, we have signalled the kinds of process involved here by noting that 'continuity hides in change; change hides in continuity' (Stewart and Strathern 2009). Assertions of continuity are bridging devices, joining past and present; assertions of change are rupturing devices, separating past and present. There is a dialectic between these devices, based on the fluctuating and conditional desires of different generations of people with regard to the directions in their life. In this case the early historical arrival of the Methodists eventuated in policies that over time 'traditionalised' the Church by pulling into it the values of the vanua, the homeland. Vanua means homeland, but it also means local territory, so that, in one sense, it can refer to the land of the whole indigenous nation, while in another sense it refers to the locally exclusive territory. Vanua thus itself bridges the local and the national, bringing them together. When the Assemblies of God first came, much later, in the 20th century, its exponents chose the pathway of rupture rather than continuity; rupture, that is, associated with pangs of renewal, expressed in the ideology of being 'born again'. Local rootedness was pitched against new globalising influences; and, in so far as people's affiliations may have been based on embodied experience rather than niceties of doctrine and doctrinal difference, new ritual forms of expression came into vogue. Coming later, and finding Methodists (and also Catholics and other Churches) already ensconced, the Pentecostalists sought, as they have done almost everywhere, to counterpoise themselves against the established Christian forms and to arrogate to themselves the appellation of Christians. The opposition of Christian versus 'heathen' was replaced by Pentecostalists versus other Churches. Pentecostalists thus intrinsically embraced the notion of conflict among Churches themselves. As Ryle points out, the 'born again' mentality also stresses the individual's relations with God through Jesus the Saviour figure. But Pentecostalists also make their own collective networks and communities of interest and commitment that strongly channel individual behaviour and conduce to a specific denominational in-group mentality. In this regard, like the Methodists, they may appropriate a valuable piece of 'tradition': the ideology of sharing, whether practised between kin or co-religionists (see, e.g. Brison 2008).

By studying, and involving herself, in the different ritual practices of the various church congregations, Ryle was able to refine her understandings of how ritual action may be efficacious. She notes, for example, the bodily effect of 'opening up' and 'surrender' that singing with arms uplifted may engender among Pentecostalists. Participation in such ritual acts can produce certain emotional effects without any specific ideologies or beliefs being attached to the acts; but the positive sensations induced by the actions may conduce further to the acceptance of the liturgically encoded representations that the leaders of church services express, linking the visceral, or embodied, domain to the cognitive world, in a way analogous to Thomas Csordas's distinction between the pre-objective (experiential) and the objectified (cultural, liturgical) domains (Csordas 1997). Ryle's focus on embodiment thus contributes strongly to this dimension of anthropological analysis.

The Catholic Church has devised its own ways of bringing together 'tradition' and its religious messages of salvation and healing. The relatively new Catholic doctrine of 'inculturation' specifically seeks ways in which local cultural forms can be harnessed to Christian purposes. (Indeed, one may reasonably argue that such an idea has belonged to Catholic practices long before this inculturation doctrine came about, at least at popular levels, with the assimilation of saints to local landscape features such as grottos and wells.) In Taiwan, among the indigenous Austronesian Paiwan people, we found the Paiwan motifs had been ingeniously incorporated into the decorations of a particular Catholic church (Strathern and Stewart 2009b). Ryle notably discusses Catholic processes of healing that link further conceptually with the politically and emotionally charged issues of forgiveness and reconciliation following the various coups in Fiji and the inter-related general questions of conflicts between the indigenous Fijians and Indo-Fijians. Ryle concludes her complexly woven narrative and analyses with a thoughtful and searching exploration of questions of forgiveness and reconciliation in the Fijian polity and the possible place of the use of traditional rituals, the healing of memories, and the promotion of ecumenism and inter-faith dialogues in such a difficult process. She interestingly problematises the conceptual bases of forgiveness and reconciliation as such – what can possibly create the conditions for them? Here, as elsewhere, religious ideas and practices can provide the foundations for either conflict or reconciliation. In the Pentecostalist vision of spiritual warfare, tinged with millenarian overtones, it is necessary to define enemies that must be defeated, thus reincorporating the idea of witches and sorcerers back into the contemporary world view. We find this situation everywhere, as much today for example in Papua New Guinea and parts of Northern Ireland as in Fiji. Ancestors become 'devils' and a part of the influence of the 'Devil', and sickness is seen as coming from the Devil rather than as an enigma or a punishment from a just Deity. In such a scenario, peacemaking would be a different exercise from one in which the ancestors were still held to retain some positive, nurturant qualities and could contribute to aspects of reconciliation between groups.

Dr. Ryle's deeply thoughtful and densely described and theorised discussions in her book make a significant contribution to the weaving of a Pacific history, like the creation of a ceremonial mat, and its presentation to her readers is a gift within the framework of what we have called here in our own title inter-denominational anthropology.

Cromie Burn Research Unit and Oatspur Research Group,
University of Pittsburgh
August 2009
PJS and AJS

References

Brison, Karen 2008. *Our Wealth is Loving Each Other: Self and Society in Fiji*. Lanham MD: Lexington Books.

Csordas, Thomas 1997. *The Sacred Self: A Cultural Phenomenology of Charismatic Healing*. Berkeley, CA: University of California Press.

Stewart, Pamela J. and Andrew Strathern (eds) 1997. *Millennial Markers*. Townsville, Australia: JCU-Centre for Pacific Studies.

Stewart, Pamela J. and A.J. Strathern 1998. Life at the End: Voices and Visions from Mt. Hagen, Papua New Guinea. *Zeitschrift für Missionswissenschaft und Religionswissenschaft* 82(4): 227-244.

Stewart, Pamela J. and Andrew Strathern (eds) 2000a. Millennial Countdown in New Guinea. *Ethnohistory* Special Issue 47(1): 3-27, Durham, N.C.: Duke University Press.

Stewart, Pamela J. and Andrew J. Strathern 2000b. Fragmented Selfhood: Contradiction, Anomaly and Violence in Female Life-Histories. In Stewart, Pamela J. and Andrew Strathern (eds), *Identity Work: Constructing Pacific Lives*. ASAO (Association for Social Anthropology in Oceania) Monograph Series No. 18. University of Pittsburgh Press, pp. 44-57.

Stewart, Pamela J. and Andrew Strathern (eds) 2009. *Religious and Ritual Change: Cosmologies and Histories*. Durham, N.C.: Carolina Academic Press.

Strathern, Andrew J. and Pamela J. Stewart 2000. Further Twists of the Rope: Ongka and Ru in a transforming world. In Stewart, Pamela J. and Andrew Strathern (eds), *Identity Work: Constructing Pacific Lives*. ASAO (Association for Social Anthropology in Oceania) Monograph Series No. 18. University of Pittsburgh Press, pp. 81-98.

Strathern, Andrew and Pamela J. Stewart 2004. *Empowering the Past, Confronting the Future, The Duna People of Papua New Guinea*. For, Contemporary Anthropology of Religion Series, New York: Palgrave Macmillan.

Strathern, Andrew and Pamela J. Stewart 2009a. Introduction: A Complexity of Contexts, a Multiplicity of Changes. In, Stewart, Pamela J. and Andrew Strathern (eds) (2009) *Religious and Ritual Change: Cosmologies and Histories*. For, Ritual Studies Monograph Series, Durham, N.C.: Carolina Academic Press, pp. 3-68.

Strathern, Andrew and Pamela J. Stewart 2009b. History, Conversion, and Politics: Three Case Studies from Papua New Guinea. In, Stewart, Pamela J. and Andrew Strathern (eds) (2009) *Religious and Ritual Change: Cosmologies and Histories*. For, Ritual Studies Monograph Series, Durham N.C.: Carolina Academic Press, pp. 309-328.

Fijian Orthography and Pronunciation

B	(mb)	bure	as in 'ramble'	(mbuhreh)
C	(th)	Cakobau	as in 'thou'	(Thakohmbau)
D	(nd)	dalo	as in 'indifferent'	(ndaaloh)
G	(ng)	Sigatoka	as in 'sing'	(Singatokka)
J	(ch)	Jale	as in 'Charlie'	(Chahleh)
Q	(nq)	yaqona	as in 'young'	(yangkohna)

For the people of Fiji who shared their faith and stories with me.

Acknowledgements

The anthropological research for this book spans the years 1993-2009. Over five fieldwork trips of 1, 4, 2, 10 and 5 months I conducted 22 months of doctoral fieldwork (1993-1998) and 10 months of post-doctoral fieldwork (2002-2004) over three fieldwork trips. In 2005 and early 2006 additional research was conducted in conjunction with my position as lecturer in anthropology at The Pacific Regional Seminary in Suva.

My doctoral research at School of Oriental and African Studies (SOAS), University of London, was generously funded by The Danish Development Research Council, DANIDA (1995-98), HRH Crown Prince Frederik's Foundation, Denmark (1995) and The Danish Research Academy. Additional fieldwork funding was granted by Knud Højgaard's Foundation, Denmark (1995); Central Research Council, University of London (1995); and SOAS Additional Fieldwork Award (1995). A Danish Humanities Research Council post-doctoral position at University of Copenhagen (2002-2005) with additional fieldwork funding enabled me to conduct new research in Fiji and update my existing data.

I thank the late Very Revd Jabez Bryce, Archbishop of the Anglican Province of Aotearoa New Zealand and Pasifika for permission to use the illustrations by Robert Park from the St John's Training Centre booklets published by the Diocese of Polynesia in 1988 and 1989. I thank Revd Dr Mika Paunga, Pacific Regional Seminary, for permission to cite from his 16 September 2005 homily; Patrick Woria SM, Solomon Islands student, Pacific Regional Seminary, for allowing me to quote from his 2005 first year exam paper; Dr Mike Monsell-Davis for permission to quote from his paper 'Youth and Social Change in the Pacific'; Prof. Konai Thaman for permission to reproduce her poem, 'Letter to the Colonel' (Thamen 1997); Nikhat Shameem for permission to reproduce her poem, 'Anomie' (Shameem 1997); the Very Revd Dr Winston Halapua for permission to quote from his book *Waves of God's Embrace* (Halapua 2008); and Netani Rika, Editor-in-Chief of the *Fiji Times,* for permission to use the *Fiji Times* quote in the Introduction and for permission to reproduce the *Fiji Times* photo in Chapter 7. I thank Continuum for permission to quote from Jonathan Sacks' (2002) *The Dignity of Difference* and Simon & Schuster UK for permission to quote from Indra Sinha's (2002) *The Death of Mr Love*. I am most grateful to Prof. R. Gerard Ward, Dr Bill Clarke and the Australian National University Cartography Unit for the excellent maps that were drawn up for me in 2001. And I thank Hawaii University Press for permission to reproduce the modified version of Map 3 from B. Lal (1992) *Broken Waves: a History of Fiji in the Twentieth Century* (Honolulu: Hawaii University Press). Earlier versions of certain sections in Chapters 1 and 5 formed part of an article in *International Journal for the Study of the Christian Church* (Ryle 2005a) and an early version of Chapter 3 was published in *Domodomo*, The Fiji Museum Quarterly (Ryle 2000).

I thank the Fiji Government for research permission, and the late Professor Asesela Ravuvu and Dr Elise Huffer, formerly Institute of Pacific Studies, University of the South Pacific, and Kate Vusoniwailala, former director of The Fiji Museum, for research association. Many thanks also to Margaret Patel, former head of the National Archives of Fiji. I am grateful to the former Research School of Pacific and Asian Studies, Australian National University, for permission to use ANU House in Suva, my Fiji base for over a decade. R. Gerard Ward, Greg Fry, Solrun Williksen and Lucy de Bruce, amongst many others, all stayed at ANU House between 1993-2005, each contributing in different ways to my research, for which I thank them, thanks also to Linda Crowl, and especially to Bill Clarke.

I thank Professors Nicolas Peterson and Francesca Merlan, Dept. of Archaeology and Anthropology, Australian National University, for granting me Departmental Visitor status for numerous visits between 1993 and 1998; and Nick Thomas, Christina Toren and Ton Otto for assistance and advice over the years; to the late Aubrey Parke for all his advice and for sharing his knowledge and experience of Fiji; to Heather McDonald in particular; Ingrid Slotte, Keiko Tamura, Chris Watson, Aileen Toohey; Margaret Burns, departmental secretary Kathy Callen, and Christine Weir.

Contracting glandular fever in Fiji in November 1995, which developed into ME/CFS, radically changed the way I was able to work in the field. The classic village study I had envisaged became untenable, and the time I spent in the village (and in Fiji) was necessarily broken up into shorter periods, and I ended up spending more time than expected in the capital of Suva. However, my research focus on connecting what was happening at the local level with broader, national processes necessitated an engagement with different field sites, and what came to be an even more multi-sited fieldwork than anticipated gave me a nuanced and multi-layered picture of Christianity and tradition in Fiji. The pattern my fieldwork took on of drawing back from and re-entering the field several times also had its own methodological and analytical qualities.

Vina valevu to the people of Naroro village, Nadrogā, for their hospitality and generosity towards me – in particular to *Bua Levu* and *Lewa,* to Nadrukoboto household, especially to my sister Merelita, to Valivalileka household, and to family members in Korotogo.

Vinaka sara vakalevu to *Tata* Paulo Tiko and *Nana* Salanieta from Lavena, Taveuni Island, and family members from Fatima village, Taveuni, for taking me into the family from the time of my first days in Fiji in 1993 – to *taciqu* Marica, Aborosio, Katarina, Veronika, Seini, Ioani, *luvequ* Levi and *taciqu* Nau.

I owe a tremendous debt to Paul Geraghty, University of the South Pacific, for invaluable advice and assistance from my first day in Fiji until the final corrections of this book, for always so generously and cheerfully sharing his illimitable knowledge of Fijian linguistics and All Things Fijian, and especially for his extensive and very useful comments on an earlier version of Chapter 3;

to Mrs Sainimere Niukula for all her help and engagement in my work, and to Jone Niukula. I thank Mrs Inise Koroi, formerly of Institute of Fijian Language and Culture; the late Kwalevu Bulou Eta for the honour of two memorable visits; the late Adi Kuini Bavadra and Clive Speed for warm hospitality, and David Routledge for lunches at a difficult time in my village fieldwork. I thank Pastor Ratu Meli Navuniyasi for his high quality transcription and translation work and many inspiring hours of discussion; Mrs Jean Costello for excellent transcriptions. I thank Aliti Vunisea, USP, for research assistance in 1998; and I thank Manfred Ernst. Many thanks to Father Denis Mahony SM and other Marist priests who were most helpful in assisting in analysing the Naiserelagi frescoes, and to Father Pat McCaffrey SSC and Mariselo Natui SSC for transcribing and translating the Hindi text in Chapter 7.

For their generosity in so readily giving me their time and sharing their thoughts, theological knowledge and faith with me in conversation and interviews I thank, in alphabetical order: Reverend Father Seluini 'Akau'ola SM, Marist College; Anaseini and Aselemo, Pius X Roman Catholic parish, Suva; Paulo Balei, Columban Mission; Reverend Tevita Nawadra Banivanua, SPATS; Reverend Dr Joe Bush, Pacific Theological College; Bishop Jabez Bryce, the Anglican Diocese of Polynesia; Father Feremo Cama, Dean, Holy Trinity Anglican Cathedral; members of the Holy Trinity Anglican Men's Group in 1998; Aisake Casimira, ECREA; Clancy, Trinity Broadcast Network; Father Pat Colgan SSC; Very Reverend Veremo Dovarua, Pacific Regional Seminary; Reverend Dr. Bruce Deverell, St Andrews Presbyterian Church, Suva and Interfaith Search Fiji; Pastor Ralph Dunn, First Church, Assemblies of God; Sister Emi Oh, Fiji Council of Churches; Reverend John Garrett; Sister Bertha Hurley, SMSM, Interfaith Search Fiji; Reverend Ledua Kacimaiwai, Association of Christian Churches in Fiji and Fiji Council of Churches; Kalini; Father Beniamino Kaloudau, Vicar-General, the Roman Catholic Diocese of Suva; Reverend Josateki and Mrs Nola Koroi; Reverend Jone Langi, General Secretary, Methodist Church in Fiji; Reverend Sereima Lomaloma, Holy Trinity Anglican Cathedral; Tessa Mackenzie, Interfaith Search Fiji; Reverend Poate Mata, Apostolic Gospel Outreach; Archbishop Petero Mataca, Roman Catholic Diocese of Suva; Reverend Jovili Meo, Pacific Theological College; Brother Mika, St Xavier's Roman Catholic Parish, Ra; Mere Momoivalu, Richard Naidu & Mika Mudreilagi, *Power Magazine*; Debby Mue, Wesley Church, Butt St; Sereana Nasome, Wesley Church Butt. St; Father John Rea SM, Lamb of God Christian Covenant Community, New Zealand Aeoteroa; Sereana Nasome, Wesley Church, Butt St; Mr Hardayal Singh, Interfaith Search Fiji; Reverend Aloesi Suguta, Assemblies of God; Reverend Dr. Andrew Thornley, Pacific Theological College; Reverend Dr Koru Tiko, Pacific Regional Seminary; Father George Ting, Our Lady of Fatima Roman Catholic parish; Dale Tonawai, the late Reverend Mesake Tuima, Royal Fiji Military Forces; Lusia Tukidia, St Agnes Roman Catholic Parish; Father Iosefo Tuvere, Sacred Heart Roman Catholic Cathedral; Reverend Dr Ilaitia Sevati Tuwere, President, Methodist Church in Fiji;

Tauga Vulaono; Meli Waqa, Reverend Akuila Yabaki, Citizens' Constitutional Forum, Bruce Yocum, Sword of the Spirit, Ann Arbor, USA; Yvonne.

Many thanks to Pastor Suli (Reverend Suliasi Kurulo), Christian Mission Fellowship, for engaging so readily with me in several inspiring interviews and conversations between 1998 and 2004, for his and Nau Mere's generous hospitality towards me, and for the warm welcome of the CMF Namadi Heights cell group. The 2005 Year 1 and Year 2 Pacific Island seminarians I taught at Pacific Regional Seminary, and many others there, contributed to this book by enriching my knowledge and understanding of their different Island cultures and the contemporary issues facing their peoples, in anthropology class discussions, written papers and in much valued *talanoa*.

For innumerable anthropological discussions over lunch at The Cottage, help and friendship over the years I thank Father Kevin J. Barr, MSC. Father Sulio Turagakacivi of Our Lady of Fatima parish, Reverend Dr Donal McIlraith SSC and Father Michael McVerry SM. I thank Sione Makasiale, Holy Trinity Anglican Cathedral, for inspirational faith, friendship and support; Father Cama, Mari and everyone at Holy Trinity Anglican Cathedral and the Bishop's Office; to the Sunday afternoon charismatic congregation at Wesley Church, Butt St for making me feel so welcome; to Malinda Tukidawa, Pita Tuisawau and members of the Patmos Christian Covenant Community for all their warm hospitality. Many thanks to Sister Ina M. Dau SOLN, Reverend Rosalyn Nokise, Reverend Alan Gibson CM for their friendship. Very special thanks to Kasanita Serevatu, Christian Mission Fellowship, and Fiona Vamarasi, Assemblies of God, for friendship and for kindly contributing written testimonies.

Ekholm and Friedman's (1985) 'Towards a Global Anthropology', Jonathan Friedman's inspiring course on 'representation' in Oceania at the height of the 'politics of tradition' debate, and my research in 1990 on Aboriginal representations of Aboriginal culture to Australian schoolchildren (Ryle 1996) sparked my initial interest in local/global interconnections and representations in time and space. I am grateful to Joel Robbins for his generosity in moving my manuscript towards publication, and to Pamela Stewart and Andrew Strathern for their insightful and constructive editorial advice.

I thank John Peel for incisive supervision of my PhD. I am indebted to Niels Kastfelt for his all generosity, time and inspiration over the past ten years. Many thanks also to Simon Coleman, Michael D. Jackson, Inger Sjørslev, Bob Norton, Eta Varani, Sai Niukula, Father John Bonato SM, Father Kevin Barr MSC, Father Denis Mahony SM, Father Paul Marx OMI, Father Thomas Mathew Nechikat OSA, Guillermo Kerber, David Routledge, Chris Gregory, Jens Peter Munk and Martin Lindhardt for help and advice and for reading and commenting on chapters. I also thank Father A. Ziggelaar SJ, Krzysztof Augustniak SJ, Father Benny Mathew CSsR, Father Lars Messerschmidt, Father Daniel Nørgaard, Flemming Røgilds, Gwendoline and Yannick Fer, Jens Peter Søltoft, Michael Voss and Oliver Larsen. Very special thanks to Ingeborg Nielsen for her work with the illustrations and help with so much else, and to my godmother, Else Schou-Nielsen. I am grateful to the sisters of Sacred Heart Convent, Sweden and Our Lady of Aasebakken convent for providing me with sanctuary during my writing. And I thank my friends for their support and sustained belief in this project.

I owe two people in particular my deepest thanks: Father Denis Mahony SM in Fiji and my parish priest in Copenhagen, Father Niels Engelbrecht, for their never-failing presence, each in different ways continuously encouraging me to stay focused and keep going, despite all obstacles on the way.

Copenhagen, April 2010

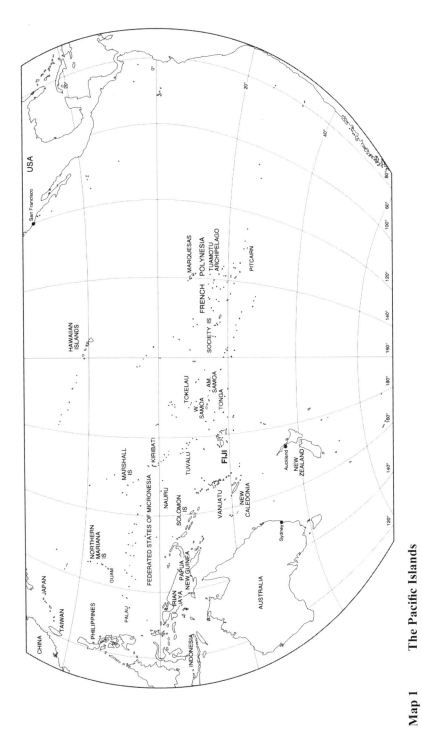

Map 1   **The Pacific Islands**

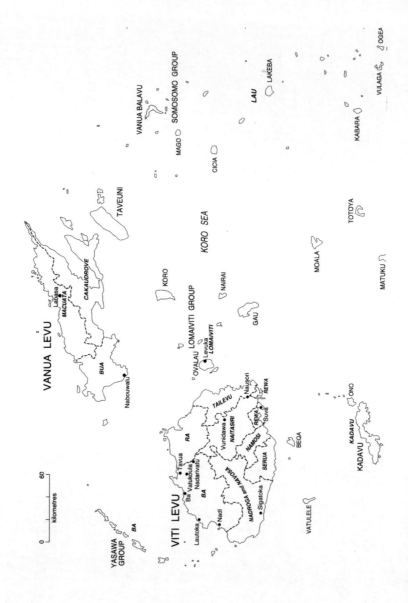

Map 2   Fiji Islands

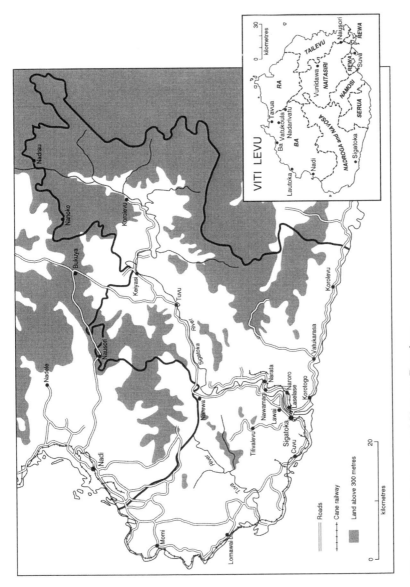

Map 3   Nadrogā and Navosa Province

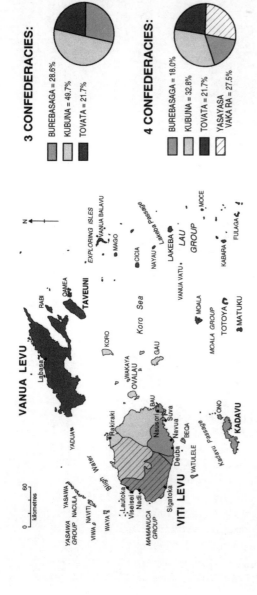

3 CONFEDERACIES:

- BUREBASAGA = 28.6%
- KUBUNA = 49.7%
- TOVATA = 21.7%

4 CONFEDERACIES:

- BUREBASAGA = 18.0%
- KUBUNA = 32.8%
- TOVATA = 21.7%
- YASAYASA VAKA RA = 27.5%

Percentage values represent the population of each confederacy as compared to the national total. Data were compiled from the 1986 Census of Fiji.

PROVINCES INCLUDED IN EACH CONFEDERACY:

BUREBASAGA

Rewa
Kadavu
Serua/Namosi
Nadroga/Navosa
Parts of Ba
Parts of Yasawa

KUBUNA

Tailevu
Ra
Lomaiviti
Naitasiri
Parts of Ba
Parts of Yasawa

TOVATA

Lau
Cakaudrove
Bua
Macuata

YASAYASA VAKA RA*

Ba
Yasawa
Nadroga
Parts of Navosa
Parts of Ra
Parts of Serua
Parts of Namosi

Map 4   Fijian Confederacies

Source: University of Hawaii Press.

Prologue
The Dust of Creation

'*Jehru*', said the young Methodist minister (*talatala*) 'is the Hebrew word for "foundation" and part of the word Jerusalem'. It was evening and Talatala Viliame, assistant minister in a neighbouring village, who had been in our village to conduct a funeral, had been invited to join an informal kava-drinking session with members of the Methodist Youth Fellowship in one of the village houses. Still dressed in his black *sulu vakataga*, the Fijian 'kilt' with pockets, white shirt, black tie and black jacket that Methodist pastors and preachers usually wear, he was sitting in the somewhat isolated position of a high-ranking guest of the house. He was positioned at the hierarchically 'highest' place in the living room at the 'highest' end of a large woven mat which covered most of the floor. Accepting intermittent servings of kava he was exchanging comments with a group of youths sitting hierarchically 'further down' on the mat, telling stories, joking, and drinking.

Tall, light-skinned and from the politically powerful eastern province of Cakaudrove, Reverend Viliame held his sermons in the Bauan dialect, also known as Standard Fijian, but which was almost a different language from the dialect spoken by the villagers which very few people outside the Nadrogā area understand. With his eastern ancestry and valued position, his pale skin, height, good looks and authoritarian demeanour, he was considered a handsome and highly eligible bachelor in the area, and the young women of the village agreed that he was very *uro* (handsome, sweet, sexy).

I was sitting cross-legged on the mat, close to the minister, yet at a respectful distance, in a 'lower' hierarchical position. It was early on in my fieldwork. Reverend Viliame was explaining his sermon of the previous Sunday to me – I had not been able to record it as the battery of my microphone had run out at the last minute. In fact, I found that I was being given less of an explanation and more of a repeat of his sermon. He spoke slowly and clearly, in a mixture of Fijian and English for my benefit, repeating his points several times, as is the style of Fijian Methodist preachers, holding my gaze firmly as he expounded in a rather loud voice what felt like an uncomfortably personal sermon. While his style made it possible for me to write excellent notes, I felt as if I were at Sunday School, rather than conducting an interview, and that I might at any minute be tested. I had hoped to discuss these things quietly and discreetly at the edge of this informal gathering and felt embarrassed that we had instead become the focal point of attention.

'*Jehru* is the Hebrew word for "foundation", and part of the word Jerusalem', Reverend Viliame repeated. 'If there is no y*avu* (foundation; house mound)', he continued, 'there can be no house. *Yavu* is our beginning; the beginning of life. We have to ask one question: where do I come from? *Dela ni yavu* (lit. place of the house mound): that is your beginning. See Genesis ch. 1-2; there are two stories of creation: God created human beings from dust, from soil (*qele*) ... [from] *vanua* and *qele. Vanua* and *yavu* are connected. They were the beginning of humanity'.

'Dust', Reverend Viliame said, accepting another cup of kava. 'If a truck runs on a dirt road you will see the dust at the back of the truck ... the wind blows that dust away ... Dust means nothing. Humanity is nothing. If humanity was created from dust ... it is where the man and the woman came from ... and where they go back to ... After forming the breath of life given by God to all people, the *yavu* was formed. Humanity comes from *vanua,* from dust ... from God'. He gave me a stern look. 'If you don't know God', he said, 'you have no beginning. In your long life journey it's important to know God'.

Unwrapping *vanua* and Christianity[1]

Fijian social and spiritual hierarchy is mirrored in spatial as well as relational terms in the positioning of the minister in what is considered the hierarchically 'highest' part of the house. In Fiji the head (*ulu*) of a person is *tabu* (lit. forbidden), the head being the highest place of the body hierarchically as well as physically; the head of a chief is therefore exceedingly *tabu*. All concepts of space and place in Fiji are centred round this concept of the head being the first and highest place. Therefore the space of houses, churches and villages are organised and considered by the same principle, being spatially divided into hierarchically valued areas of 'above' and 'below' (cf Ravuvu 1983: 18, Toren 1990: 29-39). The highest and most private part of the house (*loqi*) is where the sleeping quarters are, usually partitioned off with a piece of barkcloth (*masi*) or curtains, from the more public part of the house, the living space and the space where guests are received, *loma ni vale* (centre of the house). Within this space, the area closest to the *loqi* area is where one would invite the highest ranking members of the household or the highest ranking guest to sit.

Homes and churches have two doors – a chiefly door in the 'highest' section of the house for chiefs and high-ranking persons such as clergy. The door that most people enter the house by, is 'lower down', close to the kitchen. People enter spaces and position themselves within them in relation to their place in the hierarchy, and in so doing physically embody that social status. To place oneself in a physically higher position than a person of higher social rank than oneself is a serious breach of conduct and an indirect, or perhaps very direct, affront to the authority of the highest ranking person.

The minister is engaged in an informal kava ceremony and his hierarchical position is also reflected in the fact that he will be served first at each round of drinking. Kava (*yaqona*) is a mildly narcotic drink made from the dried

---

1   This Prologue introduces the main themes of the book and outlines its aims.

and pulverised roots of the piper methysticum plant that plays a central role in traditional ritual and ceremonial in all Pacific Island cultures (see e.g. Lebot and Lindstrom 1992, Canberra Anthropology 1995). It is presented in a polished half coconut, the traditional kava drinking bowl (*bilo*).

Kava was traditionally a drink restricted to chiefs and priests only. Essentially neutral in property, it is prepared ritually and shared to seal clan transactions, to right an offence to ancestral spirits and between clans, or used in traditional healing. But prepared and drunk alone kava can also be used to invoke ancestral power and efficacy (*mana*) in sorcery (cf Katz 1993). Although an important element of *vanua* values and practice, kava is now increasingly consumed by both men and women in informal contexts, although the spiritual, and thereby potentially dangerous properties of the drink are still acknowledged, albeit less strictly, in the ritualised fashion in which it is served and drunk even on such occasions.[2]

Vanua means many things to Fijians. It means land, place, clan, people, tradition and country. To talk of *vanua* is to talk not only of land in its material form, but land as Place of Being, as Place of Belonging, as spiritual quality. *Vanua* is both land and sea, the soil, plants, trees, rocks, rivers, reefs; the birds, beasts, fish, gods and spirits that inhabit these places and the people who belong there, bound to one another and to the land as guardians of this God-given world. *Vanua* is a relational concept that encompasses all this, paths of relationship, nurture and mutual obligations connecting place and people with the past, the present and the future.

All Fijian clans trace their lineage and history back to the 'house-mound' or 'house foundation' (*yavu*) of their founding ancestor. This is a genealogical and spiritual link to an actual place in the land. In pre-colonial times chiefs, who were considered to be divine, and non-chiefly clan members who often became deified figures to their descendents in death, were often buried in the foundations of their house. The category of *vanua* that *yavu* belong to is also known as *vanua tabu*, literally 'forbidden land'.

'*Tabu*', writes Reverend Dr Ilaitia Sevati Tuwere, former President of the Methodist Church, 'can be applied to a place, person or object, which should therefore be approached with the appropriate ritual by those who belong to a special group. Outside this group, *tabu* implies prohibition or unlawfulness. *Tabu* refers not to a thing but to a state of being under the influence of supernatural forces' (Tuwere 2002a: 136). *Vanua tabu* therefore implies an area of land that has a specific spiritual quality, is sacred or holy to a particular group of people and out of bounds to others outside of that group – or forbidden territory except at certain times and in accordance with certain rules.

This in part explains the *tabu* nature and spiritual power of such sites that the minister speaks of, while simultaneously intertwining Christian theology of Genesis with traditional understandings of *vanua* so that God is understood as the creator of *vanua*.

---

2   See also Toren 1994, Turner 1995, Tomlinson 2004, 2009.

Vanua **and church**

People's belonging to church, that is to say the Methodist Church, and *vanua* were emphasised in almost all church services in Naroro village in western Fiji, where I did fieldwork, which like the majority of Fijian villages, was predominantly Methodist. When my brother in the family I had been adopted into was due to leave for United Nations peacekeeping duties in the Middle East he was farewelled in church with speeches and prayers and the service was followed by a communal feast. At this important moment in his life, a clan elder from another village addressed Mitieli on behalf on his *vanua*:

> Sirs … we come to worship and to farewell one of our relatives about to … go and serve in the land that God had chosen for him to do services in … We are requesting that you, Mitieli, put on the armour of God. If there is anything that should be foremost in your life, it should be the worship of God … you are a young man from a chiefly household in an honourable *vanua* … set a high standard of good conduct, let nothing spoil your good name. Because if you spoil your reputation in that country it will not only bring shame to your mother and father, but it will bring shame upon this people and *vanua* also. (Transcribed and translated by Mosese Vatoga)

The links between the individual and his place of belonging, his belonging to his people, both the living, the dead and the unborn are emphasised, for the *vanua* also comprises the ancestors of the clan and those not yet born. Thus past, present and future exist simultaneously within the understanding of *vanua*. One belongs to a place and people, wherever one is in the world, with the support and responsibilities this entails. And one belongs to God and to his calling.

The strength of spiritual and emotional belonging to *vanua* and the ties between the person, faith, God and land the minister so vividly described to me that evening in the village and described above, were echoed in a similar fashion by a Methodist minister I later spoke to in the capital of Suva:[3] 'You cannot differentiate a Fijian and his religion', Reverend Tuima told me,

> My faith … is part of myself … like spirit, soul and mind … The soul is of God – what we believe, the Holy Spirit, the Spirit of God that works within us, to guide us, tell us the right thing and the wrong … Together with that you cannot differentiate a Fijian and his land – vanua. The vanua is part of me; I am a part of the vanua … it's a given gift of God to us. So we have to thank God. We worship God because of this value … like the saying by Ratu Sukuna, eh? 'noqu Kalou, noqu vanua'… my God, my land.

---

3   The late Reverend Mesake Tuima, Royal Fiji Military Forces, interview 1998.

... and politics

The term 'my God, my land' was coined by Ratu Sir Lala Sukuna, Fiji's much revered first statesman. It describes how Fijians see themselves as bound to their land and their Christian faith. And it symbolises the sense of pride and national feeling that Ratu Sukuna embodies in the minds of Fijians, especially Fijian soldiers. Yet these same words jar in the minds of many Fijians today. Sukuna's once spiritually evocative saying has for many people become equated with racist politics and violence, tainted as it is by its use in divisive, nationalist, ethno-religious rhetoric and attacks on Indo-Fijians in the coups of 1987 as well as in the coup of 2000. '*Noqu vanua* and *noqu kalou*' writes Anglican Bishop Reverend Dr Winston Halapua (2003: 108) '... manipulated a majority of Fijians because of the apparent appeal to the deep cultural values of the Fijians. In reality such a cry was a smoke screen for naked power grabbing and wealth accumulation'.

The interweaving of *vanua* with Christianity (*lotu*) in Fiji is historically linked with a third entity, *matanitu*, which originally denoted chiefly governance, developed into meaning colonial government and now, somewhat ambiguously and unclearly, relates to government and nation as well as traditional chiefly power. This tripartite structure, known as the Three Pillars, comprises the overarching ideology of Fijian society, around which village life centres, which people in urban as well as rural contexts constantly refer to, and which is also constantly referred to at national level and in the media. Yet this is a predominantly Fiji Methodist religio-cultural ideal structure that came into being during the colonial period (1874-1970).

Contemporary interpretations of this structure converge in a highly volatile political issue prevalent in Fijian nationalist politics since 1987 and exacerbated during and since the coup in 2000: whether Fiji should constitutionally be declared a Christian state. Critics warn that in a multi-ethnic, multi-religious country with a non-Christian population of some 36 percent, this ideal is incompatible with freedom of religion and respect for the dignity of difference in society. The late Reverend Niukula, former President of the Methodist Church in Fiji, is quoted as having said that 'The issue of a Christian state has nothing to do with Christianity, but rather the strengthening and accumulation of power and wealth by those in power'. (Niukula in Casimira, 30 November 2002) Similarly, the monthly magazine *Islands Business* in no uncertain terms warns against the politicisation of Christianity in Fiji and the Pacific Island region and its use in national politics:

> Christianity profoundly influences every part of the region. It is not just that at weekends church ministers can count on preaching to congregations that fill their churches. It is that the Pacific's governments fervently proclaim themselves to be inspired and directed by God. In the Pacific, Christianity is a powerful political influence that must be reckoned with. In Fiji, it has been distorted and wielded to illegally change governments. (Fiji Islands Business January 2006: 8)

Changing patterns of church adherence

The Methodist Church in Fiji, with just under 300,000 members (cf 2007 census, see Appendix 2), that is to say almost 35 percent of the total population, has always been the dominant church in Fiji, and is still by far the largest denomination in the country. However, according to the 2007 Fiji Census, the number of adherents of what are termed 'other Christian' denominations and members of the Assemblies of God Church (i.e. Christians who are neither Anglican, Catholic, Methodist nor SDA), in relation to the total Christian community of Fiji, has risen from 15.8 percent in 1996 to 24.9 percent in 2007. Bearing in mind that this figure is not differentiated and would include the Baptist and Presbyterian Churches, The Salvation Army, the Mormons and Jehovah's Witnesses, the significant growth recorded of 'Other Christian' denominations would primarily concern membership of Pentecostal churches. The findings of the 1996 census indicate that at that time one sixth of Christians in Fiji belonged to non-mainline churches. According to the 2007 census *one in every four* Christians in Fiji now belongs to a non-mainline Christian church.

A rise of such significance over the past decade in the percentage of Christians belonging to non-mainline churches, many of which are critical of many traditional Fijian cultural values and practices, gives an idea of the radically changing face of Christianity and tradition in Fiji today. The ideal of a Fijian way, dominated by Methodist values as represented in the Three Pillars structure, is now seriously challenged. And with the important role Christianity in general plays in Fiji at all levels in society, the values, spiritual, social, strategic and political, of charismatic and Pentecostal churches, are increasingly influencing Fiji society as a whole.

Complexity and connectedness

This book explores themes of connectedness and relationality. As social, cultural and historical beings we and the cultures and societies we are part of, are interconnected in time and space, our actions part of interacting wider processes and realities. For many of the people whose words, faith and actions make up this book the religious and spiritual aspects of their being in the world are that which connects them with others. This is expressed in many different ways in the following chapters. Within the framework of the relations between Christianity and tradition each chapter offers different perspectives on relatedness and connectedness in time and space: expressed in representations, rhetoric, ritual and experience. These connect people to particular social, cultural or faith communities and shared values; are used strategically and politically to exclude through emphasising or creating boundaries; or used in inclusive ways to build bridges, generate hope, reconcile and heal.

Christianity in Fiji is highly complex and multi-faceted. It may in fact be more accurate to speak of diverse *Christianities* (cf Peel 2000, Robbins 2003a,

Cannell 2006). These Christianities are all different, yet historically and culturally interwoven and interconnected – at deep existential levels, in practice, in rhetoric, ritual and in terms of religious experience – with people's ideals and experience of what is traditional and what role tradition, traditional practice, the past and notions of change and transformation play in contemporary Fiji. These complexities reflect not only the entwining of the past in the present, but also the inevitable entanglement and representation of the local and the global.

My research draws on fieldwork in Methodist, Pentecostal, Catholic and Anglican contexts, and ecumenical and inter-faith dialogue. Christian teachings and traditional beliefs and practices of reconciliation and healing, as ritualised ways of connecting the past with or disassociating it from the present, and as reconciling and healing relationships, form a pervasive theme throughout.

In Robert Borofsky's (ed.) beautifully crafted *Remembered Pacific Pasts* he points out that his book does not and cannot provide a complete account. 'But', he writes, 'it does provide points of reference for readers to think *with*. It offers tools to assist readers in weaving further narratives and developing further conversations'. (Borofsky 2000: 29) This book does not claim to give a comprehensive picture of the complexities discussed. It is a contribution to academic scholarship and debate among western and Pacific Islander scholars alike on relationality, interconnectedness, Christianity, tradition and change, in the Pacific Islands in particular, in studies of Christianity in general.

I see it as an ethnographic mosaic of the rich, diverse, complex and contested relations between Christianity and tradition, faith and politics in Fiji that I experienced during my main research periods between 1993-2006, with some updating to 2009. And it is my sincere hope that, as a representation of a particular time in Fiji's religious and cultural history, this book may be of value, providing points of reference for a more general Fiji and Pacific Islander audience to use in 'developing further conversations' around these themes.

My aim has been to write a 'different' ethnography in a style that encompasses and connects many different fieldwork sites and experiences. The book's particular contributions lie, I believe, in its wide scope, its multi-sited and multi-disciplinary approach to this field of study, drawing on ethnographic data from several different Christian denominations. In order to reflect the complexity of the issues discussed and to explore ways of expanding contemporary ethnographic writing I juxtapose many diverse perspectives in a consciously genre-blurring style and structure. I locate Fiji as a multi-cultural, multi-ethnic country within a Pacific Islands, regional and globally interconnected context. And I draw on the work of Fiji and Pacific Islander academics, theologians, poets, writers and song-writers, who in different ways discuss many of the issues I write about, reflecting the multi-cultural dynamics of Fiji society, and reflecting what the majority of local (mainly urban) people were reading about in the English language media and debating during the years of my research.

I wanted to write a book that, while based on solid ethnographic research, is inviting to read, accessible and relevant to a wider audience. It is my hope that this book may contribute to a broader understanding of the immense value of anthropological methodology, description and analysis as tools in social analysis and social interaction. The themes of relationality and interconnectedness, though particular to a Fiji and Pacific Island context, are relevant to other disciplines and also to non-academic readers. The rhetoric, emotions and the theological and political arguments that have emerged over the past decades in the Christian State debate express much of the cultural, religious and political complexity of contemporary Fiji. Similar polarisations and tensions exist in different guises and have exploded elsewhere in the Pacific Island region and reflect issues of growing concern at local, national and global levels across the world on the increasing polarisation of liberal and fundamentalist views within and between the world religions, within politics and civil society, and between religion and secularism.

The concluding chapter, Chapter 7, discusses ecumenical and interfaith dialogue and different Christian methodologies of reconciliation, forgiveness and healing. Three of the most vocal Pacific Island theologians of my research years, a Fijian Methodist, a Fijian Catholic and a Tongan Anglican, offer approaches to reconciliation based on the importance of cultural roots and interconnectedness, of listening and dialogue, the richness and dignity of difference, of reconciliation with God and the environment. These theologies do not only pertain to the situation in Fiji but are universally relevant and applicable in inter-personal and political reconciliation contexts as well as in relation to the global climate crisis.

Re-representing representations

In my research I was touched by many of the things that people shared with me, often things that were precious to them, and I value how positively they engaged with me in discussing their beliefs and visions. Many different voices and many different standpoints and practices concerning Christian faith, experience and practice and the role of tradition are expressed here. They are fragments, stories that continue to unfold outside the confines of this book, stories of which there are so many others that for lack of space or simply because I have not heard them, are not included here. What you see and what you come to learn depends not just on who you are and where you see things from but also where you happen to be at any given time, which people you meet, and which stories you hear.

I consciously make extensive use of quotations, endeavouring to give people as much 'voice' as possible and emphasise the multiple and different voices I recorded, and to create methodological transparency in my ethnography. At the same time I am aware that however honestly and genuinely I, as a *palagi* [European] academic, may wish to write about Fiji, I remain an intrinsic part of a long history of intervention, colonisation and representation (cf Keesing 1992b: 7) – and therefore will always be critiqued as such from some quarters. However, Keesing maintained that as anthropologists 'we can and should … ask where cultural symbols come from … and whose interests they serve, as well as what they mean'. (Ibid.) And I consider an outsider's representation – a complementary view to local views – to be of potential value to Fiji Islanders and Pacific Islanders. (see also Hereniko 2000) Gewertz and Errington, writing at the height of the so-called politics of representation debate in the Pacific Island region (cf Introduction), express this point most succinctly:

> At this period in history, ethnography, although an endeavour compromised by the politics of representation, can be justified so long as it sustains an anthropology that focuses on the encounter between systems: on infiltration, negotiation, clash, transformation, and resistance. As ethnographers, we may be part of the problem of hegemony, but not to write ethnography is not part of the solution. It is because Ethnography is inherently political that it continues to have potential value. (1991: 209)

My experience and voice is the 'voice-over' that permeates each page of this book, and any mistakes or misinterpretations are of course mine. As the anthropologist, although I try to facilitate what people do and say to others, I am aware that to some degree I will always 'stand between the facts and the analytical results'. Those whose thoughts and actions I have recorded are participants in a dialogue, but one initiated by the anthropologist'. (Cf Hastrup 1995: 47) I can only hope, despite the anthropological way I have represented their words, that those who shared their thoughts and faith with me will feel I have been true to the spirit of our conversations.

In Fiji and the Pacific Islands, the metaphor of 'paths' first and foremost denotes the interlinking of kinship relations and allegiances, past, present and future through exchanges of material and symbolic wealth and nurture across land and sea. The paths of Christianity and tradition in Fiji, in allegiance, in opposition and as complementary to one another, are similarly dynamically interwoven in time, space and relationships – as are past and contemporary ways in which they are represented, including this book.

Place and people

The terms used to regionally define the Pacific Island region are contested elements of contemporary discourse on Pacific Islander cultural and national identity. Whereas formerly 'the Pacific' has been the most widely used term, theoretically including Australia and Aotearoa New Zealand , but in practice denoting Pacific Island countries and cultures (including the Maori and large Pacific Islander population of Aotearoa), a number of Pacific Islanders and non-Pacific Islander academics, inspired by Hau'ofa's (1993) thoughts on the symbolism of the two different terms are now using 'Oceania' to define the area, *The Pacific*, according to Hau'ofa, indicating a western view of a vast, empty ocean with isolated islands, *Oceania* indicating an interconnected whole. While this term is increasingly used, it is somewhat ambiguous, as Oceania has often been used to include Australia and New Zealand and also sometimes the Pacific rim countries. I have chosen to use the term *Pacific Islands*, cf among others Oliver 1989, Lal 2000, and official acronyms such as PICs (Pacific Island Countries) and the East-West Centre's PIDP (Pacific Islander Development Project).

The 1997 Constitution gave the term 'Fiji Islanders' as a common name for all Fiji citizens. In this book I refer to indigenous Fijians as 'Fijians'. When referring to Fiji Islanders of Indian descent, following Brij Lal's example, I use the term Indo-Fijian. In Fiji, people use the terms Fijians and Indians and the term 'race' rather than 'ethnic group' (cf Geraghty 1997). In addition to the two main ethnic groups in the country Fiji Islanders of Fijian and European descent are classified as 'Part-European' or, in Fijian, as *Kai Loma* (often perceived as a derogatory term). Many people, especially in urban contexts, are also of mixed Pacific Islander descent, several of mixed Fijian and Pacific Islander or Chinese descent. A colloquial term people of mixed ancestry often use to describe themselves as is 'fruit salad'. The highly sensitive and politicised nature of ethnicity in Fiji explains why the 1997 Fiji Constitution's term *Fiji Islanders* is such a potentially valuable addition to the language, although it has not yet gained much popularity.

When referring to 'tradition in Fiji' in the context of this book, I am referring to indigenous Fijian tradition. Standard Fijian words are denoted in *italics* and words in the Nadrogā language are in underlined *italics*.

Introduction
Interwoven Representations
of Past and Present

Ravuama Vere (FT 1/8) says Indians have India and as such, we should not
mess with politics in Fiji. When I was a student in India, my colleagues (from
India) told me I was a Fijian and not an Indian because I was not born in India.
At home in Fiji, I am known as an Indian. Some even call me an Indo-Fijian.
The constitution of my beloved country tells me that I am a Fiji Islander. An
important part of our country's history has made us, or at least some of us, a
confused lot. (Neelesh Gounder, Letter to the Editor, *Fiji Times* 13 August 2003,
see also Ratubalavu, *Fiji Times* 5 October 2004: 3)

October 1993. The Indo-Fijian taxi driver who drove me from the Suva bus
terminal was amiable, although rather low in spirits. He spoke of how tough
things had been in Fiji over the past years since the coups of 1987, economically
and in terms of ethnic relations. Many Indians had left, he said. For those who
had no option but to stay, things had not been easy. I was struck by a sense of
heaviness, depression and sadness, and an underlying tension.

Suva was celebrating the closing months of the UN Year of Indigenous
Peoples. 'Tradition' and 'culture' were terms referred to again and again in the
English language newspapers and in speeches by prominent figures in Fiji society
at various ceremonies in connection with festivities at many different venues in
town, broadcast on radio and the new medium of the TV. By 1993 the Indo-
Fijian population in Fiji had decreased markedly after the military coups of 1987
reinforced and legislated Fijian political paramountcy in the country, toppling a
labour-led government that had sought greater political equity between the main
ethnic groups. Large numbers of Indo-Fijians, in particular well-educated Indo-
Fijians, had emigrated to New Zealand, Australia, Canada and the States.

In Fiji the idea of the Year of Indigenous Peoples became inverted to emphasise
the indigenous character, not of a marginalised group, but of the politically and
culturally dominant ethnic community, the Fijians. As *itaukei ni vanua* (literally,
joint owners of land who share a common descent), their identity so closely
connected with tradition, culture and the land meant that, historically, to Fijians
the conception of being *landless* was ultimately equated with being *culture-less.*
Without any belonging to the land, Indo-Fijians therefore did not truly belong

to Fiji,[1] an understanding still pervasive among many Fijians today and used in ethno-nationalist rhetoric.

This chapter discusses examples of how representations are ways of creating boundaries and demarcations, emphasising connections and continuities, or signifying dissociation and change – all of which are culturally and historically interwoven, touch on deep existential issues, and often also express social and political strategies.

Boundaries, connections, continuities and change

'I am a Samoan and my culture is *here*'. The young man stood up and faced the class, slapping his hand onto the region of his heart and solar plexus, 'And it doesn't change', he added emphatically, looking hard at me.

My first attempt at unwrapping contemporary anthropological understandings of the fluidity and changing nature of 'culture' and 'cultural practice' to a class of first year seminarians from eight different Pacific Island countries at the Pacific Regional Seminary[2] in Suva in 2005 did not go down very well. These theories challenged not only this young man, but the whole class. This student, as most of his classmates, came to greatly appreciate anthropology and to see its value in becoming more culturally aware and in analysing cultural practice and traditions, but we had a somewhat rocky start.

In my classes I explained anthropological theoretical concepts and frameworks of analysis, asking the students to contribute ethnographical examples from their cultures. This way we all learnt a great deal. In a similar discussion on understandings of culture a young Fijian man in the class told us that the presence of Indo-Fijians in Fiji [since the late 19th century] had had absolutely no influence on Fijian culture or traditions. When the discussion turned to what food people in Fiji eat today, however, the Fijian students agreed that *curry* is a popular dish among Fijians.

Yet these two statements are concerned less with explaining the *content* of Samoan or Fijian culture, traditions and cuisine, but are examples of cultural boundaries – of how we as humans demarcate ourselves in relation to others and in relation to a perceived threat of change or intrusion from external sources. In these examples the emphasis is on an ideal of strength in persisting and unchanging cultural values and practices. Here, change is viewed as negative and diminishing, weakening the strength and power of tradition and that which is traditional. Yet similar statements might just as easily be voiced to emphasise the exact opposite

---

1 I thank Claire Slatter, University of the South Pacific, for pointing this out. (pers comm. 1993)

2 Pacific Regional Seminary affiliated with Pontificia Universitas Urbaniana in Rome, trains Pacific Islanders for the priesthood. In 2005 there were about 150 seminarians. In 2005 two nuns attended classes, studying for a Diploma in Theology.

view: of change as innovative, positive and powerful, and lack of change as negative and limiting, conservative and reactionary.

These two opposite ways of viewing change are evident in the representations of Christianity portrayed in the following chapters. To conservative Methodists the forms of Christianity increasingly practised in Fiji by Pentecostal Christians represent a threat to traditional values and hegemonic relations in Church and society. Pentecostals on the other hand consider their forms of Christianity to be powerfully innovative and forward-moving. I discuss the discrepancies and dynamics between these views in several of the chapters, in most detail in Chapter 5. And yet, this book is not concerned with focusing on *oppositional* categories as such, although they are evident in many of the discussions, but in describing and analysing the different ways in which such categories and people's representations of them, are interwoven, and often complement each other.

When I experienced opposition among my students to an understanding of culture as being in movement, I was reminded of what a Samoan academic friend said on my first day of teaching: 'If I were one of your students', he said, 'I would want you first of all to explain why you as a *palagi* [foreigner – *valagi* in standard Fijian] are standing there, telling me about my culture'.

Although said gently, the meaning was quite clear. Those words and my classroom experiences brought me straight to the heart of the 1980s paradigm shift in anthropology that definitively led anthropologists away from former functionalist/structuralist understandings of societies and cultures as synchronic, static and isolated entities and changed for ever the previously unquestioned authority anthropologists had to represent the lives and cultures of people they had been privileged to live with or engage with at more or less deep levels. It was no coincidence that two Samoans had questioned my authority as an anthropologist, given the history of the Meade/Freeman controversy. The student later gave a very good, if indignant, account in class of that controversy.

I was never for a moment in doubt of the inherent challenges and potential pitfalls of my position as a European lay-woman, lecturing in anthropology in a Developing country Catholic seminary. While anthropologists for the past 20 years or more have been questioning the reification of 'culture' in selective representations, to the Pacific Islander seminarians I taught their culture was indeed something highly tangible, precious – and definitely not there to be questioned or tampered with.

In those first months of their studies they were all suffering from the culture shock so familiar to anthropologists on first arriving in 'the field'. They had been transposed from their cultural roots, known cultural contexts and social relationships to the context of a seminary for men from all over the Pacific Islands – for the majority of students they were suddenly seminarians in a foreign land and culture, doubly so, as in addition to this they were also living in close proximity to people from many different cultures in the relatively enclosed culture of Catholic seminary life – and with a *palagi* lay-woman as lecturer. Understandably, this was a challenging experience, especially in that first year. And the importance of demarcating positions, traditions and differences therefore became all the more poignant.

The rapid political, cultural, social and economic changes wrought by the post-colonial era in non-western countries and the fast pace of globalisation across the world is rapidly changing our ontological realities and challenging traditional structures and values. And not least Pacific Islanders, as other former colonised peoples, have been concerned at many different levels with unraveling and redefining the ways in which they as peoples and cultures have been represented – or misrepresented – by westerners over time: by explorers, scientists, painters, missionaries, colonial officials and governments, by historians and anthropologists, aid agencies, journalists and foreign politicians.

My position as yet another contributor to the long history of western intervention in the Pacific Islands was especially stark when I lectured on the history of the peopling of the Pacific, even though that history tells of the unimaginable courage, tenacity and navigational skills of people such as the Austronesians, who sailed thousands of miles from South East Asia to the far reaches of the earth's greatest ocean. Even geographic terminology – for instance, the 'Far East', which is not east of the Pacific Islands – is euro-centric and acts to diminish the place of the Pacific Islands in the world. Similarly, the Pacific Islands as small markings on a vast expanse of blue paper have a tendency to disappear off the edges of or into the middle join of most atlases, a fact highlighted by the Australian-produced 'Upside-Down Map of the World' that centralises Australia and the Pacific Ocean at the top of the world and Europe at the bottom, in effect inverting euro-centric representations of the world.

Yet, unexpectedly, I found I had to tenaciously argue my case of how the Pacific Islands were peopled against views from several of the students that their ancestors did not, as I maintained on the basis of scientific evidence, migrate from ancient Papua and in a later wave from South East Asia – but sailed to the Pacific from Egypt. This understanding is based on what has since been revealed[3] as a myth, generated by Methodist missionaries in the 19th Century who trained Fijian ministers in Fijian history. There were no oral traditions concerning the settlement of Fiji, presumably because Fiji had been settled hundreds or thousands of years before. So the missionaries constructed a history of the settlement of Fiji, based on popular anthropological theories of the time which maintained that Melanesians derived from Africa, incorporating into the myth the names of real Fijian ancestor gods, such as Degei and Lutunasobasoba. The pupils at this training centre became the first history teachers in Fiji, and through them the so-called Kaunitoni Myth spread throughout the Islands and has survived, largely unquestioned, right up to the present. (Geraghty 2005, n.d. b)

Again, when I lectured on Darwin's theory of evolution, it was quite unacceptable to these first year seminarians. My teaching was in accordance with the teaching

---

3   Cf France 1966, 1969, World Council of Churches 2001, Geraghty 2005 and n.d. b.

of the Catholic Church, which acknowledges the scientific fact of evolution by descent.[4] My students, however, were unconvinced. And the irony was not lost on me that I as a European academic in 2005, on the basis of contemporary western scientific knowledge and contemporary Catholic theology, was refuting the Eurocentric 19th century representations of Christianity that European missionaries once coerced indigenous Pacific Islanders to adopt in replacement of their traditional creation myths.

The situations recalled here emphasise the deeply ingrained and highly charged complexities of cultural interaction and engagement, the inherent political nature of representations – and their interconnectedness through people's agency and relations in history, across time and space. Where do we as anthropologists enter this longue durée (Cf Peel 2000) and 'freeze' a particular moment for study? And what should we beware of in the process and in the subsequent process of re-presentation of our studies? Where, in fact, does a story *begin*?

'There are no individual stories'

> You can't just say, "My story starts here". It's older than you. It has a thousand beginnings, each of them in someone else's life … You can't just say, 'It ends here' … Our stories begin before their beginnings and continue beyond their ends … really there are no individual stories, only *the* story, coiling and weaving through all our lives. (Sinha 2002: 25)

Although the character in Indra Sinha's novel is Indian, to say that there are no individual stories is perhaps a very poignant point to make when talking about Pacific Island peoples and cultures. For people's life experience in the Pacific Islands is always embedded in webs of kinship and social relations. And as the examples described above emphasise, people's actions, cultural engagement and relations anywhere in the world are likewise embedded in social histories that began to be entangled long before we ourselves came to be part of those processes.

In stories we re-member and re-present memory, experience, hopes, dreams, the lived, the imaginary, the fictitious. We re-present aspects of our lives or the lives of others in particular ways in particular situations to particular people. Yet among all humanity even the individual telling of a story, as Sinha's character expresses above, does not exist alone, in isolation from others. It is part of many other stories and comes into being in the situation of its telling, thereby implicitly existing in all other stories. The storyteller and the listener or listeners are all part of the whole.

---

4   Cf Coyne (2005), then Director of the Vatican Observatory, who refers to a 1996 declaration by John Paul II to the Pontifical Academy of Sciences, and to early Christian writings on Genesis. Coyne argues against the view that random evolution is incompatible with belief in a creator God, emphasing that science reflects God's infinite purpose. See also Ayala 2005, Spencer 2009, Alexander 2009, McMullen 2009.

The story, as Michael Jackson (2002: 23) writes, citing Hannah Arendt (1958), 'comes into being within an already existing web of human relationships'. And as J.D.Y Peel emphasises (1995: 584), referring to Carr (1986), 'we live narrative before we tell it; or rather, our living and our telling of narratives are deeply and continuously implicated with one another'.

Storytelling, Jackson continues (ibid.), 'mediates our relation with worlds that extend beyond us; the important thing is not how we name these other worlds but how narrative enables us to negotiate an existential balance between ourselves and such spheres of otherness'. He points out that although the stories that are approved in any society tend to reinforce extant boundaries, 'storytelling also questions, blurs, transgresses, and even abolishes these boundaries'. And within and across these relationships storytelling and narrative are expressive of power relations – power relations that may be confirmed and strengthened through narrative, or may be challenged and usurped, strengthening or changing the story-teller, as well as the listeners. As Peel writes (1995: 584, 593) 'narratives are not only representations of the past, of things presumed to have happened or existed, but also sketches of possibilities, prophesies or scenarios for things that might be … just as narrative is an expression of power, it also works to empower those who can achieve it'.

In 1946 Collingwood similarly emphasised the relationality of representations of history, and how historians as contemporary figures are enmeshed in the re-presentations they make of the past. For although history is based on 'fact', it is nevertheless a story, a re-presentation; the past can only ever be accessible from the present:

> Every present has a past of its own, and any imaginative reconstruction of the past aims at reconstructing the past of this present, the present in which the act of imagination is going on, as here and now perceived ... the historian himself, together with the here-and-now which forms the total body of evidence available to him, is a part of the process he is studying, has his own place in that process, and can see it only from the point of view which at that present moment he occupies within it. (Collingwood 1992: 247, 248)

The past is only accessible from the here and now, in all its relational and contextual complexity. Collingwood's words apply in fact to all representations, whether history, theoretical reflection, prose, poetry, political writing or religious testimony. Whether describing the past, the present or the future, our stories are contextually, historically and humanly interwoven. With religious testimony, another dimension is added for those who share a common faith: a spiritual dimension that intertwines stories with individual and shared spiritual belief and experience.

Collingwood's words are particularly poignant in relation to debates on the meaning and uses of history and tradition that have formed such an important part of Pacific Island academic discourse over the past quarter of a century. As early as 1968 historian H.E. Maude warned against the unchallenged dominance of Eurocentric representations of Pacific Island histories and the post-colonial nationalistic backlash experienced elsewhere:

> The need for a more island-oriented historiography would seem urgent if our work is to stand the test of time and not be rejected as imperialistic rationalization by the people of the independent nations that are coming into being in the new Pacific, as has happened in India, Africa and the West Indies, where we are witnessing a reaction from excessively Eurocentric history towards an equally extreme national version – what has been termed decolonized history. (Maude 1991: xix)

One might here compare Tongan anthropologist Epeli Hau'ofa's contemporary perspective on this:

> For Pacific scholars the main factors for the reconstructions of our pasts are events determined by Euro-American imperialism. Our histories are commonly structured on the temporal division of the past into precontact, early contact, colonial, and postcolonial or neocolonial periods ... Our histories are essentially narratives told in the footnotes of the histories of empires. (Hau'ofa 2000: 456)

Maude's words of 40 years ago ring very true in relation to the academic debate on history, tradition and nationalism in the Pacific Islands over the past 20 years.[5] The issue of continuity, change and transformation in notions of tradition and thus also in history has been at the centre of some of the most debated points of view in historical and anthropological analyses of Pacific Island societies. The different ways of representing this and the inherent politics of such representations, and whether western scholars should or should not participate in these debates have been hotly debated amongst western and Pacific Islander scholars alike,[6] reflecting the general debate in anthropology in the 1980s on the politics of representation and the 'invention of tradition'.[7]

---

5   Cf for example, Biersack 1991, Carrier 1992, Foster 1995b, Otto and Thomas 1997.

6   For example Keesing and Tonkinson (eds) 1982, Keesing 1982, 1989, 1990, 1992a, 1992b, 1994, Linnekin 1983, Handler and Linnekin 1984, Hanson 1989, Wilford 1990, Freeth 1990, Nissen 1990, in a debate sparked by Hanson's article, claiming that certain elements of Maori culture were constructed by European scholars. See further comments in Linnekin 1991, Trask 1991, Keesing 1991. See also Borofsky 1988, 2000a, 2000b, Gewertz and Errington 1991, Linnekin 1992, Friedman 1992, 1996, Neumann 1992, Obeyesekere 1992, Jolly and Thomas (eds) 1992, Jolly 1992a, 1992b, Ryle 1996, Jourdan 1996, Jourdan (ed.) 1997, Hereniko 2000, Borofsky (ed.) 2000. Several of the key articles in the debate were re-printed in Hanlon and White (eds) 2000, see Introduction for a stimulating overview.

7   E.g. Wagner 1975, Hobsbawm and Ranger 1983, Fabian 1983, Marcus and Fisher 1986, Clifford and Marcus 1986, Clifford 1988.

Plunging *medias res:* Anthropology, Christianity and the longue durée

The study of history in non-western contexts, as Maude emphasises, has had a deeply Euro-centric bias and tended to base 'first contact' experiences of local peoples with westerners, as the *starting point* for history per se in a given locale – as in the pre-'discovery' *terra nullius* perception of the Australian continent as completely void of human existence until the coming of the whites. 'First contact' is a heavily loaded word that from an Islander view, as Hau'ofa points out, 'describes accurately the first and early encounters between Oceanians and European sailors as carriers of dangerous diseases that wiped out large proportions of our populations in the 18th and 19th centuries'.[8] Similarly, the study of Christianity, writes Peel, 'does not start at the beginning, but has to plunge *medias res* ... We come in on people in a predicament, in the *middle* straits of something... ' (Peel 2000: 24 in Barker nd).

In a similar vein Fenella Cannell, in her phenomenal introduction to *The Anthropology of Christianity* (2006) points out that rather than focus on an assumed religious, socio-cultural and historical rupture caused in societies by the advent of missionisation, the point after which nothing will ever be the same (Cannell 2006: 44) we should focus more on the indigenous expression given to different 'Christianities' and their interrelations within a particular historical context. Pointing to the inherent paradoxes within Christianity, Cannell emphasises that what emerges in the meeting of a particular Christianity and a particular cultural and historical context, will always be unique. And no matter how orthodox a particular form of Christianity is, it can never merely contain one message with one possibility of interpretation (Cannell 2006: 43). 'If we can stop presupposing that Christianity changes everything forever, we may be able to begin to see the experiences of Christianity, in all their diversity, complexity and singularity, for what they are' (Cannell 2006: 45).

The past two decades have seen a spate of writing on the historical tensions within the discipline of anthropology concerning the study of Christianity and the reluctance of anthropologists to engage with Christianity other than as a negative and destructive influence,[9] and the marginalisation or omission of Christian beliefs and practices in many earlier ethnographic texts. This has, as Douglas has pointed out at length, been particularly true of ethnography in the Pacific Island region.[10] While 'the importance of Christianity has often functioned in anthropological accounts as something set in opposition to local culture, or as an avenue by which

---

8   Hau'ofa 2000: 455, see also e.g. Jackson 1998: 108-124, Borofsky 2000b, Schieffelin and Crittendon 2000 and Douglas 2001.

9   E.g. Harding 1991, Ewing 1994, Douglas 2001a, 2001b, Drooger 2003, Robbins 2003a, 2004a, 2007, in press, Cannell 2005, 2006, Coleman 2004, 2007.

10   Cf. e.g. Barker 1992, Douglas 2001a and 2001b; and comments on Douglas' 2001b paper from Austin Broos 2001, Barker 2001, Fabian 2001, Jorgensen 2001, Knauft 2001, Orta 2001, Peel 2001, Stewart and Strathern 2001, Trompf 2001

one can advance one's pragmatic or political interests' (Tomlinson and Engelke 2006: 19), and this has been particularly true of the Pacific Island region, since Barker's (1990a) call for more research into Christianity in the Pacific Island region, over the past two decades an increasing number of anthropological studies, centred on contemporary Pacific Island practices of Christianity, have emerged.[11]

'What is "new" in the [emerging interest in the anthropology of Christianity]', as Tomlinson and Engelke (2006) note, 'is not the study of Christianity itself. What is new is a more self-conscious engagement with Christianity as a cultural logic [cf Robinson 2003a, 2004a]' (Tomlinson and Engelke 2006: 19). This leads to discussions of whether Christianity as a belief-system and as practice, for example, was merely subsumed into already existing cultural and religious structures, or whether those structures were changed for ever by the advent of Christianity?

Robbins, clearly influenced by his own research among the Urapmin of Highland Papua New Guinea, for whom the recent adoption of Baptist Christianity has affected significant socio-cultural rupture, argues that anthropology as a discipline has sought to focus on *continuities* rather than rupture, in a desire to see the communities we study as resilient towards western influence.[12]

The chapters of this book juxtapose many different ways in which continuity and change in relation to Christianity and tradition are drawn on, experienced and represented by Fijians and Pacific Islanders.

Oceanic representations of space and relationality

Hau'ofa describes the mapping of the Oceanic region and its compartmentalisation into particular areas as the work of European outsiders, whose quite different perceptions of place and space have had lasting influence on how the Pacific Island region has been, and still is imagined and defined, by Pacific Islanders as well as outsiders.

> There is a gulf of difference in viewing the Pacific as 'islands in a far sea' and as a 'sea of islands'. The first emphasizes dry surfaces in a vast ocean far from the centres of power [stressing] the smallness and remoteness of the islands. The second is a more holistic perspective in which things are seen in the totality of their relationships. It was continental men, namely Europeans, on entering the Pacific after crossing huge expanses of ocean, who introduced the view of 'islands in a far sea'. From this perspective the islands are tiny, isolated dots in

---

11   E.g. White 1991, Burt 1994, Robbins 2004, Scott 2007, Eriksen 2008, Tomlinson 2009.

12   Robbins 2003a, 2004, 2007, see also responses to his 2007 article by Barker 2007, Cannell 2007, Coleman 2007, Eriksen 2007, Garma 2007, Harris 2007, Howell 2007, Keller 2007, Luhrman 2007, MacCormack 2007, Maxwell 2007, Peel 2007, Schieffelin 2007, Zehner 2007.

> a vast ocean ... it was continental men, Europeans and Americans, who drew
> imaginary lines across the sea, making the colonial boundaries that, for the first
> time, confined ocean peoples to tiny spaces. These are the boundaries that today
> define the island states and territories of the Pacific ... our ancestors, who had
> lived in the Pacific for over 2000 years, viewed their world as a 'sea of islands',
> rather than 'islands in the sea'. (Hau'ofa 1993: 7)

'Early islanders may have perceived the Pacific as a sea of islands. To continental
man it is often envisaged as an empty expanse of ocean', write Levison, Ward and
Webb (1973: 62), suggesting that these diverse spatial interpretations were founded
on quite different oceanic experiences. 'The expanses of the empty Atlantic and
eastern Pacific ... formed the ocean images of Europeans, but people entering the
Pacific from its western margins might well expect the seas to the east to be as
island-studded as the margins they knew'. (Ibid.)

In a paper on the changing geographic conceptions of Oceania, Ward (1999)
outlines the differences in knowledge and Eurocentric perceptions of space,
distance and remoteness that underlie early mappings of Polynesia by de Brosses
in 1756, de Rienzi in 1831 and d'Urville in 1832. The map in current use, from
1938, is the only version by a Polynesian, Te Rangi Hiroa (Sir Peter Buck),
celebrated Maori anthropologist. By contrast with the other versions, Ward writes,
'his Polynesia has an implicit message with the Polynesian triangle pointing
strongly eastwards as an arrowhead – symbolising his message of "Vikings of
the Sunrise", exploring eastwards, reaching the Americas, and returning. It
celebrates Polynesian technology, courage and sense of worth'. (Ward 1999: 3)
This corresponds to the vast oceanic world of the great Tahitian chief, Tupaia,
whom Cook and Forster met in 1769 and whose mental map of his world consisted
of over 130 islands, stretching from the Marquesas and Tuamotos westwards as far
as Samoa and Tonga.[13]

> One might set forth in almost any direction, confident that islands, known or
> unknown, will rise over the horizon to meet one ... [in an] expanse ... equivalent
> to the area bounded by the Baltic, the Mediterranean, Ireland and the Russian
> Urals. This remarkably wide world was the combined product of a strong
> marine technology, systems of navigation anchored by mental maps and spatial
> concepts of stars, islands, winds and sea roads, and a tradition of oral history and
> remembering. (Ward 1999: 8, 10)

In his paper, Ward suggests a further reconfiguration of Te Rangi Hiroa's map
to include the 'new Pacific Islands' of urban centres such as Los Angeles and
Auckland, indicating the continual ebb and flow of demographic movements, and
the continually changing Pacific Islander senses of identity and belonging within
and across expanses of ocean and land.

---

13   Cook in Beaglehole 1955: 294 and Dening 1963: 133-136 in Ward 2000: 8, 10.

According to Hau'ofa, like Aboriginal Australian songlines, Oceanic sea routes were mapped in chants:

> that identified sequences of landfalls between points of departure and final destinations. Distances were measured in how long it generally took to traverse them … Our landscapes and seascapes are thus cultural as well as physical. We cannot read our histories without knowing how to read our landscapes (and seascapes) … It is essential that we do not destroy our landmarks, for with their removal very important parts of our memories, our histories, will be erased. (Hau'ofa 2000: 466-467)

Halapua, in his recent compelling theological reflection, uses *moana* (the sea in Tongan and other Polynesian languages) as a metaphor of pre-Christian and Christian journeying, connecting Pacific Islanders in time, space, spirituality and community with their ancestors and with God:

> The *moana* holds mystery because of the depths of the ocean and its hidden life. Here is experienced the presence of the gods of the ocean and the spirits of the ancestors. Even in the perils of the ocean there is always a sense of affinity with those who have crossed the ocean before. In the midst of the *moana* there is a sense of being embraced – we are not alone. There is a strong sense of awe and of being in the presence of the heavenly bodies – the sun, the moon and the stars. (Halapua 2008: 5)

European representations of otherness

On many of the early European voyages of discovery, such as the Cook voyages, the records of illustrators, painters, scientists, botanists, naturalists and intellectuals played a central role in the ways in which Pacific peoples came to be represented in European contexts (see for example Thomas, Guest and Dettelbach 1996). Yet Smith (1985, 1992, 2000), transposing Said's (1978) discussion of Orientalism to visual representations of the Pacific Islands, describes how many of the accuracies of such illustrated recordings were later changed, to conform to European imaginings of otherness, exoticism and degrees of primitivism and savagery.[14]

Nicholas Thomas (1989b) discusses the conceptions of French navigator Dumont d'Urville, whose map of Oceania in 1832 drew up boundaries between Melanesia, Polynesia and Micronesia on the basis of evolutionary ideals regarding the physical attributes of the Islanders and the degree of hierarchical structure of societies, as well as their disposition towards Europeans. The Polynesians were

---

14   See also Hereniko and Wilson 1999 who, cf Hanlon and White (2000: 2), 'refer to a 'Pacific Orientalism', suggesting an Orientalist discourse that takes distinctive forms in the Pacific Island region.

My God, My Land

hospitable and light-skinned, while the Melanesians were characterised by their blackness, savagery, and lack of political organisation:

> These blacks are almost always grounded in very fragile tribes, the chiefs of which exercise arbitrary power, often in a manner as tyrannical as that of many petty African despots. More degraded towards the state of barbarism than the Polynesians or Micronesians ... all their institutions appear still to be in their infancy; their dispositions and intelligence are also generally inferior to those of the tan race. (d'Urville in Thomas 1989b: 30)

In discussing the origins and significance of the Melanesia/Polynesia division, Thomas 1989b: 27) argues that the racism inherent in these still permeates anthropological discourse on Pacific studies: 'discredited ethnological typifications of peoples and societies seem to live on in the use of the labels "Melanesia" and "Polynesia" in contemporary anthropology and Pacific studies'. Pacific societies have been characterised, he writes, (1989b: 33) 'in terms of the presence or absence of some kind of centralization or hierarchy'.

Fiji, with its confluence of Polynesian and Melanesian traits, both in terms of physicality and of political organisation, proved a classificatory problem for Europeans. The Fijians of the eastern islands, the Lau group especially, were considered very close to Polynesians. They were lighter in colouring, taller, and considerably more hierarchically organised than the darker-skinned, more Melanesian types of western Fiji, and the interior of Vitilevu. In 1858, Wesleyan missionary Thomas Williams described his problem as follows:

> Differences of colour, physical conformation, and language, combine to form a separating line between the East and West Polynesians sufficiently clear, until we reach Fiji, where the distinguishing peculiarities seem to meet, and many of them to blend, thus betokening a confluence of the two races ... Excepting the Tongans, the Fijian is equal in physical development to the islanders eastward, yet distinct from them in colour, in which particular he approached the pure Papuan Negro; to whom, in form and feature, he is, however, vastly superior. Many of his customs distinguish him from his neighbours, although he is by language united to them all. (Williams 1982: 17)

Before the arrival of missionaries, beachcombers, survivors of shipwrecks, or trading agents deployed on the islands, were the first Europeans to live among Fijians. Unlike the missionaries and settlers who came there in the years to follow, these people lived with Fijians, conformed to Fijian ways, and in many cases married into Fijian society. William Lockerby, sandalwood trader from Liverpool, spent over seven years in the Pacific, writing a detailed journal (1808-1809) that includes vivid descriptions of warfare, widow-strangling and cannibalism in Fiji. (Im Thurn and Wharton, eds 1982) He considered his hosts on Bua island in a quite different light than that of cannibals ... In war they are fearless and savage to the utmost degree, but in peace their disposition is mild and generous to their friends, and the affection they bear towards their relations is very seldom found among Europeans. (Lockerby in Scarr 1984: 11)

While the processes of deconstructionism in Western academia in recent decades has challenged and changed its perceptions of its authority, its self-perception and representations of others, such representations, including missionary narratives, have had lasting effects on the ways in which Pacific Islanders see themselves and 'westerners'. Howard (2006: 14) writes that 'concern for the misrepresentation of Pacific Islanders in western media dating back to the 18th century was a motivating force' behind Rotuman anthropologist Vilsoni Hereniko's making of the film *The Land Has Eyes*. (*'Pear ta ma 'on maf'* 2004, see Hereniko 1994: 413)

While you're talking, we're sinking[15]

The hegemonic classification of Oceanic societies by the Western world as isolated, small and insignificant, 'unable to rise above their present condition of dependence on the largesse of wealthy nations' (Fry 1996: 4) continues. One example is the 'doomsdayism' of contemporary Australian imaging of the South Pacific and of Pacific Islanders described by Greg Fry. He maintains (1996: 1, 28) that 'the doomsdayists [the bureaucrat, the politician, the foreign affairs journalist and the academic economist], like earlier Australian "framers" of the islands, are engaged in a system of knowledge that implicitly denies self-determination [of Pacific Islanders] while claiming to advance it, and promotes superiority and exclusion while claiming to advance equality'.

The catastrophic situation of Pacific Island nations in relation to global warming, especially nations such as Tuvalu, the Marshall Islands and Kiribati already experiencing the serious effects of climate change, their land quite literally sinking as sea levels rise, is drawing Pacific Islanders into a new web of geographic, demographic and political global interconnectedness. However, unless Pacific Island nations are given proper places at the negotiating table as equal partners with the rich and powerful industralialised nations, and their needs in relation to mitigation goals and the financial and technological means for adaptation to climate change are met, Pacific Islanders run the risk of being 'framed' anew by the industrialised world: as 'disappearing worlds', isolated, passive victims of climate change.

Yet Pacific Island nations can make an impact through coordinated local and regional agency. The churches of the Pacific are aware of their own people's 'failure to be faithful to the requirements of the covenant [cf Genesis 2] ... to care for [God's] created world and be responsible stewards of the resources therein' (Pacific

---

15   Peter Emberson, Pacific Conference of Churches (PCC), in Kristeligt Dagblad 15 May 2009. World Council of Churches website, accessed October 2009.

Conference of Churches Environmental Programme). But, like churches across the world, the Pacific Conference of Churches points to the industrialised nations' over-production and over-consumption as the basic cause of anthropomorphic climate change. The PCC emphasises the injustice that those countries that pollute least, will suffer most, and call for global solidarity and justice in response to the crisis. 'A lot of people are talking about adaptation and mitigation and talking about saving the trees but there's not that many of us thats [sic] talking about looking for other places to live', Pacific Conference of Churches General Secretary Fei Tevi pointed out during the COP15 climate summit in Copenhagen in December 2009. And Jim Marurai, Prime Minister of the Cook Islands commented during the COP15, 'Sadly Mr. President, from what I have been hearing, some parties are not willing to respect our right – our right to survive'.[16]

Drawing on Pacific Island and Christian metaphors of connectedness the Statement from the 9th Assembly of the Pacific Conference of Churches on Climate Change declares:

> Our Moana, our Oceania is our gift from God ... We are a part of the Body of Christ.[17] When our low-lying atolls of Oceania are affected by the effects of climate change, we all suffer as a result. We stand at the Turanga Wae Wae (place of ownership/guardians of the gift) of the Pacific Ocean and as guardians of this Ocean, it is our duty to protect and safeguard this gift for our future generations ... We call on our sisters and brothers in Christ throughout the world to act in solidarity with us to reduce the causes of human-induced climate change. We issue this call particularly to churches in the highly industrialized nations whose societies are historically responsible for the majority of polluting emissions. We further urge these countries to take responsibility for the ecological damage that they have caused by paying for the costs of adaptation to the anticipated impacts (Halapua 2008: 96-97, see also the PCC Environmental Programme and the Moana Declaration (PCC 2009), Emberson 2009a, 2009b).

Talking about tradition

Talking about 'tradition' and the past is an important part of everyday life discourse in Fiji, as it is in countries right across the Pacific, a way of linking the past with the present:

---

16   http://climatepasifika.blogspot.com/2009/12/message-at-copenhagen-fei-tevi.html. See also http://www.pcc.org.fj/index.php?id=1, http://www.oikoumene.org/fileadmin/files/wccmain/2008pdfs/WCC ClimateChange_BackgroundInfo2008.pdf, and http://www.youtube.com/watch?v=oUyZOgcHn-Q&feature=related for Tuvalu representative's speech at COP15, 'The Fate Of My Country Rests In Your Hands'.

17   Cf 1 Corinthians 12 'In the one Spirit we were all baptized into one body ... if one member suffers, all suffer together with it'.

In the Fijian and Tongan languages, the terms for past are *gauna i liu* and *kuonga mu'a*, respectively; *gauna* and *kuonga* meaning "time" or "age" or "era"; and *liu* and *mu'a_meaning* "front" or "ahead"... The terms *liu* and *mu'a* may be used as verbs, as in *au sa liu* and *teu mu'omomu'a*, meaning, "I am going ahead of you", or ... "I am taking the lead" ... the literal translation of *au sa liu*. The past is then going ahead of us, leading into the future, which is behind us ... a conception of time that helps us retain our memories and to be aware of its presence ... The past is alive in us, so in more than a metaphorical sense the dead are alive – we are our history. (Hau'ofa 2000: 459-460)[18]

Samoan poet Albert Wendt alludes (below) to the continuous discussions, diverse practices and representations of tradition and custom, ideologies such as 'the Pacific Way', *kastam* ('custom', 'our tradition'), the *fa'a Samoa* (the Samoan Way), the 'Melanesian Way', in Fiji often known as *vakavanua* (the way of the land), *vakaviti* (the Fijian Way). These practices and ideologies all contain common elements of communal sharing and caring, of the interwoven nature of kinship ties and belonging to the land which, intertwined with Christian values and belief, form the basic threads in the fabric of Pacific Islander life.

Like a tree a culture is forever growing new branches, foliage, roots. Our cultures, contrary to the simplistic interpretation of our romantics, were changing even in pre-papalagi [pre-European] times through inter-island contact and the endeavours of exceptional individuals and groups who manipulated politics, religion, and other people. Contrary to the utterances of our elite groups, our pre-papalagi cultures were not perfect or beyond reproach. (Wendt 1976: 52 in Clarke 1999: 193)

The desire and need of Pacific Islanders to accentuate and re-define notions of tradition and Islander cultural identity in terms of what is 'traditional' and 'authentically' part of past culture, following independence from colonial rule, has strongly influenced politics and social life throughout the Pacific. And the dynamics between people and institutions, between practice and ideals, between the old and the new were – and still are – seeped in power relations, in who has access to definitions and re-formulations of tradition. As Wendt points out, challenging the propensity among many people in the Pacific Islands to see tradition as solid and un-changing, socio-cultural life in the Pacific Islands has always been in flux. And as Hereniko (2000: 27) emphasises:

No single individual or ethnic group has a monopoly on the truth. After all, everyone is an insider sometimes and an outsider at other times. To refuse to acknowledge the shifting nature of our subjective positions in different contexts,

---

18   Hau'ofa (2000: 459) quotes Kame'eleihiwa 1992: 22-23, who gives the same explanation for the Hawaiian terms for past and future.

the multiplicity of voices among a seemingly homogeneous group or the vast
differences in points of view between Western-educated Pacific Islanders and
farmers at the village level, is to ignore the truth of our personal experiences.

So people 'talk about' tradition, reflect on tradition, and 'do' or 'have' traditional
practices, all of which mean different things to different people at different times
in different contexts. Tradition, then, is an open field of diverse, contested and
negotiated discourses, practices and representations. Traditions were always
fluid and malleable. Oral traditions, Tonkinson writes (2000: 172-177), were by
nature variable in content and interpretation. Yet at the national level of societies,
tradition is likely to be reified or objectified as timeless and primordial, and
contrasted strongly with foreign elements, politicians being the 'embodiment of
contradictions inherent in political uses of tradition and the agents who attempt to
resolve those contradictions'. (Ibid.) The widening gap between the rich and the
poor, between urban and rural communities and the emergence of new powerful
elites in Pacific Island societies means that tradition will be increasingly evoked
'as a strategy for justifying such inequalities'.[19]

In Fiji *vanua*, as a lifestyle based on the nurturing of kin, is usually posited in
opposition to other ways, such as 'the way of Europeans', or 'a way of life in the
manner of money' (Toren 1989: 142), or 'the way of Indians' (see also Thomas
1990b). Yet, however 'highly reified as a reference point for practice' (Thomas
1992c: 324), *vanua* is not a static construction: "'The way in the manner of the
land" is not a mere leftover from an earlier era, but is itself being continuously
constructed and transformed'. (Toren 1989: 714) Positing *vanua* against 'the way
of Indians' has developed since the coups of 1987 into an understanding of *vanua*
as a dominant culture of *itaukei* within which the element of Christianity is 'all
too frequently expressed as intolerance towards Hindu or Muslim fellow citizens
[combined with] … the interests of the new chiefly class whom Rabuka claimed to
represent during the coup' (Kaplan 1990: 143).

Representing tradition in Fiji research

Much research on tradition in Fiji has focused on missionary and colonial
misapprehensions and misrepresentations of Fijian tradition, since perpetuated in
Fiji politics and legislation, and in people's understanding of their history and
identity. This is particularly pertinent with regard to issues of land tenure.

Peter France's (1969) ground-breaking study on Fiji colonial history
established that British misinterpretations of Fijian social structure and systems
of land tenure frose former fluid systems into a legislative 'orthodoxy' which still
exists today (cf. Jolly 1992b). Many studies on tradition in Fiji have since focused
on colonial constructions of Fijian traditionality, '… a way of life … constructed

---

19   Ibid. See also Bendix 1967, Otto and Pedersen 2000.

on the foundations of village life and buttressed by bureaucratic-administrative regulations and procedures' (Rutz 1987: 557 and 1995), and their centrality in contemporary politics of identity. Margaret Jolly contrasts, for example, the focus on continuity between past and present in Fijian tradition with the rupture and revival which characterises *kastam* in Vanuatu, linking these different understandings with the legislative *inalienation* of land in Fiji and *alienation* of land in Vanuatu during the colonial period. Clammer (1976), referring inter alia to France's 1966 documentation of the Kaunitoni Myth, notes ways in which colonial models of Fijian tradition permeated scholarly research, being uncritically re-presented as authentically Fijian.[20]

The dynamics between Fijian appropriations of or resistance to colonial and missionary influences and impositions in Fiji and their importance in the present, has also been widely discussed[21] Kaplan's work, in particular 1995a, describes how Fijians, through syncretic appropriations of colonial and missionary discourse and imagery and Fijian myth, in the cultic figure of Navosavakadua and his *Tuka* movement, actively resisted and redefined colonial authority to their own uses. In elegantly blending historical narrative with contemporary ethnography, Kaplan shows how history is continuously being remade by individuals and groups, using selective elements of the past in their constructions of past and present.[22]

Ambiguities and transformations

Despite the appearance of *vanua* and Christianity as a solid whole posited in opposition to non-Fijians and non-Christians the relationship between church and chiefly power is ambiguous. Architecturally, this is expressed in Methodist churches retaining a separate chiefly door and place for the village chief and elders in the *loqi tabu* area (the sanctuary) at the back of the church, the hierarchically 'highest' (*icake*) position, where the pulpit, often raised, is located (see also Tippett 1968: 169-171, Thornley 1979: 110 and Toren 1988). Originally, this emphasised the divine sanctioning of chiefly authority and the separation of people and chiefs. (Thornley, pers comm. 1997)

This spatial lay-out is not found in Catholic, Anglican or other churches in Fiji. High Chief Ratu Sir Kamisese Mara, who converted to Catholicism, who converted to Catholicism as a young man, is said to have initially expressed surprise at having to sit with the rest of the congregation in church, rather than in a chiefly place, spatially hierarchically above the people (Father K.Barr, pers

---

20 E.g. Roth 1954 and Geddes 1945, who had both worked in the colonial administration.

21 Cf Thomas 1990a and 1992b, Kaplan 1988, 1989a, 1989b, 1990a and 1995b, Kelly and Kaplan 2001.

22 See also reviews by Ogan 1997 and Wilde 1998.

comm.). In Methodist churches it is only when the minister stands at the pulpit that he is physically and hierarchically higher than the chief. Only for a moment, I was told, does he symbolically become the chief:

> We are the chief ... at that very moment, eh? ... in the church. But when we come out, we are a normal *talatala*, but the respect of the people is still there. We are equivalent to the chief ... the *talatala* is the representative of God ... so our ways of life will always put God as a chiefly figure ... In that area ... [*loqi tabu*] they both of them have to complement each other ... if they don't ... there will be a conflict between the chief and the *talatala* ... which sometimes happens. (Interview, Tuima, 1998)

Christina Toren's (1988) rich analysis of the Middle Eastern rugs depicting da Vinci's picture of the Last Supper, found in Methodist churches and homes on Gau island, she argues that the image of Christ at the table, offering the wine and bread to the Apostles, in a number of ways mirrors the hierarchy of Fijian society, as reflected in the spatial positioning of ranked men and the paramount chief in a *yaqona* ceremony – symbolising the hierarchy of Fijian society, including the invisibility of women in ritual life. Christ symbolises the paramount chief of a *vanua*,

> the relationship between God and Christ, his son, 'the word made flesh', may be likened to that between the ancestor gods (*kalou vu*, lit. root gods) and the paramount chief of a country ... the orientation of the viewer and of figures in the 'The Last Supper' confirm the transformation of the balanced reciprocity of *veiqaravi* [lit. facing one another] inscribed in the space of the village, into the unambiguous hierarchy of 'attendance' on chiefs – inscribed in the space of the house on the axis of 'above' and 'below'. (Ibid: 698 and 709)

Toren's analysis is a detailed discussion of the continuity and malleability of tradition in Fiji. 'What constitutes a living tradition may reveal an extra dimension to the past, one whose validity is not a matter of "what happened" but how it may be understood' (1988: 696). Social meaning, Toren argues, is constituted in social relations, and so tradition is also constituted and mediated in social relations. Understandings of Christianity are therefore seen primarily in terms of the continuity and transformation of social relations within particular social spaces and contexts. Thus external influences, such as Christian symbolism and values are internalised, domesticated in Fijian terms.

As Toren also points out, there is a certain irony in the significance of a Roman Catholic image of the initiation of the Eucharist in the Da Vinci tapestries in churches that so rarely celebrate Holy Communion, her point being that meaning is continuously transformed. Catholic symbolism is transformed to become an intrinsic part of Methodist tradition. '"The coming of the light" did not violate indigenous cultural practice but revealed the inherent Christianity of the Fijian people. The process of constructing the past neither denies nor distorts it. Rather it reveals a dimension to the past that historians and anthropologists have overlooked' (ibid: 696).

I have seen tapestries depicting this same picture in Methodist churches in both Tailevu and Nadrogā Navosa provinces, in a Roman Catholic church on Taveuni island, Cakaudrove Province, and in Methodist and Seventh Day Adventist homes in Naroro village in Nadrogā Navosa. This underscores the importance of Toren's observations and the significance of her analysis as perhaps not only pertaining to Methodist perceptions of this image in Fiji, but to Christians from several different Churches.

I discussed Toren's interpretation of Christ's spatial positioning in the picture as representing a mirroring of traditional chiefly status and hierarchy with a Fijian Methodist minister who, though finding Toren's ideas interesting, offered a significantly different interpretation. He saw *The Last Supper* as depicting the traditional ideal of chiefly leadership in Fiji: Jesus as the chief, by handing the bread and wine to his disciples, is shown in a momentarily *subservient* position, selflessly serving his people (cf Matthew 20: 20-28):

> Jesus, the chief of chiefs, so to say, eh?... ready to wash the disciples' feet ... Ready to serve the others, eh?! ... That's a good image! The chief is the chief of the lower down class. He is there for them ... chief of the servers (turaga nei kaisi) – yeah, we translate it like that. That was the earlier concept of the chiefly system in Fiji. It was unfortunately taken out when power came into it. (Banivanua, interview 23 July 1998)

Several Pacific Island theologians (cf Forman 2005: 120) have related the kava ceremony to the Christian Eucharist, the themes of self-sacrifice, leadership and service being elements of both rituals (see e.g. Fa'asi 1993 for a Tongan perspective).

Gospel journeys of land and ocean

For more than 30 years Pacific Island theologians have been discussing the dynamics of Gospel and culture, developing particularly Pacific-oriented theologies and re-orienting themselves from the euro-centric evangelisation that so often trampled insensitively on Pacific Island traditions, values and beliefs.

Thornley (1979: 161), Referring to R.H. Green, Methodist missionary in Nadrogā in the years just preceding the independence of the Methodist Church in Fiji in 1964, notes that 'the effect of sustained mission endeavour to shame Methodist followers into a rejection of all links with the past produced a profound silence on spiritual matters not considered in conformity with the orthodox'. 'Their religion was a closed religion', writes Uriam (2005: 297), 'and they had no place for anything that was not part of *their* church ... Their church was the centre of the world, and the world should listen to them, for they knew what was best for the world'.

> They tried to get local people to adopt a way of life that is not theirs ... it seemed that this was development ... but it was modernisation ... they were actually trying to get people to convert to *their* way of life and did not respect that we had out own way of life ... and our own conscience that was given to us by God. They were not trying to develop the God that was already present in us, but they were bringing this white God into the black people of the Pacific, and not realising that God was already present there. [People] just needed transformation, they just needed conversion [from] some of the way of life that was not really reflecting the love of God to other people. (Interview, Paulo Balei, Fijian Catholic lay missionary, 12 October 2004)

Pacific Islander theologians (cf Forman 2005: 120) point out that their ancestors' strong beliefs in a divine presence and in the afterlife made them very open to Christian faith and produced a remarkable strength of belief. Islanders' deep awareness of the spiritual realm is a particular gift they bring to Christianity. (Cf. Puloka 1987, Raku 1988, Rimon 1988, Talapusi 1995)

Drawing on anthropological and 'church and culture' theories, a young first year Solomon Islands seminarian and novice of the Catholic missionary order the Society of Mary (SM) gave the following answer to an anthropology take-home exam at Pacific Regional Seminary. Responding to the question of whether he as a missionary in a foreign country would preach the Gospel in the same way as he would preach it in his own village, he wrote:

> I have experienced ... the model [of evangelisation] 'Christ against culture'. It left my society naked, without cultural identity today ... It destroyed most of our ways of life. Therefore as a missionary to another country, I would preach in the anthropological way – 'Christ of culture'. Respectful and sensitive towards people and cultures. In Makira province, Solomon Islands, Christianity [has] done away with most of the ways of life, the way we [lived] and did things. Missionaries entered and denounced almost everything: custom dances, war games, feasting, spiritual fishing adventures Today, there are said to be Christians without self-identity who are confused, are abandoning one faith [for] another, and there is [an] underground movement of fanaticism. All [this] happened because of some missionaries who are disrespectful and less sensitive ... I would prefer to be understanding of the complex nature of life[,] the world and its people. (Patrick Woria, April 2005)

In 2001 Pope John Paul II addressed Catholics in Oceania, taking issue with past mission insensitivities, acknowledging the inherent strength of religiosity of pre-Christian Oceanic cultures, and stressing the importance of cultural respect and of making the Gospel message contextually relevant:

When the missionaries first brought the Gospel to Aboriginal or Maori people, or to the island nations, they found peoples who already possessed an ancient and profound sense of the sacred. Religious practices and rituals were very much part of their daily lives and thoroughly permeated their cultures ... The missionaries at times sought to impose elements which were culturally alien to the people ... Inculturation is born out of respect for both the Gospel and the culture in which it is proclaimed and welcomed ... The process of inculturation is the gradual way in which the Gospel is incarnated in the various cultures ... The Church teaches the unchanging truth of God, addressed to the history and the culture of a particular people. Therefore, in each culture the Christian faith will be lived in a unique way ... An authentic inculturation of the Gospel has a double aspect. On the one hand, a culture offers positive values and forms which can enrich the way the Gospel is preached, understood and lived. On the other hand, the Gospel challenges cultures and requires that some values and forms change. (*John Paul II, Eccelesia in Oceania* 2001: 8 and 17).

The Catholic Church's 'theory of syncretism, currently known as inculturation', writes Cannell 2006: 25, 'presents quite a sophisticated attitude to local culture, claiming that local forms of approaching God may all be acceptable, and even necessary, as long as the presence of a transcendent deity presiding over all is acknowledged'. Inculturation – and contextual theology for that matter – raises questions of how best the Gospel and Christian values can be presented to different peoples in different contexts. Which aspects of tradition are supportive of Christianity? Which aspects of tradition relate to the 'seeds of the Gospel'? Which are challenged by Christianity? Which aspects of tradition should be questioned? The sharing and caring between kinspeople, so fundamental within Pacific Islander cultures, is expanded within Christianity to concern everyone. Everyone is our neighbour, even those people we don't like. (Father Kevin Barr MSC, pers comm. 2005)

At the Second Vatican Council (1962-1965) the Roman Catholic Church revised the former Latin Mass rite which can now be celebrated either in Latin or in the vernacular. At the same time the Church opened up for the inclusion and use within this rite of traditional cultural symbols and rituals of the many different peoples and cultures within the universal Church. Elements of local tradition, cultural symbolism and practice have now become integrated and valued parts of Roman Catholic liturgy and worship – and are expressed also in the design and architecture of Catholic churches. In some Catholic churches in Fiji for example, the tabernacle, where the consecrated Host, believed to be the actual Body of Christ, is kept, is designed as a *bure kalou,* a pre-Christian 'god house'. In this instance the architectural form of a traditional sacred place is used to house the most sacred element of Catholic belief. In this way traditions of the past are woven into a contemporary Christian present. Their meaning is thereby retained, although transformed to become part of Christian symbolism. The past

Figure I.1   Catholic Charasmatic Renewal Convention, Suva, 1998

is not cut off from the present but, as the roots of the present, is part of that which gives the present life and meaning.

Some years ago in Fiji during Holy Week, instead of performing the ritual of feet washing that is part of the penitential rites of Holy Thursday, Catholic Archbishop Mataca instead served kava to his priests. Usually he himself would be the most honoured guest in a kava ceremony. For the Archbishop to place himself in the position of actually serving the kava to those hierarchically 'lower' in rank than himself, is a profound inversion of roles, and a very clear statement of humility. By this, Archbishop Mataca expressed, as Christ did by washing the feet of his disciples, his own humility and servitude towards others. (Father K. Barr, pers comm. 2005) The Archbishop hereby incorporated strong Fijian cultural symbolism and ritual of servitude and community into Catholic liturgical rites. In Figure I.1, during the final mass of the Catholic Charismatic Renewal Convention, held in Suva in 1998, the chalice is carried to the altar at the Offertory by a Fijian in the traditional dress of a warrior, making a traditional presentation.

Figure I.2　　'Black Christ with Worshippers', triptych mural by Jean
　　　　　　　　Charlot, St Xavier's Catholic Mission, Naiserelagi (centre)

'Black Christ with Worshippers'

A particularly striking visual rendition, albeit by a European artist who spent much of his life in the Pacific Islands, of the inculturation of Fijian and Indo-Fijian cultural symbols and values with Catholic symbolism, is found in a rural church in Vitilevu. Perched on the top of Navunibitu Hill at the foot of the Kauvadra mountain range in Ra, northern Vitilevu, and with a panoramic view across the azure blue expanse of Vitilevu Bay, lies the small church of St Xavier's Catholic Mission, Naiserelagi. Built in 1918 from soapstone carved from the top of the hillside, it houses an unusual treasure, a striking triptych murial, painted by French artist Jean Charlot. In 1960 the priest of the mission, Monsignor Franz Wasner (former private chaplain to the von Trapp family singers) commissioned Charlot to paint an altar panel. Monsignor Wasner's vision was an altar panel that depicted the different ethnic groups in Fiji, united in Christ. The triptych 'Black Christ with Worshippers' was painted between October 1962 and January 1963; two additional frescoes 'St Joseph's Workshop' and 'Annunciation' were later added. (Fiji Museum nd)

Against a backdrop of luscious palm fronds, green taro leaves, *yaqona* (kava) plants, banana palms and green sugar cane the triptych beautifully depicts a rich fusion of Fiji, of cultural and Christian symbols all focused towards the central figure of a crucified black Christ. As with Salvador Dali's famous painting *Christ of St John of the Cross* (1951) no nails pierce the hands or feet of this Pacific

Figure I.3   'Black Christ with Worshippers', triptych mural by Jean
Charlot, St Xavier's Catholic Mission, Naiserelagi
(left-hand side)

Figure I.4   'Black Christ with Worshippers', triptych mural by Jean
Charlot, St Xavier's Catholic Mission, Naiserelagi
(right-hand side)

Islander Christ on the Cross, his Sacred Heart aflame in his breast. He is depicted wearing a loincloth of brown Tongan-style patterned bark-cloth (*kumi*) used in chiefly burials. The *kumi* has the words *omnis honor et gloria* (all honour and glory) printed on it and it is decorated with symbols of the Holy Trinity: a Star symbolising the birth of Christ; a dove, symbolising the Holy Spirit; and the fish, symbol of Christ from the early church, the Ancient Greek word for fish, *ichthys,* an acrostic, meaning 'Jesus Christ, God's son, saviour', also used in the shortened version IHS.

Immediately to the left of the crucified Christ figure is a wooden *tanoa* (kava bowl). The *magimagi* (plaited coconut fibre string) of the *tanoa* that traditionally would be laid along the ground to point directly towards and honour the chief or highest ranking person present at a kava ceremony, is pointing to Christ as the High Chief. Three large shiny white cowrie shells, rather than the usual one, adorn the end of the *magimagi*, symbolising the Holy Trinity. To the left of the *tanoa* a Fijian warrior in barkcloth and pandanus palm *sulu* is presenting Christ with a *tabua* (whales tooth). Behind the warrior a Fijian woman carries a presentational roll of woven mats, symbol of women's labour and love. And to the far left a local school girl, in bright blue and white uniform dress, faces Christ, symbolising the importance of the mission's work on education and its role for the next generation.

On the right hand side an Indian woman in a soft blue sari holds a garland of flowers to present to Christ. Behind her, amidst bright green, young sugar cane, we glimpse an Indo-Fijian man, leading a pair of oxen, pulling a wooden plough. Here we sense the import of Indo-Fijian skill and labour in working the land and farming cane, the holiness of the cow in Indian culture, connecting to ancient beliefs in their distant former home across the ocean, the image also emphasising the importance of the Catholic ministry to the Indo-Fijian community in this area.

To the far right of the triptych is a young boy, an acolyte, in a red cassock and white surplice, holding a lit candle. Behind him the curved Bishop's stave is propped against a palm tree. Saint Francis Xavier, the patron saint of the parish of Naiserelagi, dressed in white lace soutane and Feast Day, gold-trimmed white chasuble and stole, is celebrating the Eucharist, holding up the white host and golden chalice, the Body and Blood of Christ.

On the left hand side of the main picture stands a young Fijian priest in white soutane – the present Archbishop Petero Mataca, symbol of the new generation of indigenous clergy within the Church. Placed next to Father Mataca, is the figure of a European priest dressed in a black soutane and cloak – Saint Peter Chanel, patron saint of the Pacific Islands, holding the wooden club with which he was martyred on the island of Futuna in 1841. Golden halos are painted above St Frances Xavier and St Peter Chanel, indicating their canonised status.[23]

23   I thank Father Denis Mahony SM and other Marist fathers for assistance in interpreting the symbolism of this triptych, and Paul Geraghty for mentioning June Knox-Mawer's (1965) descripton of the frescoes and her visit to Monsignor Wassner (see also Klarr 2005 and Varea n.d.)

The symbolism of inculturation in this triptych suggests a Christianity that embraces diverse cultural values and traditions and complementary expressions of faith and worship. The strong images in the triptych of land, the fruits and produce of the land and the working of the land underscore the ideal of inculturation as grafting the Christian message onto the strong roots of tradition, the object of mission being 'not to destroy but to fulfil'. (Cf Barr 1979)

'The contemporary message [of] mission is that you need to go out to other people and show them the love of God. Show them [that] whether you are a Hindu, a Muslim, you're an Indian, a Rotuman or you are Chinese or whatever, God loves you just the same as he loves me … For us the contemporary understanding of mission is that we believe that the Christ we want to bring to other people is already present there'. (Balei, interview 12 October 2004) As MSC missionary and anthropologist in Papua New Guinea, Carl Laufer, expressed: 'When we approach a person of another culture and of other religions we have … to [take] off our shoes, because the place we enter is holy [Cf God's command to Moses, as he approached the burning bush, Exodus 3: 5-6]. Otherwise … we might forget that God has already been in this place before us'. (Janssen in Barr 1979: 16)

Treading with such reverence this triptych interweaves a complementary landscape of Fijian and Indo-Fijian cultures, of ancient and holy values and traditions, of lives lived and given in love and faith.

The *mana* of the Gospel

In 1988 and 1989, not long after the first coups in Fiji, the then Dean of Holy Trinity Anglican Cathedral, Winston Halapua from Tonga, commissioned a series of illustrations for theological training. St John's Training Centre, under the Anglican Diocese of Polynesia, published two booklets of passages from the Gospels, strikingly illustrated by Robert Parkes. The theme of each passage is conveyed simply in one sentence on the page opposite the illustration, in English, Fijian, Tongan, Samoan and Hindi. These languages 'reflect the multi-lingual and multi-cultural richness, and yet complexity, of our Diocese', Bishop Bryce from Tonga, Archbishop in Polynesia, writes in the foreword of *The Resurrection and Pentecost*. The Gospel events, Holy Week and the time from the Resurrection to the Ascension, are placed in different, familiar Pacific Island contexts. 'In attempting to make the unfamiliar familiar, retelling the Gospel Story in this new way, the overriding hope is that this work will be a witness to Christ's *mana* (his abiding spiritual presence) which transcends all the differences, unites all the diversity and fulfils all aspirations'. (Ibid.)

The publication of these illustrated booklets at that specific time in Fiji's history was particularly significant in terms of preaching a Gospel message of inclusivity and caring and sharing among peoples of different cultural backgrounds. Not

Figure I.5 **'In fellowship Jesus shares his last supper' [Luke 22: 14-20]**
Source: *The Love of God Among Us: The Easter Story* (St John's Training Centre, 1988).

least the fact that Christ and his disciples were depicted as people belonging to all of these four cultural groups facilitated a powerful message at a sensitive time. Bishop Bryce continued his foreword, describing the illustrations in the book:

In the first illustration (Figure I.5) Jesus is depicted in the core male Pacific Island situation of sitting round a kava bowl, *talanoa*, telling stories, talking and listening and drinking kava. Jesus is sharing his Last Supper with his disciples, but it is particularly significant in a Pacific Island context (cf former discussion) that *he* as High Chief is serving the others. What is also notable is that although the recipient is about to *cobo* (the ritual clap a recipient makes in acceptance and thanks prior to taking the cup) Jesus is not presenting the kava formally, as a server would, kneeling in front of the recipient, but handing the *bilo* to the other, as one friend to another. One senses not hierarchy here, but people in communion on equal terms.[24]

Figure I.6, 'The Road to Emmaus' could be in Savi'i in Western Samoa. Christ strolls with two of his unsuspecting and dejected followers, all dressed in the customary lavalava [sulu in Fijian]; one disciple bears his traditional body

---

24   See Halapua (2009), Chapter 7 on *talanoa*.

Figure I.6   'The road to Emmaus' [Luke 24: 13-35]
Source: MANA: The Resurrection and Pentecost (St John Training Centre, 1989).

tattoo. Each carries a leaf which has been used as an umbrella'. (Bryce in St John's Training Centre 1989) At the Ascension (Figure I.8), 'Christ's followers truly represent the diversity and reality of the Church in the Pacific. One can see the Fijian *sulu* (or Samoan *lavalava*), the Tongan *ta'ovala* [fine, woven mat for church and ceremonial use, cf Chapter 3] the Indian sari and the European woman's *vinivo* (Fijian for dress). All bring gifts in the traditional way, coming to bid Christ goodbye'. (Bryce in St John's Training Centre 1989) This image of Christ taking leave of his followers on shore of the ocean brings to mind Pacific Island pre-Christian conceptions of the journey of the soul by river or sea westwards towards the after world (cf Chapter 3)

The last illustration of the booklet, with the text 'empowered by the Holy Spirit, Peter attests to the faith within by willingly preaching the truth in boldness [Acts 4: 1-22]', depicts the usually peaceful foreshore in Suva, Queen Elizabeth Drive. A missionary is led away by a Fijian soldier, the papers in his hand scattering on the ground as he is arrested (suggesting that although the messenger may be removed and imprisoned, the message will remain and, like seeds of the Gospel, scattered on the ground, will grow). This must have been an extremely powerful image at that particular time, so shortly after Suva had

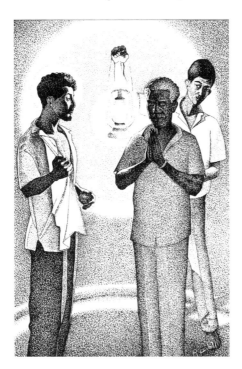

Figure I.7   'Thomas assuming the Hindu gesture of devotion having seen
for himself the wounds of Christ's suffering' [John 20: 26-29]

Source: *MANA: The Resurrection and Pentecost* (St John Training Centre, 1989).

been full of soldiers during of the coups in 1987. Although it relates to a biblical
passage concerning evangelisation, the illustration also vividly captures the
force of military power, injustice, loss of freedom of speech and imprisonment,
the power and domination of some over others – all painful themes of the coups.
This illustration also depicts the repression or removal of that which is different
and unwanted – alluding to the oppression suffered by Indo-Fijians and by those
who spoke out against the injustices at the time of the coups.

'It is hoped', concludes Bishop Bryce in his foreword, 'that the viewer will
look anew at his or her reality, at that of others different from themselves, and
then look again at the meaning of the Kingdom of God as it relates to life, culture
and the world'. (St John's Training Centre 1989) This example of inculturation
emphasises at one and the same time the richness and diversity of community-
based Pacific Islander values, the spreading of the Christ-centred Gospel message
of salvation, love, forgiveness and inclusiveness, and makes explicit reference

Figure I.8   'The Ascension' [Acts 1: 8-11]

Source: *MANA: The Resurrection and Pentecost* (St John Training Centre, 1989).

to the use of force and oppression in society – and the necessity of speaking out courageously against such injustice.

Theological journeys of land and sea

Liberal Pacific Island theologians are re-defining and re-contextualising the Gospel message as rooted in Pacific Island soil, as part of the land and seascape of the Pacific Islands.[25] Their theologies emphasise connectedness, relationality and inclusivity. 'The seed of *Pacificness* is that of survival, it can only grow if survivors understand that 'life', the goal, is always in transition from self-centredness to relation-centredness', writes Havea. (1993: 15) While these theologies are rooted in the land, they are simultaneously Christ-centric, cf Prior (1993: 32-34) who describes a Trinitarian theme in 'coconut theology' of Christology, *Kairos* (fulfilled time, God's time, God's grace, cf. Mark 1: 15), and Communion.

---

25   June Knox-Mawer's (1965) description … Wassner. (see also Klarr 2005 and Varea n.d.).

Tuwere's theology of the land seeks (cf Forman 2005: 116) to meld the Christian dualism of the physical and spiritual by placing the spiritual within the land. The history of salvation in Fiji is seen as the continuous work of God, 'first in the history of the land, its beliefs and value systems, and then in the coming of Christianity and the growth of the Church. Christ stands at the centre of this history. Fijian culture is therefore not the final reality'. (see also Gilles nd) So just as the minister in the Prologue described the creation of *vanua* as the work of God, Christianity is seen as the beginning and fulfilment of *vanua*, of all that went before:

> When the Yahwist writer says 'And the Lord God formed the man from the dust of the ground'… it brings into play the total meaning of the *vanua* … man's origin is in a piece of earth. His bond with the earth belongs to his essential being. The earth is his mother. He comes out of her womb. From it he has his body'.[26]

Tradition and Christianity, land, sea and spirit are interwoven in this prayer, expressed in images of Samoan cultural values and practices such as kava drinking and tattoos – and of journeying together on the ocean:

Atua[27]
Allow us to drink from the tanoa of Your peace,
Right the course of our canoes
to overcome the currents of violence, hatred, war, abuse
Give us peace of being at rest, so that peace prevails
over any wind that gusts through our islands,
Tattoo in our hearts Your righteousness and purity,
Through all cultures and walks of life, we pray
as instruments of peace and as the people of Pasifika.

The holistic basis of Pacific Island theologies have much to offer in relation to our understandings of the global climate crisis – which highlights the fragility and interconnectedness of the earth's environment, and the necessity and empowering potential in working together to combat the problems. Contemporary discussions within the Pacific Conference of Churches concern developing a theology of hope. (Cf R. Nokise, Bird, Casimira, pers comm. 2009) The prayer of hope and supplication below, as Halapua 2008 and the prayer by Aunoa, draws on images of people's strengthened journeying together on the ocean to redeem the Fonua:

---

26   Tuwere 2002a: 97, see also Tugaue 1994 in Bush 1995d: 81, compare Cadogan 2004, and see Longgar 2009.

27   *Atua* means 'God' in Samoan and other Polynesian languages. Prayer by M. Aunoa, American Samoa (*International Day of Prayer for Peace 2008, DOV Pacific Focus*). World Council of Churches.

Loving God,
provide a voice for our struggles.
Provide extra paddles to bring us together.
Grant peace to our hearts, our ears and our eyes
to forgive and to love our neighbours and our enemies.
O Lord, give us a chance to redeem the Fonua
and to reclaim paradise.[28]

Pacific women's theologies

The importance of inclusivity and equality, of all people being equal in Christ, expressed in contemporary Pacific Island theologies questions and calls for transformation of fundamental aspects of patriarchal structures of gender, hierarchy and age inequalities and oppression in Pacific Island cultures. Roman Catholic nun Sr Keiti Ann Kanongata'a (2002: 35)[29] writes of the valuable contributions Pacific Island women have to offer contextual theologies through their particular experiences. Women are, she writes, increasingly speaking out and acting against their marginalisation in decision-making processes and many other aspects of society, and against the widespread domestic violence towards women and children that takes place across the Pacific Island region:

> Today, we do not just tell our stories we have launched into actually making things happen. The women are so much involved in the struggle against violence especially domestic violence against themselves and our children; in the struggle for justice and in the struggle for liberation from cultural and social enslavement.

A fascinating collection of innovative reflections by Pacific Island women theologians (Johnson and Filemoni-Tofaeono (eds) 2003), weave together personal, cultural, church and scriptural strands (ibid: 14-15), celebrating traditional values and practices, stressing the need for equality and inclusivity, and highlighting social justice issues:

> We as women need to address our pre-conceived ideas about the sanctity of our traditional Fijian village life, and ask whether it builds our relationship with God and our response to God's call ... Full and equal participation in the life of the community and the Church, irrespective of gender, creates the essential and crucial ministry of Jesus, to which he called all his followers. His mission

---

28   Fonua is Tongan for vanua. Prayer by Reverend Valamotu Palu, Fiji. *Ecumenical Prayer Cycle: In God's Hands*. World Council of Churches.

29   See also Kanongata'a 1992, 1996,

was to bring redemption to the whole of humanity. In such a mission we can all participate. (Soronakadavu 2003: 163-164) [30]

Michiko Ete-Lima (2003: 24, 29) describes a 'discourse about God using the concepts and ideals of the *feagaiga* (the sacred relationship between the brother and the sister in the Samoan context) ... The personhood of God is made explicit in the *feagaiga* as both the brother and the sister. This relational concept of God allows one to embrace the unique feminine and masculine attributes of God'.

Valamotu Palu connects the commitment, dedication and sacrifice of individual women tapa-makers, working closely together over long periods to create a whole tapa,[31] with that of the Christian's faith journey:

> To be real to the people, salvation must come as it is defined by Pacific people in their own cultures ... I believe we can glimpse a clear picture of God's relationship to humans through the relationship between the women and their tapa ... The careful following of each step until a long, beautiful and colourful ngatu is complete reflects God's relationship with creation, especially with human beings, a story of repentance and rebirth ... Tapa makers give life to the world through their creative work. God can be imagined as a potter in Palestine, as well as a tapa maker in Tonga. (Palu 2003: 62, 70-71)

In another reflection, love, belonging to, responsibility towards and care for the land is equated with love and belonging to God:

> For the Maohi people, to love the land is an affirmation that we love God – the divine land owner. God is portrayed as present in the land. Like the mother's womb, God entrusted new life in the womb of the land, providing everything needed to sustain and enrich the life of humankind ... the Church implores the people not to sell our lands, for they are our mother's and God's particular gift to the Maohi people. It is for this reason that we stand against nuclear testing in our land. (Hoiore 2003: 44)

Céline Hoiore connects this deep sense of belonging to the land and to God with the call to be born again (John 3:5),

> to return to the motherland to rediscover our identity and the fullness of life in the womb of God. A *taata A'ia* can never be uprooted from his or her place of birth. Wherever we go, our motherland is always calling us to return home. God has named us, we are the *taata A'ia* of God. (Ibid: 45)

---

30   See also e.g. Oh 2003, Meo 2003, Mansale 2003, Sovaki 2003, Tapu-Qilio 2003, Costello-Olsson 2003, and see e.g. Malogne-Fer 2007 and Eriksen 2008 on women and contemporary Protestant Christianity in the Pacific Islands.

31   Very large piece of printed bark cloth, see Chapter 3.

All reflections focus on the transformative and communal nature of faith as connecting people through God to one another, to their traditions and to the land:

> The Fijian presentation ceremony is an act of transformation. It, transforms ordinary objects, such as the *tabua* /sacred whale's tooth), *yaqona* (kava, our ceremonial drink), artifacts, food and even human beings from an inferior state to a superior state. When these objects or human beings are offered in a ceremonial way, their quality is transformed to a higher, more sacred level. They are transformed into sacredness. Furthermore, what was once personal has become public. What was once small and unimportant is transformed into something of greater value.
>
> In this process, the quantity and quality of life's resources and the value of relationships and human well-being are made more valuable, more precious, because they are deemed to be complete and whole through the ceremonial presentation. In the same way, through the presence of Jesus in our lives, individuals and communities can be transformed and made whole. (Sainimere Niukula 2003: 208-209)

And Leseli Raitiqa's (2003: 105 and 106) reflection on the Book of Ruth, parallels its themes of sickness and healing with *vanua* sickness in Fiji, thereby linking the themes of this chapter with the themes of belonging to the land discussed in Chapter 1, of healing the land in Chapter 2, and of reconciliation and healing in Chapters 6 and 7:

> *Vanua* sickness is the result of the removal of blessing (*mana*) from the land ... [causing] it to be empty ... With courage and faithful action Ruth ...restored the family and healed the land ... I liken Ruth to Christ, the ultimate redeemer of the land and of all life. Through Ruth God healed her family and their land. ...Jesus, the true *mana*, is the healer of *vanua* sickness and brings life back to all his people'.

Chapter 1
Paths Across Space and Time

Belonging to the land

'People belong to the earth, *na qele* [the soil]', my mother in the village said. 'We are born of it and are buried in it when we die. We should honour and respect the *vanua*', she said, referring to the Pentecostal church in a related, neighbouring village which rejected many of the values of *vanua*. She was saddened, she told me, that her youngest daughters [as members of that church] had turned away from the *vanua*.

'Land for me is like a mother', a woman told Reverend Dr Tuwere. 'When the soil is thrown carelessly all over the place when one has already dug a wild yam, it hurts because it is part of me'. (Sanaila of Levua, Wailevu in Tuwere 2002: 35) 'The *vanua*' writes Tuwere, 'is a 'social fact' which for the Fijian people holds life together and gives it meaning. To be cast out from one's *vanua* is to be cut off from one's source of life'. (Tuwere 2002: 36) He notes that in several Pacific languages the word for land is related to or identical with the word for placenta, e.g. in Samoan (*fanua*), Tongan *(fonua)*, and Maohi Nui or Tahitian *(fenua)* or Maori [*whenua*], [having] parallel meanings with the Fijian *vanua* 'But *vanua* is also physical in the sense of being a piece of land that a person nurtures and gardens – and these connections between land, life, nurture and person are particularly emphasised when a father plants a coconut tree on the spot where the umbilical cord (*wa ni vicovico*) of his newborn child has been buried'.[1]

This chapter concerns Fijian people's deep sense of belonging to the land, to *vanua,* and how this became intertwined with belief in God, Yahweh from the start of the Methodist mission. It outlines the historical and political backdrop of my main research trajectory, from the first 1987 coup to the coup of 2006, and discusses the interweaving of church and politics in contemporary Fiji in relation to the Christian state debate.

The flesh of the land

The people of the land in Fiji are known as the *lewe ni vanua,*[2] the flesh or inner part, the very substance of the land. *Vanua* is thus likened to a life-giving body

---

1 Tuwere 2002: 36. See Hoiore 2003 in Halapua 2008: 6, Cloher 2004, Bergin and Smith (eds) 2004 for similar Polynesian perspectives, and see McDonald 2001 Chs 1,2, 8 re: Western Australian Aboriginal concepts of land, people and spirits.

2 Cf Ravuvu 1983: 76, Toren 1995a: 164, Abramson 1999b: 268-272, Tuwere 2002: 35.

that would be incomplete without the people as its inner flesh. People are part of the inscription of *vanua* in the land, just as *vanua* is emotionally and symbolically inscribed in the bodies and spirits of the people who are part of it. 'Without the people, the *vanua* is like a body without a soul'. (Tuwere 1992: 21 in Halapua 2003: 84, Tuwere 2002: 35)

Vanua in its material sense is divided into four main categories: *yavu* (ancestral house sites); *qele ni teitei* (garden areas); *veikau* (forest, foraging, hunting land); and *vanua ni qoliqoli* (fishing grounds). (Tuwere: 2002: 35, Ravuvu 1983: 70-84) *Yavu,* as described in the Prologue, means 'house foundation' or 'house mound'. *Yavutu* means literally the place of the original house site of the founding ancestor, the place of the origin of a clan. Capell 1991: 239 notes that this means to stand, to be in a place. More precisely, Geraghty (pers comm. 2006) points out that *yavutu* is made up of the words *yavu* and *tu* which is 'a suffix meaning "main", as in *suitūu* "spine" (main bone), *wakatūu* "taproot" (main root)'. I therefore suggest the term *yavutu*, and the reverence with which people talk of *yavutu* indicates a sense of belonging, and of being rooted, to a particular place.

The pre-Christian Fijian practice of burying kinspeople either beneath their house foundations or close by their houses, took place, according to Ravuvu, in order to feel comforted by living in close proximity to one's kin and staying close to the superior spiritual power of the deceased. The dead, writes Trompf (1995: 130) of Melanesian societies, 'are almost always conceived as remaining part of society – which is a community of both the living and the dead ... constitute powerful and watchful participators in rites ... are usually crucial for group support, yet not confused with deities worshipped or other spirits placated'.

People did not fear their ancestral spirits, Ravuvu writes, but respected them for their potential contribution to the welfare of the clan. It was through missionisation, he maintains, that a fear of death and the dead as 'malefficient' was developed. Colonial government legislation prohibited grave sites to be within villages. (Native Regulations 1877-1893, Lawa 14, 1877 138)

This meant that people's fear of being socially separated from the rest of the group in death was compounded by the thought that they would be buried away from their living kinspeople too. (Ravuvu 1988: 56) Thomas (1990a) describes colonial legislation on the 'improvement' of village life, based on Victorian notions of order and hygiene, which to a large degree reflected colonial images and fears of heathenism and savagery. These included enforcing that burials took place in designated grounds at a distance from villages, the spatial re-ordering of villages and even moving villages from areas considered to be unhealthy to 'better' locations.

The practice of burying the dead beneath the house of the living evokes a sense of the land of a person's clan as a life-giving womb and a tomb to which people are returned as bodily representations of the symbolic clan body, as nourishment for the land, to be transformed into renewed and strengthened *mana* for future generations. As Toren (1995a: 176) writes, 'The tangible substance [of the dead became] part of the foundation of houses to constitute immanent ancestral efficacy (*mana*)'.[3]

In a similar way to the way in which whales teeth and other valuables traverse historical paths from clan to clan across the land and sea, linking people in reciprocal obligations, so too did the bodies of clan members travel as the substance of kinship and the *mana* of ancestral spiritual connections, in death as in life, and, in their laying to rest in the *yavutu*, linking place and people, past, present and future. (Cf Chapter 3)

The old mana: land and gods

In pre-Christian Fiji, the world existed as an expression of the *mana* (divine power, efficacy) of the gods, of which the chiefs and their divine rule (*matanitu*) were living representatives. It was maintained through respect for this *mana*, the *tabu* (literally forbidden – sacred, holy) places, their symbolism, and the ways in which people lived and cared for *vanua*. There was a creator god, Degei, who had the form of a snake and lived in the rugged Kauvadra mountains of northern Vitilevu. There were numerous other gods, *kalou-vu* (literally root gods) of particular clans belonging to particular places. The spirits of dead ancestors, *niju* in the Nadrogā dialect, *vu* in Standard Fijian, or *kalo yalo* (deified mortals) of the many different clans across the islands were likewise revered and feared.[4]

Fijians in pre-Christian times existed within this polytheistic cosmology, maintained by a balance of ritual and political power between people of the land, *itaukei* (literally owners of the land) and the chiefs (*turaga*) they installed. These chiefs were 'stranger-kings', seen to come from across the seas, were considered *tabu*, and were believed to embody divine powers (*mana*) linking them to the *mana* of ancestors. (Cf. Sahlins 1985: 73-103) They were thus seen as links between the people and the divinities. This complementary opposition of 'land' and 'sea' was 'not only geographical but also implied autochthony versus foreignness, and "ownership" of land versus rule over it' (Kaplan 1990b: 129), an appropriation and domestication of potentially dangerous and powerful *mana* from outside. Although Fijian society was – and is – hierarchically structured, this is inextricably linked with concepts of complementarity and reciprocity. (Cf Toren 1994: 213)

Routledge points out that there was no original fixed pan-Fijian system of social structure prior to Cession to Great Britain in 1874. Social units had different meanings in different parts of the Islands (Routledge 1985: 29), yet contemporary Fijian social structure is the result of the forcing of a heterogeneous situation into a homogeneous structure, for ease of administration by the colonial government.

---

3   Compare Gewertz and Errington 1991: 127, see Tomlinson 2009: Chapter 2 re 'cleansing the soil' of house foundations of malign ancestral spiritual power.

4   See e.g. Williams 1982 [1858]: Thomsom 1895: 216, Hocart 1912, on totemism see Capell and Lester 1941, Becker 1995.

According to this, the basic unit was the *yavusa*, derived from the word *yavu* (foundation). Membership of this group gives access to natural resources, the supernatural powers of the ancestors, and the allegiance of other members of the group. Symbols of identification with the *yavusa* include a name, a common founding ancestor (and his efficacy), and a place of origin where the founding ancestor first settled. A higher-level organisation is the *vanua* (chiefdoms or federations), further divided into *mataqali* (clans), *mataqwali* in Nadrogā.

Mataqali are again divided into smaller lineage groups, known in Standard Fijian as *tokatoka*, *bito* in Nadrogā, the lowest social unit being the *vuvale*, household, *were* in Nadrogā. Although groupings of villages will make up a *vanua*, village boundaries do not correlate with kinship group boundaries. *Vanua* were divided into different units: the *turaga* (chief); *matanivanua* (spokesman, literally, eye of the land); *bete* (priest); *bati* (warrior); *mataisau* (carpenters) and *gonedau* (fisherman). Of these, all but the *turaga* were hereditary units and only the *turaga* and *matanivanua* are officially in use today. (Tuwere 2002: 140)

Vanua are headed by a chief (*turaga*), who formerly was installed by the people, linking him with the locality of the *vanua*. (Routledge 1985: 28) Since colonialism, the hereditary principle has tended to dominate over other claims to title succession, such as prowess in war or other capacities, particularly in the case of high-ranking titles.

The late 18th century saw further developments in power allegiance in the form of *matanitu*, 'flexible and fragile alliances', held together by the force of powerful chiefs through conquest and tributary relationships, the political constitution of the *matanitu* intimately connected with the tenure of land. (Routledge 1985: 28, 30)[5] In the colonial period, meanings of *matanitu* as chiefly authority became intertwined with colonial authority and came to mean 'government'. Since colonialism, it has come loosely to mean 'state' and 'government', yet to most Fijians these are vague terms of reference, and so *matanitu* retains an ambiguous quality of distant authority, still somehow connected with *vanua*.

The new *mana*

All ships until the 19th century approached the Fiji islands from the east. This was partly because it was easier to follow the trade winds (Ward, pers comm. 1996), partly because Australia and New Zealand were newly colonised, and partly because of Fiji's fierce reputation. Colonial influence and Christianisation spread from east to west. Vitilevu remained unexplored until 1865, when it was first crossed by Europeans.[6]

---

5   On land in Fiji see inter alia Ward 1969, 1995a, 1995b, 1997, Kamikamica 1996, see also Abramson 1999a, 1999b.

6   See Brewster 1922, Hooper and Roth 1990, Tischner (ed.) 1984, Clunie 1986, Gordon 1879, 1986.

Although Tahitian teachers first brought the message of Christianity to Fiji in 1825, its history there began in earnest with the arrival of English Methodist missionaries David Cargill and William Cross and Tongan missionaries, who came from Tonga in 1835. Roman Catholic missionaries arrived from Uvea (Wallis) in 1844, but never matched the success of the Wesleyan mission. The imperialist ambitions of the powerful Wesleyan high chief of Tonga, Taufa'ahau, came to play a particularly important role in the first phase of conversion and the simultaneous complexities of high-chiefly politics and wars in Fiji. Entangled with this were the aspirations, ambitions, economic and political resources and sectarianism of the European missionaries.

The Fijian language was written down by Wesleyan missionaries David Cargill and William Cross in the 19th century, who were closely connected to the high-chiefly island of Bau and to paramount chief Cakobau. The language spoken on Bau was taken by the missionaries to be the Fijian language. In their efforts to convert and educate Fijians by providing them with a written language, the Methodists entangled themselves in Fijian politics, coming to support the power of eastern Fiji by standardising Bauan as the Fijian language.[7]

The distinction between contemporary understandings of *vanua* and those of pre-Christian Fiji is blurred, but when the Christian missionaries came to Fiji there was already a cosmological understanding of a supreme creational power, as well as of earthly priestly mediators. Furthermore, the mythically-based idea of people of the land being governed by stranger-king chiefs from overseas could have facilitated the comparatively easy acceptance of this new spiritual power and its advocates and the merging of Christianity with *vanua*. Yahweh, the Christian God, was added as supreme god to the pantheon of deities within the Fijian cosmology. (Cf also Kaplan 1995a)

Despite the efforts of the missionaries, most other elements and understandings of *vanua* were retained and tacitly came to exist as an ancestral shadow land of place, kinship relations and spiritual power, alongside Christian beliefs and practice. For mainstream Christian Fijians today this is not necessarily problematic. As described below, Tuwere's Christological theology of the land draws on aspects of pre-Christian spirituality. However, as described in Chapter 2, Fijian Pentecostals' understanding of ancestral spirituality and the land is markedly different. Describing the spirituality behind the Fijian word for God, *Kalou*, Tuwere writes:

> *Lou* (second syllable) is normally used of a yam garden when leaves of young yams spread all around the garden, covering the soil. This is the time when the gardener is filled with joy: a time when the *were* (garden) is *lou*. It means that God is creator and source of all life. (Tuwere 2002: 59. see also Tuwere 1998)

---

7   See e.g. Clammer 1976: 14-28, 28-33, Thornley 1979: 104-105, Tomlinson 2009: 38-41.

He explains: 'There is no such thing as a god or spirit without a place or *vanua* in Fijian belief. Each attains a status in Fijian origin and is connected to a holy place. Because of this, *mana*, like *tabu*, is a basic land-related concept'.[8] And all components of *vanua* are connected in ritual. In ceremonies, 'one belongs simultaneously to the past, present and future ... the ancestors, God and future generations are all either named through speech ... heaven, earth and *bulu* or the underworld, are one'. (Tuwere 1992: 184) Tuwere sees the concept of *mana* as bridging the gulf between *vanua* and *lotu* – *vanua* 'with its focus on place and the image of the sacred; [*lotu*] with its emphasis on time, conversion, and change. Rituals of both are often juxtaposed, affecting thought and action in everyday life. The advent of the *lotu* was [widely] perceived as the arrival of the new *mana*'. (Tuwere 2002: 136)

New boundaries and categories of land

Sir Arthur Gordon, first governor of Fiji, shocked by the dispossession of the New Zealand Maori, was determined to avoid the same thing happening in Fiji. The first Fijian government, the government of Cakobau, set up in Bau from 1871, was particularly oriented towards the interests and needs of the European settlers. By the time Gordon arrived, large areas of land had already been sold to settlers who were developing agriculture and recruiting labour from outside Fiji, from the Solomons and Vanuatu. Gordon, impressed by the hierarchical structure of Fijian society and the conversion of Fijians to Christianity, saw Fijians as having the potential to move up the evolutionary ladder. He set out a policy to 'insulate Fijian tradition against the disintegrative effects of a market in land and labour', resolving 'to return all lands alienated prior to Cession to their customary owners, and to stop Fijians from being recruited for plantation work in favour of indentured labourers from India. (Jolly 1992: 338)

However, in order to render Fijian lands as inalienable, the colonial administration in effect institutionalised British interpretations of Fijian kinship systems and systems of land ownership. This changed what previously had been a fluid complementary system of chiefly/commoner relations into a frozen (and misinterpreted) European top-down hierarchical model, thus channelling considerable power to the chiefly elite.[9]

British colonial policies in Fiji in the 19th century sought furthermore to spatially re-order the colony through imposing Victorian cultural and moral values. (Thomas 1990b) The introduction of indentured labourers from Indian from the late 1870s (until 1916) to work in the sugar cane plantations created

---

8   Tuwere 2002: 142. Re: *mana* see also Thomson 1895: 111-112, Hocart 1912, 1914, Sahlins 1962: 228-235, Clammer 1976: 34-37.

9   See France 1969, Clammer 1976, Rutz 1987: 557, Kaplan 1989a, 1989b, 1990a and Thomas 1989a, 1990a, 1990b.

an underclass of landless people who worked the land, yet remained outside the genealogical systems of land tenure. In 1940, the Native Land Trust Board (NLTB) was established, empowered to grant leases for agricultural land not in use by indigenous Fijian owners. This resulted, Jolly writes (1992: 340), in the removal of rights from lineages, placing them in the care of the NLTB, as an administrative agent for the benefit of the Fijian owners.

In 1976, in an effort to improve protection of tenants, the former lease act ALTO was amended to become ALTA (Agricultural Landlord and Tenant Act), providing new leases for a minimum of 30 years and extending existing leases for 20 years. These leases began expiring in 1997. Many Indo-Fijian families have been forced to leave land that they have worked on in generations, have lost their homes and their livelihoods. In 1997 when I asked Indo-Fijians in Sigatoka town and the local [Indo-Fijian] sugar cane farmers their view of the new Constitution[10] and the hopes it generated, they said that it was worth nothing really if the issue of land and ALTA was not solved. Solving the problem of these expiring leases and the problem of the increasing deterioration of land-owner/tenant relations and creating some sense of security for Indo-Fijians has therefore been one of the most pressing and contentious issues in Fiji for years.

'I work the land', a farmer shouted to me above the roar of his tractor, as we descended a steep hill from the cane fields with a heavy load of stacked cane during the 1997 harvesting season. 'I have worked this land and made it what it is, but it is not my land. My lease is due for renewal soon. If they don't renew it, I have nothing. I have no security', he added sadly, 'no security at all'.

Church and chiefly power

The success of missions, and the lives of the Methodist missionaries and their families, were highly dependent on establishing and maintaining good relations with chiefs. In both Tonga and Fiji missionaries were unable to keep Church and state separate and were 'unavoidably [drawn] into complex power struggles to the point where the missionary's preferred role of advisor was indistinguishable from his image as collaborator'. (Thornley 1979: 8) The Wesleyan mission did not, however, make any significant headway until paramount chief Cakobau converted in 1854. Sahlins (1985: 39-40) argues that Cakobau's conversion came only as a 'tactic of despair', to save his position of power in a 12-year feud with the chiefdom of Rewa and to secure Taufa'ahau's allegiance. (see also Routledge 1985: 83) In

---

10   Ratified in July 1997, 'abrogated' after the coup of 2000. Court cases in late 2000 and early 2001 ruled that the 1997 Constitution was in force, that it had not been 'abrogated' – and Bainimarama accepted this. But in April 2009 Bainimarama claimed again to 'abrogate' the Constitution after the Appeals Court ruled his regime to be illegal. However, legally it remains valid, although through coercion and threats Bainimarama introduced a new order, signing on judges and lawyers afresh. (Norton, pers comm. 2009)

the years that followed Cakobau's adopting of the *lotu*, so many Fijians converted that the mission was almost unable to keep pace.[11]

From the time of Cession, the term *matanitu*, formerly understood as the most powerful manifestation of divine chiefly governance, came to be equated with colonial governance; yet it was never divested of its chiefly connotations. Since Fiji's independence in 1970, *matanitu* has come loosely to be understood as *state*, although the term *vanua* is also at times equated with vague understandings of *the state*. 'The unity of *vanua*, country, *matanitu*, chiefly authority, and *lotu*, the Christian religion, took on an almost trinitarian solemnity in the inner life of Fijians', writes Garrett. (1982: 114) 'The text "Fear God, honour the king" (1 Peter 2: 17) has become part of the heraldic apparatus of Fiji. It stands for a freely honoured union of chiefs and people within the Christian faith'.

So from the very first, church and chiefly governance, which quite quickly became intertwined with colonial administration, became inseparable entities. Fijian society, in pre-Christian times, bound together through the service of the gods and of the chiefs as embodiments of ancestral *mana*, now became interwoven in the service of church and chiefs and *vanua*. Much of the reverence shown to chiefs, was likewise shown the missionaries. (Thornley 1979) In many ways the *vanua* had absorbed the *lotu* (Tippett 1955: 216), had re-defined it from the start within a Fijian conceptual framework and spatial symbolism within village life.

The close connections between Methodism and chiefly power on the one hand and the colonial regime on the other, 'resulted in its failure to accommodate movements of protests and thus act as spokesman for the disaffected'. (Thornley 1979: 161) The Gospel-based preaching that had been the focal point of missionary John Hunt, was given less emphasis in the Methodist mission after his premature death, during an era of great inter-tribal warring and violence, which the Church in part condoned. Christianity became instead associated with power struggles and violence. (Thornley pers comm. in Barr 2004a: 26) As Forman (1996: 6 in Barr 2004: 24) writes: 'British Methodism had stressed an intense individual experience in the context of the sovereignty of God; Pacific Methodism stressed the sovereignty of God more than the individual experience'. (See also Gunson 1978) This possibly casts some light on the search among increasing numbers of Methodists, especially young people, for forms of Christianity founded on a personal relationship with Christ.

Thornley also points out (2005: 150) that the focus of missionaries in maintaining complete control of the mission, keeping Fijian ministers firmly in subordinate positions in the background, their opinions largely ignored, meant that:

---

11   Re: the history of the Methodist Church in Fiji, see Thornley 1979, 1996a, 1996b, 2000, 2002, 2005a, 2005b, Thornley and Vulaono (eds) 1996, Munro and Thornley (eds) 1996, Ryle 2001: 194-212, Tomlinson 2009.

These missionaries moved forward with blurred vision, or in the well-known biblical phrase, they viewed events "through a glass darkly". Their determination to retain ownership of the Fijian church led inevitably – and in many respects regrettably – to a missionary-dominated church agenda for the next half-century, an agenda that was to be increasingly out of touch with the needs and aspirations of Fijian people.

These significant points give the image of a Church with limited vision and great focus on power and containment which, in its rapid institutionalisation, became shackled to dominant power structures and figures of power. This pattern was maintained when the Church finally became independent in 1964. In its need to maintain conformity to hierarchical structures of leadership, the Methodist Church was unable to address the spiritual insecurities and social needs of individuals within its aegis. It is perhaps this lack of dialogue and accommodation of grassroots expression within the Church that has enabled strong figures to dominate its direction and politicise it so much in the past two decades.

Transgression and transition: 1987-2006

Anomie

> I leave this land where I was born
> this sunny warm May morning.
> History has been unkind
> to take no note of this bond
> between me
> and this land of mine.
>
> Misted porthole
> I look out, I leave my soul,
> I cry my farewell
> to home and friends and a life well-known.
> For what? I think with fear.
>
> Yes, I am scared and angry too.
> How can I start afresh?
> In a country not seen before
> what little choice I have.
>
> Your home is not your home, they said.
> Repatriate them! they called.

Ten more minutes to touch down
Is that you my heart that pounds?
I wait at the airport, clutching my suitcase
and struggle with tears.
No job, no work permit, what do I do?
Where will I go?
No home.
No place to hide.

How do I heal my wounds?

Head held high I remember
The *Syria.*
Through my veins flows
Girmitiya blood.[12]

If they could do it
so will I.
Do your damnedest
I will survive
in this new land
New Zealand.

Nikhat Shameem (1997)

A divine mission

I believe it's [the coups][13] a divine mission given to me by God, as it stated
clearly in the first chapter of Jeremiah – "Before you were even conceived, I
knew you. Before you were born I called on you and appointed you to be a

---

12   *Girmitya* refers to indentured Indian workers, brought to Fiji to work on plantations
between 1879 and 1916. The indenture system itself was abolished and the last indenture
contract expired 1 January 1920. (Lal and Fortune (eds) 2000: 110. See inter alia also
Gillion 1962, Mayer 1963, Ali 1979, 1980 and 2004, Lal, B.V. 1983, Naidu 1980 and 2004,
Munro 2005, Lal, Reeves and Rai (eds) 2006: 370-382). The *Syria* was wrecked on a reef
off the coast of Fiji in May 1884. As 'the worst disaster in the history of Indian migration
to Fiji' (Gillion 1962: 64) it came to symbolise the inhuman conditions, great suffering and
resilience of Indians under the indenture system.

13   Re the 1987 coups, see e.g. Roberston and Tamanisau 1988, Scarr 1988, 1990, Lal
B. (ed.) 1990, Lal, V. 1990, Lawson 1991. See also *The Review* May 1997: 12-36, *Pacific
Islands Monthly* 1997: 18-24, Griffen (ed.) 1997, review, *Fiji Times* 7 May 1998.

> prophet of mine". I believe that's the same sort of prophesy that God put in my life. (Sitiveni Rabuka, quoted in Dean and Ritova 1988: 162)

> The coups … brought to the surface a presumption that had for some time been lying dormant beneath the surface of relative peace and harmony … the pre-eminence of Fijian rights over the rights of all other communities in Fiji. This direction follows the path of confrontation, divisiveness, self-destruction and isolation from the rest of the world. (Kamikamica 1996: 288)

The sentiments of the two quotes above are worlds apart, yet they both highlight the same issue in contemporary Fiji history and politics: the centrality of Fijian notions of their cultural, political and religious supremacy over the non-Fijian population of the country, a right to supremacy believed to be divinely accorded, based on traditional, hierarchical structures of chiefly power and land ownership.

The ideological position behind the 1987 coups was that non-Fijian communities were *valagi* (strangers, visitors), to be shown benevolent hospitality by the *itaukei* (owners of the land) in the way of the land (*vakavanua*) and according to Biblical, Old Testament traditions. (Weir 2000b)

> Fijians categorise the population or inhabitants of the country, or any locality or village, into two main divisions. A person is either a *taukei* (indigene or owner) or *valagi* (visitor or foreigner) in any place. It is a relationship of mutual obligations and clearly defined roles in which one does not count or begrudge his or her contribution to communal life. Depending on the goodwill of the people involved, it can be a gracious partnership of host and guest, or a hostile relationship of landlord and tenant. (Tuwere 2001: 171-172)

Ravuvu (1991: 83) writes: 'All along the Fijians have been tolerant and generous hosts'. And as the Fiji Constitution Review Commission (FCRC) noted: 'Time and time again Fijian submissions [to the FCRC] likened Fiji to a house. The owner will gladly invite his guests to join him in the living room but not to share the family's private quarters. How then can Indo-Fijians think they have a right to take part in the country's government?'. (Reeves, Vakatora and Lal 1996: 56) This parochial, introvert view focuses on the *maintenance* of traditional values, structures and difference. From 1987 onwards it became closely linked with extreme ethno-nationalist and ethno-religious sentiments.

Against this is posited a universalist, one-country, one-people, *forward-looking* ideology of democracy, rights of citizenship and political equity, connecting Fiji with modern politics and seeing the country as part of international economic and political dynamics. This is the main Indo-Fijian position. Between these two extreme positions is a third, conciliatory position which seeks to build bridges between the Fijian and non-Fijian communities, recognising 'the prerogative of the Fijian chiefs in the Council of Chiefs … together with a reciprocal responsibility of indigenous people to meet the needs of the non-indigenous'. (Norton 2000a:

112) These two polarisations reflect the ideological and political positionings in Fiji society since the drafting of the 1970 Constitution and Independence, and form the backdrop to the unfolding political events between 1987 and 2000.

Tippett (1955: 215-217) accurately predicted that growing industrialisation and urbanisation in Fiji would continue to weaken the *vanua* and its ties within the Church, and eventually lead to a serious rift within it between the traditionalist, chiefly line of thinking and the democratic Western model. It is the presence of these two concepts, pointing in quite different directions, that helps explain much of what has happened since. (Garrett 1997: 392-393)

'The political logic of accepting difference is inventing and supporting institutions that help difference to be maintained', Indo-Fijian writer Subramani wrote in 1995. 'It is not necessary to create one people and one nation; rather, we should learn to view a system of difference as our unity'. (Quoted in Norton 2000b: 83) The problem Fiji faces, Norton (2000a: 84) wrote in the optimistic political climate following the ratification of the 1997 Constitution, 'is to reconcile a concept of indigenous paramountcy with the development of an equitable national society for which Indian labour, capital, and skill have long been crucial'. At that time there was considerable hope for the future, 'the constitutional reform [1990] had reconstructed, perhaps more surely than ever before, an institutional and ideological framework for containing ethno-nationalism and encouraging inter-ethnic political co-operation'. (Ibid.: 114) There was a real sense of moving forward.

In the general elections of April 1987, the Alliance Party, which had held power since Independence in 1970, was defeated by a Coalition of the National Federation Party (NFP) and the Fiji Labour Party (FLP), both overwhelmingly Indian in their support, led by Dr Timoci Bavadra, a Fijian of commoner descent from western Vitilevu. The Coalition promised democratic and social reform, greater equity of political power between Fijians and Indians, and a correction of government funding imbalances between the eastern and western parts of the country. Although the Coalition had won mainly on the basis of Indian votes, contrary to Fijian nationalists' claims, the Coalition victory did not give Indians control over Parliament. (Norton 1990: 135)

Demonstrations and rallies were, however, organised by nationalists who claimed that Fijians had lost their country, their security and their power. (Norton 1990: 137) One of the strongest voices of these protesters (who called themselves the *Taukei* movement) was Apisai Tora. He was quoted in the *Fiji Sun* as saying: 'the paramountcy which the Deed of Cession [1874] guaranteed and which the fathers of the present constitution undertook to protect for all *Taukei* forever … this sacred covenant is now broken … we cannot remain silent as our traditions are endangered … we cannot become strangers in our own land. (*Fiji Sun* 22 April 1987 in Norton 1990: 137)

In fact the Deed of Cession does *not* guarantee Fijian supremacy, Norton (pers comm. 2009) points out. However, despite the rhetoric levelled at the Indian community and widespread genuine fear of loss of their control over the land and thus loss of identity, the protests against the new government also concerned ancient chiefly politics and rivalry between the strong eastern confederacies and those of the west. In particular, the Coalition government was a serious threat to the power of defeated Prime Minister Ratu Sir Kamisese Mara. (Garrett 1990: 87)

On 14 May 1987, one month after the elections, in a military takeover of Parliament, Colonel (later Major-General) Sitiveni Rabuka entered the scene. Well trained in the Fiji Battalion of UNIFIL in south Lebanon, Rabuka exploited the fears of indigenous Fijians and growing ethno-nationalist sentiments to justify the coup, maintaining that he had acted in order to avoid bloodshed. Indeed the coup was almost bloodless, as was the second coup in October 1987 when he declared Fiji a Republic.

Rabuka was acting in a dual role: being of the commoner *bati* (warrior) clan, he was acting as traditional defender of his chiefs against the *vulagi* (foreigners), as well as modern military commander and Prime Minister from 1992-1999. Intertwined with these roles was Rabuka as Methodist lay-preacher, moral adjudicator and self-styled Old Testament prophet. Paralleling the notion of the Israelites as God's chosen people, his speeches were replete with Biblical references and narratives linking Fijians as a divinely chosen people, in sacred covenant with the land.

Rabuka's roles, in fact, represent the Three Pillars ideology of *vanua, lotu* and *matanitu*. Yet, as Garrett (1988, 1990) and other analysts have remarked, despite being the main actor, Rabuka was acting within traditionally-defined structures and had to chart a careful political course, maintaining a balance between the extreme position of the *Taukei* movement, his own political ambitions, and the authority of the chiefs.

Towards a new era: 1995-1999

> The only thing left with the Fijian people is leadership of this country. In business we are behind, in education we are behind. Therefore leadership should be in indigenous Fijian hands. (Pita Nagusuca, Submission to Constitutional Review Commission, 27 July 1995)

> We Indians are not happy, because we are part and parcel of Fijian people. How we are omitted? [from the 1990 Constitution] ... When Fijians are photo, Indians are frame. When Fijians are shirt, Indians are buttons. You take the frame out, the photo drops. You take the buttons out, shirt looks ugly and useless. (Parmanand Singh, Submission 024044 to Constitutional Review Commission. Quotes from Norton 2000b: 83)

The polarisation of the Fijian and Indian leadership in the years following the coups developed during Rabuka's years as Prime Minister into dialogue on how to reach a middle ground on the sharing of government. This shift was largely due to the positive rapport between Rabuka and Opposition leader Jai Ram Reddy. (Norton 2000: 85) It became clear that the 1990 Constitution, which in legislatively securing Fijian political paramountcy, openly discriminated against the Indo-Fijian community, would need to be changed.

Between 1995 and 1996, the Fiji Constitution Review Commission, which comprised former Anglican Archbishop and Governor-General of New Zealand, Sir Paul Reeves (of Maori descent), Fijian Tomasi Vakatora, successful businessman and former Speaker of the House of Representatives, and Indo-Fijian academic Brij V. Lal, undertook a review, inviting submissions from organisations, institutions and individuals. Their report was submitted in September 1996, after which the Joint Parliamentary Select Committee, headed by Rabuka, worked through the recommendations and finally reached agreement on them in Parliament and with the Great Council of Chiefs (GCC).

The new Constitution was ratified in July 1997 and Fiji was re-admitted to the Commonwealth two months later, with Rabuka presenting a whale's tooth as a traditional Fijian *isoro* (atonement) to the Queen.

The main outstanding challenges of land leases and the amendment of ALTA (Agricultural Landlord and Tenant Agreement) still, however, seemed as remote from solution as ever. With increasing numbers of land leases coming up for renewal, the insecurities and concerns of Indo-Fijian farmers grew, as did those of the Fijian landowners. In early 1998, a severely misjudged 20 per cent devaluation of the Fiji dollar caused food prices to rocket. The effects of a severe drought and the Government's tardy and insufficient help to the many mainly Indo-Fijian sugar cane farmers and small-holders in desperate situations led to great hardship. It was into this scene of growing dissatisfaction in both communities that the VLV (*Veitokani ni Lewe ni Vanua Vakarisito)* Party, the Christian Democratic Alliance entered. Its ethnocentric emphasis was on *itaukei/valagi* (landowner/visitor) imagery and rhetoric, re-fuelling the Christian state debate.[14]

The elections of May 1999 proved to be a watershed. The Fiji Labour Party achieved a landslide victory on the basis of both Indo-Fijian and Fijian votes. Rabuka and Reddy, brokers of significant political reconciliation, lost heavily, voters on both sides feeling that each leader had sold out to the other. The Fijian side, in particular, was deeply divided. As Norton (2000: 114)[15] points out, Labour not only won because of its politics and ideology, but also due to the 'unprecedented political fragmentation of Fijians, partly provoked by ethnicist resentment against Rabuka's compromising with Indian demands.

Mahendra Chaudhry, former trade unionist and leader of the Labour Party, was elected as Fiji's first Indo-Fijian Prime Minister. His political style and rhetoric and the radical and hasty changes in legislature his government adopted, grated with the traditional Fijian 'kava-bowl' style of lengthy and more allusive discourse. (Lal 2000: 2) Significantly, Chaudhry had worked single-mindedly towards achieving

---

14   See e.g. *Fiji Times* 10 March 1998: 1, 10 March 1998: 6, 14 March 1998, 15 March 1998: 10, 17 March 1998, 18 March 1998: 5, 24 March 1998: 6, 27 March 1998: 5, 28 March 1998: 2-3.

15   See also Lal 1999.

greater equity between the communities, to uncover corruption and to deal with the complex and sensitive issue of land.

Tragic déjà vu: the 2000 coup

The events of May 2000, when on 19 May the democratically elected government of Mahendra Chaudhry was forcibly overthrown in the name of the *vanua* by a group of rebels led by disaffected businessman George Speight, and 30 ministers were held hostage in the Parliamentary Complex for 56 days, brought to an abrupt end the lengthy process of reconciliation and hopes for a multi-ethnic political future for Fiji. It also brought to an end the slow economic recovery from the coups of 1987.

What the messy and chaotic situation of May 2000 showed was that there was no simple explanation as to what happened, who took part, who was behind the scenes and who was in charge. There were significant silences from important and influential figures in politics and among the chiefs, to indicate who supported what was going on. Analysts familiar with Fijian political complexities recognised emergent themes, and the use of the Indo-Fijian community as a scapegoat for indigenous Fijian internal conflicts. 'The problem with Fijian nationalism' Teaiwa wrote (2000: 1) 'is that there is no Fijian nation. There are Fijian provinces and confederacies, but the two military coups of 1987 and the current hostage crisis illustrate with disturbing insistence the erosion of indigenous Fijian social order and the fragmentation of indigenous Fijian leadership'.[16]

Whereas the brutality that emerged in the 1987 coups was directed only against the Indo-Fijian community, the coup of 2000 exposed many different levels of tension, not least among Fijians. The anarchy Fiji witnessed in 2000 was on a hitherto unprecedented scale. The looting and arson of primarily Indo-Fijian owned shops that took place in central Suva on 23 May, estimated at some $30 million, was to a large degree perpetrated by ordinary Fijians, including families. (Robertson and Sutherland 2001: 17-18)[17] The Fijian crowds that rampaged through the streets of Suva on 23 May, looting and pillaging, broke out of a march organised by Taukei Movement leaders and prominent Methodists. 'The image of a humble, God-fearing, dignified and hospitable people marketed by the Fiji Visitor's Bureau is chillingly contraverted. The chiefs

---

16   On Fijian chiefly leadership see e.g. Nayacakalou 1975, Ravuvu 1991, Dakuvula 1992, Lawson 1997, and on chiefly leadership in the Pacific Island region see e.g Lindstrom and White 1997.

17   Since 1987 breaking into and desecrating Hindu temples has become a regular occurrence, e.g. *Daily Post* 13 November 1996, 27 October 2003: 1, 29 October 2003: 3, 6, *Fiji Times* 30 June 1997: 3,6, 30 October 1997, 31 March 1998: 5, 1 April 1998: 2, 15 April 1998: 5, 10 June 2003: 4, 27 October 2003: 3, 3 November 2003: 5, 26 September 2005: 5.

and church ministers stir their people but the simple truth is they do not control them'. (Teaiwa 2000: 5)

The political reverberations of the coup extended far beyond Fiji, giving an unfortunate example to smaller Pacific Island nations, who look on the country as a leader in the region. As Fry (2000) noted, the situation affected all countries in the region, including Australia and New Zealand: 'While democracy is a hard system to run in a multicultural society, the alternative being proposed by the hostage-takers of an ethnocratic state maintained by force would take the region down a very fraught path'. A mere week or so later, the crisis in the Solomon Islands exploded into a coup there.

> The complexities of contemporary Fiji, caught between tradition and modernity, converged in tragic style in the 2000 coup. Among Fijians, there are the old confederational alliances and power struggles between east and west within indigenous chiefly politics. Then there is the issue of the power of the Great Council of Chiefs in relation to government and to the growing powers of a new self-styled, upwardly-mobile urban elite, highly influential in business, commerce and politics. This clash between old, aristocratic Fiji and the new self-made elite, was personified in the differences in style and leadership of the High Chief Ratu Mara and the commoner soldier/statesman Rabuka.[18]

In social terms the anarchy surrounding the coup accentuated the intense disaffection among indigenous Fijians towards their leaders. In particular, it highlighted the growing numbers of 'angry young men', from both villages and towns, searching for meaning and direction in their lives. These men are no longer willing to be subordinated within the rigidity of *vanua* structures run by male elders, yet are unable to make their own way in the rapidly changing society of modern Fiji. With no inspired traditional leadership to follow, they are seeking other routes, many of which lead through crime, violence and anti-social activities. In following Speight, they felt they were doing something and going somewhere. These events highlighted the growing schism between the rich and poor in Fiji, and between urban and rural communities, between the greed of those who have made it in the modern world, and the plight of the majority of impoverished Fijians.

The role of the Methodist Church in indigenous politics was yet again highlighted. Its leadership was weak in neglecting to advocate Christian values, and showed lack of vision in not addressing the pressures and challenges of a rapidly changing society. Church leaders were heavily criticised by the Fiji Retailer's Association for negligence during the coup: 'Christian leaders have a moral responsibility to assume a much more active role in ending the violence ... At the very least ... they should speak out strongly and point out daily on all radio

---

18   Teaiwa 2000: 2, see also ECREA 2001a: 12, Tuwere 2001, Lal 2000a, 2000b, Lal and Pretes (eds) 2001 Tuika (ed.) 2002, Hereniko 2003, Trnka 2008.

stations and on television that such violent behaviour is completely contrary to God's law and totally unacceptable'. (*Fijilive* 13 June 2000)

Finally the events emphasised inter-ethnic tensions and differences, and the discrepancy between what interim Prime Minister Qarase later described as 'communal democracy' and 'liberal democracy': that is, Fijian ethnocracy versus an inclusive non-racial system of political representation. At the Pacific Leaders' Conference in Hawaii in February 2001, Qarase was reported as questioning whether Fiji would ever want to accept 'liberal Western democracy', saying that to do so would its destroy culture and traditions. (*USP Pacific Journalism* Online 1 February 2001) This point has since been repeated many times by influential figures within Fiji society, politicians as well as Methodist and Pentecostal church leaders.

Dramatising the 2000 coup: the role of the media

One of the several notable differences between the coups in 1987 and the 2000 coup was the clear sense that the events of the 2000 were enacted on a global stage. The role played by the media, national as well as international, was expressive of increased globalisation and strengthened ties across countries and continents through media and internet networks. In 2000 there was no censorship of the domestic media and no control by the Ministry of Information of the international media.

In 1987 Fiji did not have television. But by 2000 villagers were used to watching Fiji TV news and also the news from Australian and New Zealand TV and BBC World. (Dobell 2001: 135) Dobell describes how the *Fiji Times* editor, Netani Rika

> reflected on the media awareness found even among villagers who staged land occupations or blocked roads: 'People know just how powerful the media is when it comes to putting your message across. That was reflected in how both the security forces and the rebels got their message across, not only here but overseas. There were even times when smaller rebel groups around the country refused to talk to the local journalists, saying "We want to see the BBC people. We'll only talk to the BBC people". It was only when the foreign TV crews came onto the scene that they would speak both to the foreign crews and then to the local journalists. (Ibid.)

George Speight, clearly chosen as front man on account of his media abilities, was able to dramatise not merely the siege of the parliament, but also to project via the media 'a leadership and institutional paralysis … Fiji's media gave Fijians much of the news needed to interpret these forces … In Speight's daily press conferences, his attack increasingly turned from Indo-Fijians to the failings of Fijian leadership …'. (Dobell 2001: 127, 132 and 131) Elements in the army, police and the chiefly structure were backing Speight overtly or covertly, but would not directly embrace him. Finally, Speight, 'emboldened by the weakness of the institutional responses and media attention ... made the mistake of believing his own publicity, and overplayed his hand after the hostages were released'. (Dobell 2001: 132)

Tragic Déjà-vu take two: the 2006 coup

Between 2000 and 2006 the Qarase-led Government was criticised from many different quarters for its unwillingness to comply with the judiciary in uncovering the truth behind who was involved in the coup. The Government, it seemed, was more focused on covering up than uncovering the truth and bringing about justice in relation to the perpetrators of the coup. The tone between the military and the Government grew more and more shrill so that by late 2005 one began to wonder just who was in control of the country, so aggressive and forthright was the tone of Commodore Bainimarama in criticising Qarase and his Government.[19]

On 5 December 2006 Fiji experienced its fourth coup in 20 years. This coup differed to those in 1987 and 2000. The coup of 2006 was not conducted on behalf of the chiefs, as were the coups of 1987. It was not concerned with strengthening the chiefly system and the power of indigenous Fijians, and it did not contain the anti Indo-Fijian rhetoric of the 1987 and 2000 coups. At its outset it was a direct response to the political impasse in the reconciliation process since the coup of 2000.

The ideals behind the coup of 2006 were said to be to once and for all uncover the truth behind the coup of 2000 and bring those involved to justice. According to Commodore Bainimarama, it was not a coup, but a 'clean-up campaign' to 'take the country forward', with the goal of eradicating corruption in government and creating greater transparency. (Lal 2007: 4) The 2006 coup d'état, Norton points out, 'presents the paradox of the army as the strongest embodiment of indigenous Fijian power supporting a project ostensibly aimed at transforming governance to serve the needs of the multi-ethnic nation, especially by eliminating discriminatory policies and practices'. (Norton 2007: 417)

Noting the immense change in traditional leadership and politics in Fiji that the turbulent events of this period have brought about, Norton writes:

> The nearly 20 years from Rabuka's coups in 1987 to Bainimarama's coup in 2006 have been a period of dramatic change in the political status of the two most important institutions embodying indigenous Fijian power: the military and the Great Council of chiefs (henceforth GCC). The former has come to dominate the political arena, while the latter, after a strengthened prominence during the late 1980s and the 1990s, has seemingly been weakened. The passing of the last of the great colonial chiefs who led Fiji to independence in 1970

---

19   See Fraenkel and Firth (eds) 2007 for in depth discussion of the 2006 election campaign and its aftermath, leading to the coup.

(Ganilau in 1993 and Mara in 2004) has undoubtedly been a factor in these changes. But the major catalyst has been militant Fijian ethnic nationalism in creating crises of political social order that have challenged the capacities of the army and the GCC to manage, and indeed have threatened the integrity of both. (Norton 2008: 1, see also Norton 2009)[20]

Church, politics and the Christian state debate

Since the coups in 1987 the Methodist Church in Fiji has been criticised from liberal Christian and many other quarters for becoming highly politicised. During Reverend Dr Ilaitia Tuwere's presidency (1995-1998) he sought to steer the Church away from politics and back on a more spiritual course,[21] with limited success, however. An editorial in the *Fiji Times* in 2001, referring indirectly to Methodist Church President Reverend Kanailagi becoming a member of the Senate, roundly condemned the Methodist Church's role in the 2000 coup and ensuing anarchy, its lack of spiritual leadership and social responsibility:

> During the political upheaval last year the Church took an active role in splitting the Fijian political parties. In effect it fragmented the Fijian voters ... religion was used by some politicians to create a racial divide and exacerbate an already explosive situation. (*Fiji Times* 28 August 2001: 6)

The Methodist Church responded defensively to the criticism, levied at it from many other quarters too, with a full page media release dated 28 September 2001, which amongst much else noted:

> The Church cannot exist in isolation from both reality and the political world. Its prophetic role cannot be confined to the pulpit only ... Today, there is the even more need for the ordained Ministers to work closely with those whose decisions have a tremendous effect on the lives of its members and the Nation as a whole. (*Fiji Times* 29 September 2001: 47)

A sermon by Methodist Church General Secretary Reverend Tuikilakila Waqairatu, preached at the Pentecostal church, Christian Mission Fellowship's main church, World Harvest Centre, emphasises these ideals, shared by the Methodist Church leadership and by many Pentecostal church leaders:

> Christian involvement in politics is a must ... the kingdom of God must be allowed to penetrate in politics to help in nation-building ... Parliamentarians, the civil service, the *vanua* and the Church must be penetrated by the kingdom of

---

20   For a comprehensive analysis of the 2006 coup see Fraenkel, Firth and Lal (eds) 2009.
21   Cf interview, *The Review*, October 1995a, 1995b.

God to help them better carry out their responsibilities. You cannot become a good
politician if you're not a Christian. The kingdom of God must penetrate into the
civil service, ministers, CEOs ... from the top to the bottom. The *vanua* as well
must be transformed by the power of the kingdom of God. The kingdom of God
must penetrate all aspects of the Church. The kingdom of God must be supreme
in all things. (*Fiji Times* 11 October 2005: 3, see also *Sunday Times* 21 August
2005: 4)

Those in favour of constitutionally declaring Fiji a Christian state see this as a
path to national unity. Boundaries and categories of Christian faith would be
extended and expanded to embrace all aspects of the secular world – government,
the legal system, the media and education. All would be based on 'biblical
concepts of law and grace' and only 'God-fearing persons' would be in positions
of leadership and authority. (Cf ACCF Review 2001: 6; Corporate Repentance
Seminar, Suva 6-9 October 2004) There would be 'freedom of religion, [but
recognition] that the religion of the state of Fiji is the Christian Church', as
General Secretary of the Methodist Church, the late Jone Langi pointed out
to me, saying that if Pakistan could function as a Muslim State, with time set
aside officially each day for prayers, why shouldn't Fiji be a Christian State?
(Interview 24 October 2002)

Strongly expressing his support for a Christian state, Reverend Poate Mata
of Apostolic Gospel Outreach International Fellowship maintained that until Fiji
returns to the 'theocratic leadership' he described the country to have been under
during missionisation and colonialism, there will never be any stability in the
country. (Interview 9 November 2004) Emphasising the importance of finding
the root cause of the disaffection and hurt of Fijians that led to the 2000 coup,
Reverend Mata explained to me the potential dangers to Fiji of western ideals of
democracy:

Democracy is a social ill to Fiji, particularly to us Fijians. Because it just goes
against our Fijian protocol ... from 1970 [since independence] up till now, how
many coups have we had, about two? That is under democracy. Democracy is
the freedom of speech. [With] freedom – there is no longer ... respect of one
another.

A Christian state, many argue, would re-establish moral standards, counter the
present erosion of traditional values and authority and combat the accelerating
levels of crime, violence, prostitution, drug abuse and sexual offences in Fiji. A
Christian state, critics say, will establish a unilateral understanding of unity, based
on a particular interpretation of Christianity.

The Three Pillars

In order to understand the foundation of the Christian state ideal in Fiji it is necessary to understand the ideal construction of the Three Pillars of *vanua, lotu* and *matanitu*. 'Fijian collective consciousness', writes Tuwere (1997b: 45), 'is made up of the inseparable union between the three strands of *vanua* (land), *lotu* (Church) and *matanitu* (state). Their union is so complete that if one is affected, the whole is affected'. Former Methodist President Paula Niukula explained its derivation:

> Before Cession, before the Christian Church grew in Fiji and before Great Britain took over the government, the Fijian community existed alone in Fiji. But when our grandfathers accepted the Church and the Colonial Government, that which bound the people together was divided into three: the Community, the Church and the Government. They became the bases of Fijian life. They are the three pillars of Fijian society.[22]

But how did the notion of the Three Pillars come into being? According to Tippett the unity symbolised in the tripartite structure did not exist before cession, but was a product of colonialism. It was, he emphasises, a unity based on the peculiarly Bauan way of life, 'as modified by Cakobau in the substitution of Christianity for the primitive polytheism which he previously maintained … it seems that if there is a Fijian way of life, it is really something more or less new, achieved by two strong factors or instruments of unification, namely, the Christian Church and the British Crown … a unity finally accomplished after cession on a basis of "Land", "Church" and "Kingdom"'. (Tippett 1955: 213 and 219)

This tripartite structure is in fact not unique to Fiji, but described by Otto (1992: 217) with regard to Baluan Island, Manus in Papua New Guinea, where the Fijian term *lotu* was introduced by Fijian missionaries into Tok Pisin, so that Baluans talk of *Kastam, Gavman* and *Lotu*, custom, government and church. Neumann (1988: 86) describes a similar structure among the Tolai of East New Britain, and Barker (2007a: 76) discusses the 'postcolonial triangle' among the Maisin, referring to other studies of this same structure elsewhere in Melanesia. Tomlinson (2002: 239) observed, as I also did, that *vanua* and *lotu* are used more frequently than *matanitu*, or used together without the third element of *matanitu*.[23]

---

22   Niukula 1994: 14-15, see also 1991, 1992a, 1992b. The Three Pillars is not the same as 'the three-legged stool'. This expression, developed by Ratu Sukuna, referred to the mutually dependent ethnic groups of Fiji society during colonialism, the Fijians, Indians and Europeans, the Fijians providing the land, Europeans the capital and skilled manpower, and Indians their cheap labour. (Lal 1988: 60, see also Sukuna 1983)

23   Tomlinson also notes that in Kadavu *matanitu* is often replaced by other words such as *viqaravi* (service) *itavi* (responsibility), *vuli* (study), *matavuvale* (household), something I did not, however, note in my research areas.

Halapua offers a radical exploration of the Three Pillars in his book *Tradition, Lotu and Militarism in Fiji* (2003), replacing *matanitu* with the expression *turagaism*, understood as ethnic chiefly (*turaga*) dominance over non-Fijians. In pre-colonial times chiefly power was historically closely interwoven with military power and connected with wars between clans for ownership and control of land. The coups of 1987 are a contemporary example of this ideal being put into practice. The fact that Indo-Fijians cannot own land in Fiji and that very few have ever been accepted into the Fiji Military Forces further enforces this.

While acknowledging the importance of the interweaving of *vanua* and *lotu* since the Christianisation of Fiji, and acknowledging the fears of those who feel their identity and way of life threatened by the economic and political influence of the Indo-Fijian community Tuwere points out that beneath the romanticised image of the harmony and unity of *vanua* and church, lie growing problems of poverty and injustice which are glossed over by these ideals of tradition:

> ... the *lotu* was absorbed by the *vanua* from the beginning. It is probably because of this union, which has been taken for granted for so long, that the necessary element of discerning their essential difference has been lost ... Their oneness is complete ... implicated and affirmed by dictums such as *Na vanua na lotu, na lotu na vanua* (The Church is the land, the land the Church).
>
> Statements with nationalistic flavour such as *Noqu Kalou, noqu vanua* (My God, my land) find expression in popular folk songs and they unconsciously help to support a ruling ideological structure, namely that the *lotu* is identical with the *vanua* and they are one ... the relative harmony which [*vanua, lotu, matanitu*] now enjoy can become a new form of escape from reality if the poor, the powerless and the marginalised are not justly treated. In the changed situation brought about by the coups of 1987, splitting the society open, the country and especially Fijian leaders are now called to move beyond the so-called point of harmony of *vanua* and *lotu* and address the plight of the growing number of poor and powerless Fijians. (Tuwere 1997b: 46)

Reverend Koroi goes even further in critically viewing the historical links between *vanua* and *lotu,* 'Tradition takes control ... and the Church is just there to honour tradition', he told me:

> The Church ... when it first came ... may have started well or properly, but was [it] the Church that Christ built or the Church that ... the missionary built? ...What is central ... is it Christ or is it the minister? The minister becomes the focus, you know ... the Church [and] ... minister's house [are] built in the village ... the pulpit [is] in the centre [of the Church] ... and everything is ... focused on the *talatala* [Methodist minister] ... Christ said God has anointed me to preach the Gospel to the poor, give sight to the blind, release to the captive and so on ... to me this is what Jesus meant by his church ... But the Church that started here is the Church that seeks to ... make ... big buildings,

to build a big institution. The poor are neglected ... Jesus's concern was the people, not the institution, not the building, not the administration. (Interview, 1998)

Reverend Koroi goes so far as to question whether the spirituality of the Church became buried from the first under the institutionalisation of the missionaries' Christianising and civilising mission in Fiji:

Taukeism is the domination of men over women, adults over children, husbands over wives and chiefs over subjects. In the field of religion, *Taukei-ism* [*taukei* meaning landowner] is the domination of Christianity over non-Christian religion or other domination over others; and even the *talatala* (ministers') domination over their members. (1992 in Ernst 1994a: 208)

And Fijian Methodist theologian, Lisa Meo, responding to this comment, points out (1994: 65-66):

Taukei can be translated in the Church to mean the indigenous Fijians' ideologies and aspirations are superior to everyone else's ... "culture-oriented" for women means they will remain marginalised and voice-less in decision making ... [this] is an obstacle to the prophetic role of the Church in addressing pressing social injustices ... [and] comes at the cost of the needs of half the population of Fiji comprising Indians and other minority racial groups.

Debating a Christian State[24]

'Give to Caesar what is Caesar's and to God what is God's', Reverend Koroi told me, quoting Matthew 22:21, when I asked him about the Christian State. 'The state has a role to play and God has a role to play. Christians ... are Christians within the state, but ... the state works by laws and rules and force ... you cannot force Christianity into ... a state'. (Interview, 1998)

From the time of cession in 1874, the term *matanitu*, formerly understood as the most powerful manifestation of divine chiefly governance, came to be equated with colonial governance, yet it was never divested of its chiefly connotations. And since Fiji's independence in 1970, *matanitu* has come loosely to be understood as *state*. Yet the Fijian term for Christian state is *vanua lotu vaKarisito*, which literally means 'land of the Christian Church' or 'land of the Christian faith'. The word used in this instance to translate 'state' with, is *vanua*, with all its complex connotations of land and tradition and the relations between land, people, chiefs and Church (*vanua, lotu* and *matanitu*). This makes for a confused understanding of the ideology behind the Christian state and its political

---

24   See also Ryle 2004, 2005, 2009 and Ryle 2001a: 212-228.

and constitutional ramifications. Attempting to clarify this confusion, Tuwere distinguishes between the terms *vanua vaKarisito* and *matanitu vaKarisito*:

> I want to see a distinction made between Christian state and Christian *vanua*, Christian land ... *vanua vaKarisito*. They are two separate things. Christian state... *matanitu vaKarisito* ...that brings in the whole question of the constitution ... a very complicated question – legally as well as theologically ... that does not need to get into the constitution. We can simply live according to the principles of the Christian faith ... [25]

During the reviewing and drafting of the new Constitution in 1995-1997 the debate on the Christian State was intense. The Fiji Constitution Review Commission invited submissions from any institution, group or private person who wished to state their views. In addition, the FCRC commissioned a number of research papers on particular issues of importance to the Constitution, including the Christian state issue.[26]

The Report of the Fiji Constitution Review Commission (Section 5.38, Reeves, Vakatora and Lal 1996: 73) recommended that:

> The Constitution should not declare Fiji to be a Christian state, but the *Preamble* should continue to record the coming of Christianity and its significance in the life of the country. It should do so in terms that reflect the importance of Christianity not only to the indigenous people and other Christians but to the cultural and spiritual life of Fiji as a whole.

The recommended wording of the *Preamble* included:

> We, the people of the Fiji islands, Seeking the blessing of God who has always watched over these islands, Recalling the events in our history that have made us what we are ... the adoption and enduring influence of Christianity and its contribution, along with that of other faiths, to the spiritual life of Fiji ...

So while the contribution of Christianity was acknowledged in the FCRC Report and the above wording (later enhanced in amendments to the Constitution prior

---

25   Interview 1998. See also Tuwere 1997a, 1997b, *Fiji Times* 28 June 1997: 1 and 6, Bush 1999a: 62, Rabuka 1999.

26   Copies of all submissions and research papers are in the Fiji National Archives. A selection of research papers were published in Lal, B. V. and Vakatora, T.R. (eds) 1997, see Bush 1995d, Fiji Council of Churches 1995, Garrett 1995, Nacanaitaba 1995, Niukula 1997, Tuwere 1997 and Bush 1995a, 1995b, 1999a, 1999b, all critical of the Christian state issue. Many of the views expressed in 1995 in favour of a Christian state were re-iterated in the 2001 Ravuvu Constitution Review Commission (Casimira 2002), see also Bush 1995a.

to ratification in mid July 1997), the 1997 Constitution did not formally declare Fiji a Christian state. This is in keeping with the place of Christianity and the state in the constitutions of other Pacific Island states. In his research paper to the FCRC, Niukula (1997: 76-77) quoted from the preambles of Western Samoa, Vanuatu, Solomon Islands, Tonga, Papua New Guinea and Tuvalu, all of which emphasise the central importance of Christianity and of Christian principles and traditional values in their histories and societies, but none include clauses, declaring their nations to be Christian states.

A chosen people: a political and spiritual Covenant

However, although Fiji was not declared a Christian State in the 1997 Constitution the issue remains central to particular sections of the Christian community.[27] Referring to the Deed of Cession of 1874, supporters of the Christian state claim that the chiefs ceded Fiji *as a Christian country* to Britain and that they had thereby signed a *covenant* of both political and spiritual character which officially declared Fiji to be a Christian country:

> … whereas the Fijian Chief Thakombau styled Tui Viti and Vuni Valu and the other high native chiefs of the said islands are desirous of securing the promotion of civilization and Christianity and of increasing trade and industry within the said islands. (from the Deed of Cession, 10 October 1874, cited in Niukula 1997: 57)

The Methodist Church in Fiji and Rotuma's submission to the Fiji Constitution Review Commission in 1995 emphasises this:

> We are merely asking that since we recognise the Deed of Cession to be a covenant not only between Fiji and Great Britain, but beyond this a spiritual covenant between our forefathers and God personified in the Lord Jesus Christ, that this recognition that Fiji be a Christian state be formally declared in the Constitution. We strongly believe, on the basis of Biblical truths, that the covenant made with the Lord Jesus Christ at Cession is an eternal one. The voluntary surrender of Fiji at Cession was a voluntary surrender that Fiji as a

---

27   During the Methodist Church Conference in 2003 the Christian State was again strongly promoted by the Methodist Church leadership, cf Fiji Times 16 August 2003, 18 August 2003, 22 August 2003, 23 August 2003, 29 August 2003, 3 September 2003, 7 September 2003, 11 September 2003, 17 September 2003, Daily Post 18 August 2003, 20 August 2003, 26 September 2003, Sunday Times 24 August 2003, 10 October 2004, Sunday Post 31 August 2003, 17 September 2004, 21 October 2004, 2 November 2004, 1 September 2005.

nation was also given over to the Lordship of Christ, hence the absolute sacred trust. (1995: 7)

Several Fijians have pointed out to me, as Tuwere also notes (2002a: 65), that the chiefs did not 'cede' the Fiji Islands to British *ownership,* but in terms of *vanua* to British *stewardship.* When the first governor of Fiji, General Sir Arthur Gordon, as representative of Queen Victoria, was sworn in on 10 October 1874, he was 'welcomed and accorded with the ceremonial that befitted only a high chief. From the point of view of the receiving culture, the occasion was seen as the *vanua* welcoming the *matanitu* in every sense into the land'. (Ibid: 51) And Macnaught (1982: 1) points out that, according to 'Fijian myth', the Fiji Islands were ceded to Queen Victoria in loving trust (*loloma*) by the chiefs, in recognition of her greater powers, through:

> ... chiefly presentation, no less, which had obliged the gratified recipient, now supreme chief of Fiji, to redistribute powers and privileges to the original donors and to assume part of the responsibility for safeguarding the prosperity and rights of the people ... the Deed of Cession, far more effectively than the Maori's Treaty of Waitangi, came to be seen by Fijians as a solemn charter for a British-Fijian partnership premised on verbal assurances (the cession itself was unconditional) that colonial rule would respect and maintain the interests of the Fijian people.

The idea of a Holy Covenant between God, the chiefs of Fiji, and Great Britain in relation to the *vanua*, resonates with the Old Testament message of the Jews as God's chosen people. Furthermore, this view claims that Fijian chiefs are chosen directly by God to be supreme leaders and authorities in Fiji. Reverend Tuima (interview 1998), pointed to the Romans 13:1-2 passage:

> Let every person be subject to the *governing authorities*; for there is no *authority* except from God, and those *authorities* that exist have been instituted by God. Therefore whoever resists *authority* resists what God has appointed, and those who resist will incur judgement.[28]

Turaga levu, which literally translates as 'high chiefs' is the term used for the English 'supreme authorities' and *turaga* (chief) for 'authority'. Garrett (1995: 2) also points out that this Bible passage is considered by some Fijian groups to mean that the Deed of Cession was sanctified by God. Tuwere takes issue with contemporary interpretations of this Bible passage and other claims of divinely sanctioned chiefly authority, linking them with 'loss of direction' in the Methodist Church since 1987. (Tuwere 2002a: 102, see also Kaplan 1990: 141 and 1995:

---

28   New Revised Standard Version, my emphasis.

158) Yet these interpretations continue to be pervasive in much Christian rhetoric, such as that of the former VLV party[29] and the ACCF.

The Association of Christian Churches in Fiji (ACCF)

> God has given ACCF the vision *"Fiji to be God's Treasured Possession"* (Exodus 19:5) to keep the Assembly focused on its most important responsibility of first turning the hearts of all people in Fiji to God. Fiji can only become God's Treasured Possession if the people of this country submit themselves to God and accept Jesus Christ as their Lord and Master and their Saviour ... ACCFs responsibility is a spiritual one of saving all souls for Christ. (ACCF n.d.: 2-3)

In 2001, as a response to the moral and spiritual disorder among Fijians brought about by the 2000 coup, Pentecostal churches and the Methodist Church formed a joint organisation, The Assembly of Christian Churches in Fiji (ACCF). Usurping the mandate of the Fiji Council of Churches which includes the Catholic and Anglican churches, this increasingly influential organisation is comprised of almost all Protestant churches, i.e. almost half the population.

The founders of the ACCF saw the main problem of the coups as deriving from disunity among Fijians, and their main purpose was to promote reconciliation and unity, first and foremost among Fijian Christians – as the first necessary step towards general reconciliation and unity in the country.[30] Newland (2006: 332) writes that after the 2000 coup the Catholic Church initiated reconciliation meetings between Fijians and Indo-Fijians, while the Methodist Church led a group of Protestant churches in reconciliation meetings between Fijians. This group developed into the ACCF. Benjamin Bhagwan, General Secretary of the Fiji Council of Churches, argues (Newland 2006: 340) that the ACCF was seeking unity among Fijian Christians but was not concerned with minority groups.

The unity the ACCF is pursuing entails the constitutional declaration of Fiji as a Christian State. Those in favour of the Christian state claim that this radical move would create unity between Christians and is the only way to create stability in the country. With reference to the essential relatedness of Fijians, the ACCF Review points out that 'the effects of certain foreign factors have contributed to the complexity of this problem' (ibid.), and emphasises

> it is imperative that the citizens of this country ... realise the root cause of their ancestral disunity – *turning away from Yahweh*, the unseen Deity who guided them to this land ... that unity would require that they, as a people, *confess their*

---

29 See Ryle 2001: 223-225.

30 Cf interviews Langi 2002, Kacimaiwai 2004, see also Newland 2006: 340-346, 2007.

waywardness and repent of their sins before Jehovah the Creator of the earth and Lord of all nations. (Ibid. All emphases in quotes from ACCF Reviews as in original)

The quotes of this Review highlight that the ACCF sees itself and its responsibility as primarily 'spiritual'. Its aim is to evangelise all the peoples of Fiji to not only convert to Christianity, but to accept Jesus Christ as their individual saviour. By seeking this path to unity for the different people of Fiji the ACCF is seeking to heal the brokenness of the past that came about through sin, that is to say by turning away from Yahweh.

Yahweh is the Creator and beginning, the 'unseen Deity' who brought the Fijians to Fiji, cf the myth of the Kaunitoni Migration. The worship of ancestral gods is seen not as part of an already-existing, pre-Christian, pagan cosmology that was replaced by Christianity, but rather as a human aberration of Yahweh's original cosmological order. This follows the biblical narrative of the Israelites, who turned away from God to worship other gods and to follow leaders who did not serve Yahweh – and who were punished by God for their sins.

While the ACCF's approach is spiritually based, it is also politically oriented in that it sees reconciliation in Fiji as only attainable through a spiritual strengthening of traditional chiefly leadership. Once chiefly leadership in Fiji truly follows the command of Yahweh, then reconciliation and healing will follow. However, referring to the right to freedom of religion in Fiji, enshrined in the (1997) Constitution, the Review sees this as the freedom to worship in a particular Christian denomination: 'individuals choose to worship in a *particular Church denomination* of their choice *but* they have no choice on being part of the Body of Christ as that prerogative belongs to Christ alone'.

> The Bose Levu Vakaturaga's [Great Council of Chiefs] mandate, the Presidential plea and the formation of the ACCF are truly representatives of the three pillars of our nation – the *Vanua*, the *Matanitu* and the *Lotu*. In unison they have committed themselves to reconciliation, unity and attainment of peace and prosperity in our land. The Church (represented by the ACCF) acknowledges the trust of both the *Vanua* and the *Matanitu* (Government) to take the lead in uniting her members who are of the *Vanua* and the *Matanitu* as well. It is a constitutional privilege of our nation that individuals choose to worship in a *particular Church denomination* of their choice *but* they have no choice on being part of the Body of Christ as that prerogative belongs to Christ alone. It is with this understanding and response to the call to unify the Body of Christ and bring about Reconciliation and healing in our nation that the Church healers have prayerfully considered a vision and mission for ACCF. (Ibid: 7)

Leading Pentecostal churches and conservative sections of the Methodist Church are in agreement as to there being a covenant between the old chiefs and God to keep Fiji a Christian country, which in turn supports the ideal of a Christian State.

It would seem then that the Christian state issue doctrinally and politically unites a large section of the Protestant churches in Fiji which in effect represent a majority of the whole Christian community. Yet beneath the surface of this common goal is a distinct and significant difference in perspective between Methodists and Pentecostals on the positioning of the elements of the Three Pillars in relation to one another. (Cf Chapter 5)

The reference to 'certain foreign factors', i.e. non-Fijians, in the above quote, as a destabilising or spiritually dangerous factor in Fiji is highlighted in many different ways in the rhetoric of the former VLV party, the ACCF and other ethno-nationalist Christian bodies. Supporters of the Christian State maintain that if Fiji is not declared a Christian state Fiji will suffer divine retribution.

The Methodist Church in Fiji submission to the Constitution Review Process in 1995 emphasised: 'We are ... of the view that if this is not recognized now then this nation is under a Divine curse'. This outlook was endorsed by the late Reverend Tuima, who considered the repeal of the Sunday Observance Decree and the accommodation of non-Christians in the 1997 Constitution, the severe drought Fiji was experiencing in 1998, and the falling price of gold, affecting the running of the Vatukoula goldmine in Vitilevu, as 'the curse of God to us ... because He has told He is the Light, there is no other God. Do not worship other gods than me ... Compare that to ... [the] sacred biblical [words] in relation to [Romans 13:1]'. (Tuima, interview 1998)

This chapter has explored the deep sense of belonging of Fijians to the land, and the politicisation of this in recent decades. Continuing the theme of people's relational belonging to the land the first part of the following chapter concerns a curse on the land, describing different approaches, traditional and Pentecostal, to eliminating its powers and healing the land.

Chapter 2
Healing the Land

The *tabua*: conveyor of death and atonement

In the Fiji Museum's permanent exhibition 'Mission' there is a glass cabinet with an old *tabua* (whale's tooth), yellowed and darkened with age, and the *magimagi* (plaited coconut fibre string) it was presented with. An exhibit note states: 'Tabua presented by chief's [sic] and people of Navuso to the Methodist Church early this century, to atone for their responsibility for the murders of Thomas Baker and his followers'. Another exhibit note, The Thomas Baker Tragedy, explains what happened:

> In 1867 Rev. Thomas Baker, a Fijian Minister Setareki Seileka and six out of eight Fijian student teachers from Davuilevu were hacked to death and eaten at Nubutautau in Central Vitilevu. While the murders of Fijian mission teachers in Fiji were not uncommon at that time, the murder of a European missionary was unique, Mr Baker being the only Methodist Missionary to be killed by followers of Fijian religion. He and his followers were not slain because they were Christians, but because the Navatusila Chief – A Christian Chief who felt slighted when Baker decided to hold a meeting at Lomanikoro instead of Navuso, and who had sent a Tabua into the mountains requesting the missionary's murder. The Baker party thus perished at the hands of pagan Fijians on the request of a Christian convert. The European Missionaries in Fiji, while they were often reviled and threatened in the early decades at the mission, seem to have been largely immune from direct attack, but the same was not true of their Fijian converts, many of whom were killed by followers of Fijian religion, particularly after Christianity began to take a hold, and to threaten the authority of chiefs and priests.

Next to the tabua in the cabinet is a colour group photograph with a note that reads, 'Reverend Thomas Baker's Great Grandniece Lynn Flaherty and her immediate family at Nubutautau, Navosa on 13 November 2003, during the Forgiveness Ceremony'. So a *tabua* was the conveyor of Baker's death, and other *tabua* conveyors of subsequent ritual atonements for the deed. The *tabua*, Ravuvu explains (1987: 23):

> represents everything that is valuable and worthwhile in Fijian society. It embodies everything that is chiefly in nature, including chiefly behaviour and social valued chiefly qualities … [it] also possesses a mystical power that makes it much more sacred than any other object of ceremonial offering … the 'whale's

tooth' is potent and has *mana* or power to effect good or ill when offered and accepted ... [causing] ... the intrinsic value of a particular 'whale's tooth' to vary according to circumstances and the relative status of offerer and recipient.

This chapter gives different examples of how human action is reflected in the state of the land and in people's relations, past and present; how human action can spiritually disturb or reconcile the land, its innate ancestral powers and their influence on people's relations and the land; how the efficacy of ancestral spirituality of the land may affect change, punishing or rewarding people's actions; and how the power of the Holy Spirit can exorcise the land of ancestral spiritual power, cleansing and un-blocking demonic spiritual strongholds.

The blessings of the land

> If my people ... humble themselves and ... turn from their wicked ways, then I will hear them from Heaven, will forgive their sins, and will heal their land. (2 Chronicles 7:14)

In November 2003 a widely and internationally publicised traditional ritual of reconciliation was staged in the area where Australian Methodist minister Thomas Baker was killed, with reports reaching Australian, New Zealand, Canadian, European – even Vietnamese – newspapers, and with coverage on Australian TV. Eleven descendents of Thomas Baker were invited to Fiji to receive, together with descendants of Baker's Fijian assistants who were killed with him, the ritual apologies of the people of Navatusila. In anticipation of the ceremony, the *Fiji Sun* newspaper, the paper that reported most extensively on this event, noted in a Comment entitled 'Lifting the curse':

> 13 November will be a day of liberation for the whole *vanua* of Navatusila in Navosa. This will be the day when they converge at Nubutautau to traditionally apologise to the families of Reverend Thomas Baker and eight other [Fijian] families [whose ancestors] were killed and eaten by their ancestors, 136 years ago. From the day Reverend Baker and his missionaries were killed, the *vanua* of Navatusila has been under a curse. (*Fiji Sun* 10 November 2003: 4)

An Associated Press news bulletin from Australia noted somewhat dryly: 'The Australian descendants of a Christian missionary eaten by cannibals 136 years ago will travel to Fiji this week, hoping to help lift a curse on the village where he was killed. Residents say they have had bad luck since Baker was consumed and they blame his avenging spirit'. (*Fiji Sun* 13 November 2003: 10)

According to the *Fiji Times* (12 November 2003: 3) some 200-300 guests attended the Baker reconciliation ceremony. The seven villages involved had spent F$10.000 on 'beautifying their settlements' (amongst other things installing new toilets and bathrooms to host the guests, including then Prime Minister Qarase), and preparing food and gifts for the reconciliation ceremony. The villagers had collected 10 cows, 30 *tabua* (whales teeth) and fine mats to be presented to the Australian visitors, the two chiefly households and the descendants of the local missionaries. (12 November 2003: 3)[1]

The ceremony started with a church service conducted by the ACCF, moved on to the traditional ceremony and ended with a lavish feast. The villagers sought forgiveness from the paramount chief of the province of Naitasiri, Turaga Qaranivalu Ratu Inoke Takiveikata, the [chiefly] Mataiwelagi household of Bau and the relatives of the local missionaries who were killed with Baker. (Ibid.)

The Sunday Post reporter noted that when the most important *tabua* had been presented by the *Tui* (chief) of Navatusila, asking for forgiveness for the deeds of his forefathers and asking for his people to be released from the curse that they had been under since,

> a prayer was said asking for the blessing of the land and its people from that day onwards. The sunny day was … broken minutes later as dark clouds hovered around the village, opening up for intermittent rain. The people of Navatusila took is as a sign … that their apology had been accepted and acknowledged by the Almighty. They linked the events to a passage in the Bible, in the Old Testament, in 2 Chronicles, Chapter 7:14: If my people … humble themselves and … turn from their wicked ways, then I will hear them from Heaven, will forgive their sins, and will heal their land … (*The Sunday Post* 14 November 2003: 13)

All three of the interwoven elements of the Three Pillars structure were in play in the *bulubulu*, as the *vanua* were present in the guise of the people and their chiefs, the Church was present, and the Government was represented by amongst others then Prime Minister Qarase. Acording to *The Daily Post* the PM emphasised precisely this, saying that the reconciliation ceremony 'brought together the three solid foundations of Fiji society: the Church, Government and culture (*vanua, lotu, matanitu*) [sic]'. (*The Daily Post* 15 November 2003: 5)

The politics of representing the past

Because Reverend Baker was a 'European' (i.e. white) missionary his killing (and the killing of his Fijian assistants) by pagan Fijians – and the fact that he was subsequently also cannibalised, as were his assistants – has been given considerably

---

1 Former Methodist President Reverend Koroi warned that this high profile event would end up creating more poverty and financial problems for the villagers (*Fiji Times* 5 November 2003: 3), see also *Fiji Times* 17 November 2003: 6, 29 November 2003: 6, *Fiji Sun* 27 August 2003: 1, 18 November 2003: 4, 27 November 2003: 4, *Daily Post* 16 October 2003: 3.

more prominence, for example in being part of a permanent exhibition in the Fiji Museum, than the killing of Tongan missionaries by the people of Kaba, publicly atoned for in a reconciliation ritual at the Methodist Church Conference in 2003. (*The Daily Post* 28 August 2003: 5)

In a letter printed in the *Fiji Times* shortly after the Baker reconciliation ceremony Australian church historian and Australian church historian Dr Andrew Thornley, who has researched extensively into the history of the Methodist Church in Fiji, brought the Baker killing into the wider historical and political context of Fiji mission history. Thornley (2002: 33-35) has a very clear account in his latest book of what happened to Baker – and why. Thornley's point in his Letter to the Editor was that the people of Navatusila in 19th century Fiji saw Baker as connected with Eastern Fiji chiefly power (as indeed the Methodist mission was) and understandably felt threatened:

> I was moved by pictures of Navosa people shown on Australian TV as they sought forgiveness from the descendants of Thomas Baker, killed at Gagdelavatu with nine Fijians in 1867. Considerable wealth in the form of traditional gifts was passed from the hands of villagers in their effort to remove what they felt to be more than 100 years of ill luck. The humility of the Fijians was clearly evident, however, the written evidence of history demonstrates that, for their part, the descendents of Baker just as much needed to seek forgiveness from the Navosa people.
>
> For Thomas Baker irresponsibly ignored advice, notably from knowledgeable Fijians, to continue his journey across Viti Levu in 1867. The people of the neighbouring district of Dawarau warned Baker that [because of] the situation inland [it] was too dangerous to proceed. For a number of reasons, but partly because the advice came from traditional non-Christian sources, Baker chose to ignore the warnings. So Baker came into Gagadelavatu, the chief town of Navosa, near the site of present-day Nabutautau, as an unwelcome visitor. He was seen as an agent of the Christian chief Seru Cakobau who had waged war and tried to conquer the interior [of Viti Levu]. The time was not rife for Baker to take nine Fijians into hostile territory. Baker knew the risk and he did not tell his wife where he was going, so unsure was he of the territory and the minds of the people.
>
> In view of these circumstances, which I have considerably summarized from my longer account in the book *Exodus of the i Taukei* ... the people of Navosa had little option but to view Baker's motives from a traditional and cultural point. The perceived agents of Bau's influence had to be removed. Baker's death was, of course, sad. More to the point, it could have been avoided if Baker had exercised reasonable judgment. So the blame for the missionary's death does not only lie with the people of Navosa. Forgiveness is needed from both sides. (*The Fiji Times* 23 November 2003: 6)

Thornley's letter highlights how closely history, the past and the present, the local and the global are linked in the ways in which the past is portrayed in the present. The entanglement and use of the past in the present are evident in the examples given here of people's desire to conduct traditional reconciliation rituals – and not least in their staging and performance, their efficacy, and the responses they engendered. The fact that we can only access the past from the present, and the interweaving of history, tradition, Christianity and politics in the different re-presentations of what happened then and in 'the present' (i.e. 1867 and 2003) are similarly evident in all examples.[2]

Burying the past

As discussed before, people in Fiji are bound to one another through *vanua*. People are always and at all times connected to one another through their belonging to a particular clan that has historical, social, cultural and spiritual ties to a particular place, a particular part of the land. Whatever a person does will reflect on all the other members of the clan in the present as well as the future, just as the actions of deceased clan members still reflect on the clan as a whole today. Crime, sin and disorder or 'brokenness' in any part of the clan or by any clan member at any time therefore reflects on the whole.

If relations among the people or between different *vanua* are in a state of disorder, so too is the land in a state of disorder. Polluted or disordered relations between people are also a polluting of the land. Disordered social relations and disordered relations to the land can effectuate *kalouca* (lit. evil spirit), sickness and death in a clan, in subsequent generations too, until the customary ritual of reconciliation has been performed and accepted. A healing of relations between people therefore involves healing the land.

In discussing the 'sacredness' of soil, Matthew Tomlinson (2002: 246) writes of how soil was considered by a Methodist minister in Kadavu to be '*bibi* ("heavy", connoting "important") because the elders are buried in it'. Essentially, the soil contains ancestral spirituality and is therefore potentially dangerous. On the other hand, it connects people of the present to the intrinsic strength of kinship relations and thus to the power of the ancestors.

This sense of 'heaviness' can therefore be viewed positively as well as negatively, depending on a person's Christian beliefs, i.e. whether being Christian entails negating that which is pre-Christian as being of the devil, or viewing one's ancestral connections as being an important element of one's identity in the present. Another man, drawing also on imagery from Genesis, gave another explanation of why soil was considered to have special significance in Fiji:

---

2   I thank John Barker for referring me to Errington and Gewertz 1995 for a comparable example of a re-enactment of the arrival of missionary George Brown to the Duke of York Islands in 1875. See also Weir 2000a.

First, God built Adam from soil. Second, ancestors fought over it. (This seems to be both a reflection and a cause of soil's importance). Third, he explained, the earth was created before everything else, according to the Bible's story of creation: before water, before animals, before humankind, land was brought into being. (Tomlinson 2002: 246-247)

Tomlinson (2002: 247) points out that 'linguistically, the sense that the land is seen to act *upon* people – that land is an agent which can affect humans, that land is *mana* – is expressed in certain phrases'. Dickhardt, who also conducted research in Kadavu, says:

In my respondents' statements [the *vanua*] appeared as something alive (*e dua na ere bula*, a living (*bula*) thing (*ere*), as something possessing *mana* ... as something with ears (*taliga*) for hearing (*rogo*) and eyes (*mata*) for vision (*rai*) ... even as something that could bite (*katija*) in the sense of a punishment for particular forms of transgression. (Dickhardt 2000 in Tomlinson 2002: 247)

People come from the earth and are bound to their *vanua*, to their place of being. They have an obligation to care for that place, to be there, an obligation to participate in the nurturing not only of the land but also of the kinship relations that are connected to that place of belonging. If they do not see to their obligations they may fall ill. If they do not care for the land they belong to they anger the ancestral gods who retaliate by causing sickness and maybe even death.

There are three different terms in Standard Fijian for rituals or ceremonies of reconciliation – *isoro*, *matanigasau* and *ibulubulu* – all of which share the same ritual structure, involving the presentation of one or more *tabua* (whale's tooth) and other valuables such as kava and mats (sometimes meat, such as cow, and drums of kerosene) by *vanua* representatives of the clan responsible for a crime, to clan representatives of the victim.

The three terms are used interchangeably, as is notable in the different newspaper reports of the Reverend Baker reconciliation and in my interviews with those involved. However, in general Fijian perceptions of reconciliation derive from the term *ibulubulu* which means burial, grave, that which covers it; that which is under the earth. *Ibulubulu* comes from the word *bulu* which means to cover with earth, to bury, and Bulu was also the pre-Christian name for the underworld of death. (Cf Williams [1858] 1982: 243) When used in relation to forgiveness and reconciliation, figuratively speaking, *bulubulu* means to bury an injury. The offering of a *tabua* as a token of peace is then also *ibulubulu*. (Capell 1991: 19 and 17)

'People talk of "bulu kina na ca" – evil being buried by it (the *tabua*)'. (Geraghty 2006, pers comm.) Implicit in this is the common understanding that once the appropriate ritual of reconciliation has taken place between clan representatives of perpetrator and the victim, grievances are considered buried, laid to rest – forgotten (a term frequently used).

Descendents of those who killed and cannibalised Reverend Baker had already performed two traditional ceremonies of reconciliation to the Methodist Church in Fiji in atonement, one in the early 20th Century, one in the late 20th Century, in the 1980s. Yet, according to the villagers, the curse had not been lifted and its effects – problematic relations with local government, lack of development, social problems, infertile land and bad harvests – continued to dominate their lives.

The ceremony performed in 2003, however, was markedly different from the former traditional reconciliations because Pentecostal and Methodist pastors led villagers in a period of prayer, prior to the actual ceremony. The new perspective of the 2003 *bulubulu* for Reverend Baker was the understanding that people could not wipe the slate clean, so to speak, by traditional rites alone. Reconciliation and healing of the land could only come about if Christian rituals of cleansing and exorcism of the land through the power of the Holy Spirit took place prior to the traditional *bulubulu*.

In some ways the *bulubulu* became the culmination of a Pentecostal Christian spiritual preparatory process, rather than the main event. On the other hand, the time-consuming and costly material preparations for a ceremony of such proportions which villagers must have spent weeks on, means that tremendous focus was placed on the ceremony itself and the complex interplay of clan relations, as well as the added power of the attendance of the highest ranking government and church leaders in the country and overseas guests. However, the unusual addition of a preparatory period of praying and fasting before a traditional reconciliation ceremony, and the ways in which the event was explained from Pentecostal perspectives, is significant.[3]

Reconciling land and people

The traditional rituals of forgiveness and reconciliation described here, concerned with the restoration of balanced reciprocal relations between people and between people and the land, resonate with similar cosmological understandings in many other cultures and among peoples across the Pacific Island region and elsewhere in the world. People's need to maintain balanced relations with their ancestors and the spirit world through observing particular rituals and rules of conduct to appease spirits, placating them through ritual sacrifices (or, as in this case, ritual presentations) remains, albeit changing over time, interwoven in people's lives in syncretic religious belief. (See Strathern and Stewart 2004: 91) This is what Gary Trompf (1994 in ibid: 93) terms as 'the logic of retribution'. Strathern and Stewart

---

3   What is also notable about the expensive 2003 *bulubulu*, arranged by the ACCF, is that the costs, I was told, were covered by the Ministry of Reconciliation and National Unity, a ministry set up to promote reconciliation between the ethnic communities in Fiji after the 2000 coup.

capture the gist of this by relating it to the popular term, 'there is no such thing as a free lunch'. (Ibid.)

In Melanesia, Trompf (1991: 158) writes, 'the dead are almost without exception understood to continue their involvement with the living. Avengement is commonly thought to "exorcise" a spirit of its inimical aspects, turning it into a supportive agent'. 'Throughout most of Oceania ... the helpful deceased are those who have received the proper funerary rites, while troublesome ghosts arise from those not properly disposed of or from those expected to carry their grievances beyond death'. (Trompf 1995: 131)

Although Trompf is describing the reasoning behind *avengement* of wrongdoing as being the means of transforming negative spiritual powers to positive, so central in Melanesian contexts, rites of reconciliation in Fiji seek to do the same. Brokenness between clans needs to be restored through rites of reconciliation that will heal social relations, relations with the spirit world and the land. That is to say, reconciliation will bring nourishment and fertility to the social barrenness of human relations and the material barrenness of the land – and will transform the powers of the spirit world from 'inimical' to 'supportive'.

Describing reconciliation as 'a prerequisite for regeneration and reproduction' Ravuvu (1987: 260) points out – in this case with regard to the situation of a couple's elopement, but his words apply to any situation of damaged clan relations:

> a 'weak link' had been created in the social fabric of the *vanua*, and the 'social debt' which the [offending] *yavusa* [tribe] ... had incurred had to be cleared if co-operation, life and prosperity were to be attained. It was the duty of those who committed an error to take the initiative and erase their tarnished image, to restore mutual respect and honour to both parties, thus reviving the good relationships which had been impaired through the abrasive act of one of their people. On the spiritual level, this non-compliance with *vanua* standards was an act of aggression against the supernatural realm of the *vanua* which arbitrates over human affairs ... Action was thus imperative. The offended *vanua* would need to be appeased if continuity of life and prosperity were to be attained. The local metaphor of *sautu na vanua* means people must prosper; the Fijian term *sautu* implies peace, happiness and the availability of abundant resources. (Ibid: 260-261)

(Bakker 1986: 200-202) notes (also in relation to the disordering of clan relations on account of elopement) that the concept of *duka* (dirt, pollution) in Fijian conceptualisation is equated with disorder of social relations, and *savasavaa* (clean, pure; cleansing, purification) with their reconciliation and re-ordering through rituals of reconciliation.

So the reciprocal relations between different clans are linked to one another and are kept in balance through spiritual links to *vanua*. In any situation of *vanua* transgression the subsequent presentation of a *tabua* from one clan to another simultaneously and immediately clears not just individuals, but clan members, past, present and future – and heals the land.

Bush (2000) describes a dramatic ceremony of *bulubulu* at the Methodist Church Conference in 1996, in which a village of 500 people publicly atoned for the sin of a deceased grandfather who had participated in the massacre of a white plantation owner and his family in 1873. The *kalouca* (evil) the village was experiencing on account of this past act was described as a 'contagious disease', spreading throughout the community. The presentation of a *tabua*, 'a symbol of confession, deeper than words', is the key to unlocking and freeing relations. Its very acceptance means that the sin or misdeed is immediately cleared, the words '*sereki galala!*' (freedom is loosed!) being called out. Bush, inspired by Tuwere, relates the traditional *bulubulu* to Christian notions of sin and salvation:

> [*Ibulubulu* illustrates] the communal nature of sin and salvation … a rite of confession and pardon … nearly sacramental in character … *Bulubulu* literally means the "burial" of the sin that has been troubling the people … Tuwere sees all sin as having to do with relationship (*veiwekani*) … brokenness in relationship in one area is thought to reverberate throughout the whole network of relatedness. It is … "contagious". Sin will always be manifest in broken relationship, and salvation will always find expression through well-being in the community. (Bush 2000: 31-32)

'The sins of our forefathers will be punished to the third and fourth generations'

The Old Testament image of a God who punishes those who disobey him corresponds to the powers attributed to pre-Christian pagan gods and spirits in Fiji. He is seen to protect, punish and oversee all that happens in this world as well as the spirit world. (Ravuvu 1983: 98) From an Old Testament perspective actions count, not only at the time they happen, but also in subsequent generations. Unless a sin has been confessed and atoned for echoes of the sin will be passed down in different form from generation to generation.

This corresponds with traditional Fijian understandings and Pentecostal doctrine on reconciliation and forgiveness. Methodist pastor Reverend Ledua Kacimaiwai, one of the ACCF pastors involved in counselling and spiritually preparing the villagers of Navatusila for the reconciliation ceremony explained:

> So we really need to go down to the root of it, get biblically taught on … what we have to do: corporate repentance, the chiefs and the families getting together, confessing[4] … Identifying our sins, through prayer, fasting for three weeks …

---

4   See e.g. Eves 2003, Robbins 2004: 231-246, Rumsey 2008 on the importance of confession in Pentecostal faith practices in Papua New Guinea.

until the *vanua* was ready to ask for forgiveness. Because it takes humility [to] ask [for] forgiveness, don't you think so? ... we have to remember too ... they were kind of proud of doing it ... Not only did they kill him ... they ate him. To talk about it ... it's suddenly gone into their spirit and in their heart ... we are ... correcting the ... past wrongs, before we ... move forward. You can't ignore this and then move forward. (Kacimaiwai, interview 1 November 2004)

But why hadn't the former two *bulubulu* performed to the Methodist Church taken away the curse in Navatusila? Why, I asked Reverend Kurulo from Christian Mission Fellowship, a leading member of the ACCF and one of the main organisers of the 2003 *bulubulu*, was it necessary to do it all again?

Because a lot of the forgiveness that had taken place was just at horizontal level, not the vertical ... we helped them with the vertical, so they have to come to God ... to ask forgiveness to God on behalf of their forefathers for what they [did] towards the man of God ... [You] see some of the curses that we inherited ... that the Bible talks about ... the iniquities of our forefathers [can] visit the ... third and fourth generations. [What was done] was [not done to the Methodist Church, it was] done to Thomas Baker, he was a man of God. So first of all they need to come and ask forgiveness of God. (Kurulo, interview 28 September 2004)

As other villages or clans, whose ancestors committed significant crimes in the past, Navatusila people experienced *kalouca*, bad luck/evil and problems with many aspects of their daily lives:

Everything that they planted was not bearing fruit. The children were not really going ahead in education ... This is what they have analysed, regarding their family tree, and regarding the land. So that really makes them really to search. They have a time of prayer, fasting and prayer, asking forgiveness, they ask forgiveness [from] God. First of all they receive Christ into their hearts, and then they ask God's forgiveness just for them personally, and then they come as a community to ask God's forgiveness for what they have done ... it was Baker and the family that was mostly affected. So we have to bring in Baker's family descendants ... this was the fourth generation of the Baker family! ... This is what the Bible talks about. So now ... the road is [being constructed] and they [have started] to plant; things are flourishing, and they see the release in their own lives. Also they see the impact of what happened. (Ibid.)[5]

Reverend Kurulo refers in the first quote to the 'horizontal level' of forgiveness, which I take to mean traditional presentations such as whale's teeth and kava offered

---

5   A missing link in this chapter is the experience of the people themselves, but the date for the Baker reconciliation was moved so many times it finally took place when I had left the country, and I was unable subsequently to visit the area.

during a *bulubulu*, focused on restoring the communal balance of relationship at *vanua* level. This level includes the ancestral spirits, yet also involves God, Yahweh, as creator of *vanua*. An important element of the traditional rites of *ibulubulu* or *isoro* is that the agency involved is ritually formalised between particular spokesmen (*mata ni vanua*) on behalf of the group or on behalf of the injured parties, who may be individuals. In these rituals it is the restoration of relations between two groups, rather than the restoration of relations between individuals, that is important.

The Pentecostal prayers of cleansing and repentance described here are concerned with reconciliation, yet they differ from traditional Fijian rituals of reconciliation, their focus primarily being on the *vertical* level, the level of the individual's relationship with God. The main focus is on individual spiritual agency through the releasing power of the Holy Spirit. In dedicating one's life to Christ and being baptised in the Holy Spirit one achieves a personal relationship with Christ. Steps towards this are taken through the identification of past sins, repentance, individual fasting and abstinence, and seeking God's forgiveness. It is this reconciliation with God which will eventually lead to reconciliation and the restoration of healthy moral and social relations in the community. Reverend Poate Mata, Gospel Apostolic Outreach Church, described the deterioration of relations in the area:

> It went to a stage in Nataleira, if one of your relatives dies, even your own sister or your own brother wouldn't come to the funeral. That now is un-Fijian … So for us to identify the root we've got to seek God's wisdom, and God's divine intervention, because he knows we don't see the root, we see the fruits … The root is spiritual. So these people here were planting marijuana … why? … Because that's their only means of income, marijuana … according to them. But for the past ten years … the police, the village elders, they tried to encourage the people not to plant or sell or buy marijuana. They did no such thing. The police had been up there, but they could not identify [a] single marijuana [plant] in this particular village, until ACCF went in there and approached the problem *from a spiritual point of view* ... We went and we fasted and we prayed. (Reverand Poate Mata, interview 9 November 2004)

Breaking the spiritual stronghold

From a Pentecostal perspective there is a 'spiritual stronghold' of evil binding these people to the sins of the past, causing them to commit sins in the present. The root of the problem is spiritual and can therefore only be solved from a spiritual perspective. Each individual Christian, first and foremost, the *individual* body as vehicle for spiritual cleansing through fasting, abstinence, suffering and prayer, rather than the communal, *social* clan body as in rites of the *vanua,* is central to this. And in order to undertake this the individual has to make a conscious decision, again unlike in communally ordered *vanua* rites, and has to pray for the will to see it through:

> The only way to break through [a] spiritual strong hold [is that] you should pray and fast, or fast and pray ... that has been the strategy wherever the committee on healing the land, whatever they move into then its necessary we must come together and .... the Lord shall renew their strength. So when you fast you are absconding from food, physical food and you want to feed your spirit with the spiritual food, the word of God. Okay, so you pray and you fast. You are seeking for God's intervention in your life, wisdom, strength, power, direction. You are telling God, I am going through something I can no longer handle, please I need your divine intervention, so I'll be fasting in front of you, I am sorry for all my sins, I am tormenting [my] flesh so that my spirit will grow. That's a very simple explanation of fasting ... And that's what they did so they came together. It's easy ... boom! Down came the power! And that saw the break-through in there. (Mata, interview 9 November 2004)

In November 2004, a year after the *bulubulu* ceremony of forgiveness and reconciliation in Navatusila, Christian Mission Fellowship's monthly magazine, *The Harvest Times* (Issue 33, November 2004: 12) ran an article on 'healing of the land' and 'transformation revival' in which a number of different examples were given of communities and areas of land that had undergone divine healing and transformation, following rites of cleansing and exorcism led by pastors from the ACCF, including the *vanua* of Navatusila, which had experienced significant changes in the past year:

> Tremendous blessing ... has come down on the people of Navatusila. From stagnant, dry weather, rain falls there ... the crops are in abundance ... there is an abundance of fruits, root crops as well as the fish in the rivers. The skin diseases, which used to inflict the people, have disappeared and even the pigs that used to rummage and damage their crops, have disappeared. The young people after having heard that their land was cursed because of the wrong deeds of their forefathers up to the present time then realised that marijuana [which they had been growing and selling for ten years at considerable profit] was one of the causes of this curse ... They then decided to pull up all the marijuana in the village ... They dedicated their land and people to God and when dedication prayers were offered [there was] this sprinkling of rainfall from nowhere in heaven just to re-inforce to those who were there that God was present in the occasion. (Ibid: 12)

The breaking of the spiritual bondage and re-infusing of the land and people with the power of the Holy Spirit affected tremendous release and change. Only through public and inner acknowledgement and confession of this bondage, as part of rites of renewal and transformation, was it possible to lift the curse of past deeds and be ritually cleansed.

From a Pentecostal perspective in order to restore social relations and material well-being in the present it is necessary to re-interpret particular sites and acts of the past and present as demonic and destructive, demarcating and dislocating them from the present. The present understood as the time now and ahead of a person from the moment they make the decision to change and give their lives to Christ. At the same time these rituals *connect* the past with the present and in fact emphasise the ever-present power of the past in the present, just as the power of evil in the world is an ever-present reality.

Embodiments of faith

John Barker (2007a: 6) points out with regard to pre-Christian beliefs in Melanesia how 'spiritual attacks by sorcerers, spirits, and ghosts [were attributed] to breeches of moral codes. In turn, many people interpreted the health of their bodies or success in subsistence activities as indices of the moral condition of their communities. (Fraenkel 1986) Landscapes, rituals or decorated bodies were also read as embodiments of the moral health of a community'. (O'Hanlon 1989)

This understanding is similar in Pentecostal Christianity where the body, as the temple of the Holy Spirit, is a symbol, representation and an individual and collective field of expression for faith – in ritual, as experience, spirituality and emotion. To many Pentecostals the body indicates the strength of a person's faith (cf Coleman 2000a: 147,148), the strength of the *relationship* between the individual and God. The body should therefore also *be* and *be seen to be* strong, as this strength and health is in itself a witness to a person's strength of faith.

Christ himself should be portrayed as the literal embodiment of health, strength and invincible power. Coleman, analysing an illustration of Christ as a body-builder in the Word of Life charismatic church in Sweden notes that the picture shows 'a healthy, strong body acting as an index of faith … a powerful and triumphalist Christ who embodies movement … the whole body … exalting in physical and spiritual power. Christ is breaking forth, perhaps even removing himself from the confines of the canvas rather than being placed in dialogue with other figures … a Christ of power who looks straight at the viewer in direct evangelical exhortation'. (Ibid.)

A Pentecostal woman explained the significance of portraying Christ as strong and triumphant by comparing Catholic representations of the suffering and broken Christ on the Cross. If portrayed at all, she said, the Cross should be empty, symbolising the victory and power of the resurrection:

> Just as there was an empty tomb, there was an empty cross … To continue to have Christ on the cross is a sign of defeat and is idolatrous … Jesus has risen … but [they're] continuing to show a picture of weakness and suffering … If there's no resurrection, there's no Christianity … [They are preaching] a

gospel of sorrow ... [their] portrayal of Christ is always [like this or] as a baby.
(Momoivalu, interview 1998)

Jesus should be shown as strong and victorious. It is the power of the victorious and
indefatigable Risen Christ, such as Coleman's tangible Christ as a body builder,
that transforms and heals individuals and communities, who through the power of
his Holy Spirit exorcises ancestral spiritual power, restores morality and healthy
social relations, brings rain, nourishment and healing to barren land.

Spiritual warfare

Pastor Kanaimawi, ACCF, explains the ACCF methodology of healing the land
(Newland 2006: 341-342):

> They go out to a village and get all the villagers, irrespective of what church they
> are, look at their problems, do a spiritual mapping, map out where the devil has
> been influential – whether it's a killing field in one place or whether it's where
> they worshipped demons in the past – and then they cleanse those out. Then the
> people repent for what they have done and ask God to come in and the whole
> village just transforms.

Fer (n.d.), referring to Jorgensen (2005), describes spiritual mapping as a
Pentecostal theology of global spiritual warfare, developed on a worldwide-basis
since the 1980s, entailing a 'come-back' of territorial spirits. Jorgensen describes
the categorising of development as both *physical* and *spiritual* by an elderly man
in Telefolip, Papua New Guinea, who argued that material development in the area
had been blocked by Satan's power, operating through traditional spirits. Only
after this power had been broken could development take place. (2005: 452, see
also Tomlinson 2009: 148, Stritecky 2001: 66)

   Cleansing exercises involving the exorcism of demonic forces from land and
community are regularly reported in the Fiji newspapers. *The Fiji Times* (4 December
2002; 5 December 2002; 6 December 2002) brought reports of the involvement of
Methodist Church members in the burning down of a family home considered to be
possessed by evil spirits, the dismantling of a community hall (*soqosoqo*) and the
burning of a *tanoa* said to date from pre-Christian times in two villages in Tailevu.
The purpose of these acts of cleansing was to exorcise and break demonic bonds
with the past through the destruction of artifacts belonging to the past or buildings
that were seen as housing spirits from a non-Christian, pagan past.

   'We are trying to ... cleanse ourselves spiritually', the village headman of one
of the villages commented, 'and we hope to bring the village, which has been
separated because of new church factions coming in, to be together again'. (*Fiji
Times* 4 December 2002: 1) While the Methodist Church head office distanced

itself from the events the 'cleansing exercise was done with the support of the *vanua* and the Methodist Church'. (*Fiji Times* 6 December 2002: 2)

A villager whose house had been identified as possessed by evil spirits was on the other hand taking legal action. 'The allegations are that there is a spirit who came from this house holding an ancient war club and spear', he said. (*Fiji Times* 5 December 2002: 3) And *The Fiji Times* editorial, emphasising the value of history and historical artefacts, pointed out that 'the deliberate burning of precious historical artifacts is probably illegal'. Some of the artifacts that were destroyed, such as the *tanoa,* 'were made long before the Deed of Cession [1874] and as such represent a vital link with Fiji's past'. (*Fiji Times* 4 December 2002: 6)

A cleansing of the land and exorcising of ancestral spirits was held outside Naroro village, where I lived. The Pentecostal Church of God pastor had a small and rather fluid community of adherents, mainly youth, who met for services and teaching in his home on the outskirts of the village. One night the pastor led his congregation to the top of Tavuni, the ruins of a Tongan fort on a hill behind the village. My sister told me about the all-night prayer vigil she had taken part in.

Tavuni was the *vanua tabu* (lit. forbidden land) of the *vanua.* There was an important message in both the pastor's choice of location and the timing of the prayers. Although people used to collect firewood on Tavuni, it was *tabu* to go there after dark and on Sundays. My 'father' told me how a soldier had once gone up there on a Sunday to drink, and had been chased away by the <u>*niju*</u> (ancestral spirit) that 'bothered' him for a long time after, until he conducted the necessary rites (*ibulubulu*) to the clan elders, to ask forgiveness of the *vanua* and reconcile with the ancestral spirits.

But the pastor had led the group of youth up the path to the top of the Fort at the dead of night. When the group had reached its destination, my sister told me, they spent the first part of their vigil exorcising the devils around them. They called out loudly, rebuking them in the name of Jesus Christ, and the devils retreated. After this rite of exorcism and cleansing, the group spent the rest of the night on the hilltop, praying. In the morning they returned to the village.

From a Fijian socio-cultural perspective this violation of traditional norms of respect (and fear) of ancestral sites and spirits is a strong statement against traditional values and mainstream Christian beliefs and practice. Furthermore the message is, in effect, a challenge to the political status quo, to the superiority of the power of the chiefly lineage group (<u>*bito*</u>) in the village (the pastor belonged to the commoner <u>*bito*</u>), entrenched in respect for tradition and the *vanua,* people's belonging to the land and to the (Methodist) church.

The Fort, an excavated archaeological site, open to the public, was beautifully located with magnificent vistas of the Sigatoka river and valley, the mountainous interior of Vitilevu to the north, and the white Sigatoka sand dunes and azure of the sea to the south. I went there often to spend time alone in the shade of the ancient, gnarled trees and write my fieldwork diary. Despite its history of fighting and cannibalism I had always felt it to be a tranquil place. I enquired of my sister whether there were only evil spirits up at the Fort; were there no good spirits there? She was astounded at my question. There was no doubt in her mind – only evil spirits were there.

Conceptualising evil

When later discussing this with Reverend Suliasi Kurulo, at that time pastor of the parachurch, Every Home for Christ, he was also abundantly clear:

> There are only two kingdoms: the kingdom of God and the kingdom of darkness – of Satan and all his fallen angels ... in the Bible these demons are called unclean spirits – and all ancestral gods [and spirits] are classified as that. (Kurulo, interview 1998)

Protestant cosmological understandings that emerged during the Reformation cut out the Catholic concept of the Great Chain of Being, asserting that the only essential realities are those of God and his created world of man. There are no intermediary spirit beings between God and man in this cosmology, such as the saints and angels of Catholic belief. In Protestant cosmology, God and man are related to each other by God's grace and man's faith alone. (Taylor 1985: 40)

Traditional Fijian understandings of the spirit world are, by contrast, holistic. The spirits and the efficacy of the spirit world are as much a part of the concept of *vanua* as the material elements such as the rocks, rivers and trees and clans they belong to and are an integral part of people's everyday lives. Ancestral spirits are essentially neutral but can be persuaded through offerings of *yaqona* (*kava*) to use their *mana* for good or evil purposes. (Cf Katz 1993) Good and evil exist within the Fijian spirit world, but are not clearly demarcated and separated, as in Christian doctrine. Using similar clean/unclean dichotomies as Reverend Kurulo, Ratu Meli Navuniyasi, pastor in Apostolic Churches Fiji, explained:

> Before Christianity people in Fiji had their own religions. They served these gods and devils ... the old beliefs came from Eve's disobedience, [from] the First Dispensation of Innocence. The spiritual teaching of the eating of the fruit is disobedience to the teaching of the Lord. God is a clean God. If you allow sinful things in, he will pull out ... [The] *vu* ... are the angels of darkness ... They don't act by themselves – they only do what they are asked to do. They can provide wealth, they can heal, they can kill. You cannot see them – they manifest [themselves] through people ... They are all evil. (Navuniyasi, interview 26 June 1998)

What is notable is that the pastors do not negate the existence or the efficacy of ancestral spirits – but they re-classify them as essentially evil forces. Many of the evangelising practices and rituals of present-day Pentecostals in Fiji, as elsewhere in the world, mirror the approach of early missionaries to the problem of the pre-

Christian spirit world. The night vigil outside the village emphasises that not only are ancestral spirits, the *vu* or *niju* as personifications and embodiments of tradition, redefined as concepts of evil and the devil, they are in fact necessary components of Pentecostal beliefs. As Caplan (1995: 124) points out:

> Unlike liberal Christianity spread by late 19th- and early 20th-century missionaries of the principal denominations ... which denied the 'reality' of evil spirits in the everyday lives of their followers and potential converts, Pentecostalism not only acknowledges their existence, but continuously demonstrates the power of the Holy Spirit to vanquish them.[6]

'Through the image of the Devil, old spirits and deities are integrated into the Protestant universe of discourse as "Christian" demons'.[7] The actions of the pastor and his flock in the village not only acknowledge the existence of ancestral spirits (or devils, as they term them), they in fact *accentuate* the reality of the spirit world. And while the public outer battle against the demonic ancestral spirits of the land is a very real battle while also taking place metaphysically (cf Stritecky 2001), it mirrors the inner battle of individuals against the ever pervasive power of the devil and demonic spiritual forces.[8]

Robbins (in press) writes that Pentecostalism often claims not to be ritualised yet is actually notable for 'an extremely high degree of ritual activity that marks its social life', and Robbins points to this as the key to understanding its success. Coleman (in press) notes that charismatic ritual has the ability 'to frame other kinds of replication, those of mimesis and mutual participation – rhetorical, embodied, spatial – among participants within and beyond the meeting hall'. Pentecostalism draws people together into an empowered and empowering ritualised community where change and transformation become readily attainable through individual action.

The 'healing of the land' conducted prior to the Baker reconciliation held tremendous transformative and empowering potential in the fact that pastors from Suva came especially to a neglected, rural area of Vitilevu and stayed for a prolonged period to work with the villagers and guide them through a programme of ritual reconciliatory interaction at spiritual and social levels. The serious attention bestowed on the marginalised people of this area and the ritualised opportunities individuals were given to act, to take charge of their life and make a conscious decision to change, is unusual and empowering in relation to the highly hierarchical norms of traditional rural Fiji society.

---

6   See also Caplan 1985, 1987a, 1987b, Barker 1990b, Robbins 1995. And see Parkin 1985.

7   Meyer 1998a: 322, see also 1992 and 1995, Newland 2004.

8   See also McDonald 2001: 157 re AOG missionary rhetoric in Aboriginal Western Australia.

It is in many ways extraordinary that Pentecostal pastors officially took part in a traditional ceremony involving rituals that link people to their ancestral spirits. I suggest that having first, in the weeks prior to the ceremony, exorcised the land of its ancestral spiritual power and demonstrated the superior power of Christianity, the presence of the pastors within the ceremony could be seen as a form of spiritual warfare. Their presence could also be seen as part of a general strategy of translating vanua values and practices to become based on biblical principles and Born Again Christian principles. And since the ACCF advocates that Fiji be declared a Christian State, entailing the strengthening of chiefly power and thereby of traditional ritual, the ACCF's organising of the reconciliation ceremony and their official presence could also be seen as a political statement.

The importance of roots, connections and relationality, of honouring and strengthening people's ties to one another in their belonging to the land, *vanua,* is expressed in the complex rituals of a village funeral described in the next chapter.

Chapter 3
A Path of Mats: A Village Funeral in Nadrogā

One Saturday evening in September 1997, an old lady in the village where I lived died. When later I reread my notes on the mortuary rites that took place, an image came to mind of a path from death to burial and beyond through mourning, paved with mats – a path of mats.

In Fiji and in all other Pacific Island cultures, mortuary rites involve complex exchanges of material wealth that affirm and reproduce kinship relationships, often thought of as kinship 'paths', through time and space – thus reproducing social life.[1] As Trompf points out in relation to Melanesia, society in this life and in the afterworld is interwoven, a 'community of both the living and the dead'. The deceased are 'almost always conceived as remaining part of society … constitute powerful and watchful participators in rites … [and are] usually crucial for group support, yet not confused with deities worshipped or other spirits placated'. (1995: 130)

In Fiji, mortuary rites emerge from, confirm and reproduce the intricate patternings of *vanua*.[2] In the funerals I attended in Nadrogā three types of traditional valuables (*iyau*)[3] were considered the most significant objects of exchange: whale's teeth (*tabua*), barkcloth (*masi*) and mats (*iō*). Of these I found mats, and their aesthetic as well as exchange value in the mortuary rites, to be of particular interest. The presentation and exchange of mats; their cultural, social, and economic value; their placing at all stages of the final journey of the dead; the consistent order in which they are placed; who are the givers and who the recipients – all these factors are visible and tangible expressions of the links or paths between people and place, between loss and bereavement and the re-affirming of social relations and obligations, past, present and future. Women are the producers of

---

1 Compare for example Hocart 1915b, Weiner 1976: 61-120, 1980, 1985, Kaeppler 1978a: 174-202 and 1978b, Strathern, A. 1981, de Coppet 1981, Strathern, M. 1988, Liep 1989, 2009: 238-252, Damon and Wagner 1989, Foster 1990, 1995a, Battaglia 1992.

2 See Williams 1982 [1858]: 187-205, Waterhouse 1997 [1866]: 226-230, Hocart 1915b, 1929: 177-184, Geddes 1945: 47, Quain 1948, in particular: 359-373, Lester 1953: 123-129, Belshaw 1964: 141-148, Sahlins 1962, in particular: 188-192, 197-202, Hooper 1982: 100-106, Ravuvu 1983: 62-69, 1987: 179-202 and 338-341, Toren 1995b, 2004, 2006.

3 See e.g. Thomas 1991: 59-82, re *tabua* 69-75.

barkcloth and mats and play key roles in their exchange and in the care of the corpse and the ritualised, collective expressions of grief during the funeral.[4]

The term *na sala ni ibe*, the Standard Fijian term for 'a path of mats' but which also means 'the path of the mat', is a term used in mat making to describe the straight weave that goes through a mat. (Inise Koroi, pers comm. 1997) This funeral could therefore be described as a point of convergence in the interweaving of *vanua* paths through time and across space.

In south-western Vitilevu, in addition to the complex matrix of kinship paths which traverse the land and sea, clans and villages are linked through particular relations known as *koi cālevu* ('paths of relations' in the Nadrogā language). Related families from different villages are further linked to particular households in each others' villages through what is known as *cālevu ni veiluveni* (lit. paths of parent/children relations). This means that when a family visits another village for a funeral, wedding or church function, for example, it is considered as belonging to a specific household in the village. This household is responsible, as a parent is to a child, for caring for the visiting family, providing its members with a place to rest, eat and sleep. This hospitality is reciprocated when the members of the host household visit the other family's village. In this way people always have a sense of belonging to both people and place wherever they go.

And while the living reproduce kinship allegiances through these complexities of mortuary exchange, the dead travel along clan-designated 'soul paths' (*sala ni yalo*) across the land to a 'jumping-off' point (*icibaciba*) from whence they jump into the river or the sea and continue their journey westwards towards the after world. (see Trompf 1995: 159, Halapua 2008: 4)

Death, as a site of loss, change and readjustment, at individual, collective and institutional levels, is where the depth and breadth of what is known and practised as 'tradition' in a society is perhaps most clearly evoked and enacted. The crisis of death is not only the meeting point between biological life and death, it is also where the paths of past, present and future social relations converge. The particular patternings of mortuary rites in a given place and context therefore reflect the embeddedness of both life and death in social relations.

In my experience three main factors were consistent in the ways people in Fiji, whether Anglicans, Catholics, Methodists or Pentecostals, talked about or referred to death: 1) that we ourselves do not know the time or the day for our death; that death comes 'like a thief in the night' (cf 1 Thessalonians 5:2), 2) that we need therefore to always be prepared and need to repent in time before God's calling, as noted in the eulogy at this funeral 3) Among the bereaved I spoke to there was a clear acceptance of God's will in their lives, never anger against God for 'taking away' a loved one. At the same time, it is likely to mainstream Christian Fijians that death may not be caused by God calling us to him, but by *vanua* sickness caused by 'sin against the *vanua*' (cf Raitiqa 2003: 103) or by sorcery.

---

4   Compare Bloch 1982: 265.

'Fijians tend to accept God's will, and death is part of God's will of course. Death is never seen as a sacrifice. However in the olden pagan pre Christian days, whenever there is a new house built for a Chief, a commoner has to be sacrificed. So it is a pre Christian practice but it is never seen that way [now]'. (Kasanita Seruvatu, formerly a Methodist, now a Pentecostal, pers comm. 2008) And another Methodist friend from Cakaudrove province noted, 'I agree with your informant … on how death is viewed by Fijian Christians. He or she has gone to be with Jesus, something everyone should look forward to because there is a promise of something beyond this life'. (Eta Varani, pers comm. 2009) Similarly Tomlinson (2006: 137) cites a sermon in which the Methodist preacher speaks of being happy about death, referring to a deceased person as 'going home … Our place awaits us in Heaven'. This gives an impression of death as a departure to a new 'place of belonging' – particularly poignant in the Fijian cultural context.[5]

While the funeral is a meeting point of kinship relations it is also a major social event, a social commentary and a performance involving a great deal of labour. Everyone has a part to play, and in what is said or not said, in the way things are done or not done, subtle – or sometimes not so subtle – points are made on broader issues, such as the value of tradition and the acceptability of change.

Nadrogā mortuary rites

Nadrogā funerary rites fall into three distinct stages:

First, the _Vura_, a pre-burial rite of leave-taking known elsewhere in Fiji as the *reguregu* (Standard Fijian). The Capell Dictionary describes *reguregu* as: '…a present of *tabua* made to male friends of a deceased person, on which occasion the visitors kiss the corpse; to the woman a presentation of mats, cloth etc. is made, and their personal attendance at the house where the body awaits burial is required. *Reguregu* – the act of making the above offering'. (1991: 172) So the term *reguregu* or _vura_ means both the situation, the act of giving, and the gift itself. In most of the funerals I attended, I found that people considered this pre-burial mortuary rite and the exchanges that take place during it, to be of greater importance than the funeral service or the burial itself.

As is indicated by Roman Catholic missionary of the Marist order Père Jean de Marzan,[6] based in western and central Vitilevu in the late 19th-early 20th centuries, the *reguregu* or _vura_ was one of the main components of pre-Christian mortuary rites in Nadrogā, and possibly the most important actual rite of leave-taking. Other

---

5   For a somewhat different view see Toren (1995b, 2004, 2006) and for a general review of ideas on exchange and sacrifice see Stewart and Strathern (eds) 2008.

6   Père de Marzan served in Vitilevu, the last area in Fiji to be Christianised, from 1893 to 1927. Re Catholicism in Fiji see Knox 1997, Garrett 1982: 286-288, 1992: 167-174, 1997: 402-404, Ernst 1994: 211-212, Newland 2006: 353-355.

rites that followed it were concerned with appeasing departed spirits (the rite of *ruku*), and redistributing valuables (the rite of *tuva ulu* or *juberi ni ulu*):

> …when the time has come to wrap up the dead person, the relatives make up the *veireguei* [*veireguci*], kissing for the last time. First they cry, then smash up objects belonging to the deceased, his kava cup, his special kava bowl, his wooden or bamboo headrest etc. They take from the deceased's head the *vatu ni balawa* (headrest)[7] which will be carried to the tribe of the mother to announce the deceased's *tuva ulu* ceremony....(1987: 50)

Second are the rites preceding and surrounding the actual burial, including the church service. Between the church service and the burial, five whale's tooth (*tabua*) presentations and the rite known as na ruku take place.

   Third is _na juberi ni ulu_, the post-burial exchange and redistribution of valuables given during the *yura*. The distribution list is divided into seven categories: the *kōvana*, their kinship ties; the kin of the *Karua ni ulu* (second *ulu*), the clan of the father's mother (FM) of the departed, and four other presentations to the *kōvana* for the succeeding post-burial feasts.[8]

Dramatis personae

The departed	Tai
The *mōmō*	the mother's brother or his direct male descendent.
The *kōvana*	Tai's mother's clan
The *itaukei ni mase*	the 'owners of the deceased', Tai's lineage group, the chiefly lineage group
The commoner *bito*	the other lineage group in the village
The mourners	relations belonging to Tai's *vanua*

Tai is the respectful Nadrogā term for grandparent or elderly person, and I will use this term hereafter when referring to the old lady who died. Tai was the sister of the chief, a former teacher and the widow of a Lauan man. They had no children of their own, but Tai's adopted son was the village catechist (*vakatawa*). One of his daughters had lived with Tai for the past few years in her house next door, looking

---

   7   Nowadays the announcement of death to the mother's clan would be made through the presentation of a *tabua*.

   8   Formerly these four presentations would have taken place on the designated days. But the labour, time, cost and practicalities of arranging four more exchange ceremonies and feasts are extensive. Today it is increasingly the norm to make joint exchanges on the day of the funeral and reserve Hundredth Night (*vakabogidrau*) as the only other large-scale post burial celebration.

after her. In Fiji, as in many other cultures, sickness and death are considered to be contextual events, embedded in kinship ties and obligations, and expressive of conflicts and jealousy between clans, lineage groups or individuals. As de Marzan (1987: 48) notes, '... before contact with whites, a Fijian could not conceive that death could arise from natural causes. This is a notion that is just beginning to take hold among them; most attribute death to other causes ... sometimes they believe that the *dinau*, debts to other tribes, cause the sickness, and sometimes death is attributed to misbehaviour. Most frequently they say that a *drau ni kau* (charm) is the cause of death'.[9] But Tai had long been weak and in need of rest. So her death was not considered suspicious or unnatural. She died in her sleep at home. Tai died, people said, because 'she was very old and needed rest'.

Two groups of kinspeople were to become key actors in the sequence of events to follow Tai's death: her mother's clan from a neighbouring village further up the valley who would be the most important people, the highly honoured guests of the funeral (the *kōvana*); and Tai's lineage group (her father's, the chiefly lineage group – *bito*), her extended family, who, for the duration of the mortuary period, were known as 'the owners of death' (*taukei ni mase*).

A third group of kinspeople who came to play an important role was the commoner *bito* of the village. In a ritual sealed in the customary manner through the sharing of a bowl of kava the elders of Tai's lineage group 'gave their power [authority]' (*holi ni lewa*), as one man told me, to this group for the duration of the funeral, that they might take charge of the practicalities of arranging the funeral proceedings. At the end of the funeral, this delegation of power from the chiefly lineage group to the commoner lineage group was ritually cancelled through the sharing of kava and the presentation of valuables from the former to the latter as a mark of gratitude for their help.

The *kōvana*

Although Fijian funeral rites vary from place to place, the maternal relatives, known in Standard Fijian as *vasu*, of the deceased hold a special position in funeral rites across the islands.

The relationship between a man and his sister's son, and to some degree her daughter, is very close. He is known as the *mōmō* and must respond to any needs of his *vasu*, whether material, financial or social, in terms of loyalty. In pre-colonial times, the *vasu* relationship was an integral part of chiefly politics and warfare,

---

9 Re: sorcery and traditional healing see Katz 1993, re: sorcery see Tuwere 2002: 161-162, Toren 2004: 133, re: death in kinship conflict, see Miyazaki 1997: 105-106, re: body and sickness within the social whole, see Becker 1995, 1994, re: illness and death due to imbalance within the 'double soul' see Thompson 1940: 114.

with chiefs demanding allegiance and loyalty from their *vasu* kin in time of war or when making particular political allegiances.[10]

But in western Fiji, the *vasu* kingroup is given a much higher status in mortuary rites than in much of eastern Fiji. In Nadrogā this group is known as the *kōvana*, a recent addition to the Nadrogā language that means literally 'governor' and is adopted from English. It means that these people are seen as the highest-ranking people of the funeral, and from the time of their arrival in the village, the *kōvana* are completely in charge of what goes on – quite literally, the governors.

The most honoured member of this group is the mother's brother, known as *vikila* in Nadrogā and *mōmō* in parts of eastern Fiji, of the deceased and in his stead, his direct male descendants. *Vasu* is used to denote the relationship between the mother's brother and his nieces and nephews, and the mother's clan in general. In parts of western Vitilevu the word *mōmō* formerly meant 'chief'[11] – this emphasises the central importance of this kinship relation and how the *kōvana* kingroup is considered 'governor' or 'chief' at a funeral. Ravuvu, writing of Eastern Fijian mortuary rites, points out that this handing over of control to the mother's clan is 'symbolic of the return of the body to the "female side" of the deceased, while its soul or spirit departs to where all other spirits are destined'. (Ravuvu 1987: 339)

Before the relatively recent adoption of the term *kōvana* into the Nadrogā language, it may possibly have been referred to as *imatai ni ulu* (lit. creator of head, or first head). *Matai ni ulu* means the first, *ulu* meaning first or top, but also, in Nadrogā, head, and in other places in Fiji, headstone. (Geraghty, pers comm. 1997) Although people knew this term and explained the *kōvana* classifications to me in terms of *matai ni ulu* as well, the term used during the funeral and in later discussions was always *kōvana*. According to de Marzan, the maternal relatives of the dead are known as *itaukei ni ulu* (lit. owners of the head) because they are presented with whale's teeth at the start of the final exchange of valuables after the burial (*tuberi ni ulu*, lit. piling up of the head or headstone), the whale's teeth signifying the start, or head, of the ceremony. (1987: 54)

The *kōvana* is a complex group divided into three hierarchical categories of relations (*ulu*) from both the maternal and paternal line of the departed, spanning three generations:

---

10   See e.g. Williams 1982 [1858]: 34-37, Hocart 1915a, 1923, 1926, Mauss 1990: 17, Routledge 1985: 35-36 and 213-214, Clunie 1986: 101-102, Sahlins 1985 Chs 2 and 3, 1991: 72-78, Toren 1990: 42, Thomas 1991: 63, 67, 195, note 22. *Vasu* relations are also very much present in contemporary Fijian chiefly politics, cf Ewins (2001), and *Fiji Times* 22 October 2005: 12 re the *vakataraisulu* (lifting of the mourning) of Ro Lady Lala Mara, Roko Tui Dreketi, in the chiefly village of Cuvu in Nadrogā, October 2005.

11   See Waterhouse 1997: 247 for pre-Christian linguistic terms and Nayacakalou 1957. 47 re. usage of the term in the 1950s.

Kōvana – *matai ni ulu* (first *ulu*, *ulu* being the name of the pile of yams which will be presented). This group belongs to the clan (*mataqwali*) of the mother (M) of the departed and are the direct descendants of the mother's brother.

Karua ni ulu – (second *ulu*), the clan of the father's mother (FM) of the departed.

Katolu ni ulu – (third *ulu*) this is the clan of the father's father's mother (FFM) of the departed.

Although the *kōvana* is considered the most important group, and the group to receive most of the valuables, all three *ulu* have an honoured status at a Nadrogā funeral. But from the way people in general referred to the *kōvana*, and the respectful, expectant hush that came over the people in the 'house of death' at the long-awaited arrival of this kingroup during the mortuary rites, it seemed fairly obvious that it is considered the most important *ulu*. A woman explaining to me at the time of their arrival how the *kōvana* would now take over all proceedings dropped her voice to a confidential whisper, describing in awe-struck tones how the *kōvana* would take up their place of honour, 'the *kōvana* is a great chief on this day', she told me.

Honoured as chiefs, the *kōvana* will sit in the hierarchically highest (*icake*) part of the house of death, 'above' everyone else, closest to what would normally be the sleeping quarters, an area that has been specially prepared to receive the coffin and the *kōvana*. The *mōmō* (mother's brother) sits at the highest place, and when he is not in the house his closest male relative. From now on, when I speak of the *kōvana* I am referring to this group.

People talk with a certain reverence about the *kōvana* of their relatives. One girl pointed out to me that her father's mother was from the village of Korotogo 'so when he goes, they will be the *kōvana*', she said. Tai's mother came from Narata village, her paternal grandmother came from Korotogo village, and her paternal great grandmother from Lawai, a village on the other, western, side of the Sigatoka river. In this way, Tai's death brought together these three generations of relations in particular but others as well. These relational paths, criss-crossing the physical landscape of Nadrogā and the temporal landscape of clan history, converged in the soil of Tai's father's clan and village where she was finally laid to rest.[12]

Everyone I spoke to emphasised the need to respect and care for the needs of the *kōvana*, because they were the 'mother's side'. Another reason could be because the *kōvana* represent three generations of wife-givers to the paternal line of the deceased: the wife of the father (i.e. M – the mother of the deceased); the wife of the father's father (FM), and the wife of the father's father's father (FFM).[13] Each *ulu* represents the clan descendants of a woman who married out of the clan,

---

12   Fijian residence patterns are usually patrilocal, i.e. women move to their husband's village. But increasingly, I was told, in this area women prefer to stay in their own villages.

13   I thank John Liep for suggesting this. (pers comm. 1998)

in the past bringing with her the rights to a piece of land belonging to her clan of birth, her father's clan. Andrew Strathern (1981: 222) writes of the importance of the mother's clan in Hagen, PNG, which must be continuously appeased, in life as in death, with material gifts: 'exchange relations are set up, not only between the living kin and the deceased, but also between the living kin and the spirits of the dead themselves. This ... shows that death does not mean an ending of obligations, but their renewal and sometimes even their amplification'.[14]

While people told me the rites and exchanges honouring the *kōvana* were solely a matter of 'showing respect', these rites emanated in former times from the need to appease ancestral spirits. Although practised today for different reasons, they still represent the connections between *vanua*, life and death, between people and place, and material and spiritual existence. And certainly the strength of contemporary practice of these rites indicates that the Christian beliefs and ritual in connection with death were subsumed into already existing patterns and practices of spiritual belief.

Writing of the mortuary rites concerning the maternal kin, the *kōvana,* of the dead, de Marzan (1987: 55) says:

> *Dra kata* (blood which bites) refers to a ceremony aimed at preventing the dead person's spirit from striking at their kin. This ceremony has been one of the hardest to extirpate ... Every man is *vasu* to one or several people, that is, related on the maternal side to several. From that, following Fijian custom, he has the right to take what he likes from his maternal relatives, who have no right to object. He takes their valuables and animals without their being able to prevent him. But once dead, his spirit is not calm in the rest of the dead, until his paternal relatives have paid compensation to his maternal kin. This compensation is the *drakata* [*drakwata*] ... a ceremony which consists in presenting the maternal kin with a feast, valuables, etc.etc., in the village of the deceased [i.e. the village of the father of the deceased] ... done most simply it consists of a live pig, raised specifically, taken to the deceased's maternal kin. So in all the villages of Navosa (Colo West) nearly all the pigs carry the names of the dead. (1987: 55)

I have no record in my notes of a live pig being presented to the *kōvana* at this funeral, but according to the villagers, the rite of *drakwata*, understood in terms of the presentation of a pig, is still practised today. Although it may not be presented at the actual *juberi ni ulu* exchange of valuables, a live pig is given as a special gift from the 'owners of the dead' to the *kōvana*. Once the *kōvana* return to their village they kill the pig and share the cooked meat in a communal feast. The intestines of the pig are cooked separately and a special kava ceremony held before the shared meal. (Aliti Vunisea, Research Notes, July 1998)

---

14   See Toren 1990: 42 re the 'path of women' carrying the 'blood of posterity' and Eriksen 2008. 71 re mortuary exchanges in Vanuatu

While a pig is still presented to the *kōvana* the *drakwata* rite itself is now replaced by the more elaborate mortuary rites of exchange described in the following, but the meaning of the rites remains essentially the same: the compensation in death of the *vasu* (mother's clan) for rights which the paternal kin members have had over the *vasu* in his or her lifetime. These rights held particular importance in pre-Christian times in relation to chiefly feuds when a chief could demand political allegiance or warriors for fighting of his *vasu*. *Vasu* relations were also created by victorious chiefs demanding the chiefly daughters of their vanquished foe in marriage, thereby enforcing their *vasu* allegiance in the next generation.

The *kōvana* kingroup receive special attention in every way – for the duration of their stay in the village, except during the final exchanges, they remain in the *werenimase* 'house of the deceased'. They are served the best food first, which is cooked separately, and they receive the first cup (*bilo*) at every kava ceremony. It is they who receive almost all the valuables (*iyau ni vanua* – lit. valuables of the land) presented during the mortuary rites; almost all the mats presented in the 'house of death'; most of the whale's teeth presented in ritual leave-takings as the coffin is carried from the 'house of death' to the grave; and the majority of valuables presented at the final exchange ceremony after the burial.

In turn, the *kōvana* have the responsibility to provide the mats and barkcloth that will line the grave. It is the men of the *kōvana* who dig the grave, who are the pallbearers, who lower the coffin into the ground and fill up the grave. It is also the *kōvana* who in former times erected the headstone on the Fifth Night after the death (*bogilima*), or as is the vogue today, place stones round the burial site or cement the grave, a ceremony known as *tuvavatu ni bulubulu* (lit. to put stones round the grave).

In other parts of Fiji (Ravuvu 1983: 67) *vakabogiva* (Fourth Night) is the first post-burial feast, while *vakabogitini* (Tenth Night), *bogilimasagavulu* (Fiftieth Night) and *vakabogidrau* (Hundredth Night, the final and biggest burial feast to mark the lifting of the mourning) are celebrated across Fiji. Each of these feasts traditionally entailed exchanges of whale's teeth, kava, and cooked food, such as pig and root crops. In Eastern Fiji where there is no large-scale exchange of valuables after the burial as in Nadrogā, the relatives of the deceased provide all who participated in the funerary rites with a feast or a portion of cooked food known as *na burua*. Further post-burial feasts and rites take place in other parts of Fiji.

When a high chief dies, the mortuary rites performed are considerably more complex and the period of mourning will include a ban on fishing in the waters of his clan for a 100-day period – a traditional expression of respect which at the same time was, and still is, a mode of environmental conservation.

In Eastern Fiji, adaptations of the elaborate Tongan style of grave decoration are found. Posts are driven into the ground at each corner of the grave and a narrow length of bark-cloth, cut into fringes, plaited pandanus and flower garlands (*sisi, salusalu* in Standard Fijian), or a fringe of coloured raffia is hung between the posts all the way round, so that the grave is encircled by a garlanded border (I did not see this form of decoration on graves in Nadrogā).

Prologue – preparations

As the elders of the village met in the chief's house the night Tai died to discuss her funeral, a carrier took her body to the hospital outside town, where it would remain till the day of the burial. The possibility of having a body kept in a morgue or 'cool box' until burial has changed the course and length of funerary events for villages close to a hospital, extending the time between the announcement of the death and the actual burial considerably. This means that more people are able to get to the funeral and from further afield, more valuables are given, and consequently a greater number of guests need to be catered for.

The elders decided that the *vura* would be on the following Tuesday and the burial the next day. How the news of this death would be announced, I was told, was that Tai's lineage group (*bito*) would tell the second village *bito*. After this, the *vanua* (chiefdom) would be informed and then it would be announced on the daily Fiji Radio broadcast of deaths. This daily service informs people across the islands of deaths, so that family members can either make their way in person with their offerings, or send contributions of money or valuables through others. The village spokesman (*mata ni vanua)* and two other men were dispatched to inform the other six villages of the *vanua,* travelling by bus and carrier from village to village. It was expected that the first village to be informed of the death, would be Tai's mother's village, the village of the *kōvana* kingroup, which was also part of the *vanua.*

De Marzan writes of the announcement of death:

> Formerly, once the death was made public, messengers (*mata*) were sent, carrying a spear or headrest of the deceased. They would come and announce the death, clapping as a gesture of respect (*vakaisausau*) [*vakasausau;* this usually means clapping with flat hands, as in dancing, while the cupped-hand clapping of respect is *vakacobocobo*] ... and offer the object to the house-owner, saying *"oqo na nonai sa ni mate ko Kalulu, sa mate"* (This is the *sa* of the death of Kalulu (supposing that to be the name of the deceased), he is dead, etc). The owner of the house would touch the object and say, "That this be the end of the dead, that we others live that way". This is still done in part of Serua and Colo West. (1987: 51)

On Sunday Tai's death was formally announced in the village church and prayers were said for her. From Monday onwards the village became a hive of activity. It had rained a great deal in the days preceding her death and the entrance to the village was very muddy. A load of wood shavings from a local furniture workshop in Sigatoka was ordered for the day of the burial. The coffin was ordered from another Indo-Fijian owned carpenter's. Groups of women and men made trips to the gardens to dig up rootcrops and vegetables, and bundle after bundle was carried back to the village. Homes were swept and cleaned and made ready to receive guests.

By Tuesday morning the rain had stopped. The sky was a dull grey; it was cold and a chill wind was blowing, but at least it was not raining. A disused half burned-down kitchen hut was taken over by the women as the cooking shelter, where mounds of cassava roots and breadfruit were peeled and cut up and boiled in enormous cauldrons. Other women sat cross-legged on the concrete floor of the hut, laboriously slicing green beans and onions with razor blades.

Meanwhile the women of Tai's clan, my family, were busy sweeping the house that had been chosen as the 'house of death'. The furniture had been removed and the house had become a neutral space to be transformed for the coming ceremonies. In the hierarchically highest part of the house, the private, sleeping quarters (*loqi*) that faced the village green, the women laid down the first set of mats, material and barkcloth given by the women of Tai's clan, presented in a brief, formal ceremony in Tai's now empty house and which would form part of the collective gift of women's valuables to the *kōvana*.

As I was carefully noting down which of us had brought which mat or which piece of material to this communal presentation, the women laughingly corrected me and said that who brought what was of no consequence; the presentation was a communal presentation, was from the *bito*, from all of us. This did not, however, correspond to what the women of the *kōvana* told me when they explained how each woman's contribution had been noted and would be carefully matched when she received the mats from 'the house of death', as explained above.

Other women have also confirmed this, and frowned when they heard that I had received nothing in return for the (F\$35; £17.50) *vabasi* mat I contributed to that first presentation from the *bito* to the *kōvana*. This was quite wrong, they told me. Had I not been given a mat in return because I was the anthropologist and therefore an outsider? Or was it because here was a chance to circumvent protocol and save giving me a mat, since I probably wouldn't know what to expect? Or was there a quite different reason? Although it would have been interesting to enquire into, I decided not to pursue this.

In the area immediately adjacent to the church building, the young men of the village were building a shelter (*covacova*) of bamboo poles and corrugated iron roof, where the many guests would eat the funeral feast. Makeshift tables and benches were erected from long planks of wood laid on stacks of concrete building blocks.

On the other side of the village, a cow lay tightly trussed, her soft, brown eyes wide with fear, nostrils dilating. When the shelter had been built, the young men, dressed in overalls and gum boots, tatty trousers and worn T-shirts, dragged the poor beast across the village green to a point not far from the hut being used as a kitchen. The village dogs smelt death and congregated as closely as they dared. The men positioned the cow on her back, her bound legs in the air, and cut her throat, her warm blood spurting over their faces and clothes. Wiping their sleeves across their faces, the young men laughed and joked and someone casually kicked the creature's side. The dogs crept closer. The men cut off the cow's head and disembowelled and partitioned the carcass, the bloody entrails laid out on the grass. The heavy pieces of meat were carried to the kitchen hut while dogs and village pigs moved in to lick up blood and scraps in the grass. In the choking smoke of the kitchen hut, the women wiped their smarting eyes and set about cutting up the mounds of bloody meat.

The group of young men responsible for preparing and serving the kava (*yaqona*) to be drunk throughout the funeral were taking turns pounding the roots with a thick metal rod in the heavy mortar. Almost like the pulse of the village, the slow, rhythmic thud, thud of the rod on the gnarled, dried roots and the occasional clink of metal on metal, is a noise as familiar and intrinsic to Fijian village life as the sounds of children and the barking of dogs. It seemed almost continuous during the days and nights of the funeral, as pounds and pounds of kava roots were pulverised for consumption. Some of these roots would be provided by the village, but most would be brought as parts of presentations of valuables for the funeral. While there were to be many different simultaneous kava gatherings in different houses, some formal, some informal, the kava which would flow in the house of death and the house where people were received on entering the village, and where they formally presented their gifts the first time, would be part of the most important ceremonies.

Kava was not grown in this area and so unless presented as a gift, kava consumed in the village was generally bought in the market in Sigatoka. The recorded amount presented to the 'owners of the deceased' at this funeral was 16.5 kilos. In addition to this was the unrecorded amount of kava given by individuals and households in the village. Almost all of this would have been consumed in the course of the funeral. By its end, three of the fathers in my family had been drinking kava continuously day and night for more than three days. Their eyes were red and swollen and they had to wear sunglasses to protect them from the glare of daylight, a common affliction from over-consumption of kava. Other afflictions apart from the extreme physical lethargy it causes, which is cumulative, is the disease known as *kanikani,* a severe drying out of the skin, irritation and itching

The *vura* – arranging the path of mats

The *vura* for Tai started sometime during the afternoon and continued all night and morning till the body was brought to the 'house of death' the next afternoon, the day of the burial.

The private area of the 'house of death' had undergone the first stages of preparation to receive the coffin and the *kōvana*. The mats, material and barkcloth which the women of Tai's family had spread over the concrete floor earlier that day had been laid in a particular order: first a large, thickly woven plain mat (*icōcō*), the kind usually found in the main area of a home; then a slightly smaller mat known as *vābasi*, edged with an acrylic wool fringe or layers of fringes in bright colours or with a broad border of embroidered wool. On top of this was placed a smaller, softer, more finely woven 'sleeping mat' (*idarodaro*), also edged with a coloured fringe. The mats were placed so that the fringes and edges of each mat were visible. A length of printed cotton was spread over this and finally a piece of barkcloth was laid carefully in the place of honour on the very top.

Material, presented in lengths or in bolts, has increasingly come to be included in women's valuables in Fiji. Material is used frequently as an exchange valuable in the area where I worked. Although traditionally bark-cloth and pandanus mats were made in most areas of Vitilevu, bark-cloth-making disappeared in most places in the 19th century, and mat-making has declined in many places. Buying material for gift exchanges is much cheaper than buying either mats or bark-cloth, and material is always available in shops in Sigatoka. Material, however, is not valued as highly as mats or bark-cloth.[15]

The sort of barkcloth used in all presentations at this funeral is known in this area as *kumi,* a brown-patterned, Tongan type of barkcloth, usually quite large with large patterning. The first layer of a bed of honour (*idarodaro*, lit. things to lie down on) had been created, with the same arrangement of mats and barkcloth as in other life-cycle rituals, such as circumcision and weddings; in this context it is understood as being a resting place prepared for the dead. In pre-colonial times the dead person would be wrapped in mats and barkcloth:

> If a sickness is regarded as serious care is taken to prepare mats and tapa on which the invalid will be laid; the invalid is stretched out on what will be used to wrap him up. (de Marzan 1987: 49)

As the mourners gathered in the 'house of death' and presented their mortuary gifts, layer upon layer of mats would be added to this first covering on the floor, each layer maintaining the same sequential order as the mats which would later line Tai's coffin and grave.

From wall to wall a cord was suspended, onto which two large pieces of barkcloth were pegged. This partitioning curtain of barkcloth is called the *vajukolo* (*vatukolo* in Standard Fijian), and forms the physical division between 'above' and 'below' (*icake, ira*), between the honoured 'private' (*loqi*) area reserved for the coffin and for the *kōvana,* and the hierarchically lower area for the other mourners. Just as the sleeping area of a house is usually partitioned off by a curtain or, in former times a piece of barkcloth, and mats are spread out for sleeping on, so the bed is prepared for the deceased to rest on in the highest part of the house in a similar fashion to the way a wedding bed is prepared by the women of the groom's

---

15   Re: bark-cloth in Fiji see e.g. Hooper 1982, Ewins 1982: 5-21, Clunie 1986: 126-140, Colchester 2000. Re bark-cloth in the Pacific Islands see Smidt *et al.* 1995, Thomas 1995: 131-150, Neich and Pendergrast 1997. See Palu 2003 for a contextual theological reflection on tapa-making in Tonga.

bito and also partitioned off with a piece of barkcloth. Until the arrival of the coffin the next day, the *vajukolo* curtain remained folded up, so that it was possible to follow the movements in the *loqi* space.

The village was buzzing with excitement. Groups of mourners (*iyatoyato*) were arriving after long, dusty journeys, clambering down from buses or carriers or getting out of taxis, the women straightening their dresses, looking around, adjusting their presentational rolls of mats and lengths of material, the men pulling out drums of kerosene, or sacks of flour or sugar.

> Until the *reguregu* presentation, kin members cannot venture into the village where [a] funeral gathering is happening, nor can they participate in any activity connected to the dead, such as women going in to weep for or kiss the corpse or men joining the *lovo* [earth-oven]-making group etc. The kin group will remain outside the village or peripheral to whatever is taking place ... until the presentation is over. The *reguregu* is like the 'branding' ... that you're one of the mourners and can now participate. But that also explains why one finds ... more people milling around, yet, the funeral service or burial are often almost empty ... to be seen to be doing something more labour intensive is much more appreciated than just sitting in the pew and participating in the singing which takes little effort ... [Attending the service] works well in urban settings because many may not have seen or met the departed for a long time and this is a time to reminisce on his or her life through eulogy. In a village setting this can still be done while cutting up meat or attending to the *lovo*. (Eta Varani, pers comm. 2009)

Members of Tai's family waited in the house, drinking intermittent informal rounds of kava while they awaited the funeral guests. In the home of the church deacon, others waited round a kava-mixing bowl for the groups of mourners who, on entering the village, would go to this house first. Here, senior male representatives of the lineage group of the deceased, the 'owners of the deceased', received the guests and their presentations of whale's teeth, drums of kerosene, cartons of bread, sacks of flour and sugar, mats and lengths or bails of material. All valuables were laid down together in the middle of the floor by the *tanoa* and presented by one of the men, with a speech. They were accepted by the male representative of the 'owners of the deceased', who in return offered the guests a cup of kava.

I spent most of my time in 'the house of death' and was able to record the number of mats and lengths of material and bark-cloth presented there, but had to rely on members of the family to record the number of valuables presented in this house, many of which would be redistributed in the post-burial exchange of valuables. My record of valuables going into the village is therefore based on what others recorded. Recordings I had been promised of which valuables went to which clan groups did not materialise, so although I have a list, in order of importance, of the clan groups who received valuables, I have no complete record of the valuables that left the village at the post-burial redistribution.[16]

After the formalities of this first round, several other informal rounds of kava might follow, as the guests settled in for a good yarn *(talanoa)*, or they might make their way to their host households. The women then took their presentational rolls of mats and made their way to the 'house of death' where they presented the mats to the women of the 'owners of the deceased', who received them on behalf of the *kōvana* until they themselves arrived and took over proceedings. In the *werenimase* there was an almost constant flow of newcomers through the door, a turning of heads and exchanges of smiles and greetings, as one group of mainly women mourners after another arrived, stooping politely as they made their way through the seated people and the clusters of sleeping children and babies to the centre of the room to present their gifts.

Tai's sister, a matron of great stature, with laughing eyes and a wrinkled face that creased into great smiles with ease, was wearing a black *sulu,* a black patterned dress and a *ta'ovala* and sat in the *loqi* area. The *ta'ovala*, Tongan formal attire, worn by both women and men, is a soft, very finely-woven mat worn round the waist and tied round the middle with string of plaited pandanus. Only members of the chiefly *bito* in the village wore this, and it was the only mark of Tongan influence evident at the funeral. The elders of the village told me that I should specify that this was a funeral of the *vanua o Henibua* (which is of Tongan extraction). Yet when discussing the rituals that took place I was told that they were all specifically Nadrogā traditions and that nowhere else in Fiji was a funeral as elaborate as in Nadrogā. In the course of my research I attended in total five funerals in Nadrogā, and there seemed to be only one main difference between the funerals in other Nadrogā villages and the funeral in our village – the *ta'ovala.* (See Kaeppler 1978a for description of a Tongan funeral).

Until the arrival of the *kōvana*, Tai's sister was the person each group of mourners approached when they had presented their mats. Although she may have been in the middle of telling a raucously funny story – she was renowned for being a great joker – she could break off at a moment's notice and immediately assume the solemn demeanour of a mourner, responding in a loud wailing to the sudden outbursts of crying of newly-arrived women who, having presented their mats, shuffled across the floor on their knees towards her, wiping their eyes with a handkerchief or small towel, sobbing and crying loudly.[17] Tai's sister comforted

---

16　See Belshaw 1964: 141-148.

17　Compare Ravuvu 1983: 64, A. Strathern 1981: 206 on Hagen, PNG, and Bloch 1982: 214, on mourning in Madagascar: 'at death people weep and should be sad: visitors before and after the death come to weep with the bereaved. Indeed, the behaviour of the mourners is often dramatic in its intensity. It is quite clear that this socially-organised sorrow usually matches emotions which to those concerned appear as internal and un-institutionally triggered. The Merina do not make the opposition that is common in European cultures

them, patting them on the back, nodding her head sadly and murmuring, '*sa moce, vācegu hō*' – 'she's asleep, she's at peace now'.

Thus the atmosphere in the 'house of death' oscillated continuously between a sense of excitement and expectation, quiet chatting, the lowering of voices and hush during formal incantations, waves of sadness, crying and grieving, storytelling, joking and laughter – combined with the rhythmic, meditative stirring of kava in the wooden mixing bowl (*tanoa*); the solemn three *cobo* (resonant claps made with cupped hands) of the giver of a cup of kava as it leaves his hands, accompanied by the people round the *tanoa,* and the single *cobo* by the recipient of the cup, the downing of it and the returning of the cup.

With each group of mourners, the arrangement of mats in the *loqi* area was re-arranged again and again to accommodate the addition of new mats, material and barkcloth, though always maintaining the same basic order – plain mats, fringed mats, sleeping mats, material, barkcloth – and always ensuring that the fringes of the mats were visible. By the time the *kōvana* kingroup arrived at about midnight, the *loqi* area resembled a veritable sea of beautifully woven, brightly coloured fringes – a temporal, flowing work of art, continuously reworked into a mélange of colour and softness.

The coming and going in the 'house of death' continued; by evening it was quite full and there was a somewhat jovial atmosphere coupled with a distinct air of expectancy. The *kōvana* had not yet arrived. People were sitting in groups, both men and women, drinking kava, joking, and telling stories; children were asleep in little bundles in between the soft bulks of mothers and aunties, fathers, uncles and grandparents.

It was close to midnight by the time the *kōvana* finally arrived. The word spread and an immediate hush fell on the assembly. People's eyes turned towards the door, conversations were reduced to whisperings as the atmosphere intensified. The members of the *kōvana* entered the 'house of death' in a formal line, politely stooping as they stepped carefully between the seated mourners, and presented the 'owners of the deceased' with their mortuary gifts: two whale's teeth, ten drums of kerosene, and three rolls of mats.[18]

One of these rolls contained the mats that would line the grave, called *ravuniqweleqwele* (lit. something you put on the ground). The second roll contained the mats that would be spread over the floor of the 'house of death' the day the *kōvana* left, taking with them all the mats that were presently covering the floor. The third roll of mats was set aside for the Methodist minister who was to conduct the funeral service. The *taukei ni mase* ('owners of the deceased') in

---

between genuine individual feelings and artificial institutionalised expressions of feeling. For them the two are complementary'.

18   A roll of mats is known as *ivavivi* in this area (*ivīvivi* in other parts of Fiji) and usually comprises ten mats in order from bottom to top of *icōcō* (large, plain mats), *vabasi* (quite large fringed mats) *idarodaro* (smaller, sleeping mats). One such set of ten mats in this order is known as *dua na susu* (literally, one mat) and is a unit for counting mats.

turn presented the *kōvana* with a *tabua*. This presentation, to formerly request the *kōvana* to dig the grave, is called *matau ni lolovo* and usually takes place in the very early hours of the morning of the burial, at three or four am. Only after this presentation will the *kōvana* consent to dig the grave.

Bringing Tai home

The next morning the weather had changed. It was warmer and the clouds were lifting and it seemed that despite all concern, the funeral would be blessed with good weather after all.

While the kava continued to flow in the 'house of death', as it had done throughout, a small group of people related to the *kōvana* went to the Sigatoka Hospital in a hired truck (in Fiji English, 'carrier' – an open-backed truck, often with tarpaulin covering) to collect Tai's body and bring it back to the village. On the way we learned of a bizarre situation – on prior inspection, the coffin that had been ordered from a carpenter in town was going to be too small. We drove to a neighbouring village where we had kinsmen, and spent several hours there, while the new coffin was being finished. While the adults of the group were immediately invited to share a bowl or two of kava with the owner of the house, the children set about gathering flowers and leaves from the surrounding garden and bound colourful wreaths for Tai's coffin. When we finally got to the hospital, it was past lunchtime and the funeral proceedings had been delayed by several hours.

The coffin, which cost F$200 (£100), was covered inside and out with material of a brown and white barkcloth pattern. When it had been taken out of the carrier and placed on the ground in front of the 'cool box' at the hospital,[19] mats and barkcloth were arranged inside it in the same order followed in the 'house of death'. The bottom was covered with a beautiful fringed *vabasi* mat; on top of this a sleeping mat (*idarodaro*) was placed, with a large piece of barkcloth on top. Tai's body, wrapped in the sheet it had been transported to the hospital in five days earlier, was lowered onto this soft bed; someone sprayed a little perfume into the top end of the coffin and the lid was nailed into place. Barkcloth, with a piece of lace laid on top, was draped over the coffin. On the floor of the carrier, mats were placed in the same order as in the coffin, and when the coffin had been hoisted onto this, the wreaths and flower decorations the children had made were placed on top.

The carrier brought Tai back to her village with the unexpectedly grand escort of an Indo-Fijian motorcycle policeman and a four-wheel drive vehicle, carrying the District Officer and the *Roko Tui* (head of the Provincial Council). The reason

---

19   When a person dies in a village, the only service provided by the hospital is that the body can be laid in an individual 'cool box' until the funeral. All other details involving the preparation of the body and its placing the body in the coffin are left to the family. A nurse checked that we were retrieving the right body, but left the rest to us.

for this honour was that the D.O. was married to a woman from Lau, who was related to Tai's deceased husband. Furthermore, Tai's father's clan was of Tongan descent and there are ancient and strong historical links between Tonga and the Lau islands, which formerly were part of the Tongan realm.

It was now about 2.00 pm and the sun blazed from a cloudless blue sky, the mud in the village hardening under the sudden intense heat and sun. It was late in the day, and the body had to be buried and the subsequent exchange ceremony (*juberi ni ulu*) completed before sundown (around 5.30 pm). The escort and carrier stopped outside the 'house of death', and a whale's tooth (*tabua)* was presented. This *tabua* is called the *na ivahobu* (lit. the taking down of the body) and signifies the return of Tai to her village. The giving of this *tabua* also acknowledges the potential danger involved in bringing the body back, 'because of supernatural complexities which might arise'. (Belshaw 1964: 142) While the coffin was carried into the 'house of death', the driver of the carrier was given the customary gift of the mats the coffin had rested on during its journey back to the village. That is to say, minus one mat, which was given to the policeman – an unexpected, and much appreciated, gesture.

A path of farewells

This chapter might perhaps just as well have been called a path of farewells (*cālevu ni tatau*), as from the time of the return of the body to the village, each step along the path from the *werenimase* (house of death) until Tai was finally laid to rest in her grave, was marked by a whale's tooth presentation, given by the *bito* of the departed, to signify the deceased's leave-taking of significant aspects of communal life.[20]

There are five such formal farewell presentations, made at various stages before and after the burial from one group to another:

- the *tarai ni yaqona*, made by the family of the departed to the *kōvana*, to give the body to them.
- the *tatau ni lotu*, made by the family to the minister after the church service, to request the deceased's taking leave of the church and its responsibilities.
- the *tatau ni vanua*, made by the family to the elders of the *vanua*, to request the deceased's taking leaving of the clan.

20   See also Deane (1921: 41-42): '…every Fijian has come to think that he will live beyond the grave. A very human custom has arisen therefore and is practised constantly among the islanders when a man is about to die, it is the *tatau* or bidding farewell (note: the same farewell is customary in Tahiti, and was known as the "tutu"'. (Ellis, *Polynesian Researchers* iii: 115)

- the *tatau ni were*, made by Tai's household to the *kōvana* to request future protection or acknowledgement of the deceased's children and grandchildren by the *kōvana*. (Although considered an integral part of a Nadrogā funeral, this presentation was not made on this occasion).
- the *vadaroi ni yago*, made by the lineage group to the *kōvana*, giving their consent for the body to be buried.

After a ceremonial welcoming round of kava (the *matakarawa*) had been drunk with the District Officer in the *werenimase*, followed by a more informal round, the men left. For a moment there was a relieved, relaxed atmosphere. Then the *vajukolo* curtain was lowered, the space behind was closed off and immediately transformed.

Wave after wave of intense wailing and crying erupted from behind the curtain. A long queue, mostly of women and children, formed outside one door to the 'private' area, filing into this space of mourning. Inside they knelt by the coffin, leaned over it, touched and kissed the glass window in the lid, their arms outstretched across it, some beating their fists on it as they wailed and cried out in violent outpourings of emotion. The long stream of figures, with bowed heads and respectfully bent backs, weaved their slow way through this dark, stuffy and crowded space, across the many layers of soft mats, the smell of sweat and flowers mingling with the wetness of tears and damp handkerchiefs.

Outside this women's world of throbbing emotion, on the other side of the *vajukolo* curtain, men had returned and were engaged in the presentation and reception of the first of the five *tabua* presentations which would mark the deceased's taking leave of successive communal contexts. This was the *tarai ni yaqona*. It was presented by the family to the *kōvana,* and is the point when the family formally presents the body to the *kōvana*. This presentation, a point in the funeral marking the leave-taking of home, has been described to me as particularly painful.

Then the six pallbearers of the *kōvana* stood up, moved towards the *vajukolo* curtain and, quite suddenly, pulled it down. Immediately the darkened space behind was exposed to the light. The men of the *kōvana* had come to take away the body; the huddled, grieving female figures clung to the coffin, their wailing and crying crescendoing, as the men stepped forward and with strong hands took hold of the coffin, lifting it away from the women.

The funeral service

The coffin was taken out of the 'house of death' (*werenimase*) and slowly carried to the church, a makeshift choir following behind, singing hymns. The coffin was carried through the main door at the end of the aisle and placed on a platform on its bed of mats, arranged in the customary order. The wreaths were arranged on top, again by the children. This arrangement of mats was to be given to the minister (*talatala*) after the funeral. The circuit minister, the 'big', i.e. senior minister and the 'small', younger, assistant *talatala* from Korotogo village all presided. They entered the church from the door behind the pulpit, reserved for ministers. The chief, Tai's brother, the D.O., and the church deacon (*tuirara*) of the small Methodist circuit were present, all seated in the honoured *loqi tabu* area of the church.

The choirmaster had chosen the hymns, which all concerned death and 'moving to the next world', as one person put it. The minister who delivered the sermon had also chosen the Bible readings, all concerning, as someone said afterwards, 'death as the door to the next world', 'the passage from this world (*bula vakavuravura*) to the next'. The sermon urged 'people to repent before God's calling'. When it was finished, eulogies were held for Tai. This was explained to me as 'the praising of the person who has died ... telling what she has been doing in her lifetime' and 'giving our traditional respect for the person who died'.

The first eulogy was by the District Officer who stressed the kinship ties between Naroro and Lau, sealed through Tai's marriage to a Lauan. The second eulogy was by the Chief, Tai's brother. His eulogy stressed the good work that Tai had done for the *vanua* through her many years as a teacher, and how she had been loved and respected by everyone. In a later conversation with me about his eulogy, the Chief likened his sister to Diana, Princess of Wales: 'Tai worked for the Church, for the *vanua*, and for the *matanitu* (government) – she served the *vanua* as a teacher ... she was loved ... like Princess Diana[21] ... because of Fijian custom, because [she did these things for] the *vanua* ... for the whole'.

I was surprised to find that I was the only member of the church choir participating in the procession and the service, all other members were otherwise engaged. On this occasion, the choir was made up of people from the other *bito* in the village, and the only people from the village who attended the service were Tai's immediate family: her brother and sister, her adopted son, his wife and their young daughter, who had lived with Tai and looked after her in her final years. Everyone else in church was either from the *kōvana* or from other villages. Commenting on this, Eta Varani (pers comm. 2009) explains differences developing between rural and urban funerals:

> While church service and burial attendance are not considered important in rural areas, in urban settings, the funeral service plays a more important role. Since people are busy working, service attendance is more appropriate because it usually sets a time limit, although formal, it ensures that you are showing your 'face' to the owners of the dead. This may mean a restriction to social interaction but it still means a lot in terms of 'face saving'. As well, congregating

---

21 This funeral took place shortly after Diana's funeral, broadcast on BBC World TV, and followed closely in the village. Tai's sister had brought her TV and video-recorder with her when she came for the funeral, a stay that lasted for several weeks. Each night she re-played the video of Diana's funeral to a shifting audience of women and children in her sister's house.

at a confined space for *reguregu* and *kana* [eating] as well as work commitments restrict what one can do in an urban funeral. One may not attend the *reguregu*, but attending the service expresses the sharing of grief with, and support to the owners of the dead.

Attending the feast is not as important as one finds in rural areas because food is not as important. However, I cannot ignore the social aspect of it whether in rural or urban settings: from cooking, food preparation, *lovo* and wreath-making etc. to grog session, they are all occasions where everyone can meet and catch up with the latest gossip. With easy access to transport for villagers to attend funerals in the city, there is much to talk about. In the village this is also a time to enjoy the food they would never have enjoyed in normal times – *bulumakau* [beef] *vuaka* [pork], chicken and fish, all at one time.

Na Ruku

When the service was over, the coffin was carried out of the church by the <u>*kōvana*</u> pallbearers. The chief, the two ministers and the church deacon of the circuit walked solemnly behind in their black *sulu vakataga* and jackets, their hands clasped behind their backs, others joining the procession behind them. Outside the church, the second *tabua* was presented. This is the <u>*tatau ni lotu,*</u> to formally request Tai's taking leave of the church and its responsibilities. It is presented by the 'owners of the deceased' to the minister and is also a thank you to the Church for having looked after Tai in her lifetime.

The procession moved on down the village green (*rara*), turned at the end and walked slowly up again. This was Tai's final journey through the village. Her family and the rest of the lineage group had long since positioned themselves on the grass outside the house of one of the family members. When the procession reached the house, it halted. The third *tabua* was presented, Tai's <u>*tatau ni vanua*</u>**,** marking her taking leave of her clan and people. This is presented by the 'owners of the deceased' to the elders of the *vanua* (*qase ni vanua*). This farewell was described to me as the taking leave of the 'family' and I was told it was the most poignant moment in the whole funeral.

These first and third *tabua* presentations are the most central points of a Nadrogā funeral, far more central than the burial itself. This emphasises the fact that the mortuary rites of passage first and foremost concern the relations between the deceased and his or her kinship ties, the taking leave of these relational contexts, and the loss to the whole of a member of the kinship group.

The <u>*tatau ni vanua*</u> was followed by a rite called <u>*ruku*</u> (lit. to walk under), in which the close family passed under the coffin. The pall-bearers at the middle, the coffin resting on their shoulders, provided a natural division of space beneath. A long line of mourners queued up on one side of the coffin, and one by one they stooped down and wove their way between the motionless men, passing once under from the left, returning in a u-shaped loop, so that for some time the line of bodies appeared as one, as if weaving a slow, serpentine dance in unison, a *meke*[22] for the dead. When people returned from this rite they appeared very moved and sat down on the grass in groups facing the coffin, many weeping and wailing loudly.

This moment in Nadrogā funerals seems to be a final marker for many people. They often remain seated, seemingly drained of emotion, while the procession finally moves on towards the grave and the actual burial. However many people I asked, though, no one gave me any other explanation for this rite than that it is a 'last respect' to the departed and that, as with the rites of *tatau*, it was something peculiar not merely to Nadrogā but to this particular *vanua*. Ethnographic descriptions from the 19th century, however, suggest that similar rites observed in Nadrogā then had links to pre-Christian spiritual beliefs:

> The body wrapped in mats leaves the house. A suitable opening is made; for chiefs, they break open a whole corner of the house. In Colo the body is half brought out of the house four times. Then those present all beat their hands against mats to force the spirit to leave … Among those who speak the western dialect this feature is replaced as follows. In leaving the house, the bearers stop in the centre of the village, and raise the body, below which the children of the relatives pass four times. This ceremony is called *ruku mate* or *tadra mate*. This superstitious practice is to prevent the deceased's spirit from recognising his house or returning to strike at some child of his kindred. (de Marzan 1987: 50)

Reverend Lorimer Fison (1888: 9) describes a similar custom he observed in eastern Fiji:

> In several parts of Fiji, when an old man dies a curious custom is observed. Before the body is carried forth to the burial, it is either lifted up by the bearers or laid upon a raised platform. A man – (the brother of the child's mother) – then takes the son's son of the deceased, passes him rapidly several times hither and thither, and under and over the corpse, and then runs away with him at the top of his speed. This is done in order to bewilder the old gentleman as to the direction in which the child is taken away, it being supposed that he will be very desirous to have his grandson with him where he is, and will therefore seek to kill him. A like custom is observed when the father dies; but it is the father's father who is especially dreaded, for it is supposed that the relationship between the paternal grandfather and his grandchild is closer than that which exists between the child and its father. This ideal can be clearly traced to the former prevalence of descent through females, which indeed is still the rule among some of the Fijian tribes.

---

22   *Meke*, traditional Fijian dance, was not performed in this village.

And Buell Quain (1948: 366) observed a similar rite in Vanualevu, eastern Fiji, in the mid-1930s:

> ... young men whom the village elders had appointed as pallbearers lashed the bundled corpse with sennit ropes and lifted it high in the center of the house so that the dead man's "small children" and his sisters' children could walk stooping beneath it; thus the souls of those who had not yet attained the sturdiness of maturity were protected against the coaxing advances of the dead man's soul when it would come beseeching them to join the souls of the dead.

The *ruku* ritual as I experienced it, though different in detail, shares many of the features seen by these three observers, our observations spanning a time period of over 100 years and a geographical area which covers the island group from east to west. All descriptions concern a pre-Christian rite of passage, establishing a boundary between the dead and the living, a way of ensuring the delimitation of the spiritual powers unleashed in death. Children were particularly vulnerable to such powers, and in thus protecting the children related to the deceased, the continued life and health of the clan as a body was ensured.

The burial

When the last person had passed under the coffin, the *ruku* was over and the pall-bearers moved on up the *rara* towards the area behind the 'house of death' where Tai was to be buried, behind her brother's house. In a clearing between some trees, a grave had been dug. It was lined with mats, whose edges were folded over the sides of the grave, their brightly coloured fringes standing out vividly against the earthy hues of the freshly uncovered soil and the bright green of the grass and surrounding trees. The coffin was placed at the edge of the grave.

It was now time for the presentation of the final *tabua*, the *vadaroi ni yago*, the last farewell, signifying the deceased's taking leave of this world. This presentation is from the 'owners of the deceased' to the *kōvana*, granting them permission to bury the body.

In later discussions with the men of the village about these rites, they listed this presentation as the fifth, and described a different fourth *tabua* presentation that, according to my notes, did not take place at this funeral. This is the *tatau ni were*, from the 'owners of the deceased' to the *kōvana*, as a request for future 'protection' or acknowledgement by the *kōvana* of the children and grandchildren of the deceased. That was the custom in former times but is now hardly ever observed.

The barkcloth (*kumi*) and lace which had been draped over the coffin were removed and laid aside and, taking hold of the edges of the mats, the pall-bearers slowly lowered the coffin into the grave, folding the brightly coloured edges of the mats over it and placing stones on them to hold them in place. It was now the

duty of the Methodist ministers to perform the final rites. The minister read out
the words from the back of the Methodist Hymn Book, bent down as he read, and
took up a handful of earth, casting it into the grave, 'earth to earth, ashes to ashes,
dust to dust'. Ravuvu writes:

> Death is the separation of the human being from the womb of 'mother earth',
> or the soul of spirit from the body. Burial …is thus the final act of separation
> and also the initial rite of incorporation as the soul enters the spirit world of
> Bulu from where it watches over the affairs of the living … Funeral offerings
> and other mourning activities are also a means of identifying with the dead and
> thus continuing the link with the ancestors. By being involved in death rituals,
> a person is closely identified with and assured of the assistance and blessing,
> not only of the living kinsmen of the dead, but also of the spirit world of which
> the soul of the departed will be a part. In this way, continuity of co-operative
> relationships with the supernatural world is assured for the sake of the living.
> (Ravuvu 1987: 299)

When the ministers had spoken these final words at the grave side and the other
minister and elders had cast handfuls of soil into the grave, the men of the _kōvana_
began to fill it while the choir stood nearby, singing hymns. As the grave began to
fill with soil, two of the young men jumped in to trample it flat. When the last of
the soil had been carefully patted down, the *kumi* and the lace were spread over the
mound. The children who had been waiting for their big moment, stepped forward
with the small wreaths and flower arrangements they had made, now wilted from
the heat and sun, and arranged them on the grave, a wooden cross at one end. Then
the children and pallbearers cheerfully took up positions for a group photo by the
graveside. Tai's granddaughter, who had borrowed a small Instamatic camera from
someone in the village, took several shots of the smiling group.

The post-burial re-distribution of valuables (_juberi ni ulu_)

When the burial was over, the guests dispersed quickly from the hot sun by the
graveside and made their way to the shelter erected next to the church to partake
of the funeral feast (_magisi_). Plates with great mounds of boiled root crops – taro,
cassava, sweet potatoes and yams – were placed in a line down the narrow tables.
Women sitting cross-legged on the grass by the enormous cauldrons of food at the
head of the table filled each guest's plate with a helping of stewed meat. Another
group of women next to them washed the dirty plates, which were then immediately
filled with a new helping and offered to the next guest. As is the custom at Fijian
feasts, the guests did not linger over their food but ate quickly and left the table,
giving up their places to the people of the next sitting.

   As the final round of guests were completing their fill of the food, the elders
of the 'owners of the deceased' met to discuss the details of the re-distribution

of valuables (*juberi ni ulu*) that had been presented to the men during the *vura* – almost all the mats presented had been taken to the 'house of death' where the women presided. The distribution was to follow these priorities, the village spokesman (*mata ni vanua*) explained: the first, and by far the most important recipient would be the *kōvana*; and the second recipient kin group would be those in other villages with kinship ties to the *kōvana* (*veiwekani ni matai ni ulu*). Third came the kinspeople of the second *ulu* and fourthly those of the third *ulu*.

The final four categories of distribution concerned presentations of valuables to the *kōvana* to mark the four main post-burial feasts, Fifth Night (*bogilima*),[23] Tenth Night (*bogitini*), Fiftieth Night (*bogilimasagavulu*), and the final 'lifting of the mourning' feast, Hundredth Night (*bogidrau*).

The village elders and the elders of the *kōvana* now gathered in the middle of the *rara* awaiting the re-distribution of these valuables, which had been displayed and arranged by the 'owners of the deceased' ready for presentation. Each set of valuables was made up of a number of kerosene drums, with one or several folded mats laid across, on top of which one or more *tabua* were placed. This *tabua* is known as the *ulu* (head). A label on each denoted to the village spokesman who was to receive what. He stood in the middle of this collection of valuables, a piece of material draped over and fastened across his shoulders and chest. This was in place of the barkcloth (*kumi*) most often worn on such occasions. It is of particular importance, an indication of respect, to wear either barkcloth or material for the first two main presentations of whale's teeth that were about to take place prior to the re-distribution of valuables: the presentation of the *tabua icegu* and the *tabua kali*.

Na icegu and *na kali ni sucu*

These two *tabua* presentations, from the 'owners of the deceased' to the *kōvana*, are considered very special and the whale's teeth used are very precious.

When a person is growing old, it is the responsibility of his or her immediate family to make sure they always have in their possession two high-quality *tabua* for presenting to the *kōvana*. They are considered so special that when they are presented they are not held in the hands but offered on a mat, held forth ceremoniously in the arms of the presenter. This way of presenting these *tabua* indicates extra respect for the *tabua* and for the *kōvana*. 'You hold the mat like you hold a baby', I was told.

Calling out across the village *rara* to the seated elders of the *kōvana* opposite, the village spokesman verbally presented the *cegu* and *kali* to Tai's *mōmō*'s (mother's brother's) son, who stood up to receive the honoured gifts, held out to

---

23   Part of the valuables received from the family was presented by the owners of death to the First *kōvana* for the *tuvavatu* (laying of the stones) the day after the funeral, which was also *bogilima*, the Fifth Night after the death.

him on a woven mat by another man. He carefully slid his arms under the mat and remained standing between the two groups.

The first *tabua* is called *cegu*, which means literally 'breath' and symbolises the life the mother gave to her child. Its meaning was explained to me like this: 'The mother gave life to her child; until the child takes its first breath it is still connected to the mother by the [umbilical] cord. God created man by breath ... women give birth... the breath [life] goes back to its mother ... when we die, our breath is finished and goes back to Heaven'.

The *tabua icegu* symbolises the connection of the deceased's body with her mother's body, her mother's clan and the mother's place. When this whale's tooth is presented to the *mōmō,* the body of the deceased is being symbolically, ritually and materially returned to the mother's clan in a gesture of reciprocal acknowledgement of the central role of this clan in giving life to the 'owners of the deceased' clan.[24] Jean de Marzan writes of the *tabua cegu:*

> ... The dead [before burial] wear a whale's tooth on their chest. If not on the chest, the whale's tooth will be in a hand; often there is one in each hand. In the west this is called *nonai cegu,* his breath ... When a man related to the mother of the deceased comes into the house, he takes the whale's tooth and replaces it with another. (1987: 49, see also Geddes 1945: 47)

Deane writes that the soul of the deceased 'was supposed to take with it the spiritual part of [this *tabua*], and, thus provided for, would travel to a tree "hard by Heaven's gate" in which tree he was to throw it as a passport on his journey to the happy land'. (1921: 84) This would indicate that these important *tabua* represented, and probably still represent material, symbolic, social and spiritual dimensions and were not merely examples of material exchange between the living.

The second whale's tooth is called *kali,* meaning pillow, or 'the hand holding the baby'. It symbolises, I was told, the care and protection the mother gave her child. 'When the baby is born the first thing it does is breathe, the second thing is to cry ... and the mother holds the baby and comforts it'. So, in the same way as the mother gave birth to, nurtured and protected her child, that child's body is symbolically handed back to her mother's place of birth and her mother's people, who formerly had relinquished their daughter and her reproductive powers to her husband's clan. The *tabua* goes back to where the child came from, that is to say to the mother's brother, the *mōmō.* It also denotes the fact that 'It's over ... Tai is no more, and all things ... go back to where they came from'.

Ravuvu, describing mortuary rites in the Wainimala River area of Tailevu, Eastern Fiji, describes this similarly, yet from a decidedly male perspective. He firstly points out the 'major structural separation of the "male side" – the "father's

---

24   In the exchange of valuables made at a wedding (*tevutevu*) the groom's clan usually gives more than the bride's clan, in expectation of the life the woman will contribute to her husband's clan.

side" – from the "female side" – the "mother's side"' that is similarly evident in the preceding series of rites I have described. He then analyses the return of the body to the mother's clan in a way that confirms what I was told – yet adds a slightly different perspective than that which the villagers (male and female) I discussed this with gave me:

> Only the flesh or the body, the 'female side' is returned and conjoined with the earth through burial. But the soul or the spirit is separated from the 'female side', the 'mother's side', and remaining with the spirits, its male ancestors. This is confirmed by the ceremony of the *tuva ulu* ('the arraying of the head') ceremony, involving the presentation of 'a number of large-sized whale's teeth by the father and brothers of the deceased to the mother's brothers, and their children after the burial. These *tabua* [are] designated as the 'head of the deceased, to be shown to the mother's brothers and their children … the 'head' – often associated with the soul or spirit predominates over the rest of the body, is always associated with the 'male side', although culturally claimed by the 'female side' to be its contribution to life. The head is the locus of one's power or spirit, and thus it is a sacred part of the body considered to be taboo (*tabu*). Since the 'head' or 'spirit' of the deceased is not returned at death, the *ulu* in this case thus forms a compensation for the spirit or soul of the deceased. It finally affirms that death had occurred and that the soul, or spirit remains with the 'male side' in the spirit world. (Ravuvu 1987: 339)

The village spokesman now set about the task of re-distributing the sets of valuables to the various groups present, starting in hierarchical order with the First *kōvana*. At the same time he verbally presented the already mixed kava (*yaqona*) in the wooden *tanoa* placed on the grass between the two clans. The sharing of this kava would finalise the exchanges about to take place and once again seal the bond between the kin groups. An elder from the *kōvana* stood up to officially accept the gifts of the *tabua icegu* and *tabua kali* presented earlier and the *mōmō* sat down with his group, the mat with the whale's teeth still resting on his arms.

And now followed the very last group of presentations to close the proceedings – three more *tabua*. The elder from the *kōvana* presented a *tabua* to 'the owners of death', a presentation known as 'the welcoming of the valuables' (*matakarawa ni yau*). Then he presented the 'owners of the deceased' with the *tabua ai tatau* as a formal thanksgiving for all that kingroup had done for the *kōvana*. The 'owners of the deceased' received this and duly presented another whale's tooth in return. This *tabua* is the final presentation called *bili ni mua*, acknowledging the finalisation of exchanges and in effect giving the *kōvana* permission to leave, and marking the end of the re-distribution of valuables.

It was getting late. The afternoon was drawing to a close, the light waning and the air cooling down. The minister stood up and said a prayer of thanksgiving. Three men from the 'owners of the deceased' were called to sit by the *tanoa* and serve the kava (*talo ni yaqona*). The first cup was served to the *kōvana*, the second to the minister, the third to the most senior member of the 'owners of the deceased'. The post-burial re-distribution of valuables (*juberi ni ulu*) was formally sealed and relations between the clans were balanced and ordered. A short period of informal drinking now commenced.

It would seem as if the departed, and the clan itself, is assisted through ritual exchanges on a journey of farewells and reconnections that start at death and continue on through the mourning period till Hundredth Night (*bogidrau*), when the mourning is lifted. The rites simultaneously symbolise a severing and reconnection of the links between the deceased and the *vanua*, that is say *vanua* as the place and people to which one belongs, of which one is, and *vanua* as encompassing all tradition, customs and beliefs – the very soil from which it came and to which it returns, 'earth to earth, ashes to ashes, dust to dust'.

Folding the mats

Immediately after the burial, *yaqona* was presented to the women of the *kōvana* and they received special gifts of soap, *sulu* (material), *waiwai* (oil) and sweets from the *weka ni mase* women of the village. This giving of gifts (*sili i wai*) was once part of a cleansing rite from former days when members of the *kōvana* would have been in direct contact with the body and would therefore have needed to be cleansed, physically and ritually afterwards in the sea or the river. Furthermore, the women of the *kōvana* stayed inside the house of death from the time of the display of the body until the burial, and did not wash until after the body was laid in the ground.

Having washed and changed, the women of the *kōvana* made a presentation in the 'house of death' of kava to the women of the deceased's family (the 'owners of the deceased') in order formerly to ask permission to 'fold the mats' (*lobi ni iō*). This, in effect, signals the very end of the funeral. Permission was granted through a speech by an elder woman of the 'owners of the deceased' kin group and was sealed with a round of kava.

After the final exchanges had taken place, the dismantling of the 'house of death' began. Just as it had been the women of Tai's *bito,* the 'owners of the deceased', who had prepared the 'house of death' for the funerary proceedings, it was now the reciprocal duty of the women of the *kōvana* to set about dismantling and clearing out the house. The pieces of barkcloth and lengths of material were removed from the *loqi* area and carefully folded in two separate piles. Each mat was shaken, folded and stacked by type. Both the mats given and received by the *kōvana* would eventually be redistributed to the women of each group who had participated in the funeral.

The woman of highest rank directed proceedings, and women were given or allowed to choose a mat of the same value as that which they had contributed to the communal presentation. If a woman gave a sleeping mat (*idarodaro*), for example, she would be allocated a mat of similar value; if she had given a piece of barkcloth, she would receive another piece of barkcloth. But a woman who had given a mat would not be given a piece of barkcloth, as that is valued higher than a mat, indeed higher than all other female valuables.[25]

Finally the empty *loqi* area was swept and the roll of mats and barkcloth the women of the *kōvana* had brought with them as their contribution and thanksgiving (*vavinavina*) to the 'owners of the deceased' were spread out in the same sequential order. Piled up in great mounds, they were carefully accounted for: there were 10 large, thickly woven plain mats (*coco*); 15 smaller, fringed mats (*vabasi*); 46 sleeping mats (*idarodaro*) and 8 pieces of brown patterned Tongan-style barkcloth (*kumi*) – in all, 71 mats and 8 pieces of barkcloth plus several lengths of material. The women were satisfied; this was considered a very good harvest. It was in fact a really big presentation, reflecting Tai's chiefly status.

Later, when the *kōvana* have left, the 'owners of the deceased' prepare a feast of food and *yaqona* called *madi ni vavi* to distribute the valuables brought by the *kōvana*.

Epilogue

Outside the 'house of death' it was dark and the cold air of evening was full of the revving of engines, the loading of kerosene drums, mats and people into the jam-packed carriers and the general commotion of departure – children running hither and thither, crying, being lifted into the arms of mothers and grannies in the carriers, dogs barking, people calling out final greetings and exchanging roars of laughter. Finally, the carriers clanked into gear amidst bellows of exhaust fumes and set off out of the village and onto the dusty road leading up the valley.

An exhausted silence fell on the village, broken by the sounds of televisions and murmuring as those kava drinkers who had not yet succumbed to heavy, drugged sleep, sat in stupefied silence round kava bowls, automatically receiving and returning the coconut shell drinking bowls. Others lay outstretched on the mats of their living room floor or had gone to bed.

As elsewhere in Fiji, a contemporary funeral such as this in western Vitilevu is made up of elements perpetuated from the past and others that have changed over time. The staging of this collective performance of tradition took up immense

25 Women gave mats, material and *masi*, and men *tabua* and kerosene. And almost all mats, *masi* and lengths of material were presented in the house of death, where mostly women were gathered. Women did also give and receive *tabua*, as noted above, but it is fair to call mats women's valuables, as they belong primarily, in terms of production, distribution and exchange within the sphere of women.

labour and time and was a very costly affair for those involved. While the deceased was honoured and taken leave of in numerous ways, almost all rites of passage were directed towards providing for and honouring the *kōvana* kingroup. In this way the individual rite of passage of the deceased was closely interwoven with relations, past, present and future, between the deceased's clan, represented by her lineage group, the 'owners of the deceased', and her mother's clan, the *kōvana*.

By comparison with these elaborate, time-consuming and expensive traditional funerary rites, the role of the Methodist church in all this seemed almost perfunctory. Although the minister and church deacons played a visible role in the procession from the church to the grave, walking immediately behind the coffin as it was carried through the village, and reading the final prayers at the side of the grave, the length of the service, the number of people who attended it, and the final prayers at the grave-side seemed of minimal consequence in the overall sequence of events. Although there was admittedly an admonition from the minister about repenting and changing one's ways before death, the funeral service seemed to be viewed not so much as an occasion of spiritual direction, expression and reflection, as one moment in a long sequence of kinship affirmations.

Was the role of the Methodist church an intrinsic and inextricable part of the traditional rites of this event, to such a degree that it is almost impossible to distinguish between the two, as so many Methodists have told me, referring to the concept of *vanua, lotu* and *matanitu* (land, church and governance)? On the one hand, yes. On the other, the Christian element in this funeral seemed to be an appendage to the activities that took place in the course of the three days the funeral lasted. This was the case in all the Methodist funerals I attended in Fiji. Only at Roman Catholic and Anglican funerals I attended did the funeral service appear to have a more central role in the funeral proceedings, Roman Catholic funeral services including the Eucharist. At a Roman Catholic funeral I attended in the next village the coffin was driven directly from the Roman Catholic church in Sigatoka to the burial site outside the village; there were no exchanges of *tabua* on the way.

In considering this and other Methodist funerals I have attended, it seems quite feasible to say somewhat tongue in cheek that a Methodist village funeral could actually take place without the church service. Omit this brief part of the other lengthy funerary rites and you would basically still have a funeral. But omit everything else and merely have the funeral service and burial – and that would make for a quite different event.

Was this the true role of Methodism in Fiji, I wondered, as I thought about the funeral – was the church more a forum for displaying, confirming and strengthening kinship ties than a place to find spiritual guidance and development?[26] I have discussed this with several Methodists, both ministers and lay-people, both men

---

26   Former Methodist Church president Koroi (interview 1998) made a similar point and Ernst also asserts that the Methodist Church in Fiji often seems to be more 'culture-oriented than Christian-oriented'. (Ernst 1994a: 211)

and women, and they agreed with this perception of the way the Christian part of funerals is overshadowed by the concerns of *vanua*, the increasing focus on material exchanges and the funeral feast.

This is not to say that there is anything to be gained per se in determining or distinguishing between what is 'traditional' and what is 'Christian' or 'Methodist'. My point is to show that although Fijians consider *vanua* and *lotu* to be interwoven, they also clearly distinguish between the two. This funeral took place in western Vitilevu where both chiefly structures and Methodism have historically always been weaker than in eastern Fiji. However, the fact remains that in relation to what is generally promulgated as a pan-Fijian ideal structure of neatly interwoven categories (*vanua, lotu, matanitu*) my observations of this funeral clearly indicate that *vanua* is by far the strongest and most important strand. This impression is bourne out by the villagers' comments in the following chapter, on which elements of the funeral were most important.

Chapter 4
Paths of Reciprocity

> One of the greatest values in our Pacific cultures is the notion of sharing or reciprocal love (*fetokoni'aki* in Tongan, *fetufaai* in Samoan and *veitokoni* in Fijian). This noble value…inherent also in the *wantok* system in Melanesia…has enabled our peoples and societies to stand tall in any situation in life [and] has enabled us to live for thousands of years. (Reverend Dr Mika Paunga, homily, Pacific Regional Seminary, 16 September 2005)

Across the Pacific Island region the cultural values of reciprocal sharing and caring for each other within a kin group and their ritualised expression through gift-giving and presentations stand out as possibly the most enduring feature of life, the values on which all else is based.[1] The structures behind the different systems of reciprocity may differ but the main values and their importance as deeply engrained elements of Pacific Islander identity are the same, as demonstrated by these two quotes. Tongan Catholic priest Father Paunga points out in his homily that despite changes taking place within Pacific Islander societies today, these traditional ideals are

> still very much alive in the new socio-economic and political culture of today even though we may not be too aware of the way [they are] functioning. We see this functioning most clearly at our wedding and funeral ceremonies. For example, last week two students came to my office, asking for money for a funeral …We can always count on our big brother or uncle to help us in need … [This] Pacific value of 'reciprocal love' is already a gospel value of the Kingdom … we must hold tight to [it and] not let it get eroded by the forces of globalisation. (Ibid.)

As this homily also emphasises, this Pacific value of caring for others and sharing with them is foundational to Christianity. However, within Christianity the Second Commandment, to 'love our neighbour', is expanded to include not just kin and family but all others. All people, including those we do not know, feel close to, or necessarily like, are our neighbours. (Father K. Barr MSC, pers comm, October 2005)

---

1   See Gregory (forthcoming) for a succinct overview of the history of theories of exchange, and with regard to the Pacific Island region see for example Mauss 1990, A. Strathern 1971, Munn 1988, M. Strathern 1988, Gregory 1982, Thomas 1991, Weiner 1992, Godelier 1999, Liep 2009, and re Fiji see e.g. Miyazaki 2000, Brison 2008.

Methodist theologian Sai Niukula points out that there are also clear connections to be made between the transformative nature of ritualised gift-giving in Fijian cultural traditions, and the transformative nature of God's gift of Jesus Christ through the incarnation, her words applicable to all Pacific Island cultures:

> The Fijian people are embodied in and defined by their ritual ceremonies of presentations of gifts, for, without them, Fijian culture and identity would no longer exist. By the same token, as Christians our existence – our identity – depends on the gift of Jesus Christ, which God gives to us in so many incarnated and transformative ways. (Sai Niukula, 2003: 209)

Nurturing kinship

In Pacific Island cultures, woven into the ideals of caring and sharing among kin is the notion of respect. The term for this in Standard Fijian is *vakarokoroko*. Following these ideals, doing what is expected is a way of showing respect and also expressing and practising relationality and connectedness. This foundational concept of traditional Fijian culture is based on notions of respect of those higher in status than oneself, of knowing one's place in the system, of extending, *giving* due respect, in conduct or materially, as befits that person.

As described earlier, the place where a person positions him or herself within a given space is dependent on that person's rank and status in relation to the other people present. Thus in one's physical positioning in relation to others, one is physically embodying the hierarchical codes of rank and respect on which Fijian society is based. In the same way, in the work you do for your chief and in what you do for those you are related to, you are simultaneously expressing and embodying ties of relationship, respect and hierarchy.

The centrality of this ideal of reciprocity was made clear to me when the men of the village were asked what they felt was the most important aspect of the funeral described in the previous chapter. From the *vura* to the burial and post-burial rites, what was most important to them? The care of the *kōvana*, the guests of honour, they replied immediately.

This kin group, the kin on the side of the mother of the old lady who died, is, as mentioned earlier, the recipient of almost all the valuables (*iyau*) presented in honour of the deceased. Caring for the *kōvana* was understood by the men to mean providing the people of this kingroup with food and ensuring they were given their rightful valuables and kava. In other words, the paramount consideration in the funeral was to show hospitality, care and respect in every way to this kin group.

This sentiment is echoed by other men from Nadrogā (research notes, Mrs Sainimere Niukula, October 2005), who emphasise that there must be lots of *iyau* and food at a funeral, and that the most difficult thing to do is to cater for visitors through food and sleeping arrangements, and that these things must be in order. In response to my asking the men of the village why it is important to do all these things for the kin group, they answered that it is because of love (*loloma*) and obligations towards the *veiwekani* (kin relations).

Fijian notions of hospitality derive from the desire to show respect at all times, inevitably linked with the desire to nurture others through feeding them. In her work in Nadrogā, Becker (1995: 57) describes an 'ethos of care' in Fijian social life which centres on

> one's connectedness with and performance of care in the social matrix of the family, the *mataqwali*, and the village. In part, the adequacy of this performance is judged by competence in providing and serving food within and outside the household unit. This competence is manifested in acts of service to and for others, encompassed in the concepts of care – *vikawaitaki, viqwaravi,* and *vilomani* – and coupled with appropriate demeanor, including knowing *varokorokotaki* (respectful behaviour and knowing one's relative social position). Although a shared understanding of correct behaviour (*itovo vina*) extends to all social contexts, this *itovo vina* is most frequently and visibly operationalized in the procuring and sharing of food resources.

As Becker illustrates in her research, this imperative to care for kin group members through nurturing and feeding them is symbolised by a general focus on providing and sharing food, on the quantity of food offered, its consumption, and the physical result of this, body size being equated with health and well-being and being cared for.

On my return to the village in 1998, after a period of some months in Europe and Australia, I was greeted with delighted cries of 'How *fat* you are, Jacqueline! How beautiful you look! You're really a *kai Viti* (Fijian) now, eh?!' I was slightly taken aback. Although I believe I may have put on a little weight, I didn't think it was that much! I really hadn't considered myself to now be *fat*, and was quite sure that in western terms I would hardly have been classified as such. However, on reflection it seemed to me that people's description of my bodily state had less to do with my actual size and shape than with the fact that people *expected* me to look different, to look healthy, strong and well after having spent time with my family in Europe. People imagined they must have fed and cared well for me during my visit, in much the same way that they themselves would have fed and cared for family members from far afield who had come home to the village for Christmas and New Year.

So in the context of the funeral, the ways in which the 'owners of the deceased' cared for the people of the *kōvana* was an expression of their literal nurturing of kinship ties through the provision of food and material goods. This social obligation is akin to the obligations a Fijian has to care for the land (*vanua*). Ideals of plenty and prosperity (*sautu*) are intrinsically connected with the responsibility to care for the land and thereby to show respect for it as a gift of God.

The degree of respect shown between kin groups is measured in terms of material quantity, first and foremost, and quality thereafter. So the number and size and the quality of the *tabua* and mats exchanged, the amount of other valuables given and the amount of food offered to the funeral guests, is vital in the outward expression of respect between clan groups. To the all-seeing gaze of relations, providing a meagre funeral feast (*magisi*) with only just enough food, or limited kinds of food, would therefore reflect a lack of respect. The same applies to the quantity of *tabua*, mats and other valuables. According to Ravuvu (1983: 42-43)

> No ceremonial function is considered complete without a presentation of food or *magiti*. A function is considered good ... if there is more than enough food for everyone attending. It is shameful if people go hungry ... The greater the hospitality, the more successful and impressive the occasion will be ... The *magiti* or food gifts should always be the best and the most one can afford ... Left-over food is an indication of prosperity (*sautu*), but it should be distributed to other households if it is not to be interpreted as stinginess.

And Aleosi Suguta (1986: 186) interestingly refers to the issue of 'leftovers' in a contrast between Fijian ideals and those of western cultures:

> This is the sort of thing that Fijians admire and even boast about because it shows how generous the giver is. But in the Western (rational) concept, such commitment is a waste of reserves which should be spared for another occasion.

But in Fiji, it is the outward appearance of quantity and generosity that counts, the outward appearance of balance between kin groups, the outward appearance of respect. Staging a magnificent funeral with all the trappings in terms of many large *tabua*, an abundance of beautiful mats and a splendid feast would generate great respect for the hosts and much pride in those who were responsible for it. As Becker (1995: 63) writes:

> The particulars of such feasts serve as a measure of the relative mutual esteem between two groups. A woman from a chiefly family in Nahigatoka [village] who is often called on to participate in such events explained, "We are ashamed ... if our contribution is only slight; it shames us".

On the other hand, she indicated her village had felt proud after ceremonies in Yavulo because 'we gave well'. The outward appearance of quantity and generosity in terms of food in particular is described by villagers as 'being respectful' towards their kinsmen or towards their guests. It is also, in a similar way to Munn's (1988: 50, 65) descriptions from the island of Gawa, a 'spatio-temporal extending process' in which food (and valuables and nurture) are converted to the 'fame' of the givers, and the 'objective gift [is converted] into subjective remembering' by the recipients.

Although the act of showing respect, as previously described, is closely linked with *vakarokoroko*, a subservient way of behaving, of deferring to authority, 'respect' also involves caring and sharing (*veitokoni*), showing compassion and love (*loloma*), generosity and hospitality. At the same time, within these values and the competition between groups to give most and best, lies the ideal of reciprocity, and within the concept of hierarchy, there is also an implicit understanding of balance. When a group such as the 'owners of the deceased' do everything in their power to honour and respect the mother's clan (*kōvana*) of the dead person by presenting them with the best foods and the largest amount of valuables, they do so in the knowledge that at some time they themselves will be the recipients of such honour and wealth.

Similarly, this balance of reciprocity exists in the ideal of chiefly-commoner relations. The people are expected to revere and defer to the authority of the chief; the chief on the other hand is expected to show compassion, wisdom and care for his people. Yet these values, traditionally so central to Fijian and Pacific Islander life, are increasingly being eroded with the competing demands of modern living.

'... a time of sadness, of pollution and of women'

When the women of the village were asked what they considered the most important part of the funeral they found it less easy than the men to answer. In their own discussions, some of the women argued that all rituals associated with a funeral were of equal importance. When asked to think in terms of the various rites that had taken place, they eventually came to the consensus that *na itatau* (the rite of taking leave of the deceased), the *ruku* (the 'last respect' to the deceased, in which people pass under the coffin) and the actual burial process were the most important parts of the funeral.[2]

However, the women also shared the men's view of the importance of looking after the *kōvana*. They said that the most important thing was to show respect to the members of this group through extending hospitality towards them and accommodating their needs. In this way, they said, the people who are very close to the deceased are honoured for the achievements of the dead person, meaning his or her achievements in relation to the clan, not his or her individual achievements.

One reason for the women considering the rites of the *itatau* and the *ruku* to be among the most important parts of the funeral could be that they are significant emotional moments to those taking leave of the deceased. The emotional side of funerals, the visible and audible nature of grieving, belongs more in the domain of women than of men. 'The men never *tagi* (cry)', one auntie told me, 'only the women do that kind of crying'. I had noticed that although it was not shameful if men did cry at funerals, and Fijian men did shed tears during particularly moving speeches in ceremonial situations at funerals and otherwise, it was the women

2   Research Notes, Aliti Vunisea, July 1998.

who particularly showed their grief – and respect – during funerals, through loud outbursts of crying and wailing.

However, there seemed to be a distinction to this in terms of closeness of relations. 'If it's a close relative we do that ... [restrained] crying ... not making so much noise', my auntie continued. 'But the men', she added with a laugh, 'oh, they just sit and drink *yaqona* – *lia lia,* eh? Crazy, eh?' 'The men cry when their real mother dies', my auntie said, '*then* they cry ... and us women, when our real brother dies ... then we can't stop crying ... When we sleep, when we wake ... *tagi, tagi, tagi* ... we cry and cry and cry'.

Such crying at funerals is not only a personal expression of grief. It is also part of a collective ritualised expression of mourning and an important element in the communal rites of passage of taking leave of the deceased. The women are key figures in this as they are in much else at the funeral. It is the women in Fiji who tend to the body in death, who in former times oiled the body, blackening men's bodies as if in preparation for battle, and women's bodies with turmeric powder; and decorating the bodies with necklaces, *masi* and turbans, in the case of chiefly men. It was mats and bark-cloth, the products of women's labour and creativity, that in former times were wrapped around the deceased and that today are used to cover the floor of 'the house of death', to line the coffin and the grave, and to lie beneath the coffin wherever it is placed, such as in the carrier from the hospital, in the <u>werenimase</u> and in church.

This linking of women with mortuary rites is seen not only across the Pacific Island region, but also elsewhere. Bloch (1982: 265) writes of Madagascar:

> both sorrow and pollution are, in Madagascar as in so many other cultures, principally focused on women ... who should weep both individually and as a group ... who take on mourning for death ... are associated with the pollution of death ... who must wash the corpse ... Individual burial is, therefore, a time of sadness, of pollution and of women. (See also Damon and Wagner 1989, Battaglia 1992)

European missionaries, writing of pre-Christian customs, described that just as in the traditional Fijian house (*bure*), dried grasses were laid on the earthen floors beneath the woven mats for softness and warmth, the graves of chiefs were lined with the bodies of strangled women, called the 'grass' for the chief's bedding. (Williams 1982: 189) The women were often strangled by their brothers, in honour of the deceased, so that he would not journey alone to the afterworld, and many women considered this fate a great honour. As in the case of valuables then and today, the greater the number of women strangled (*iloloku:* literally act of mourning) to accompany the dead, and the higher their rank, the greater the respect shown. According to Williams' sources, sometimes men were strangled too. Further acts of mourning for the deceased were the amputation of the first joint of the little finger, in both women and men. Capell (1991: 151) notes the term *mudu ni liga* as 'land given to a man who has had a finger joint chopped off in mourning for a dead chief'.

Williams (1982: 195-198) describes how at the death of the *Tuicakau* (literally, chief of the reef, the high chief of Cakaudrove province of north eastern Fiji) in Somosomo in 1845, people shaved their heads or beards and 100 fingers were ordered to be amputated. In this case, only two women were strangled and buried with the old chief, due to the missionary's pleas to spare the lives of the others.[3] Hocart writes (1929: 180) that in the Lau Islands a piece of land known as *wa ni kuna* (literally, the strangling rope), was given to the kinspeople of the strangled woman to recompense her death. Together with cannibalism these acts of mourning rated highest on the list of practices the missionaries most fervently sought to abolish when they arrived in the islands. With the spread of Christianity, they died out.

According to de Marzan (1987: 59), the complexity of mourning rites and *tabu* practised in pre-Christian Fiji were all done to propitiate the ancestral spirits: 'No people more greatly honour the dead, yet no people fear them more; unfortunately, since all is due to fear, there is very little love, very little respect for the dead among the Fijians'.

Acts of mourning carried out today include a *tabu* on eating the food which made up the deceased's last meal, refraining from drinking *yaqona* or smoking, not shaving, and not having one's hair cut. No such *tabu* were observed in relation to Tai's death in the village. This was because she was so old, people said – over 80. Mostly such *tabu* are practised in connection with sudden deaths or the deaths of children. But at a Hundredth Night ceremony I took part in, in Ba town, the son of the old lady who died, who came from Tailevu province in eastern Vitilevu, had indeed refrained from eating the food his mother had eaten as her last meal, and had not cut his hair, drunk *yaqona* or smoked for the 100 days of mourning. He and his wife had also worn a black ribbon on their sleeve to show that they were in mourning. All such *tabu* are lifted at the ceremony of *vakataraisulu* on Hundredth Night (*vakabogidrau*).

Another reason why the village women were less immediately sure than the men about the most important part of the funeral could be that almost all of them had married into the village from other villages with different traditions and different values. In marrying into this clan, they had adopted the values and traditions prevalent there, but had perhaps formerly been used to other traditions.[4]

The beauty of mats

I asked the women whether there was any particular part of a funeral that seemed beautiful to them. Their immediate response was the mats, 'especially the mats

---

3   See also Thomas 1992a on the negative consequences of such missionary intervention.

4   I thank John Peel, for suggesting this.

for the *kōvana*', they said. According to the women of the *kōvana*, with whom I discussed mats at length throughout the funeral, the mats which were most patterned and most colourful, with several layers of different-coloured acrylic wool fringes (*vabasi* mats) or multi-coloured friezes of embroidered wool (*vunisipi* mats), were those most highly valued. This was partly because the more colourful the mats, the more beautiful they were seen to be,[5] but also because the amount of work put into making such a mat was valued.

On the other hand, women at the *vakataraisulu* ceremony I attended in Ba town rated the large *coco* mats highest, as they are biggest and more rare than the smaller, fringed *vabasi* or *davodavo* mats. The size of those mats, of course, signifies a considerable amount of labour, but they have no decorations. Several women pointed out how hard it is to maintain the coloured fringes of *vabasi* mats. They get dirty very quickly and so the plain, thicker *coco* mats will last longer and age better than the smaller, fringed ones.

The village women talked about how many mats the *kōvana* had brought to the funeral, and the number they received, in terms of *ivavivi* that is, complete sets of different styles and sizes of mats arranged in the same order as the mats used elsewhere in the funeral, and presented together with a piece of bark-cloth. It was clear that the amount of *ivavivi* at a presentation indicates the richness and magnitude of the gifts. This corresponds with the ideal of plenty and the variety of foods presented in feasts (*magisi*), described above.

When the women were asked, in response to people's complaints about the burden of traditional obligations, what it would mean to them if fewer mats and valuables were presented at funerals, their answer was that 'the time will come when there have to be fewer'. Many considered it a waste to put mats in the grave. 'Times are hard', they said. 'We have to do too much'. But although there was consensus that in these financially difficult times some rituals could be done away with, the women did not consider that the numbers of valuables given to the *kōvana* should be reduced. One example of such a desired change is the situation where kin members have the obligation to perform rites for people who live away from the village. (Research notes, Aliti Vunisea, 1998)

To save money, women in this area increasingly give lengths of material, mostly printed cotton, instead of mats or bark-cloth. In the house where I stayed, the mother went to a *vura* for a young mother who had died of cancer in the neighbouring village, taking a short length of printed cotton with her as her contribution to the communal presentation from our village. When she returned, she told me she was very ashamed (*madua*) as so much had been given at this *vura*. 'There were so many mats!' she explained, 'and many big *tapa* [bark-cloth] and so much *karisini* [kerosene]! The men [from our village] gave many drums of kerosene, but there was only one mat from us women'. She shook her head and

---

5   Interestingly, the opposite applies in Tonga where the plainest mats are considered the most beautiful. The most important mats in a Tongan funeral are Samoan fine mats. (Cf Kaeppler 1978b)

repeated that she was *madua*. In fact she had two new large *coco* mats folded up under her bed, one of which she had received at the Hundredth Night of her son-in-law's mother in Ba town. She and her husband had brought one of their pigs as their contribution to that feast and she had received a *coco* mat in return. The other mat was one she herself had woven from dried pandanus strips I had brought her as a gift from the market in Suva.[6] I had hoped she would use this mat in the house since the one in use was so worn, but when she had finished weaving it, she immediately folded it up and put it aside.

It would seem that certain pragmatic strategies are employed concerning the status of the person who has died, with regard to clan relations, determining how much one gives, and whether to 'sacrifice' the best or only mat that one has, or keep it in case it is needed for a more prominent death offering. There is constant pressure to be seen always to give generously, and at the same time the risk of the shame of not doing so. So there is a desire to do things as they have always been done, to maintain a sense of continuity with past traditions, to do things in the best possible way. There is considerable competition between groups to be seen to be most generous and most true to tradition. But there is also a sense that things are changing, that selective strategies must be employed, increasingly perhaps, in the practicalities of giving that conflict with ideals of practice. People seem aware that it will not always be possible to do things the way they have been wont to – or the way they would like (perhaps it never was).

'Tradition is tradition'

As described in the previous chapter, when the body of the old lady who died was returned to the village a *tabua* was presented by the 'owners of the deceased' to those who brought her back to the village, the ritual known as <u>na ivahobu</u> (literally, the taking down from the shoulder). In discussing the course of events the day after the funeral with one of the women, married into the chiefly clan from a neighbouring village, she was adamant that this particular presentation had been omitted, or at least not done correctly. She said she had overheard the women in charge of the proceedings say that the presentation of the whale's tooth was not necessary since those who were to collect the body were only the youth and children of the village. 'I was hurt by their lack of respect … I had suggested that as they would be giving the *tabua* back to us, as we were family … we could just give it back without anyone knowing, and they could use it again later'. But not to give it at all, she told me, would bring shame on the clan. 'Tradition is tradition. How can we teach our children to do the right thing if we don't do the right thing ourselves?' I was puzzled at her account of things.

---

6 Rolls of dried strips of pandanus leaves from e.g. Taveuni and Kadavu are available at the Suva Market, though they are quite expensive.

I checked with others, but they firmly believed that this presentation *had* taken place. When I asked this woman about this some weeks later, I became even more puzzled when she retracted her earlier view and implied that perhaps things had been 'done right' after all. However, whatever happened or did not is of no real consequence here, as her former claim raises a number of interesting and pertinent points:

Firstly, it describes the tension between different ways of following tradition. Doing things *the right way* in Fijian thinking implies doing things *in the same way*, as a group. However, although there may be a given procedure or order of rites, people do not always agree as to how to follow this, or indeed whether to follow it at all. Secondly, the consequences of not doing the right thing reflect on the whole community, not just on the individuals who may have chosen a short-cut through customary procedures. So 'tradition' is really never just 'tradition', it is always contextual, a process of negotiation between different possibilities and pressures and different interpretations of what it is and what purpose it may serve in a given context. Thirdly, those who participated in the funeral all experienced its events in different ways. At no time was there just one stage. Different things were being enacted and observed in different places by different groups of people at the same time.

And finally, the suggestion by one of the women that the *tabua* be given formally, yet returned afterwards behind the scenes in order to be used again later, exemplifies the importance of the public, performative aspect of reciprocity as a display of respect. Ensuring that everything appeared in order outwardly during the different ritual parts of the funeral was very important in order to explicitly and clearly show the degree of respect accorded to the members of a clan. How that outward effect was achieved was, at least in this example, less important.

A person is never just an individual but always sees him or herself and is always seen, in relation to others, in terms of kinship allegiance, rank and status. A person's acts never merely reflect on the person alone but on their kinspeople too. For the hosts to show lack of respect in a funeral situation could seriously reflect on their kin group's standing in relation to other kin groups. The importance attached to showing respect in all details of a funeral is noted by Miyazaki (1997: 111) who comments on mortuary exchanges at a funeral in Suvavou village outside Suva:

> the nature of gift exchange during the mortuary rites confirmed the nature of relationships between the two parties. Both hosts and guests were expected to meet properly the anticipation and expectations of others. Therefore, speeches made during gift exchange put emphasis on each others' respectfulness (*doka*) and faithful involvement (*veiwaitaki*), and confirmed (*deitaka*) the tie (*ivau*) of relationship and the thickness (*sosoko*) of blood (*dra*).

Each element of the mortuary rites at a funeral is a moment in the continuing confirmation of relational ties. For these ties to be considered right and proper (*savasava*, literally, pure, clean) and in balance, respect for protocol or tradition must be shown at all times. Not to have enough *tabua* to offer in mortuary exchanges is shameful (*madua*). Bakker (1986: 200) describes how a state of imbalance of relations between clans 'brought about by deliberate performance of an unclean act, such as elopement', termed as polluted (*duka*), must be restored through rituals of cleansing (*oga*) to a pure and clean (*savasava*) state.

Finally, the story of the possibly missing *tabua*, on a par with the ideal of 'tradition is tradition', also raises the question of whether things are ever done in exactly *the right way*, and indeed whether they were ever done correctly in that oft-romanticised past that people in any culture refer to when they criticise the apparent deterioration of present values. Perhaps the illusory aspect is an intrinsic part of the ideal of tradition? As a colleague once pointed out to me, there is always someone who takes it upon him or herself to be the adjudicator of whether a ritual is performed correctly or not, and whether it is itself part of the ritual.[7] In any ceremonial or ritual there will always be debate, and often dissension among participants as to whether things were done in *the right way*, following a given protocol.

In a way, this is an intrinsic element of any ritual, since ritual in itself implies a repeated course of action, a repeated way of doing things. Since nothing is ever done in exactly the same way by exactly the same people, ritual will always be open to criticism. Often in a similar manner to romanticising the past, people will point out that *in the old days* things were done in the right way, but these days things have become slack.

What is interesting, then, is not so much whether this *tabua* presentation did or did not take place. More interesting are the reflections the possible omission generated: the considerations of *the right way* of doing things and people's collective responsibility to adhere to the markers of traditional respect. What also emerges from this account is the issue of pragmatism. When I told this story to other women in Suva they were not surprised. They nodded their heads and said that yes, they too had experienced similar things, that 'nowadays people often don't do things the right way'. Because there are more and more demands on people, the women told me, often people do not reciprocate presentations of *tabua* in the customary way, by giving as many in return as were received. Instead they hoard them. This means that there are fewer *tabua* in circulation, which leads to people having to buy them, rather than acquire them through traditional exchange networks.

So three problems present themselves in this situation: the pressure of collective expectations to adhere to traditional protocol; the socio-cultural consequences of not doing so and thereby disrupting the balance of reciprocal exchange in kinship relations; and pragmatic considerations such as the economic cost of following tradition.

---

7   I thank Jonathan Schwartz for pointing this out. See Sjørslev 1992 re 'mistakes' and non-symbolic elements in ritual.

Where I come from [Cakaudrove province] people (usually women) [often remark] on or [make] references to other women whose faces are often seen in funerals as an excuse to obtain or get material wealth such as tapa or mats. Funerals are opportunities for women who usually become part of the *bikabika* (vigil) to amass traditional wealth. This wealth may be only one or two pieces of items but the perception of the kin is interesting ... [also regarding] who gets what, how much and the quality of the *masi* or mats, even to the details of who got a particular item that was part of the presentation from a particular *reguregu* group. They especially watch ... what the leader(s) of the *bikabika* gets. This 'disease' (of material greed) is also encroaching on men. In a funeral I attended, it was related to me how some men were wondering where a big *tabua,* presented to the *matanivanu*a had gone when they needed it to present to one of the *reguregu* group. Men have become more aware of traditional wealth, or they have always been but have never really voiced their interest until recently. (Eta Varani, pers comm. 2009)

The dilemma of kinship

We're not like you gang, you know ... you can just go to a funeral ... For us, it's very hard. The law of the land is hard ... we can't go to all funerals, you know ... you go to one ... you miss one. (Elder of the *Henibua* clan, November 1997)

It was November 1997 and I had asked one of my classificatory fathers why we would not, after all, be taking part in the Hundredth Night celebrations (*vakabogidrau*) of the death of an old lady whose funeral my family and I had attended in a nearby village. I had counted the days until Hundredth Night and had looked forward to returning to observe how the important lifting of the mourning rites would be celebrated in the village of the chief of the *vanua* (clan). 'You can't go here and there all the time', my father said, 'you can't just go and drink *yaqona* ... you have to bring something – kerosene, mats ... it all costs. We gave two cows for Tai's funeral, that's F$300 ... then there was the funeral in LaseLase ... and last week the funeral in Malevu'.

My father's explanation differentiates between Europeans, who can attend funerals without having to contribute valuables, and Fijians who, following traditional obligations, should contribute financially or materially to any funeral they attend (and often those they don't attend). Quite simply, Fijians cannot afford to go to all funerals.

The temptations of tradition

My translator in Suva, a former Methodist from Nadrogā, now pastor in a Pentecostal church, Pastor Ratu Meli Navuniyasi, views the Fijian focus on traditional funerary rites and exchanges as a form of spiritual temptation. It draws people's attention away from God, and is therefore morally and spiritually dangerous. A person's time, Pastor Navuniyasi said, would be better spent in developing their relationship with God:

> We need to do away with these customs. [They are] a big drawback in Fijian society ... you just sit there drinking grog [kava] ... better to be studying the Bible, reading hymns ... If we think out our time ... the sooner you bury someone, the better ... After joining the Pentecostal Church I read my Bible ... my spiritual being tells me what to do. If I go to a funeral, I make my presentation ... a mat from the wife and drum of kerosene from the husband. If [it is] close family [you bring] *bulumakau* (cow), bags of sugar (40-50 kg, about F$40-50) [£20-25], bags of flour, *tabua* ... If they have tea[8] for me, I have that, otherwise [I] just take the next bus [home].

Pentecostal journalist Mere Momoivalu defined Pentecostal interpretations of Fijian funerary rites even more sharply:

> We must re-look at traditional Fijian ways ... Sometimes we honour the dead in an idolatrous way. Why put on a show – [F]$10,000 down the drain when someone dies? ... Why pay respect to a person who's dead? ... We come to idolise the dead [in that way]... and [by the focus on] food ... There are things that people practise that are not of God [such as] *yaqona* drinking and over-indulgence ... the standing of a person is dependent on how much food you can lay out ... how much you can take away ... There is an element of greed [in this] ... [many people] go [to a funeral] with the intent of getting something back from it. (Momoivalu, interview 16 June 1998)

This comment reflects in particular two central points of Pentecostal beliefs: firstly the issue of 'idolatry' and 'idolisation of the dead', and secondly the issue of the body and consumption of food. This perspective has historical roots in Protestant condemnation of Roman Catholic practices of praying for the souls of the dead, seen as tantamount to worshipping the dead, as blasphemy and akin to the ancestral worship in paganism.

The 'double death' of bereavement

Fijian notions of doing things, 'the Fijian way' or 'in the way of the land' are almost always posited in hierarchical opposition to 'the way of the Indians' or 'the way of Europeans', implying that because of their system of kinship, Fijians care

---

8 A generic term that could mean tea, coffee, cocoa, Milo, often accompanied by bread and butter or sandwiches or boiled root crops; or it could mean a main evening meal. Pentecostals [and SDAs] do not drink any form of stimulant and do not categorise cocoa as such.

more for each other than do Indo-Fijians or Europeans. Among Fijians there seems to be competition for where the most elaborate and most traditional ceremonies take place. In the village where I lived, I was told that funeral rites in that area were by far the most elaborate in all Fiji. However, Momoivalu's description of Fijian mortuary customs inverts the ideals of Fijian tradition, questions their contemporary use and validity, and criticises what she terms as the Fijian community's 'preoccupation with food and goods':

> The Fijian death business has become very expensive and has been likened by some to a party in comparison to the subdued style of other communities … Fijian deaths have been called in some circles as the *mate vakarua* (double death) where one who has a death in the family also experiences a financial death. (Momoivalu in *Fiji Times* 8 November 2006: 7)

Momoivalu's views of 1996 are echoed in a 1998 newspaper article on a prominent Methodist funeral in Tailevu province which, in accordance with the wishes of the deceased, had been very low-key, with next to no traditional exchanges. This funeral was noted in *The Daily Post* (21 June 1998: 7) as 'being honoured as the ice-breaker on death tradition':

> It is time we reassessed our Fijian tradition in time of a death. The tradition is a ritual which has embedded itself so deep in the hearts of the indigenous Fijians that change is hard. It's a delicate issue that needs reassessing. But as one family has shown, change need not hurt the bereaved or the memory of the deceased.

Former Fiji Consul-General to New Zealand and retired university lecturer Meli Waqa is quoted as saying:

> Traditions to do with death are crippling indigenous Fijians – financially and psychologically. It boggles the mind to think of all the unnecessary aspects [of a funeral] that many a time are not attributed solely towards the deceased or the bereaved family … it's a double blow on the family when it comes to funerals – the sad loss of a family member and the financial burden of catering for all that come to offer condolences. (*Daily Post* 21 June 1998: 7)

In an interview with me Meli Waqa (21 July 1998) elaborated on this. He explained how the system of reciprocity in Fijian society is eroding, at the same time as people, especially those living in urban areas, have to buy many more of the goods they formerly would have either grown or borrowed for funeral contributions:

> I feel it's gone overboard now … we feel that the people who are the relatives of the dead suffer twice – one they've lost a loved one and two, they are lumbered with a lot of this … wastage … particularly costs … whereas previously … things tended to just be brought from what you possessed … most of the things

now have to be purchased ... Basically, the men take *tabua* ... the women take mats and *tapa* ... [to a funeral]. And a group will take food, usually *dalo* [taro] and maybe a pig, depending on ... how you are related to the dead person. Now all this has to be purchased. Previously the whale's teeth circulated and ... if you had nothing you went to a person and borrowed, in the knowledge that when he is short, he will come back to you.

Now it doesn't happen. People go and borrow, but there is no reciprocity, or very little, particularly with *tabua*. And in some areas of Fiji, you may have learnt, when you present one, one is given back to you. Now [when] you present a *tabua,* they give you *yaqona*. Which is not what was done in the past, at least not in my area. So because there is no reciprocity, you tend to go and purchase, and *tabuas* are being sold now. And Fijians measure things by size – the bigger, the better – and for *tabua* to a funeral, you are talking about [F]$100 [£50] and above, for one *tabua .* And with food – you have to buy the *dalo* [taro] ... a pig, or [a] bullock ... all these amount to a lot. Besides, it's not only the people who are going, it's also the people who ... have to feed these thousands or hundreds [of guests] ... when you go to a presentation you expect, and are expected, to eat. And then this is a modern version, not only do you eat, sometimes you sleep there. And in some cases, particularly in the urban areas, you take food back with you.

Almost 10 years later a letter in *The Fiji Times* expressed similar sentiments (J.B. Raiova, 13 September 2005):

The expression 'Fijian traditional values and democracy are at odds' as uttered by the powerful to the powerless should not be allowed to exist in the public domain unchallenged. Tradition is an illusion of permanence. Nothing under heaven remains the same, including the evolved contemporary Fijian so-called traditional obligations, such as ... *bulubulu, somate, reguregu* ... If it wasn't for democracy and Western culture, the form that all these ceremonies stand for would be quite different ... from that practised by our forefathers, let alone practised at all. Ironically today, if it wasn't for Western technology such as refrigeration and air travel we would not have our dearly departed *Tutua* (grandfather) in the morgue while we waited for *Tubuna* (grandson) in the British Army to fly in from Germany and hence prolong our *somate* (funeral gathering) for two weeks while the grieving feasted free on Tubuna's hard-earned pounds, shilling and pence for the similar duration.

A view of traditional funeral rites as being wasteful and a hindrance to economic development was also put to me by Pastor Navuniyasi:

The most important point is the burial, the putting in the ground. [That is the] last thing I can do for that person. All other things are exchanges between the living: exchange of words, material, food. He (the dead person) doesn't know

[about what goes on] ... we have to bury him. Finished. Everything else is a
waste – time, energy, money ... (interview 29 May 1998)

This pragmatic view of traditional funeral rites and obligations emphasises the cost
in money and labour, and the waste of resources expended on rites that are directed
mainly towards the living. Preserving these rites is seen as shackling Fijians to
the past, restricting them in moving ahead in contemporary society, and holding
them behind other ethnic groups, like the Indo-Fijians, in business and commerce.
Pastor Navuniyasi continued:

The longer we ... preserve these rites the lesser chance we give the Fijian ... it
keeps them clinging to these rites. The *reguregu* should only be half ... [there
should be] less [of] everything. (Ibid.)

Pragmatics aside, this approach tallies well with the focus in many Pentecostal
churches on the individual's necessary break with the past in order to embrace a
new future in Jesus Christ. It also ties in with Pentecostal emphasis on moderation
versus over-indulgence. The pastor goes on to view funerals from a developmental
point of view:

Fiji is very young and too old at the same time. [If] we want to reach the level of
exchange (development) ... we have to *bridge* [the old and the new] ... [There]
has to be some forum [for] Fijians, making legislation [regarding funerals].
People have to be buried [by] the fifth day. The arm of modernisation is [the]
government – [the] Western system. [There should be] a bridging program from
the government between Westernisation and [tradition]. The NLC [Native Land
Council] and the NLTB [Native Land Trust Board] and the BLV [*Bose Levu
Vakaturaga,* Great Council of Chiefs] are bringing modern things to tradition.
The protocol in villages never wears out – modernisation has to be brought in
by people from within who have been educated ... Like in Cautata in Tailevu
[where funerals are conducted in a much reduced fashion].

The idea of Fijian ceremonial obligations incurring the waste of resources at the
cost of development is not new. It was a focus of the colonial government. (Cf.
Burns Commission in Belshaw 1964: 126 and Spate 1959: 22-27) However, in
the 1960s Belshaw (1964: 52-53), from an economic anthropological perspective,
took issue with the modernist colonial view on traditional obligations, stating that
they did not in fact hinder development. On the contrary, Belshaw maintained that
the demand for ceremonial goods also creates production.

It would seem obvious, however, that the more money Fijians feel obliged to
spend on traditional obligations, the less there is for them to invest in business
or the development of villages. This is a common view in urban Fijian circles.
At the same time, although Pastor Navuniyasi points to the need for government
legislation in this area, he also recognises that change must follow traditional

patterns of authority, must come from chiefly leadership within villages, and must be passed down to the people. Like Meli Waqa earlier in this section and the comment in *The Fiji Times*, he also refers to the contemporary extension of the period between death and burial, and the increase in expenditure this engenders on all sides.

Changing traditions

The village of Cautata in Tailevu province to which Pastor Navuniyasi refers as practicing a reduced style of funeral customs, is located in a verdant corner of south-eastern Vitilevu. With (in 2005) 100 households, 4 *mataqali* (clans) and 13 *tokatoka* (lineage groups), it is one of the largest villages in the province. For more than 35 years Cautata has conducted funerals in a different way from traditional Eastern Fijian mortuary rites. According to the village spokesman in a discussion with Mrs Sainimere Niukula and myself in Cautata in October 2005, the then ruling chief and elders of the village decided as far back as 1966 to cut down on funeral rites to minimise the financial burden on the bereaved. Some families could afford lavish funeral arrangements, he said, while others could not. Those who could not afford grand funerals felt ashamed (*madua*). In an effort to avoid this division between the well-off and poorer families in the village, the elders suggested a number of radical amendments to tradition, which were put to the villagers. There was general consensus as to implementing these changes.

Firstly, it was decided that the *reguregu* was to take place over a limited number of days only. If the burial is on a Saturday, then the *reguregu* is not to start before Thursday afternoon or Friday. This is something that is made clear in the announcement of the death on Fiji Radio. Furthermore, during the *reguregu* (*vura cālevu* in Nadrogā) the family of the deceased are not obliged to feed people from the village. This counts out a large number of the closest kin. Food would only be provided during the *reguregu* for those who come from outside the village. Secondly, the *burua* was seriously cut down. Eastern Fijian mortuary customs include a large post-burial feast, and the re-distribution of raw meat, known as *burua*, from the 'owners of the deceased' to all the gathered mourners, in reciprocity for the mortuary gifts they bring. Cautata village, I was told, changed this ceremonial distribution of raw meat into one of cooked meat in the form of a funeral feast for the mourners. So Cautata limited the *burua* to just the post-burial feast.

In a high-profile funeral I attended elsewhere in Tailevu in 1996 there was a delicious and extravagant meal for all mourners after the burial. This was followed by the *burua*: a large number of portions of freshly cut, raw cow's meat were placed in a long line on the grass, and the village spokesman ceremoniously called out the name of each clan that was to receive a portion. This was in addition, it should be noted, to the food and *yaqona* consumed by the same clan members over the days of the *reguregu* before the actual day of burial. This costly re-distribution of mortuary gifts, then, is one of the things that Cautata have cut out of their funerals.

According to the elders of Cautata I spoke to, as a further restriction no *yaqona* is drunk in the village on the day of the interment, until the actual burial. After it, before the funeral feast, male members of close relatives gather in the community hall for *na gunu*, a ceremonial drinking of *yaqona* that is limited to only 10 *bilo* (cups presented to hierarchically-honoured kin members) and 10 *rabe* (cups in between each *bilo* to less hierarchically-important men). The 'owners of the deceased' thus present the close relatives with this *yaqona* and with cigarettes and matches – nothing else. After the feast comes the end of the funeral.

A Fijian woman from another area, hearing of these particular rites of exchange, commented to me that it would surely be more sensible to exchange flour, sugar and rice, necessary products for a whole family's consumption, rather than cigarettes that are unhealthy and generally only used by men.

Bogi va (Fourth Night (corresponding to *bogi lima*, Fifth Night in Nadrogā rites)) and *bogi tini* (Tenth Night), both involving extensive exchanges and drinking of *yaqona*, were cancelled. According to the village spokesman, 'if the close relatives want to do just a little to remember the deceased on these two occasions, they can, but they are not obliged to cater for anyone else'. The gifts that one *tokatoka* (which in this area generally consists of about six families) would expect to give or receive in a *reguregu* in 2005 amount to the following: 1 pig (at a value of F$3-400); 10 mats; 10 bundles of taro (at a value of F$100), 1 *tabua*, and 1 kg *yaqona*. A typical *reguregu* would nevertheless cost a *tokatoka* (lineage group of about 6 households) about F$800.

How had people from outside responded to such radical changes? I asked. Some of the women told us that when they had married into the village they had at first been ashamed of these restrictions, but then had grown used to them. 'Some think we are not doing justice to the dead', a man conceded. 'They say this outright when they come'. But on the other hand, another man commented: 'It's not stopped people coming here'.

Similarly to the men of the village in Nadrogā, the men of Cautata were in no doubt as to the most important aspect: 'how we are going to feed the people coming to the funeral'.

Kerekere and the cost of tradition

The ideals of 'sharing or reciprocal love (*fetokoni'aki* in Tongan, *fetufaai* in Samoan and *veitokoni* in Fijian …) inherent also in the *wantok* system in Melanesia' (cf quote by Father Paunga at the start of this chapter) are in Fiji based on the notion of *kerekere*. As described earlier kin members give to others through love and respect for kinship ties, secure in the knowledge that when one day they will need help, they will be able to turn to kin members and receive the same. In a University of the South Pacific collection of papers from 1986 on urban life in Fiji, Suguta (1986: 186) describes this ideal of kin-based giving and sharing:

> Giving is central to the Fijian way of life ... [and] allied with this concept is another – sharing. What is given is shared by others ... Whatever a person possesses is shared by others of his kin, so in the Fijian world view there is no such thing as 'ownership' in the Western sense, only possession. This concept of possession is built around the institution of *kerekere* which essentially means that whatever one possesses may be transferred to another for the latter's use. The donor need not worry, for his turn to become a donee will come around sooner or later! (see also Rika 1986)

Described somewhat tersely by Capell (1991: 85) as 'a system of gaining things by begging for them from a member of one's own group', the *kerekere* system[9] is supposed to be reciprocal, yet this deeply revered cultural value has always been open to exploitation through greedy and anti-social behaviour and misuse by individuals who seek to sponge off relatives and not repay their debts (*dinau*) – debts understood more as favours than cash.

In many cases the *kerekere* system sadly does not work as smoothly or ideally as Suguta implies. Some people see *kerekere* merely as an easy means of gaining new things. A young mother in the village told me how one should never flaunt anything pretty such as clothes, since people would then inevitably ask to borrow them, and you would never see them again. Another woman told me how her collection of nice crockery and kitchen utensils inevitably disappeared into other homes while she was at work, '*kerekere*'d' by other villagers, never to be returned.

Even though the system of reciprocity did not always function very well in practice, and people understandably complained, villagers invariably described to me with pride the ideal of sharing and caring they felt was such an important value in their lives. Yet these ideals are increasingly being eroded by the forces of globalisation and the spread of Western values such as individualism and consumerism, the desire for individual acquisition and accumulation – and the greed and anti-social behaviour that tends to go with it.[10]

It is very difficult to refuse a *kerekere*: to do so is, in effect, to refuse to nurture and care for a kin member, and goes against all ideals of *vanua*. Many Fijians believe that such violations of kinship ties and the way of the land may bring about punishment, such as illness, from the ancestral spirits (*mate ni vanua*) or worse misfortune. At the same time *kerekere* is also invariably given the blame for the lack of incentive, enterprise and economic development in the Fijian community,

---

9   Compare Spate 1959: 24-25, Sahlins 1962: 203-214, 314, 1993, Toren 1990, Barr 1990: 121, 130, Thomas 1992a: 72, 1992b, 1993, Sahlins 1993, Monsell-Davis 1993.

10   Teaiwa (2000) discusses this aspect of greed and the eroding of morals in relation to the looting that took place during Cyclone Gavin in 1997, at the site of the Air Fiji flight 121 crash on Vitilevu in 1998, and during the coup of 2000.

since anyone making money from a job or investments will be pressurised to contribute financially to one kin member after another.

Momoivalu (*Fiji Times* 8 November 1996: 7) criticises the costly nature of Fijian traditional obligations:

> You know you're truly back home when traditional financial obligations known as *oga* jolt you from your holiday reverie ... It's public knowledge that we Fijians live in a perpetual cycle of [*oga*] ... Fijians constantly lament and despair about the cost of keeping up with these traditions and many urban Fijians in particular are of the view that they have become cumbersome and financially ruinous in some cases.

This article and other articles and letters already referred to reflect the concerns of a growing number of urban Fijians, many of whom have spent most of their lives in towns rather than villages, and who consider the complexities of traditional kinship obligations a heavy burden. As members of the new urban elite of educated Fijians, and as clan members earning good salaries, they experience endless demands to provide materially for their less well-off kinsmen to help meet the costs of funerals, weddings and the like. In 1986, Vusoniwailala wrote similarly (1986: 166) of the financial cost of kinship obligations:

> After six years in the United States, my family returned to Fiji early in 1982. Our early weeks back home were spent doing the social rounds visiting friends and relatives. There were customary feasts known as *vakamamaca* ('the drying') accorded to kinsfolk who have just returned from across the seas, with kin on my father's side as well as with kin on my mother's side. There were two similar feasts arranged by my wife's kin; again, one prepared by her father's side and another by her mother's side. As it is customary ... we had to reciprocate with gifts or Fijian valuables. But since we had just returned from America, we did not have any traditional valuables ... [and] we had to reciprocate with cash ... As we met relatives, we were also acquainted with their individual and collective economic problems ... Tradition expects a Fijian to respond positively to lighten the economic woes of kin.

Vusoniwailala describes the changing values and priorities of urban Fijians in particular, and emphasises how what, ideally, is a traditional system of reciprocity enabling material goods and foods to be circulated between clan members easily becomes a one-sided system of cash-flow from the 'haves' to the 'have-nots'. While this is a comment from more than 20 years ago, it is even more valid in today's Fiji, with the increasing move from rural to urban areas, increasing unemployment, leading to lack of opportunity and growing poverty.

Vusoniwailala outlines a number of reasons explaining why keeping up these communal kinship obligations is paralysing many Fijians. The principal ones he cites (1986: 169) are an expansion of the 'geographical area of the kinship field' due to easier transport between the islands and telephone and mail communications; and 'the widening of Fijians' perception of the kind of persons and social networks requiring communal participation'. Whereas, as Vusoniwailala points out, Fijians formerly tended to practice endogamous marriage alliances more or less within the same area, Vusoniwailala (1986: 170) sees greater mobility as bringing about changes in these marriage practices and thus broadening kinship networks. As Vusoniwailala also writes, kinship obligations include extending hospitality to unemployed relatives.[11] Then distant family members may suddenly turn up in the village and ask to stay. Children who are sent to school in Suva may also spend years living in the household of a city uncle. Friends of mine with well-paid jobs in Suva told me in 2005 that they put aside part of their pay each month so that they always have ready cash for relatives in need. Yet however much they put aside, it is never enough.

Why, asks Vusoniwailala (1986: 176-177), do people continue to maintain such traditions when they are becoming increasingly expensive and difficult to keep up? He points to a number of factors: that people feel that 'tradition wills them to'; that whatever it may cost them, they are proud to do their utmost to maintain their communal obligations; that Fijians, like other Pacific Islanders, have a predisposition to wish to share what little they have with their kinsmen; and that many people are maintaining traditional obligations because of the social pressures and stigma attached to turning their backs on them. Vusoniwailala points to the element of 'social entertainment' in communal gatherings as weighing heavily in favour of maintaining traditional obligations; and finally 'the Fijian's need to retain his ethnic identity in multicultural Fiji'.

A recent comment from a Fijian woman academic, formerly resident in Sydney for many years, highlights, however, a quite different and important perspective to funeral gatherings:

> While I entirely agree with comments by Momoivalu, Vusoniwailala and your Pentecostal informants on sustaining or eliminating traditional practices that are irrelevant and uneconomical, they have overlooked … the psycho-emotional side of the funeral gathering of kin networks. I became acutely aware of this when both my parents died. Isolated from the rest of the family network support, I developed a depression. The numerous telephone calls and visits to Fiji have helped a great deal but it brought on home to me the importance of kinship network. Just the thought of sitting and enjoying each others company, catching up with everyday gossip, participating in other life-rituals without necessarily making an attempt to consciously address my grief, are a therapy unto themselves. (Eta Varani, pers comm. 2009)

---

11   See, in particular, Gounis and Rutz 1986, and Barr 1990, Monsell-Davis 1986, 1993, 2000 and nd regarding urban youth, unemployment and poverty, Bryant and Khan 1990, Bryant 1993, Schade 1999, Khan and Barr 2003, Barr 2005a, Narsey 2006, Rakuita 2007 on poverty.

Tradition and the forces of globalisation

'Times are hard', villagers told me when discussing the logistics of contributing to funerals. 'We have to do too much'. But at the same time people were proud of their traditions and couldn't really see how to change things. Maintaining tradition becomes for many people a difficult balance between keeping up traditional obligations and having enough money for essentials. 'You can only do what you can; you cannot "spear the moon" (*cokacoka na vula*)', as someone once said to me.

Maintaining tradition not only has a financial cost, but may also result in the diversion of necessary funds for food, medicine and education, as *The Fiji Times* (18 November 2002, quoted in Halapua 2003: 151) comments in relation to a Great Council of Chiefs meeting. This addressed the problem of the cost of tradition for many Fijians:

> Too often the cost of these social obligations become too big a burden on the family budget but [are] viewed and accepted as necessary. Some families cut back on family money budgeted for food, education and medicine to meet the demands of the extended family or the traditional community. It puts a lot of pressure on the family to meet these commitments which they cannot afford but are too embarrassed to admit.

Halapua remarks (2003: 151) in relation to this: 'Never before in the history of Fiji has the abyss between the "haves" and "have-nots" been so wide'. A decade earlier Monsell-Davis (n.d.: 13), discussing the pressures of dealing with traditional obligations, pointed to a growing clash of values in Fijian society between normative pressures for equality and sharing, and the reality of the scarcity of monetary and material wealth. 'While money has become a part of the presentations on all kinds of ceremonial occasions, it is not redistributed through the community in the same way as economic necessities in former times'.

And at the same time as traditional structures of reciprocity seem to be eroding in the face of increasing economic pressures, and the financial cost of keeping up kinship commitments is increasing, the staging of funerals and other life-cycle rituals has become more elaborate. Indeed, more than 20 years ago Bakker (1986: 196) noted with regard to ritual practices in urban settings, 'ceremony, far from decreasing in complexity and incidence [in urban contexts] is in fact both more complex and significant than ever before'. (1986: 196)

For example, although commitments to mark a death traditionally end with the Hundredth Night celebration of the lifting of the mourning (*vakataraisulu*) people also increasingly mark the first anniversary of the death. New family celebrations have been added to the many existing traditional life-cycle feasts – for example a child's first, 16th and 21st birthdays, the last two of which are particularly elaborate affairs in which both traditional valuables are exchanged, Western style wrapped gifts are given, and a large feast is provided for relatives by the family of the offspring. In addition to this, well-commercialised special days such as Mother's Day, Father's Day, Grandfather's Day and Valentine's Day are increasingly celebrated, giving rise, as does Christmas and to a lesser degree the Indian festival, Diwali, to infinite opportunities for spending and consuming. As Father Kevin Barr from the ecumenical organisation, ECREA, points out, 'the real scandal is how many of these goods purchased on special occasions for Christmas, Easter, Mother's Day, Diwali etc, are then later repossessed?'. (Barr, pers comm. April 2006)

In rural villages, far from urban centres, villagers still rely mainly on traditional foods grown in village gardens, fish and shellfish from the sea or rivers, pig and occasionally beef. The proximity of an urban centre to the village I lived in meant, however, that the temptation to buy food like bread, margarine and frozen chickens was considerable. Eating bread and butter or margarine saved time in preparing meals and was therefore increasingly popular, but it was also expensive, since the amount of bread needed to satisfy Fijian appetites, used to mounds of root crops as their staple diet, is quite considerable. Cassava from one's garden costs nothing.

The desire to buy Western foods and accumulate consumer goods influences people's life styles and changes their eating habits – a problem throughout the Pacific Island region. The impact of American-style fast food on the already heavily starchy diet of Pacific Islanders is considerable, resulting in a dramatic increase in diabetes and heart disease. (See e.g. *Pacific Islands Monthly*, May 1998: 22-23) Especially urban Pacific Islander diets have become progressively unhealthy, and are increasing the need for ready cash in household budgets. *Islands Business* January 2006: 7 notes that one of its first cover stories, published more than 20 years ago, entitled 'Diet of Death', is even more relevant today:

> It dwelt on the damage that Pacific Islanders were doing to themselves by poor diet. They were forsaking nutritious traditional food, mainly local vegetables and fruit, for imported sugary junk. Obesity, heart disease, hypertension and diabetes rates were climbing alarmingly … With just a few updates here and there, Diet of Death could be reproduced in next month's *Islands Business* as still being a valid commentary on the region's present state of health.

In addition to annual church payments (especially Methodist Church members), to which each household has to contribute considerable sums, luxury foods and goods are adding to the increasing expenses households have to meet with cash payments. They include school fees, school bus fares, uniforms, books, electricity bills, and, for urban households, rent. Halapua points to the break-up of leadership values based on reciprocity and generosity since the coups of 1987 as being the cause of poverty in Fiji:

> *Vanua* is a legacy of the past generations in trust for the future. The *turaga* (chiefs) were supposed to be the custodians of reciprocity and generosity of the *vanua*. But the modern day *turaga*, the Fijian ruling class emerging after 1987,

completely reversed the process. Their interests came first; the others' interests came much later. Poverty, as a consequence of accumulation by the Fijian ruling classes and the bourgeoisie, signals the reversal of the integrity of the *vanua*. (2003: 151)[12]

Chapters 3 and 4 have described and discussed the vital role gift-giving and ceremonial presentation plays in the dynamics of Fijian and Pacific Islander social relations and sense of identity, and how these ritualised expressions of connectedness and belonging link people to each other and to the land, nourishing kinship relations and bringing the past and also the future into the time of the present.

Chapter 4 has also discussed changing attitudes to traditional ceremonial, and criticisms of the financial burden kinship obligations also represent to many people, as Fiji society experiences increasing globalisation, urbanisation, a fast-growing consumer culture and an ever-widening gap between rich and poor. Connecting with comments by Pentecostals in this chapter, in Chapter 5 Pentecostal Christians, as members of a spiritual community which distances itself from many traditional practices, discuss how best they can balance their faith and identity as Pentecostal Christians with Fijian tradition. The chapter discusses how *spiritual* gift-giving and reciprocity, expressed through the ritualised core Pentecostal practice of testimony, connects people to each other and creates new networks and relationships through the sharing of spiritual experience.

---

12   See e.g. Norton 2007 on the changing role of the Great Council of Chiefs since 1987, Lawson 1997 on chiefs and politics in Fiji.

Chapter 5

Roots and Powerful New Currents: Redefining Christianity and Tradition

The foundation this nation was built on

On a hot and humid Sunday morning in Suva in November 2004, in a packed church holding more than 3,000 people, Reverend Suliasi Kurulo, Senior Pastor at World Harvest Centre, made an impassioned appeal for his church's 'mission to the unreached' in rural Tanzania.

World Harvest Centre, the flagship of the highly successful Pentecostal church in Fiji, Christian Mission Fellowship (CMF), is an enormous round building with an interior design akin to a modern amphitheatre. It houses up to 3,800 people on terraced seating extending steeply upwards and outwards from a half-moon-shaped stage. Flags from all over the world hang down from the ceiling. Sitting in the midst of the church you have a strong sense of being connected to the whole world. A woman from the church 'cell group' I attended in the course of my research, explained to me: 'Sometimes we pray for particular countries', she said, 'and then when we look up and see the flag of that country we feel even closer to the place'.

Sitting there that morning beneath the colourful canopy of flags I too experienced a clear sense that we were indeed connected to the world. The service was being transmitted live on radio and TV via Trinity Broadcasting Network Fiji, housed next to the church, and reaching out to private homes in Vitilevu. We were part of a big, powerful, expansive and influential church. We were part of a church that really feels as if it is spiritually and materially closely linked to the world, a church that is really Going Somewhere.

As a rather different introduction to his sermon, we were shown a short video of Reverend Kurulo's (or Pastor Suli as he is fondly known within the church) mission trip. This was projected mega-size onto the extensive section of wall behind and above the stage where usually the texts of Bible passages and songs were projected during services. First the camera zoomed in on a map of the green Fiji Islands in the blue expanse of the South Pacific Ocean. Then an impressive stripe, coloured in the yellow and black, green and blue of the Tanzanian flag, flashed from Fiji right across the world to East Africa, symbolising the 'fast-track mission route' that is Pastor Suli's vision for the Church's future mission engagement in Africa.

Christian Mission Fellowship had at this time two missionaries in Tanzania, as well as missionaries in Burkino Faso, Tonga, Papua New Guinea, Australia, New

Zealand, the United States, Canada and England. Pastor Suli's sermon of more than an hour focused on *mission* and 'our responsibility as Christians' to take the Gospel out to the 'unreached', those who, he said, have not yet heard the Word of God. He links the values, changes and development that conversion to Christianity brought to Fiji in the 19th century with the responsibility of people in Fiji to take the Gospel out to others:

> The reason why we have the standard of living we do today in Fiji is because our forefathers were given that possibility ... in the name of the Gospel of Jesus Christ. When our forefathers ceded Fiji to Great Britain it was their wish that Fiji should remain a Christian nation – why? Because they understood that the importance of the Gospel wasn't just religious, but was the foundation that this nation was built on. (Kurulo, World Harvest Centre, 7 November 2004)

While he did not speak of Fiji being constitutionally declared a Christian state, Pastor Suli implicitly referred to the historical circumstances that those who promote the ideal of a Christian state in Fiji use as their main argument: that in the 1874 Deed of Cession between the Paramount Fijian chiefs and Queen Victoria, it was stated that Fiji should remain 'a Christian country'.

This chapter is concerned with how Pentecostals in Fiji[1] in their faith and faith practices relate to and redefine notions of *vanua*, tradition, continuity and change. While Methodism is closely interwoven with maintaining and strengthening clan ties and relations to the land, Pentecostals are first and foremost connected to God and one another and to global spiritual networks through a personal relationship with Christ.

Testifying in gratitude to the empowering qualities of this relationship and bearing witness to the strength of faith is a core ritual practice among Pentecostals. Testimony connects people to God and to each other and is where the boundaries between past and present, between a person's past values and actions and a person's changed spiritual self and their actions in the present, their experience and representation of transformation, conversion and change, are most clearly articulated.

This personal relationship to Christ which connects Pentecostals *through* Christ forms the lives of Pentecostals in Fiji, more than their belonging to *vanua*. At the same time, corresponding to the paradoxical nature of Pentecostalism, Chapter 2 described how some expressions of Pentecostalism in Fiji connect with the land: in the belief that the spiritual, moral and social relations of a community are reflected

---

1   See Newland 2006: 362-364 re Christian Mission Fellowship in Fiji, and for a critical view of Pentecostalism in Fiji see Barr 1998. Re Pentecostalism in the Pacific Island region see inter alia Ernst 1991, 1994a, 1994b, 2006 (ed.), Robbins 1995, 2001, 2003b, 2004a, 2009, Eves 2000, Fer 2005a, 2005b, 2005c, 2006, n.d., Stritecky 2001, Jorgensen 2005, Malogne-Fer 2006, Stewart and Strathern 2000, Stewart and Strathern (eds) 2001, Strathern and Stewart 2009, Telban 2009.

in the state of the land; and through exorcising demonic forces from the land. These central aspects of Pentecostalism – local/global relations and testimony, and the ways in which Fijians negotiate their identities as Pentecostals in relation to *vanua*, are the focus of this chapter.

Links through time and space

Pastor Suli's stories of his visit to Tanzania and the photos flashed onto the wall during his sermon were a modern version of 19th century European mission narratives from Africa and the Pacific Islands. Similarly to the narratives from a visit by Nau Mere[2] and a group of CMF women to highland Papua New Guinea, the focus on supporting CMF mission work and bringing the 'unsaved' to Christ in Tanzania, was accompanied by a 'heart of darkness': civilising imagery. By the grace of God, the Gospel of Christ and civilisation was brought to Fiji long before it reached the tribal peoples in Tanzania and highland Papua New Guinea. This gift of God calls for gratitude and service towards spreading Christianity and civilisation to those less fortunate. Mission work and evangelisation is also part of the global Pentecostal project (cf Coleman 2000b: 18) of fulfilling the 'Great Commission of spreading the Word to the whole world'.

Pastor Suli's sermon, its visual presentation and rhetorical imagery in the setting of World Harvest centre, with its canopy of national flags, captures and symbolises the dynamics and connectedness of time and space, the local and global, the roots of early mission work and the new seeds of contemporary evangelisation. It truly touched the hearts and evoked deep feelings in many people in the congregation, especially when he referred to the coming of Christianity to Fiji, and his linking of that and the responsibility of Fiji's people to bring the Word to the 'unreached'.

People were very moved, and several had tears in their eyes. A couple of women started to cry. One very devout woman from my cell group lay down prostrate on the floor in front of the stage, weeping loudly. Others, especially young people, on impulse went quietly down the many steps to the stage to lay a gift of money there for the mission work. When the three-hour service ended a friend from my cell group, who held a leadership position within the civil service, turned to me with shining eyes and deep commitment in her voice. She said: 'I am going to Africa. It's my calling. I know I am going'.

I was reminded of the testimony of another woman in the cell group. She comes from a village on the small island of Viwa, off the east coast of the largest island, Vitilevu, where one of the best-loved and most respected of English Methodist missionaries, John Hunt, lies buried. Hunt, one of the most visionary and culturally sensitive missionaries to Fiji, preached a strongly Gospel-based message of peace,

---

2   Pastor Suli's wife. Nau, was the respectful term for a pastor's wife used among church members.

translating the New Testament into Fijian before his premature death at 36 in 1848. (See Thornley 2000, Barr 2000: 26)

This woman told us how she had recently returned to her village on Viwa island for the first time in seven years, and how she had visited John Hunt's grave there. She expressed how moved she had been, standing there thinking about how young he was when he died; how he had brought the Gospel to her great, great grandfather, and had translated the 'English Bible' [New Testament] into Fijian. There is a hill there where John Hunt used to go and pray, and she had gone up there and prayed for four hours, reflecting on his life and thinking of the sacrifice he had made for her forefathers' sake. She explained to us how she felt an enormous debt towards John Hunt and the other missionaries who came to Fiji, and a tremendous responsibility to carry forth the Light that they had brought to the Islands. This woman clearly saw herself connected through her clan history and as a Christian to John Hunt and the coming of Christianity to the Islands – very clearly connecting past, present and future and her responsibility as a Christian to continue John Hunt's ministry. Now it was her generation's turn to bring the Gospel to others, she told us. (Cell Group meeting, 22 October 2003)

This understanding of Christianity is common in Fiji. The coming of Christianity in people's minds belongs to a not-very-distant past and is an essential part of their cultural and historical sense of identity. To carry forth the Light to others through evangelisation is part of the responsibility that Pentecostals, especially, feel. To maintain and strengthen the Christian and moral values the missionaries brought to Fiji is another part of that responsibility. The woman's testimony binds together past, present and future, the spiritual and material, church and *vanua* in the image of actually standing on the land where John Hunt lived and preached the Gospel to her ancestors – while expressing her sense of calling to bring that same Gospel message out to others beyond the boundaries of Fiji. Possibly even to 'take the Gospel back to where it came from', as Reverend Kurulo called for in another sermon on 'Power Evangelisation' (World Harvest Centre 17 August 2003), pointing out how much Europe is in need of re-evangelisation.

In addition to the Christian obligation and desire to evangelise, the perspective of Fijian and Pacific Islander notions of reciprocity would, I suggest, make this gesture of returning the gift of faith to the descendants of those who first brought it to Fiji, now themselves grown spiritually poor, appear particularly appropriate. It must also be an empowering thought for a Fiji Christian that Fiji, though small in geographic terms, ranked among the Developing nations of the world, and with little impact on the global political stage, is in possession of a strength of Christian faith and spirituality now lacking in the rich, industrialised countries who once evangelised the world.

Reverend Kurulo's sermon illustrated the links between past, present and future, between historical and contemporary processes of globalisation. His words create a view of the past that emphasises the roots of the past, the perpetuation and maintenance of religious and cultural inheritance, yet simultaneously draws on the outward movement of evangelisation, of conversion, radical change, transformation and development. The Pentecostal movement itself, in doctrine and practice, embraces this simultaneous and paradoxical doubleness of deep conservatism, radical change and movement.

Local/global juxtapositions

Robbins (in press) outlines three basic criteria for why Pentecostal Christianity is so successful: that its rapid expansion across the globe indicates an ability to easily and quickly transcend cultural and linguistic barriers; that it is able to build strong and flourishing institutions in places where other institutions find it hard to gain a foothold, let alone grow; and that Pentecostalism is characterised by a high level of ritual activity.

Robbins, drawing also on Albrecht (1999) and Collins (2004) points to the shared coordinated bodily rituals in Pentecostalism, such as singing with arms upraised, as being easy to learn and follow, enabling people to quickly embody the framework of faith that connects them with others. This framework is encompassing, but is a moveable framework (cf Coleman in press) of ritualised behaviour that can be established between people in any situation or context, affirming people in their shared spirituality. 'It is Pentecostalism's promotion of ritual to the center of social life', Robbins writes,

> that has allowed it to travel so well and to build institutions so effectively even in socially harsh environments … its global spread and institution building capacities [depending] on its elaboration of a ritualized approach to social life (ibid: 25) … without the rituals, the institutions would not survive. Pentecostal doctrine on its own could not produce them successfully. (In press: 16)

Pentecostalism's 'moveable, ritual framework' (Coleman in press), evident in the healing of the land described in Chapter 2, is never more clearly expressed than in the staging, performance and experience of open-air evangelisation crusades which, despite their anonymity, enable people to feel actively part of a global spiritual community.

The transnational, unboundedness of Pentecostalism as a global religion and culture[3] that 'holds its shape as it travels' (Robbins 2001: 7) became particularly clear during German evangelist Reinhard Bonnke's *Fiji Fire Conference* in 2003. As is his style wherever he goes, Bonnke's visit caused a media uproar even before

---

3   See e.g. Ernst 1991, 1994a, 1994b, 2006, Poewe (ed.) 1994, Hexham and Poewe 1997, Marshall-Fratani 1998, Coleman 2000a, 2000b, Stewart and Strathern (eds) 2000, Robbins 2001, 2003b, 2004b, in press, Martin 2002.

his plane had landed[4] that continued throughout his stay and reverberated for weeks after his departure.

The excellently organised event attracted record numbers of people, special conference buses enabling thousands of people from rural areas and towns all over Vitilevu to participate in the three evening crusades at the National Stadium. An estimated 112,000 people attended the final evening. (Kurulo, interview 2003) An enormous team of counselors from different churches worked on the ground among the participants during the three evening crusades, offering support, guidance, counseling and prayers, handing out Bonnke *Now You Are Saved* booklets that offer advise to converts regarding the next steps to take after having decided to give their life to Christ. A young woman, studying at the AOG Bible College at the time, describes her experience:

> In terms of Personal Worship the Conference served [to build] my faith (even more) in God. It was a time for me to reflect upon His greatness and what He was able to do through me while I served at the conference. A time where the "still small voice" was as audible as ever, leading and guiding me every step of the way throughout the massive crowd which (apart from the believers), also contained many inquisitive, troubled and even demonic spirits that were amongst the people ... In terms of Co-operate Worship ... each individual, though involved in their various fields of responsibility, knew they were connected to God and through one another.
>
> ... Being a counsellor ... was an awesome but challenging experience. Awesome, because I got to be a part of one of the biggest events ever held in Fiji, and the fellowship I shared with other believers (who I met there) has been life-changing and very productive. Challenging, because culturally I was young, and I was a woman. (Although I am not a native Fijian, Fiji is my country of birth, and somehow the tradition and culture of the Fijian people is a part of me). Being able to counsel those older than me, and even drawing respect from the menfolk, speaks of the things that God can make possible in His own unique way. (Fiona Vamarasi, written testimony 2010)

While in no doubt of the superiority of God's power as protection and weapon, continuous demonic attacks are a reality Pentecostals face and deal with at all times (cf Chapter 2), such attacks being particularly strong and dangerous during crusades. Prior to and throughout the *Fire Conference* teams of on site Prayer Warriors conducted continuous spiritual warfare to protect the locations used and the people present from the demonic forces that would inevitably seek to disrupt

---

4   Cf *Daily Post* 19 September 2003: 1, 26 September 2003: 6, 27 September 2003: 7, *Fiji Times* 20 September 2003: 1,6,9, 23 September 2003, 24 September 2003, 25 September 2003: 6, 27 September 2003: 6, 30 September 2003: 2, 1 October 2003: 50, 2 October 2003: 6, 23 October 2003: 6, *The Sunday Post* 21 September 2003: 2,3,4, 28 September 2003: 6. See also Gifford 1992.

and destroy this manifestation of God's power. (Kurulo 2003, pers comm.) Critical representations of Bonnke and the Crusade by the *Fiji Times* were considered demonic attacks, and the Association of Christian Churches in Fiji (ACCF) responded from a spiritual warfare perspective: a full page announcement in the *Daily Post* (27 September 2003: 30) accused the *Fiji Times* of demonic actions and called on all ACCF members to boycott the paper for a month.[5]

A spiritual community of the moment

The Bonnke crusade's ritual framework facilitated an interwoven web of experience of the spiritual flow of divine power and energy, connectedness and community – personally between the individual and the divine; communally among the people present; from the evangelist and evangelism team on stage to the participants; and between participants and the imagined spiritual community the evangelist represents in the testimonies and stories of his evangelisation narratives. A spiritual community of the moment – yet with lasting reverberations for many.

Drawing participants in a series of different directions in a short space of time gave an empowering sense of travel and movement and infinite possibilities for change and transformation. Bonnke continuously referred to stories from many different African contexts and from his childhood in Europe. One minute we were hearing about a crusade in Kenya, the next we heard of the poverty of Bonnke's childhood in Germany during the Second World War and later in a refugee camp in Denmark, next we were in Congo, then in the Solomon Islands, London, the United States, South Africa.

The continuous shifts between past and present, between one geographical location and another, interwoven with strings of biblical narratives that likewise shifted seamlessly between Old and New Testament locales and landscapes, had the effect of creating a vast and ever-expanding imaginary landscape of opportunity, action and empowerment, of connectedness between peoples and nations. At certain points, though not often, Bonnke and other evangelists in his team made explicit reference to the Pacific Islands or to the ocean that connects them, these local images bringing us back to base, so to speak, giving us a momentarily familiar sense of who and where we were, inserting us into his narrative before the next story drew us somewhere else:

> Fiji is a small country, I know. But don't forget: the last shall be the first, and the smallest the greatest. That is just how God thinks of things. And you have all the potential that any other mighty nation may have … here is enough potential …

---

5   See *Fiji Times* response, 'Are those who merely ask questions now agents of the Devil?' 1 October 2003: 50.

Figure 5.1   Prayers, crusade night, *Fiji Fire Conference*, September 2003

to unhinge the gates of Hell a thousand times, in Jesus name! (Bonnke, teaching
session, 19 September 2003)

In Chapter 6 I argue that in an overseas Catholic charismatic priest's healing
services the blending of the liturgically and spiritually extraordinary, the turning
upside down of a particular spatial, bodily and social order in the familiar spatial
and social setting of a local church, enabled participants to open up to extraordinary
religious experience.

In this context participants may have heightened religious experiences for quite
different reasons: the combination of the overseas evangelist's *unboundedness*
of narrative, the *unboundedness* of spatiality and the relative *anonymity* of the
crusade, the enormous numbers of people present, the unusually loud music, noise
and bright lights, the large screens giving close-up views of the stage, accentuating
emotions and a sense of simultaneous dislocation and connectedness all combine
in creating a sense of individual spiritual and emotional empowerment. The

**Figure 5.2   Being prayed over, crusade night, *Fiji Fire Conference*,
September 2003**

atmosphere was at one and the same time orchestrated and ritualised, but within a
framework that afforded space for spontaneity of expression.

Flow and movement

In a similar, although obviously more low-key way to Bonnke's evangelisation
narratives, Reverend Kurulo's sermon about 'reaching out' to the 'unreached',
described at the start of this chapter, full of narratives from Tanzania, juxtaposing Fiji
everyday life and values with life in the African bush; the map of the world, projected
on the wall, that connected Fiji and Tanzania; the photos from Reverend Kurulo's
mission trip; and the flags of the world hanging from the roof, all contributed to a
similar sense of connectedness with people and faith communities elsewhere in the
world. Here again was a heightened sense of opportunities and possibilities, of the
possibility and necessity of movement and affecting change – evidenced for example

in the response of my friend, who felt so strongly at that moment that she had a calling to leave her comfortable life in Fiji and engage in mission work in Africa.

Coleman (2000b: 21) writes that the rhetoric of '"reaching out" assumes the presence of, and thereby also imaginatively constructs, an ... explicitly *globalized* religious landscape ... of evangelical agency and religio-political dimensions ... activated by movement: not only the motions of the body in explicit worship, but also forms of travel across nations of the world'. Bonnke himself is the literal embodiment of this. Yet in sharp and effective contrast to his expansive globalising narratives Bonnke also drew on tangible, domestic metaphors of enclosure and openness, drawing us back to the familiar:

> If it is true that the Holy Spirit is always blowing, why is it that some Christians don't feel it? ... [Because] when the Holy Spirit started to blow [they] locked all the windows in their churches, they closed all the doors. Outside the Holy Spirit was roaring! ... You don't need to fast for 40 days to get the wind inside your church: just open the door. Open the window and He will come in. He's been waiting for so long. He will come in, and what will happen? That musty air of religious tradition will be blown out, and resurrection springtime will be blown in – Hallelujah! May every church in Fiji be ventilated by the wind of the Holy Spirit! The old out, the new in![6]

Bonnke juxtaposes that which is enclosed and literally shut-off, a church with closed windows and doors, *containing* the tamed 'musty air of religious tradition', *keeping out* the wild, untameable, uncontrollable power of the Holy Spirit that roars like a lion or spiritual cyclone outside it – with a church with open doors and windows (a familiar image in the Pacific Islands), ventilated by the fresh and life-giving air of the Holy Spirit. Juxtapositions by Fijian Methodists and Pentecostals in the following likewise draw on metaphors of stability, movement and flow, openness and closedness, to express faith as rooted in the land; floating and unstable; as flowing rather than still water; as breaking down barriers.

A sermon by Christian Mission Fellowship pastor Arthur Morell (World Harvest Centre, 26 September 2004), preaching on John 5:1-10, the story of the cripple by the gate to the Bethesda pool, focused on the fact that this man had been stuck in the same situation as a crippled beggar for 38 years. The story was symbolic of not seeking to change and move on. 'The pool had no outlet. What is stored becomes stagnant ... This is a nice description of the churches we have today: lots of meetings, lots of water, [but] no outlet for the water'. Ezekial 47, the pastor continued, speaks of 'a temple with water flowing from it'. Like the image of the Holy Spirit roaring outside the church, here is a contrasting image of strength and movement, the current of the water moving it ever onwards. 'The life and monitor of the nation is the Church ... the deeper this church goes, the stronger the water flows', Pastor Morell emphasised.

---

6   Bonnke, evening crusade, 20 September 2003, see also Newland 2006: 342-344.

He later explained to me that the point of the story is that we cannot just stay still in our lives and expect to receive help, we have to make a conscious effort ourselves to open up to the power of God. Indeed Jesus asks the cripple 'Do you *want* to be healed?' And when the man answers yes, Jesus *commands* him to pick up his bed and go. These themes of movement and flow and conscious agency, as opposed to the containment of the 'stagnant pool' [that in this interpretation symbolises mainstream Christianity] signify spiritual empowerment and growth of individuals, churches and Christianity.

My kingdom is not of this world

In the Prologue, Methodist minister Reverend Tuima likened the links between spirit, soul and mind in Christian thought to the interweaving of Fijians with their land and tradition (*vanua*) and their Christian faith (*lotu*), two of the Three Pillars of Fiji society:

> You cannot differentiate a Fijian and his religion. My faith … is part of myself … like spirit, soul and mind … The soul is of God – what we believe, the Holy Spirit, the Spirit of God that works within us, to guide us, tell us the right thing and the wrong … Together with that you cannot differentiate a Fijian and his land – *vanua*. The *vanua* is part of me; I am a part of the *vanua* … it's a given gift of God to us. So we have to thank God. We worship God because of this value … like the saying by Ratu Sukuna, eh? '*noqu Kalou, noqu vanua*'… my God, my land. (Interview 1998)

Pentecostal Pastor Ratu Meli Navuniyasi, formerly a Methodist, similarly draws on the concepts and imagery of the Three Pillars construct. Yet here the pastor makes a distinction between what he considers sacred and profane elements of the construct, saying that *lotu* (faith, spirituality, the Church) is divine and must be considered separately and held apart from the worldly categories of *vanua* and *matanitu*:

> The concept of *vanua* is very broad and very deep. When you come to understand the revelation of the Lord [you understand that] the land (*vanua*) and *matanitu* are together … [but] this *lotu* is a heavenly matter, it's *spiritual*. *Vanua* and *matanitu* … are of the world. [Jesus said] *noqu matanitu e vaka lomalagi* – my kingdom is not of this world [lit. my kingdom is in Heaven] … Man consists of body, soul, and spirit. Body and soul are well fitted into this government [*matanitu*] and *vanua* – the spirit never. (Navuniyasi, interview 12 June 1998)

There are two salient points in this representation of the relations between Christianity and tradition. One is that the Three Pillar construct is redefined as a triangular relationship, with *lotu* as the apex, *vanua* and *matanitu* as the base. This redefinition was also stressed by Pentecostal pastors at the ACCF-led 'Corporate

Repentance Workshop' held during 'Reconciliation Week' in 2004: 'As long as the church is first, government and *vanua* can be interchangeable', I was told, 'but the church must be on top'. (7 October 2004) The second salient point is the words '*when you come to understand* the revelation of the Lord'. Reverend Tuima (first quote) implies that a Fijian's interwoven sense of Christian faith and sense of belonging to *vanua* are innate, God-given qualities of *Fijianness*.

By contrast, Pastor Navuniyasi's point is that understanding the revelation of the Lord is not an inherent characteristic, but the result of a *process* of recognition and discernment. The Lord leads the believer through a process of transformation to a point where he *reveals* a deeper understanding of *vanua, lotu* and *matanitu* which at a personal spiritual level indisputedly sets the spiritual apart from the worldly. This indicates that such revelation is *acquired* knowledge, based on spiritual maturity: 'When you are spiritually matured ... the spirit will urge you to do [his work]'. (Navuniyasi, interview 5 June 1998)

Redefining Christianity and tradition

Pentecostal Christians in Fiji as elsewhere in the world consider mainstream churches to have lost the true spirit of Christianity, to have become spiritually 'dead'. The faith of mainstream Christians, their ways of worshipping God, their values and morals are considered to have deteriorated, to have become a façade. Mainstream ministers are not 'spirit-filled', congregations have lapsed into mechanical recitations of static liturgies that are no longer meaningful to people. People merely go through the motions of Christian worship, they are not true believers, their faith is not the determining framework of their lives.

By becoming born again in Christ and experiencing a personal relationship with Christ, people are 'birthed into a new life in the Spirit ... every day is a day of commitment to the Lord, you're not just a Sunday Christian'. (Momoivalu, interview 1998) In contrast to how they see mainstream Christian worship, Pentecostals often describe their form of worship as 'hot', 'alive' and 'noisy': 'In ... praising, we make noise. Let everything that has breath make noise! Praising God, rejoicing ... In the time of [the] sermon we sit and listen ... the Word of God is not cold, it's hot – we call [Pentecostal preachers] spirit-filled preachers, filled with power, *mana* – God's *mana*!'. (Navuniyasi, interview 12 June 1998)

The Christian message, Pastor Navuniyasi points out, has become 'loose', muddied and moulded to fit practices of Fijian tradition – and even they are only a façade nowadays. People have lost their respect for authority, both that of God and of chiefs. The linking of Christianity with the concepts of *vanua* and *matanitu* in the ideal of the Three Pillars, the pastor implies, goes against the teachings of Jesus, whose kingdom is spiritual and 'not of this world'. The flow and movement towards God and a righteous way of living in Pentecostalism is also a flow and movement *away* from a particular Other. This is, as Coleman points out (pers comm. 2009) a common characteristic of Pentecostal theology, of seeing itself in opposition to a particular Other.

Pastor Navuniyasi links what he sees as the deterioration of Christianity in Fiji with what he terms as the 'Fijianisation' of the Methodist Church. People should behave, he emphasised, in a 'Godly way', and yet he felt that nowadays they had 'no respect for God, no respect for men – [or] for chiefs …'

> They are *liu muri* [lit. front/back, meaning façade], people are behind a façade. How they respect the Church … is not real … When something comes to Fiji it becomes Fijianised – the *vakaviti* way … [like] the Fijianisation of the Church … Things get loose here … Pentecostals are trying to pick [things] up … [do things] the Apostolic Way. That's why we call the church 'the Apostolic Church', the Way of the Apostles …. (Navuniyasi, interview 12 June 1998)

Pentecostals are trying simultaneously to tighten and open things up; to bring Christians back on track, clarify the Christian message and disentangle it from all the trappings of Fijian tradition. 'We shouldn't let tradition be a hindrance to the way we serve God', as Pentecostal journalist Mere Momoivalu told me. (Interview 1998)

All Pentecostals I met emphasised that *vanua* and *lotu* must be clearly separated. 'You can only serve one master', the Pentecostal pastor in Naroro village said. (1997) It is not possible to be *pure* in serving God if you have to follow *vanua,* I was told by a young missionary from Christian Mission Fellowship, who held a prayer meeting in the village:

> The Methodists go to church and then they sit and drink *yaqona* and get drunk and swear and tell filthy stories … that is not being pure … It is not possible to balance the two ways [*vanua* and *lotu*], sometimes the one [*vanua*] comes out on top of the other … and that is not good. (July 1997)

The criticism levelled by Pentecostals at the lack of spirit and vitality in mainstream churches, the problem of *yaqona* drinking among Methodist clergy, and slackness and lack of responsibility towards their congregations, is echoed here by former Methodist Church President Josateki Koroi:

> The preacher who preaches in the morning has been drinking *yaqona* all night or maybe he only had one hour, two hour's sleep because he had to get up to lead the service. What can he preach? Nothing … they don't prepare their sermons … So young people are not interested in going to church. They don't know or understand anything, or the *talatala*'s sermon contains nothing … [no] spiritual message … So [people] become spiritually hungry. They are searching for satisfaction and when [these new] groups come in to show some lively and important scriptures and things like that – then of course they go. (Interview 1998)

'Your church is from overseas'

The Pentecostal focus in doctrine, rhetoric and ritual on movement and individual transformation and conversion is sharply contrasted to Fijian Methodism, which continuously emphasises the importance of kinship roots, connectedness and the maintenance of traditional obligations. (Cf Prologue) Comparing themes in Methodist and Seventh Day Adventist preaching, Miyazaki makes a similar point:

> Methodist preachers construct a problem out of the contrast between past and present and emphasize the maintenance of the rituals of the past. In contrast, Adventists present the state of the person as a problem in need of a solution and show greatest interest in the need for change in the present and in the coming end of the world in the future. (Miyazaki 2000: 36, see also Tomlinson 2006 and 2009)

Many Methodists and the Methodist Church in general view Pentecostal churches as foreign impositions and un-Fijian, saying that they do not respect Fijian culture and tradition. 'Your church is from overseas', one Methodist woman told her niece, 'this church was born and bred here'. (Momoivalu, interview 1998)

> We call those [Pentecostal] churches *na lotu vulagi* [visiting or foreign churches] … they don't believe in our culture, our customs are not acceptable to them … Pentecostalism to me is like bringing a pot plant to Fiji. See, the pot plant comes from Australia … that plant [must] be planted [in] Fijian soil … They are not looking at their teaching like that. But to us, the religion is coming from overseas; [if] we take away the overseas clothes and clothe it in ours, then it can be part and parcel of us … [Pentecostalism] is like a tree floating in water, eh? It will be unstable at all times. It has no roots. You have to put roots in the ground, in our religion and everything else … to really grow. Otherwise it just remains in that pot plant. (Reverend Mesake Tuima, interview 1998)

With its truly Pacific metaphor of roots and water this Methodist point of view illustrates what Methodists in particular consider to be an intrinsic superficiality in Pentecostalism: in its doctrine, structure and its forms of worship it is not rooted in the land, in Fijian culture. Unlike Methodism, deeply embedded in the past, in the soil, the place and people of *vanua*, Pentecostalism floats on the water, unstable, unanchored. It will therefore always be *vulagi* (foreign) and rootless.

And yet, as discussed before, Pentecostals emphasise this very fact of not being anchored. They are non-denominational, not bound within a particular tradition or to a specific place, but part of a global network of egalitarian, dynamic and independent churches that, transcending cultural, religious, geographical and national boundaries, are expansive and ever on the move. Unhindered and unadulterated by the heavy shrouds of history and the constricting hierarchical structures, ritual and rhetoric of mainstream Christianity, Pentecostals, fuelled by the power of the Holy Spirit, see themselves as recovering the spiritual enthusiasm and empowerment of the early Christian Church.

Devil worshippers

In the early days of Pentecostalism in Fiji when the Assemblies of God, as the oldest Pentecostal church in Fiji, first came to the Islands in 1926, and for many years hence, the new churches were known as *lotu tagitagi* – literally 'church of crying or of tears' or *lotu qiriqiri*, literally 'church of the guitar'. Both names are evocative of the unusually expressive and emotional style of worship of these churches. Often when Pentecostals, filled with the Holy Spirit, were praying, singing and worshipping, Methodists would throw stones onto the roof of the building they were in, calling them 'devil worshippers'. Churchgoers of the new faith were persecuted and ridiculed; people in villages who joined the new churches were beaten and thrown out of villages, and most AOG churches ended up being built outside villages. (Pastor Ralph Dunn, AOG, interview 2002)

Among Pentecostals there is still a deep sense of hurt and pain in relation to the animosity and abuse – verbal, emotional and physical – they experienced from their kin and former Methodist church families, who did not accept their change of faith lightly. This enduring hurt and lack of reconciliation with Methodists was one of the issues CMF pastors pointed out to me during the AACF-led Corporate Repentance Workshop during 'Reconciliation Week' in 2004. At the same time the pastors also conceded that there had been cases of insensitivity on their own side too in the establishment of new churches in rural areas. This deep desire for Fijian Christians to reconcile and in so doing help the country to reconcile, was (cf Chapter 1) one of the main reasons for founding the ACCF.

The 'loudness' and emotionalism of Pentecostal worship was, and is, particularly provocative to many Fijians. In Fiji quietness, strict rules of bodily comportment and the positioning of a person's body in hierarchically organised space is part of formal etiquette and equated with respect for and subservience to chiefly authority – and ultimately, in church worship, to God as High Chief, these fundamental cultural values having been woven into mainstream church worship from the start.

Methodists and members of other mainstream churches value their quieter forms of worship and liturgy, which many people feel are more in line with traditional Fijian values than the expressive and exuberant Pentecostal styles of worship. In a comment in the Fijian language daily, *Nai Lalakai* at the time of the Pentecostal Festival of Praise in 1998 Methodist Church President Tuwere compared the respect a chief might rightfully expect from his subjects – the deference, bowed head and silence observed during important ritual – with the respect accorded God as expressed in the quiet order of Methodist structures of worship. Pentecostal styles of worship, he said, are out of place in Fiji, representing, at the very least, irreverence towards God. But his comment also seems to express a sense of loss of control:

> We have our own Methodist style of worship which we believe in and practise
> … For those Methodists who attended last year's Festival two questions arose:
> Is God really revered (according to Fijian belief) in this kind of worship? In
> a ceremony accorded to a chief, are we allowed to shout, yell, clap, run here
> and there, stand and rock before him? If we cannot act like this, how can we
> Fijians with our culture and custom let this happen to the Lord of Lords? It is
> this Almighty God who should be accorded the highest glory on earth and in
> Heaven. (*Nai Lalakai* 19 March 1998: 2)

A critical 2002 editorial in *The Fiji Times* warned of the divisive aspects of these new churches: 'These sects have the potential to seriously damage the quality of spiritual life, especially in the rural areas. They divide communities rather than unite them. (*Fiji Times* 20 November 2002, 3, 6, see also 21 November 2002: 6) And the *Fiji Times* (13 August 2003: 1) quotes former General Secretary of the Methodist Church, the late Reverend Jone Langi, as saying that legislation should be tightened in relation to the registration of new churches. 'Many of these new churches do not want to get involved with tradition and so this will cause confusion with the people on choosing which path to follow'.

The *Fiji Times* editorial of 13 August 2003 agrees, although also stressing the constitutionally enshrined freedom of religion: 'There are too many break away groups causing confusion and dissent, particularly in rural areas. Modern sales techniques are in danger of replacing traditional evangelism as the pressure to expand the various congregations mounts. And the overwhelming aim is to expand the church first and the Kingdom of God second'.[7]

Henry Rigamoto, Coordinator of Interfaith Search Fiji[8] (*Fiji Times* 16 August 2003: 6), responding to Reverend Langi's comments, called on chiefs in rural areas to seek dialogue with representatives of new churches, in order to understand them. This would lead to mutual respect and tolerance rather than confrontation. Religious freedom, he emphasised, is constitutionally enshrined (Section 35, 1997 Constitution) Restricting the numbers of religious bodies in the country would, Rigamoto said:

> infringe the rights of those who are attracted to new religious ideas. Surely
> the fact that people are moving to the newer churches is a wake-up call to the
> traditional church organisations to look for genuine renewal among themselves.
> The Methodist Church should remember that it is itself the product of a renewal
> movement.

---

7   *Fiji Times* 13 August 2003: 6; see also 14 August 2003: 3, 30 August 2003: 6, 3 November 2003: 3, *Daily Post* 20 August 2003: 3.
8   See Chapter 7.

Reverend Langi's comments reflect the general inability of the Methodist Church leadership and the majority of its members to respond other than confrontationally or defensively to Pentecostalism. Methodists in general have little or no understanding of what it is Pentecostal converts are searching for, and what they seek to distance themselves from in the Methodist Church.

Breaking with tradition

> Before CMF I used to attend the Methodist church in Fiji. Then – church to me was just a ritual – something that you had to do on a Sunday. I felt obliged to go to church every Sunday because I believed that people would be looking out for me to see whether I was in church or not. I was just a church attendee and every activity in the church was just part of the act. After some time I stopped attending church at all and would use Sunday to just lie in, read books and rest. I only attended church when I went to the village because you would look silly if you didn't attend church and people would talk about you. My parents were very strict about church (like all Pacific parents) and every Sunday we all had to attend Sunday school, choir practice and church services. I suppose I moved to CMF because I was hungry for God and I wanted to know more about God and I wasn't getting that in the Methodist Church. (Kasanita Serevatu, written testimony 2009)

This explanation for converting to a Pentecostal church is typical of many Fiji Pentecostals. In contrast to following socially and culturally prescribed communal norms of church-going, based on what is often experienced as empty ritual and rhetoric, which may give little or no space for individual spiritual experience, people seek and find in Pentecostal churches ways of being Christian, based on a personal experience of the divine. Pentecostals often express that a 'hunger' for God, for learning more about the scriptures, a longing for a more personal experience of faith and church-going, for more spiritually expressive worship forms, led them to convert:

> I grew up during the "conservative" era of the Methodist church. We couldn't clap our hands or even raise our voices (in praise) during a church service. As I began to attend the AOG church, I felt that I had the freedom to worship, and the privilege to share this with other believers. [I] decided that this is how I wanted to be with Christ – I wanted to be able to express my feeling. (Fiona Vamarasi, written testimony 2009)

Discussions of conversion and the degree to which Pentecostal converts break with the past has been widely debated among anthropologists over the past decade or so,[9] although, as Lindhardt (2009c) points out, there is a general consensus that converts do not sever all ties to their past and begin a wholly new life in the Spirit, but on a continual basis in their spiritual journey discard old characteristics of their life and embrace new.

Lindhardt (ibid.), referring to Austin-Broos (2003) and Norris (2003), emphasises that 'religious conversion involves both the assimilation of new meanings *and* the development of new ritual dispositions or of new embodied, holistic knowledge, acquired through participation in ritual'. As the testimonies of conversion here show, and Engelke (2004, in print) points out, this may be a gradual process, perhaps of many revelatory, not necessarily dramatic moments of conversion:

> [Pastor Suli] did an altar call – my spirit really wanted to go but I couldn't get my body to move up so I stayed put in my seat! After the church service I told my cousin that I wanted to meet the Pastor – I did and Pastor Suli invited me to their home for lunch. We talked for a long time and that was the beginning – like [with] you he didn't try to convert me, he just advised me, listened and talked to me. What really drew me to the church was Pastor Suli's personality and his genuine interest in me as a person and not just a church member. He would ask for me everytime he saw my cousin and when I turned up to church (once in a while) he would smile at me, shake my hand, ask about my welfare and talk to me. Never once had he asked me where I'd been or why I haven't been coming to church more regularly – never once! I liked that! He also would invite me to his home for dinner occasionally with my cousin and after I met Nau Mere, they both had an impact in my life through their genuine care and concern over my welfare. Even though I wasn't a member of the church, Pastor Suli was always prepared to give me advice when I needed it ... After a few visits to the church, the church atmosphere really appealed to me and I felt at home. That made my decision for me. (Kasanita Serevatu, written testimony 2009)

Although undoubtedly some Pentecostal churches in Fiji advocate a sharp cut with one's past life and with tradition and *vanua*, my research gives an impression of Pentecostals breaking with some aspects of their past and *vanua* ties and obligations, yet retaining others – in effect *redefining* Christianity and tradition. Reverend Kurulo explained that while some aspects of tradition are negative and need to be done away with in order for people to move forward in a changing world; others are positive and should be preserved:

> ... It's a mind-set ... how you have to do things, you're not allowed to do things in this way, you have to do it in that way ... people don't understand the time that we live in ... that's holding people back in ... business, in ... education ...

---

9   See inter alia Meyer 1998a, Robbins 2004a, 2007, Engelke 2004, in print, Lindhardt 2009a, 2009b, in press.

a lot of areas. There are a lot of things that are good, that we have to preserve, but there are things that are no good, that we really have to cut off. (Kurulo, interview 1998)

Fijian traditions of hospitality, and respect for the elderly and for chiefly authority are valuable traditions that should be preserved:

Caring for the elderly; and like when you come to the village as a visitor, people bring [you] food, those are good things, you know? And when somebody dies people come in and help, because it's all community … like when you eat in the village, we don't close our doors, we just open our doors and we call everybody [to come and share the meal] … there is love and caring, all of that … like the respect we need to have for people, for the chief. Those are good things that people need to be taught because those are biblical principles. (Ibid.)

The challenges of a Pentecostal Christian in Fiji

The challenges and difficulties of leading a Christian [i.e. Pentecostal Christian] life in a society that is based on quite different values [i.e. *vanua*], was the subject of a discussion one evening in the CMF cell group I belonged to.

The Namadi Height cell group, led by Pastor Suli, met every Wednesday in his home in an affluent area of Suva, made up of broad streets and large two storey houses. The evenings were usually divided into four main parts: a period of praise and worship, i.e. singing to guitar accompaniment; a period of praying, often in small groups, people's spoken prayers building up in volume and intensity – the loudness and increasing spiritual intensity an important part of the ritual and efficacy of prayer, as also in charismatic Catholic prayer.[10] This was followed by the giving of testimonies; teaching, mainly following a 4-step manual of spiritual growth; final prayers. Sometimes tea and cake were served afterwards.

In 2004, when I had returned to the cell group after a break in Europe, it had grown so much that it had been divided into two groups, one basic, the other advanced. The basic group met in a living room space on the first floor. The advanced group's meeting was held in part of Pastor Suli and Nau Mere's living room on the second floor. The discussion here took place in the advanced group, led by Pastor Suli or in his absence by Nau Mere, among people who were mature in age, i.e. in their thirties and forties, as well as mature in their faith and spirituality.

'As Christians', a man in the group said, 'we should not be ordinary Fijians'. Fijians are not analytical, he continued, but they should learn to review their lives, see how they have changed over time. 'We must allow the Word to transform our lives', one member said. Such transformation could only take place if people

---

10   Loud praise, Csordas (2001: 109) maintains, transforms a group of individuals into a single collectivity and helps interweave spiritual and bodily experience, cf Chapter 6.

stayed close to the Word of the Lord, someone else emphasised. This was the way of dealing with the daily challenges of e.g. relating to non-Christian [i.e. non Born-Again] friends. 'Sometimes our culture is the biggest stumbling block, particularly for us Fijians', someone added. 'Conversation is always top-down, we lack the ability to express ourselves', another member pointed out. People agreed that there is a 'culture of silence' in the country, i.e. that most people do not speak out, but follow leadership from above.[11] 'The challenge', a man finally stressed, 'is whether we are Christians first or Fijians first'.

This comment highlights a significant difference between Pentecostals and mainstream Christians in Fiji: that Pentecostals consider themselves first and foremost Christian, and secondly, Fijian. Implicit in this comment is the pressure that Pentecostal Christians experience in drawing back from traditional commitments and relationships and holding fast to their commitment to Christ as the paramount focus of their lives. As Coleman and Collins point out, to Pentecostal Christians 'faith and practice … is not necessarily limited in any contextual sense …[but] an aesthetic consistency characterises and informs all practice and leaches into all social fields'. (Coleman and Collins 2000: 326) One might also say that a spiritually and morally informed framework characterises all practices and reflection among Pentecostal Christians and indeed many other practicing Christians.

Pentecostal Christians in Fiji face the difficulties of being different, of thinking differently and of not following traditional expectations and obligations, of setting themselves apart from traditional community life in a culture when homogeneity is a core value. People in the cell group discussed how difficult it was to maintain good relations with their non-Pentecostal families and friends, especially when they had first joined the church. People couldn't understand or accept, for example, that they didn't want to partake in kava-drinking; they made fun of them and tried to goad them into drinking with them, or were deeply offended. But with time, as this testimony from my friend in AOG expresses, the families and friends of converts came to accept their change of faith:

> My conversion was not taken seriously by my (extended) family members, for many Reasons. My mother is a descendant of the first Tongan missionaries to Fiji, and my (maternal) forefathers were Methodist ministers. My father was also a Methodist minister. Even though my parents respected my decision, it was the 'family' that couldn't accept it (in my culture, family opinion is important). However, all that has now changed, and I am able to freely express my faith amongst my family. I believe it was the testimony of living in Christ that changed things. My family saw that it did me good, and this led them to a change of heart. (Fiona Vamarasi, written testimony 2009)

---

11   The term 'culture of silence' is used by NGOs in Fiji to e.g. describe how social injustice and abuse in families and at the national level remains unsaid because people do not speak out against authorities.

Pentecostals usually see a mission in challenging that which they turn away from as not being of God, in witnessing to their beliefs and trying to inspire others through their way of living, to turn towards the same path. The young preacher at a CMF Youth Service emphasised that 'Christians are God's light in a corrupt world. Christians should stand out in the community like stars in the night. And you can only stand out in the community if you proclaim the Gospel in your everyday life'. (Sermon, CMF Youth Service, 10 November 2002) However, he warned that Christians should not set themselves apart from others, judge them and 'do the right thing at the wrong time', such as preaching to fellow workers in work time, as some people did.

'Faith has got a public face. As Fijians we tend to be conservative. We've got to be able to stand out and confess our faith', Reverend Kurulo said. (Cell group meeting 27 October 2004) But Christians will be challenged, he also pointed out, 'Faith that is not tested is not faith. [We are] tested to see whether we trust in God. We should expect to meet challenges, without these situations we would still [be in the same place]. We [should] endure – by the time we are through, we are in a different place'. (Reverend Kurulo, cell group meeting 27 October 2004)

To continually bear witness to one's faith is a core element of *being* a Pentecostal. What may appear to others to be an everyday, secular activity is an intrinsic aspect of Pentecostals' being in the world.[12] Pastor Navuniyasi's words (1998) that 'there are no Sundays, every day is a Sunday' express succinctly the erasure of distinctions between the religious and the secular that is characteristic of Pentecostals, who embody a faith framework or faith '*habitus*' (Coleman and Collins 2000) which informs all aspects of their being in the world.

Cleansing the past

> When you talk about God ... God is Holy ... God has a clean spirit ... and he makes us ... become holy ... good because God is good ... But the devil, you know, he has an unclean spirit. The meaning of unclean is dirty. If he comes into the life of a person he makes them miserable, dirty. (Kurulo, interview 1998)

Such transformation and healing in a person's life can only come about by confronting the past, opening up for inner cleansing through the power of the Holy Spirit.

> It's important to deal with our past – otherwise the devil will use it to bring shame or fear to our lives ... we cannot change the past but we can effect the present ... our mind determines our behaviour. This is what happened to me in the past, but I have to let it go. We have to forgive those who have done some [wrong to us]. For the good of your soul you have to let it go. Deliverance is

---

12   See also Coleman and Collins 2000: 322.

[a] healing of the wounded spirit, of the emotional hurt people have in them.
(Kurulo, cell group meeting 22 October 2003)

In one of the weekly cell group meetings at Reverend Kurulo's house in Suva not long after Reinhard Bonnke's *Fiji Fire Conference* had taken place, he focused on how baptism in the Holy Spirit cleanses people of their past, renews them and empowers them to transform their lives:

Baptism [in the Holy Spirit gives us] empowerment ... The Holy Spirit will always guide us to the truth. John 16: 12 – "And when you know the truth, the truth will set you free".

1) The Holy Spirit is a person, someone we can relate to, talk to, befriend.
2) He is the truth
3) He speaks not on his own authority [but on the Father's]. He will glorify Jesus.

The Holy Spirit is God's representative here on earth. From the Father to the Son to the Holy Spirit to us. The Holy Spirit is the sole administrator of God's wealth. God is the ultimate source – all in the store room. To get what's in the store, you just have to know the storekeeper – the Holy Spirit. The special key is the Cross of the Lord Jesus Christ. You need to get acquainted with the store keeper.

As Reinhard Bonnke told us: There was no mix-up with the flames of the 120 [apostles at Pentecost] – each flame was tailor-made. There was a rushing of fire and wind at Pentecost. The Holy Spirit comes into our lives and burns away all impurities, cleans our lives, cleanses us. The wind comes to blow the impure ashes away. The Holy Spirit does not do a half-way job. (Cell group meeting 22 October 2003)

Reverend Kurulo refers here to Bonnke's vivid, oft repeated and popular enactment during the teaching sessions and crusade nights of the *Fiji Fire Conference*, of how the Holy Spirit descended on the Apostles at Pentecost, lighting an individual flame above each of their heads. This point emphasises the uniqueness of each individual and the individual and personal relationship each person is granted through the Holy Spirit, to Christ, when baptised in the Spirit. As in Acts of the Apostles 2:1-4 'the Holy Spirit manifests himself in the body of the believer through tongues, prophesy and healing' (Harding 1987: 180) and when a person is Born Again in the Spirit they are (cf Corinthians 1:12-14) granted a gift (charisma).

The gift of speaking in tongues (glossolalia) is a gift that Pentecostals generally believe is given to all who experience being baptised in the Holy Spirit and serves as an external sign of baptism in the Holy Spirit. Other, individual gifts are the gift of healing, of prophesy, of discernment, or of preaching. These God-given gifts are to be used to inspire others, to live out and spread the Word of God. Echoing

Pastor Morell's words that the individual must make a conscious decision to open up to God's power, Kasa Seruvatu explains:

> We believe that everything is in God's hands … Being baptised in the Spirit stems from the person asking God for the experience. You have to desire in order for it to happen … it came because I had desired it. So the longing has to come from you. (Kasanita Seruvatu, written testimony 2008)

> I have always wanted to speak in tongues. I decided one day in 2004 that I would fast and pray about it and ask God to help me experience it. Every day in a week I asked God for this gift and one morning while doing my quiet time, I heard myself speaking in a foreign tongue. I was thinking something in English but the words out of my mouth were foreign – it sounded German to me and I couldn't stop myself – the words just kept flowing. It is a great experience. Spiritually you feel that you are on a different level. You know what you are thinking but the words are foreign – it just flows. You know that you are speaking a different language. In my case, also after that when I pray in English I hear myself in an English accent. It's amazing. I cannot speak English in that accent everyday no matter how hard I try but during that time I could pass for an English woman!!![13]

'As a Born Again Christian the Word of God is our spiritual food', Reverend Kurulo told the cell group, 'we need to study, obey and practice it. Confess it – you have to learn to speak to your situation'. (Cell group meeting 27 October 2004) But although baptised in the Spirit and cleansed of the past, Pentecostal Christians are still open to the dangers and temptations of demonic forces in their efforts to live a life committed to Christ. 'Satan is throwing all sorts of rocks in our way', Reverend Kurulo warned, responding to a testimony, 'Our mind is the battlefield of the devil', he pointed out, 'between spirit and carnal mind. Our spirit should be in line … You cannot prevent a bird from flying over your head, but you can stop it laying its nest on your head. The battle is about whether the thoughts take root in your life. If we win the battle of our mind, we win our life … We have the free gift of choice. The Holy Spirit will lead us, but we have the choice whether to follow'. (Ibid.)

Testimony: 'You are the Bible others read'

Spiritual transformation at an inner level affects positive transformation in a person's relationships and life in general. Testifying to this transformation is a core ritualised practice among Pentecostals. Lindhardt (2009b) argues that testimony as

---

13   Kasanita Seruvatu: written testimony 2009, see also Coleman and Collins 2000: 323.

narrative is part of an 'ongoing process of constructing the religious self ... People learn to organise and situate their life course and experiences within a biblical narrative and time-line'. Citing Peel (1995) Lindhardt sees narrative as providing 'a sociocultural form in which an arch of memories, actions and intentions 'may be expressed, rehearsed, shared and communicated'. (Peel 1995: 582-583) The author of the narrative is empowered by having a certain 'definitional and categorical' control over his or her past. Yet testimony as a form of communication is also strongly context-based, depending on the interrelations between speaker and audience.[14]

At the same time continuous inner spiritual transformation changes a person's depth of understanding of their life, and their narrative constructions of their past consequently continuously change and mature in an ongoing process of conversion.[15]

Testimony is the externalisation of an inner experience, the making public of something that was essentially personal. A personal spiritual experience becomes part of public spiritual *knowledge*, the shared knowledge and also shared embodied spiritual *experience* of speaker and audience. The inner desire of the speaker to share their spiritual experience, the situation of testifying, and the response the words engender in those listening, merge to form a shared (and yet also simultaneously individual) experience of the reality of God's power:

> When I give a testimony I am acknowledging that God is great and that He is the source of my strength and the reason I can do what I am doing. It is to acknowledge His gifts to me and also to tell others of what this God has done for me ... In a way I am telling people – look this also can happen to you if you trust God fully!!!! ... For example one day I was testifying about Jeremiah 33.3 about how God showed me what to do and it helped a sister ... My testimony gave her ideas and she knew that if God can do it for me, He can also do it for her. (Kasanita Serevatu, written testimony, 2009)

The ritual language used in testifying to the working of God in people's lives, writes Csordas, is 'not only utterance but also experience ... The formal criterion that distinguishes sharing from ordinary experience is that its contents must have some spiritual value or edifying effect. These contents may be experiences, events, problems or thoughts'. (Csordas 1997: 228 and 176-177)

Many testimonies in cell group meetings were about God's place in people's everyday lives. People related what happened to them on a daily basis as a result of the efficacy of the Holy Spirit in their lives and the daily gifts they felt they received from God which they wanted to share with others. Other testimonies were about conversion or immediate healings, such as a woman whose son had

---

14   See also Coleman (2006b: 43), summarising points made by Keane (1997: 7) on the contextual nature of the circulation of words and things.

15   Coleman 2003 in Lindhardt 2009b, see also Lindhardt, Introduction (in print).

been healed by watching a Christian service on the TV, or a woman who had been healed in prayer in a phone conversation with Reverend Kurulo. Encouraging others to trust in the transformative power of God is important:

> In every human heart there is a seed, there is a potential, there's ability that needs to be encouraged, so that people can reach the total maximum of potential. Here, a lot of people have this kind of inferiority complex … in Fiji and all over the Pacific people always put themselves down. Even though they have the potential, the ability, they need someone to encourage them … Throughout all my years of ministry I have witnessed a lot of people who said they were nothing, but you know after you begin to teach them and encourage them, they've been promoted, got into areas which they didn't dream they could reach. So to me that's very encouraging, when I see someone rise above his circumstances and be able to make a difference in society, in his family and the place where he lives. (Kurulo, interview 1998)

Brother Mika from my cell group, for example, testified one evening that he had given his life [to the Lord] in 1991 and told us of the radical changes that had occurred in his life since then, how he had worked hard to be able to study and had worked his way up through the system to now be on six months' probation as General Manager in his company. 'I know I can do it with God's help', he said, 'I just wanted to give you this encouragement. Whatever he can do in my life, he can do in yours'. (Cell group meeting 23 July 2003)

> When] we apply the word of God into our lives, and we see the impact of the word of God in our lives, it becomes our testimony, and that helps to know that God is alive … as I always say, the Bible was not meant first for interpretation, but the Bible was meant for application. So when we apply and then we teach, we are teaching something that is real to me. It has worked in my life, and that becomes a very powerful weapon to the listener. (Kurulo, interview 2003)

A testimony in the Pentecostal magazine *Power Magazine* by the popular rugby hero, Waisale Serevi, captain of the Fiji rugby team, describes his excellence on the rugby field as the manifestation of God's power and love. His words express faith and humility in the acknowledgement that his achievements are not of his own doing, but granted through the grace of God. Serevi gives thanks to God for the talents granted him. This testifying to the power of God is a form of praise and also evangelisation, seeking to reach out to, encourage and empower others to believe that if they trust in God they too may have similarly powerful experiences of the divine in their lives:

> One day all this rugby will come to an end but this unique relationship with Jesus Christ is eternal ... I just want to thank God for protecting me, especially the talent that he has given me to be a rugby player. Different talents are given to us …

He has only given [me] one and that is to worship Him in the best way I know
... through playing rugby ... When people tell me that my game is excellent, I
always remember ... that the praise is not for me but for the Lord because He is
the one who gave me the strength and talent to play my best ... I just want to say
that wherever you are right now, if you accept Jesus Christ to be your Lord and
Saviour, He has lots more things in store for you which He wants to bless you
with. (*Power Magazine* May 1998: 16-20)

With a verse from Philippians emblazoned on their shirts, 'I can do all things in
Christ which strengthens me' (Philippians 4:13), Fiji won the 1998 Hong Kong
Sevens and returned as heroes. 'God was the 8th player', Serevi was quoted as
saying. (*Fiji Times* 30 March 1998: 1, 36) 'We won the World Cup through Christ',
he told *Power Magazine*, 'We have the trophy but Jesus must have the glory ...'.
(May 1998: 19, 20)

Testimonies of moral reform, on the other hand, often describe a Pauline
experience of conversion in which the individual experiences a sudden and
overpowering awareness of their sinfulness, leading to a sense of division of their
life along a spiritually temporal line into a pre-revelatory 'before', often described
as a dark and sinful past, and a spiritually enlightened present. The testimony
below and the article it is part of, which adds that Pastor Mata went on to form his
own church, describes the dramatic, instant transformation the power of God can
affect in a person, so powerful that, the article indicates, a reformed sinner like
Pastor Poate may (like St Paul) become an important tool of God:

Pastor Poate, once a drunk and violent man ... attended a Christian meeting
while completely intoxicated. That same night, he emerged a totally changed
man. "Two miracles happened to me immediately," says Mata. "The first was that
I became instantly and completely sober. The second was that I never used to say
a sentence without swearing and that very day God cured me of that" ... Mata
went on to form the Apostle's Gospel Outreach Fellowship International.[16]

Sharing the Spirit: testimony as gift and prayer

As a central, ritualised expression of faith and a vital tool of evangelisation
testimony is a two-way process of spiritual empowerment:

Testimony is really at the centre of faith. You can always argue about doctrine,
but you can never argue about testimony, because it is based on *experience*. And
testimony is not just for yourself, it is for the encouragement and support of

---

16   *The Review* November 1997: 60. See also *Power Magazine* 1998 May: 46-47,
1998 June: 42.

others. As you water yourself, so you water others. (Reverend Kurulo, cell group meeting 16 July 2003)

In one sense testimony is a form of prayer – a public and ritualised prayer of thanks for the working of the Holy Spirit in a person's life. The person who testifies is inspired by the Holy Spirit to testify, so is receiving spiritual nurture from the Holy Spirit at the same time as giving spiritual encouragement and inspiration to others. The person testifying serves therefore as a connection between the divine and others. Testimony can be seen as both prayer, gift and evangelisation:

> My belief is that it isn't what I can do that matters; it is who I am in Christ. Integrity and perseverance play a great role in my walk with Christ, but these two things can be fulfilled if I truly love God with all my heart, mind and soul. I must have faith and trust and believe in His promise, and hold to the Hope that I have in God that one day I will be with Him in eternity. (Fiona Vamarasi, written testimony 2009)

The efficacy of this way of sharing one's faith is that the words and act as a whole trigger responses in both those listening and the person who makes the act of speech. The words resonate within the person saying them, confirming that person's faith, 'watering yourself', and radiate outwards, 'watering others'. And the faith narrative is embodied by those listening who hear and interpret it in relation to their own faith context, and subsequently share it with others. In this way, like rings in water after a pebble has been thrown into a pool, the act of testifying circulates outwards in a faith network, becoming part of other people's narratives, testimony, and spiritual outreach to others.

Coleman (in press) asks the question in relation to charismatic rhetoric, 'What might be the perceived links – not merely theological but also ontological – between persons united by devotion to a common, sacred language? How indeed might words mediate not only between God and believers, but also between believers themselves?'

> To 'speak out' sacred words that have been stored in the self is not merely to communicate to others in a semantic sense; it is also to recreate and extend one's person in the act of giving an aspect of the self to others – an aspect that is never truly alienated from the giver … Among Word of Life adherents, not only is the Bible seen as a source of objective truth, but the words of an inspired speaker can also be regarded as truth incarnate. (Coleman 2006a: 165, 168)

Sacred words, like gifts, writes Coleman, have qualities similar to objects, enabling them to circulate in a kind of spiritual gift economy. Mauss argues in relation to reciprocity and the gift in Pacific Island cultures, that 'the gift contains some part of the spiritual essence of the donor, and … this situation compels the recipient to make a return'.[17] Coleman argues that part of the charismatic qualities of the speaker travel with the words to others, the reciprocal element of this exchange being not that the recipient is in debt to the speaker in the Maussian understanding of reciprocity, but that the speaker believes that the words said will have effect. Drawing on Thomas (1991: 14), Coleman (2006a: 173) writes that 'words, like gifts, must be activated to take effect, put into a kind of verbal circulation, and speaking is the most common way to convert language from its latent to its active form'.

This concluding testimony indicates a clear awareness of testimony as an extension of the whole self to others, as embodied experience and the embodied gift of a person's faith and spirituality to others. It is clear from this that faith is lived in the consciousness of relations with others, of sharing one's faith experience with others, and is a way of *being in the world*:

> Testimony is the ability to live and witness in and through your life what God has done, is doing and will do – and the ability to share this experience with others. It is also the lifestyle and characteristics that you portray. After all, 'you are the Bible that others read'. Testimony is not just talking about Christ, it is walking in Christ and doing as He desires. (Fiona Vamarasi, written testimony 2009)

Embodied experience of the power of the Holy Spirit and testifying to the transformation this brings in people's lives, and the importance of faith in relationship, is also central to Catholic charismatic ritual life, as the following chapter shows.

---

17   Coleman 2006a: 173, see also Parry 1986: 453-458, Gregory 1982, cited in Coleman 2006a.

Chapter 6

Healing Brokenness: Catholic Charismatic Rites of Healing and Reconciliation

Healing the spiritual and social body

> Please, Father, pray for me because I am a sole parent to my daughter who is 6. Bless me and my family. I never *forgave* her father for leaving us and committing adultery but today I *forgive him* in Jesus name. We have been separated for 2 years now. PRAISE HIM. (From written testimony by young woman re healing of two years of body aches. St Michael's Church, Nadi, 20 August 2003)

> Please, Father, Pray for the striking miners here at Vatukoula[1] … [who have experienced] 13 years of frustration, disappointment and pain. Please Jesus set them free from this situation. (From written testimony by miner re: healing of eye problems. Our Lady of the Immaculate Heart Church, Vatukoula, 22 August 2003)

In 2003 a visiting Catholic charismatic priest from Kerala, South India conducted over 50 healing services in overflowingly full churches in almost every Catholic parish in Fiji, as well as a handful of services in Anglican parishes and one in a Methodist church.

Commenting on a talk Father Thomas Mathew Nechicat OSA gave on his healing ministry at the Catholic seminary in the capital of Suva (3 September 2003), a seminarian complained about how churches were always far fuller during healing services than for ordinary Masses. This must be due, he surmised, to people's lack of understanding and lack of depth of faith, and that people think healing services are especially powerful.

Father Thomas replied: 'When *we* [share] our convictions, we are thinking intellectually. People come with *feelings*. People have lots of sensitivity. We theologians have a heavy approach. People want to *touch*', he said, recounting the Gospel story of the bleeding woman, who touched the fringes of Jesus' robe in the midst of the crowd, believing that if she just touched part of his garment, she would be healed. (Mark 5:25-34) 'To theologians', Father Thomas said, 'meaning comes from the head. To Jesus meaning comes from compassion'. He added that he had passed by an outdoor Pentecostal service some days before: 'I looked at the

---

1   Emperor goldmine in Vatukoula, Vitilevu. See e.g. Emberson-Bain 1994.

National Stadium on Sunday and saw men like us with their arms in the air. And I wondered: why are we so reserved?'

This chapter explores the centrality of the body in the ritual space, movement and language of the charismatic healing services celebrated by Father Thomas throughout Fiji in 2003 – as ideal, locus of faith and spirituality, and as vehicle of experience and instrument of or obstacle to change, transformation and empowerment in the lives and social relations of the participants.

Over a period of some six weeks I participated in 21 of these healing services. After the first services, my initial engagement as a relatively discretely placed participant observer in the congregation (except for the fact that I was usually the only European present) evolved to travelling round with Father Thomas and a Fijian Catholic nun, Sister Ina M. Dau SOLN, delegated to escort him from parish to parish. Somewhat naïvely I had anticipated a role as the anthropologist in the background, but I soon discovered that although I was introduced as an anthropologist doing research, people in the various parishes saw me as an integral part of the ministry team. Most people thought I was a nun, addressed me as 'sister' and, as they did with Sister Ina, sought my confidence and help with their problems. Others thought I was a medical doctor, doing research on healing, and would be able to explain their ailments.

Father Thomas soon asked me to also take photographs of people who had been healed, which I did, if granted permission to. Father Thomas used these photographs in his ministry, in addition to the narratives he told of healings, the written testimonies people gave him, in one case x-ray photos of a woman's broken arm that had been healed, or letters by patients or doctors, indicating changes in people's condition. He also drew on people's brief descriptions of healing, written on Healing Testimony Forms that were handed out to the congregation at the end of the, to be filled out before people left. Father Thomas used these testimonies to document healings, but also, he explained, to inspire people to have faith in what could happen.

The approach to healing advocated by Father Thomas emphasises the healing power of Christ through the inherent power of the Eucharist, through communion, i.e. the ingestion of the host and wine, transformed by the power of the Holy Spirit, through the priest to what in Catholic belief is understood to be the actual body and blood of Christ, while retaining its outer form. Healing can only take place through confession and reconciliation at both vertical and horizontal levels; that is to say with God as well as with one's neighbour. This approach follows teaching in the Catholic Church since Vatican II on the multiple wounds of sin in need of inner healing and 'presents the sacrament of penance as a sacrament of healing, bringing varied healing for the multiple wounds of sin'. (McManus 1984: 42)

People are social creatures, enmeshed in social relations that, if broken, must be restored, in order for them to be healed by God. Healing is therefore never merely related to the individual. It is always contextual and has to take place at many different levels: spiritually, emotionally, socially and physically – and encompasses the past and present of a person's life. At the same time healing *connects* these different levels. It is through the individual's agency through discernment of the sin or wrong-doing, confession to God and in relation to others, especially in relation to those he or she is related to, that healing takes place. This draws a line of continuance of agency and the sense of empowerment it engenders from the space and sanctity of the church and the ritual and context of the healing service into the home and hearth, the family space, the space and time of everyday life. (see also Csordas 1997: 198-199, Lindhardt 2004: 262)

This understanding of healing corresponds to understandings of the faithful as the limbs of the Body of Christ (the Church). People are inextricably connected to one another in and through Christ. If there is brokenness in one part of the body, it will reverberate throughout the whole body. When one part of the body is healed, the whole is healed. (1 Corinthians 12:12-26)

In many ways this corresponds with indigenous Fijian understandings of sickness and healing as deriving from the pollution or brokenness and restoration of social relations between different clans. People are connected to one another and to the land through their belonging to a particular clan that is historically, socially and spiritually linked to a particular place, to a particular part of the land. 'Self and other are located in a socio-cosmic matrix as much as they are bound to one another'. (Becker 1995: 103)

The Catholic charismatic renewal movement in Fiji experienced its heyday from the mid 1970s till about 1990/1991. At this time charismatic worship was based on an idea of strong ecumenical ministry between the three mainline churches, The Methodist Church in Fiji; the Roman Catholic Church and the Anglican Church, organised by an ecumenical team, ICHTHUS. Each year a National ICHTHUS Convention was held in Suva with Catholic, Anglican and Methodist speakers. Anyone could be a member of ICHTHUS, and individual members of Pentecostal Churches also joined in the services. Although all Methodists were welcome, it was the Butt St. Methodist Circuit in the capital of Suva (an English-speaking circuit that has always been oriented more towards European-style Methodism than other Methodist circuits in Fiji) that was part of ICHTHUS. Mainline Methodist Church leaders opposed ICHTHUS, which does not now exist, but there are plans to revive it. (Interview, Father John Bonato SM, October 2002)

In 2008 almost all the 33 Parishes in the Catholic Archdiocese of Suva had a strong Catholic Charismatic Renewal (CCR) presence. The CCR in Fiji has a National Service Committee which meets twice a year and guides the CCR in Fiji and there is a regionally-based Leaders' Training Programme (Labasa, Suva, and Lautoka). The annual conventions draw people from all over the Islands and, while focused on spiritual renewal, are also social occasions for meeting up with family members from other parts of the country. In 2007 the CCR convention was held in the town of Ba – over 1,500 people took part throughout, over 2,000 attending the final Open Air Healing Mass. (Cf Father John Bonato SM, former leader of ICHTHUS team, CCR chaplain in Fiji since 1980 – interview October

2002; pers comm. 2008) In 2008 an estimated 1,800 people took part in the CCR convention held in Suva. (Father Denis Mahony SM, pers comm. 2008)[2]

Although the focus of the Catholic Charismatic Renewal in general is on developing a personal relationship with God through Jesus Christ, in the Pacific Island region this is expressed in a more Pacific-style spirituality that is communally oriented and more intertwined with the family and the parish. (Cf Father John Bonato SM, interview October 2002) So the approach to sickness and healing employed in these healing services corresponded to familiar cultural and religious values and perceptions. At the same time the rituals employed challenged Fijian cultural and religious understandings of space, place and hierarchy and challenged people's usual ways of positioning and comporting themselves as social, gendered and religious bodies and people in the space of the Church.

The power of the healing services Father Thomas led to momentarily or permanently affect transformation and empowerment of participants was, I argue, in large part due to the dynamics and tension between the taken for granted and familiar and the radically Other and different – not merely the radically different rituals, but also an expansive experience of the spiritual, sacred Other. (see also Berger 1979: 39-46)

The familiar conceptual framework of sin, sickness, confession, reconciliation and healing through God's forgiveness, the known physical space of the church building and the familiar liturgical and ritual flow of the Mass formed the backdrop of the healing experience. Posited against this were the radically different rituals people engaged in within that space. There was the overseas priest with a different rhetoric, and healing narratives and testimonies from many different parts of the world, yet at the same time in many parishes there was also the security of the familiar in the participation of the local parish priest. As Father Thomas points out, the healing services in which the local parish priest participated, were the most successful.

There was a sense of disconnection and temporary rupture of people's taken for granted, familiar reality, yet there was also a sense of familiarity. I argue that the tension between a radically Other spiritual experience and the familiarity of physical space, symbols and ritual in these healing services created an openness in many people which enabled a heightened experience of the sacred. This spiritual experience was first and foremost an experience of the spiritual as embodied – individually and socially.

The body and religious experience

'At the heart of the religious phenomenon', writes Berger, 'is prereflective, pretheoretical experience'. (1979: 36) 'The sacred', writes Csordas (1994: 5), 'is

---

2   For an overview of the history and development of the Catholic charismatic movement, see Csordas 1997: 3-40.

an existential encounter with Otherness that is a touchstone of our humanity. It ... defines us by what we are not – by what is beyond our limits, or what touches us precisely at our limits ... this sense of otherness itself is phenomenologically grounded in our embodiment'.

In attempting to analyse the ways in which these healing services, people's experience of them and their experience of the transcendent within them dissolved, merged or inverted perceived cultural, hierarchical, social, spiritual and religious perceptions and demarcations of self-other *the body* necessarily becomes the focal point. As Michael Jackson points out, 'While words and concepts distinguish and divide, bodiliness unites and forms the grounds of an empathetic, even a universal, understanding. This may be why the body so often takes the place of speech and eclipses thought in rituals'. (Jackson 1981: 341)

The body, according to Lock and Scheper-Hughes, could be described as 'simultaneously a physical and symbolic artifact, as both naturally and culturally produced and as securely anchored in a particular historical moment'. (Lock and Scheper-Hughes 1987: 7 in A. Strathern 1996: 2) So the body does not just exist within a given moment as belonging to a particular person, as directed by individual cognitive processes. The body does not *merely* mechanically internalise, learn and perform particular movements, gestures and their timing, such as the bodily movements of religious worship within the space and time of religious ritual. The body *experiences* and remembers, is effected and brought into affect, is transformed by experience – an experience that encompasses rational, emotional, sensual and spiritual expression and feeling.

In Csordas' seminal paper on embodiment 'as the existential ground of culture' (1990: 5), further developing Mauss, Merleau Ponty and Bourdieu's theories, he writes that 'perception (the preobjective) and practice (the habitus) [as] grounded in the body leads to the collapse of the conventional distinction between subject and object' (ibid: 39) ' ... [the body is] at once an object of technique, a technical means, and the subjective origin of technique'. (Ibid: 7) And to Geertz's theories of religion as a system of symbols Csordas (1994: 5) adds that religion is 'articulated in a system of social relationships ... [and] acts to establish long-standing moods and motivations ... The method to get at these moods and motivations is to be found in the phenomenologists' notion of Otherness'.

So the body is not just an individual body, but always a body in relation to others. '*Embodiment*', Andrew Strathern points out (1996: 2), referring to Seremetakis (1994), '... reminds us of the concrete, the here-and-now presence of people to one another, and the full complement of senses and feelings through which they communicate with one another'. And Strathern emphasises Lock's point in her 1993 article that 'any anthropology of the body must include a theory of the emotions, and the first step toward such a theory is to recognise how arbitrary the Cartesian separation between "reason" and "emotion is"'. (A. Strathern 1996: 7) Lock cites Michelle Rosaldo's argument (1984) that 'emotions inevitably involve both meaning and feeling ... emotions cannot simply be captured as either cognitive judgements or visceral reactions'. (Lock 1993: 139 in A. Strathern 1996: 8)

Charles Davis (1976: 3) emphasises that 'Since the human self is both intelligent and bodily, spiritual and material, its spontaneous responses are indissolubly both intelligent and bodily, spiritual and physiological'. (Ibid: 13) And he suggests that in order to understand the body from a religious and spiritual perspective we must clarify the difference between 'emotion' and 'feeling' and dissolve the dichotomy between intelligence/feeling and rationality/feeling:

> ... A feeling differs from mere emotion in being an intelligent, insightful relationship with what is felt. It is not just a bodily reaction to a physical or imaginative stimulus. It is a spiritual, rational response ... (ibid: 6) Prior to any conceptual formulation, however, there is a direct, intelligent apprehension of the object, the insightful grasp of what is felt. Intelligence is present and operative even before the mind formulates in concepts what is intelligently apprehended, and the intelligent grasp of the object may and often does run deeper than what can be clearly formulated ... Feelings are spontaneous responses ... the stirring of our intelligent, spiritual, embodied affectivity toward whatever is presented to it. ... affective responses are themselves cognitive insofar as they reveal those features of reality we call values. Nevertheless, feelings presuppose as already given a factual presentation of the object. (Davis 1976: 7)

Spiritual feeling is facilitated and nurtured by ritual practice, by the aesthetics of religious experience within a given context: the aesthetics of sound, smell, seeing, moving, touching, being. These embodied aesthetic, sensual experiences, i.e. in the ways in which people move in relation to each other, the ways in which their bodies respond to different parts of religious rites, are central to people's participation, response and experience in religious worship. And they are central to the ways in which people bring their experience in the context of e.g. church worship, with them into the world of other social relations in ritualised practices that stem from their experience of the ritual in these communal contexts.

Drawing on Mauss's essay, 'Body Techniques' (1979), Asad, in discussing the embodiment of ritual in monastic life, suggests that embodied practices (including language in use) form a precondition for varieties of religious experience' (1993: 76) and talks of the 'mutually constituting relationship between body sense and body learning'. (1993: 77, see also Lindhardt 2004: 259) Lindhardt emphasises that 'essential to ritualisation is the production of ritualised bodies, which in turn produce ritualised practices'. (2004: 260) Bell, he points out, inspired by Bourdieu's notion of the socially informed body, 'suggests that a ritualised social body comes to possess a cultural "sense of ritual" or a "ritual mastery"'. (Bell 1992: 107 in ibid.)

> Such practical knowledge is not an inflexible set of assumptions, beliefs or body postures; rather it is the ability to deploy, play, and manipulate basic schemes in ways that appropriate and condition experience effectively. It is a mastery that

experiences itself as relatively empowered, not as conditioned or moulded. (Bell 1992: 221)

I agree with the idea of 'ritual mastery' as empowering, as a form of practical knowledge that empowers and is relevant in analysing charismatic ritual and people's experience of these healing masses. But I am trying to go beyond this and argue that a powerful creative force comes into being in the embodied experience of the sacred: I call this *spiritual agency* – 'agency' to emphasise the creativity, intentionality and inner 'drive' that manifests itself in relation to other people and ritual and other activities that I see as an intrinsic part of spirituality. People who engage in religious ritual and experience the transcendent engage with the transcendent at that moment and, inspired by their experience, bring it with them in their continued ways of experiencing the world and of engaging with others in the religious community and with the world outside the community. This engagement that I term *spiritual agency* could be similar to what Davis describes here as 'religious feeling':

> Religious feeling is the arousal of our personal being – our intelligent and bodily, spiritual and material selves – in what is, though variously mediated, a direct relation to transcendent reality. Religious feeling is constitutive of every truly personal religious experience, because without it religious responses are reduced to words, gestures, attitudes borrowed from others and repeated without personal involvement. By religious feeling a particular experience is intrinsically, not just extrinsically, for example merely verbally or socially religious. (Davis 1976: 25)

To speak of religious feeling or spiritual agency as being embodied is to see it as part of that which makes up a whole person and their ways of being in the world. It is an active component of people's daily life, their agency in life, the choices they make, the challenges they face, the way they relate to others and their surroundings, the way they engage bodily in their faith, the rituals they participate in or perform, the words they say, their reflections, the emotions and feelings they experience. It is such spiritual agency that is central to people's actions and responses in the healing services described in this chapter, and how people connected their experiences within the context of the healing services with their daily lives: how the empowerment they experienced during the services affected change in their lives and in their relations with others.

Global links: the overseas visitor

It was the unusually physically expressive nature and spiritual intensity of the healing services that Father Thomas celebrated that challenged many people within the Catholic Church in Fiji, laity as well as clergy. Yet it was also this turning upside down of conventions and norms and the ways people through this came to perceive themselves and use their bodies and voices within the space of the church, and the ways the sacred space of the church was transformed through the rites performed that made these healing services so efficacious and popular.

Originally invited to give a retreat to the Fijian SOLN (Sisters of Our Lady of Nazareth) order of nuns Father Thomas' retreat had been such a success that he was invited back and given permission by Archbishop Petero Mataca to conduct a healing ministry in the country. Word of Father Thomas' healing services and the many healings that occurred in the course of the services spread quickly from parish to parish, mainly through the loosely organised parish charismatic groups, but also, through the close network of extended family relations in Fiji.

In many cases parish priests worked with Father Thomas. But in some cases parish priests did not want to be involved. According to Father Thomas a greater degree of success of these healing services was achieved when people saw their own parish priest actively participate in the healing services and concelebrate Mass with him. Several parishes invited Father Thomas back to conduct a second service, and word of this also spread, so that by the time he left the country, parishes were still ringing to ask him to return and celebrate another healing service.

In addition to this, many, many people contacted Father Thomas via the mobile phone he was lent by a parishioner for use while in the country. An ever-growing stream of people came to the Presbytery in the parish where he was based in Suva, to talk to him and be prayed over or to ask him to come and visit sick relatives. Many calls were received each day on the Presbytery phone. And on a daily basis Father Thomas also received phone calls from relatives of people who had attended these healing services, based as far away as Australia, New Zealand, the States and Canada, and he conducted healing prayers over the phone with them. In addition, he went on daily sick visits to people and conducted healing prayers for families or parish groups in their homes.

However, in the midst of all the excitement the healing services brought with them, there were also sceptical voices to be heard, at the time and later. Criticism of Father Thomas' ministry focuses in part on the fact that he operated in a very individual manner. He did not seek to connect his ministry with the ministry of charismatic groups in Fiji; nor did he give any guidelines for how these groups could follow up his ministry and build on it. As one very critical priest told me, the charismatic group of his parish had had no idea what to do after the hype and excitement of the occasion had passed. Furthermore, someone who had been healed during the service, died three days later. There was, this priest said, no mechanism in place in the charismatic group for explaining this.

Nor had Father Thomas shown much cultural awareness or sensitivity to Fijian cultural protocol, such as presenting a *sevusevu* and *vakavinavinaka* (presentational kava roots given by the visitor and presented at the start and end of a visit to ask permission to be in a place and to thank for the hospitality extended). This priest pointed to the whirlwind nature of Father Thomas' ministry. He felt that Father Thomas had been too much the centre of attention in the healing services, and that he in his ministry didn't challenge the deep problems of society. (Father Pat

Colgan SSC, interview 24 September 2005) But despite these and other criticisms, for a variety of reasons, Father Thomas' ministry was a great success.

Despite the Catholic Church being the most outspoken Church against social injustice in Fiji, particularly in relation to the injustices to Indo-Fijians at the time of the coups in Fiji in 1987 and in 2000, the hurt and sense of vulnerability among the Indo-Fijian community, especially since the coup of 2000, in which many Indo Fijians suffered violence and abuse, make Indo-Fijians almost invisible in Catholic parish contexts.[3] Indo-Fijians mainly attend *Misa Puja*, Masses held in Hindi, explicitly Indian in their cultural expression.

Father Thomas sought to reach out to the Indo-Fijians, but had little success with this, even after a programme on the healing services on the Indian TV channel in Fiji. He was an outsider with little knowledge of the highly complex cultural and political context in Fiji, but on a few occasions Father Thomas did specifically focus his rhetoric towards the particular, sensitive ethno-political situation in Fiji. At one healing service at which there were a good number of Indo-Fijians, some of whom were Hindus, Father Thomas emphasised: 'God does not discriminate between Hindus, Muslims, Christians. The healing God does not discriminate. We are the ones who discriminate. God created only one race. God created only one colour – colourless … For God, Indians and Fijians are the same. For God Hindus, Muslims and Christians are the same'. (St Joseph the Worker Church, Tamavua 14 September 2003) And at a *Misa Puja* Father Thomas prayed these words of encouragement, 'Grant us, Lord, the strength to persevere as we walk together in love, peace, hope and harmony … Rekindle in us the spirit of love, reconciliation, peace, unity'. (St Agnes Church, 23 August 2003)

The intensity of Father Thomas' ministry and the rumours of healing that abounded from it, were such that people walked for miles across difficult terrain in the interior of the main island to get to the healing services; that people in other rural areas paid large sums of money to hire vehicles that could bring them to the town or coastal churches where healing services were being held; and that people waited patiently for hours and hours in churches to participate in the healing services. Most churches were overflowing – with Catholics, as well as mainstream Protestants, Pentecostals and Hindus.

A number of factors played into the wave of excitement that Father Thomas' ministry affected within Catholic parishes. In addition to attending Mass, which for those living in towns is often on a daily basis, Catholics in Fiji are very focused on devotional practices. These practices include praying the Rosary, Adoration (where a consecrated host is exposed in a monstrance on the altar for a period each week and people spend long periods in front of the altar in prayer); praying in front of the Tabernacle (where the consecrated host is kept); praying Novenas (nine day prayers for a particular intention); holding daily family prayers, and praying prescribed prayers such as the Divine Mercy prayers at certain times of the day.

---

3   To counter this problem, since 2005 the order of Saint Columban (SSC) have engaged in a special ministry among Indo-Fijian communities in Fiji.

Father Thomas' healing services, with their focus on communal recitation, added to the devotional practices of ritualised communally spoken prayers, particularly popular among Fiji Catholics.

Secondly, apart from a relatively small elite of well-educated and wealthy people in urban areas and also people who attend non-mainstream churches such as Pentecostal churches, most people in Fiji, especially in rural areas, will generally seek traditional healing or religious healing first and seek medical help only as a final resource. In many cases, people whose lives might have been saved by proper medical attention in time, die because their relatives have tried all sorts of non-medical intervention before taking the patient to a doctor or hospital. Thirdly, the fact that Father Thomas was an outsider and came from overseas, added to the perceived efficacy of his healing powers.

Because Father Thomas came from overseas his authority as a priest and his perceived efficacy as an instrument of God's healing was, I would argue, considered different and exotic. His healing services were to some degree so popular precisely because they were the work of a visiting 'stranger' from overseas. A local charismatic Catholic priest would not have achieved the same level of interest or enthusiasm. The perceived power of innovation, difference and freshness the outsider inevitably brings with him through his mere being there and through the narratives he brings with him of a different world played a role – but so, I suggest, did the deep-seated Fijian mythological understandings of the powerful 'stranger-king'. (Cf Sahlins 1985: 73-103)

Despite the increasing physical, material and social criss-crossing and linking of Fiji Islanders and Pacific Islanders across the world through work and family connections, television, telephones, mobile phones and the internet, an outsider in person still has a certain amount of kudos and could be seen to emanate particular or even superior spiritual powers. To many of the poorer participants with little educational background in rural areas, who only see their parish priest once a month or even less (since Catholic priests in rural areas often minister to parishes stretched over very large areas) the spiritual energy and drive of Father Thomas' healing services provided unprecedented stimulus and inspiration, as they also did for isolated, overburdened rural parish priests.

The structure of the healing service

At the start of each service Father Thomas emphasised a number of Biblically-based central points: 1) that he does not heal: only Jesus heals; 2) that he has merely been given the gift of facilitating or passing on that healing; 3) that in praising the Lord you are asking God to touch you and heal you; 4) that healing can only take place in the name of Jesus Christ – 'In my name they will drive out demons' (1 Corinthians 5) that healing is dependent on the acknowledgement of individual sin (Psalm 41:4) 'I said I have sinned against you' 6) that healing is dependent on the powerful Word of God (Psalm 41:3) and 7) that 'God will touch you and set you free from your anger'. (Ephesians 4:26)

Each healing service was structured in the same way and based on the liturgical rhythm and flow of an ordinary Catholic Mass, yet was at the same time completely different to any ordinary Mass. In chant-like, almost meditative style, line by line, Father Thomas led people to loudly repeat the words of a lengthy healing prayer. Through this,[4] people are led to 1) become conscious of their need for the healing touch of God by becoming conscious of their mistakes and sins; 2) to open their souls through praising God; 3) this will in turn lead them to be open to hearing the Word of God, that is to say the liturgy of the Word through Bible readings and through the homily or sermon; 4) in praying for others and themselves people are confirming their relatedness through God to each other and to the world; and this all leads up to 5) the sacrifice of the Eucharistic celebration, Holy Communion – the pivotal point of an ordinary Mass and of these healing services.

The healing prayer expressed the individual's praise and adoration of God, individual acknowledgement of sin; and supplication for forgiveness and healing. Interwoven with this were Bible quotations that Father Thomas or members of the congregation were asked to read; and testimonies were given by people who had experienced healings in former services, as well as of those participating in the present service.

Within each healing service was a Eucharistic Mass. The start and end of the Eucharistic Mass was clearly indicated by Father Thomas and clearly demarcated, partly by the break while the altar was prepared for Communion; partly by the initiatory and concluding liturgical words and movements of the priest or priests; but also by the fact that while engaged in the Eucharistic celebration Father Thomas and the concelebrant priest wore Eucharistic vestments. Before and after the Eucharistic Mass Father Thomas was dressed in a simple white soutane, occasionally also wearing a stole.

The pivotal and most striking event that took place during each healing service, which took place directly *before* the start of the Eucharistic Mass, was the invitation to people to come up to the sanctuary and kneel round the altar. During some of the healing services, Father Thomas invited people up to the altar during the Eucharistic Mass – this was after the homily or sermon, before Communion. This timing is important, since the invitation to come to the altar was an invitation to people to bring their sins and sorrows, pain, anger, illness and so on, as a sacrifice to lay on the altar before the mystery of sacrifice of the Eucharist.

Very little singing took place during the actual Mass and Father Thomas discouraged any form of clapping, as he felt it disturbed the flow of the Holy Spirit and the flow of people's concentration: 'I am trying to bring people to aloneness with God. If they start clapping, they will start sitting, looking left to right', he pointed out to me. (17 September 2003) 'The noise scatters people's thoughts', Sister Ina said, 'He's helping them to tune in, to meet God'. (Ibid.)

---

4   Cf Father Paul Marks OMI, interview, Copenhagen, 2007

Figure 6.1   Individual prayers for healing, St Peter's Church, Nakavika, Namosi, 26 August 2003

Figure 6.2   Individual prayers for healing, Our Lady of the Immaculate Conception Church, Vatukoula, 22 August 2003

This did indeed differ from the usual form of worship in Catholic charismatic meetings and charismatic Masses I participated in in Fiji, where the use of guitars, clapping and louder, more expressive singing is prevalent. Only in one healing service that Father Thomas conducted, in an Anglican church, did I see anyone 'rest in the spirit'. This aspect of charismatic practice was something he discouraged, and when an Indo-Fijian woman fell to the ground in a 'sacred swoon' in the sanctuary after having testified to the healing she had experienced at the previous healing service in that church, Father Thomas deflected any focus on the situation by asking one of the team members to discreetly take the lady to one side and counsel her.

At the conclusion of each healing service long lines of people sought individual healing from Father Thomas. Each service lasted from between three to five hours, including – or rather very much because of – these sessions of individual healing afterwards; the longest service I attended lasted all of seven hours.

In his conversations with people in these individual healing sessions, Father Thomas felt their pain in his own body for a moment, as inner visions about illness or accidents concerning the person or people the person is related to – and he was usually right when he asked whether people had been operated on or had a knee injury or had had an accident, or whether someone in the family had had an abortion, committed suicide, committed murder, all of which could be elements causing illness or blocking healing. In this way for a brief moment healing facilitator and those seeking healing are fused together, connected in joint bodily or spiritual pain. Physical and emotional relief and release comes when the spiritual bondage is released through acknowledgement of one's sins.

Raising one's hands to the Lord

Each healing service started with Father Thomas calling on people to raise their arms high up in the air, and loudly and exuberantly repeat over and over the words 'Praise the Lord!'. Many people were clearly most uneasy about this to start with, although those who had prior experience of these healing services slipped into it without problems. It was not easy for the majority of people: for one thing, to most people it was alien and suspect to perform such explicit and expressive bodily actions as to raise one's arms high up. And secondly, it was challenging to speak so loudly and exuberantly in church.

There are cultural reasons for why many people in Fiji find this type of worship challenging. As has been discussed in previous chapters in Fiji quiet or silence, strict rules of bodily comportment and the positioning of a person in relation to others in hierarchically organised space and social relations is part of formal etiquette. No one may stand or sit taller than a chief. It is therefore extremely rude and offensive to stand up when those to whom you should defer are sitting, or to stretch over the area above their heads, the most *tabu* part of the body, or to sit on a higher seat than those you should defer to. The physical and symbolic ordering

**Figure 6.3   Praising the Lord, St Peter's Church, Nakavika, Namosi,
                  26 August 2003**

of people within space in Fiji, equated with respect for and subservience to chiefly
authority – and ultimately, in church worship to God as the paramount chief of all,
were woven into mainstream church worship from the time of Christianisation.
The importance of silence as expressing respect and reverence in traditional Fijian
ritual is borne out by the absolute silence and stillness of body comportment
maintained at the death of a high chief.

However, despite people's initial suspicions and reluctance or shyness to
participate, to raise their arms and hands so high in the air and for such sustained
periods, in the course of the services I attended almost every single person present
let go. Even in parishes where the majority of people initially were negative
towards the idea, they ended up joining in fully.

The explicit use of lifted hands and arms in the course of the service, we were
told, is an invitation to God to come into our lives. The palms raised upwards
meaning also an uplifting of joy or of burdens or sins to the Lord, essentially an
uplifting of everything we are and have to offer to the Lord. Raising our hands
up in worship is, Father Thomas told me, a *two way process*. We are 'waiting on
the Lord' and 'inviting the Lord to come into our lives' … We are 'asking the

[Holy] Spirit to come down'. At the same time we are 'reaching out to the Lord', are 'lifting ourselves up to the Lord'. (Interview 22 August 2003) We also make ourselves physically vulnerable. We surrender ourselves. Indeed, as someone once pointed out to me, this gesture is internationally recognised as indicating unconditional surrender.

You become truly open and there is a sense that the openness also lays open your sins and wounds before God. And this links with the main thrust of the services: in order to be cleansed and healed you must lay open your sin and brokenness. And this too follows the understanding of the Catholic rite of reconciliation, which is based on the acknowledgement and confession of sin and wrongdoing and the genuine intention to change that leads to absolution and forgiveness from God. Despite – or perhaps because of – the laying open of a person's conscience and sense of sin, wrongdoing and brokenness this becomes an empowering gesture – perhaps because physically the movement gives release and a sense of freedom. Perhaps because in surrendering themselves totally to God and feeling God's forgiveness, participants feel liberated.

'At the beginning I wasn't used to it and I told myself that I will never do that', a Pentecostal friend recalls about raising her hands in the air when she first joined Christian Mission Fellowship (CMF). 'But … once I began to realise how much God had given me and how much more He could give me, you become emotionally involved in every song and prayer that is said in church or where ever. I do it not because it is a requirement, but because I feel good acknowledging what God has done'. (Kasanita Serevatu 2009) A young man from CMF told me, when I asked him what he felt when he held his arms up in this way, that he felt a closeness to God. 'But', he added, 'I only hold my arms up like that if I feel clean inside and at peace with God'. A Catholic charismatic told me that unless you feel close to God – or desire to feel close to God – it is almost physically impossible to raise your arms up in this fashion.

In a highly hierarchical society such as Fiji's, where much cultural value is placed on conforming to given norms and where individuality and being different is seen as suspect, one could argue here that this would make it difficult for individuals to go against the flow of spirit and bodily movement during an event like this, and not raise their hands. However, I had a very clear sense that when they had overcome their initial awkwardness at such expressive behaviour, people truly felt empowered and spiritually touched by performing these movements which were indeed physically energising to do.

A rural parish priest warned us when we arrived that his parish was very anti-charismatic. Yet the repeated request by Father Thomas to people to raise their hands up high ended up with the whole congregation doing so. The parish priest said afterwards that he himself had felt negative towards the whole thing to start off with, but found himself transformed during the evening:

'[People have been] using [their] mind, [having] an intellectual way of understanding [their faith] … judging intellectually', he told us, '… People have grown complacent in their faith here ... During the course of the Mass [service] I let go of my intellect – and my heart was touched' ... '[We have to] let go and experience the experience', he added. (Father Pita, Mary of the Immaculate Conception Church, Solevu, 22 September 2003)

Reconciling and healing brokenness

To Father Thomas physical sickness is mostly connected to spiritual illness or 'brokenness' and sin in a person's life, and particularly in their family relations. Sickness and healing are therefore not individual phenomena as such, but linked with the life and social relations of the individual – present as well as past, and are linked with the actions of the individual's relations, those living as well we those of former generations. We are all related – in time and space.

Similar to the image in 1 Corinthians 12 of the Church as a body needing all its different parts in order to function, Father Thomas pointed out to people: 'We are all related to one another and to God. When one of our members is hurting, we are all hurting. When one of our family members is far away from the Lord, the whole family is far away from the Lord ...'. (St Joseph the Worker Church, Suva, 25 August 2003)

This relatedness, Father Thomas emphasised, also means that the consequences of one's sinful actions will be handed down through the generations:

Do not abuse one another, respect one another. If you are hitting your wife, stop it in the name of Jesus Christ – or your sins will go into your children. (St Peter's Anglican Church, Lautoka, 26 August 2003)

... the children will continue the bondage of their parents, Exodus 20:5 ... We carry bondages from one generation to another ... just like bricks glued together, a continuous chain ... (Holy Trinity Anglican Cathedral, Suva, 8 August 2003)

[See] Nehemiah 9: ... They stood before the Lord and confessed their sins. Do you confess the sins of your ancestors? The sins of our forefathers ... [See] Exodus 20:5 ... [will be punished] to the third and fourth generations ... We have to pray for our parents, [for] our ancestors. (Holy Family Church, Labasa, 24 August 2003)

Father Thomas explained that to open up for healing one must embark on this process of recognition and acknowledgement of one's mistakes and sins. We have to ask for forgiveness from God but also from those we have hurt in our lives, and forgive those who have hurt us. Only then can we expect healing to take place. If we hold on to anger, bitterness and hurt in our lives, we will not be able to open up to either spiritual or physical healing. Family members holding on to anger or trauma, or who have committed sins, can keep another member of the family locked in physical illness or depression.

Much of this approach ties in well with traditional Fijian understandings of identity. An individual is never merely an individual. The Fijian body, as Becker points out, is first and foremost social:

> Among Pacific Island societies the self is not so much conceived of as a body, but 'as a locus of shared social relationships, or shared biographies' (Lieber 1990: 74). The Melanesian person is construed as a 'composite site of relationships' (M. Strathern 1988: 13) that is not 'coterminous or even synonymous with individual bodies'. (Foster 1990: 432 in Becker 1995: 4)

One is, as we have seen in previous chapters, always and at all times connected to one's clan and clan members and whatever a person does will reflect on all the other members of the clan in the present as well as the future, just as the actions of deceased clan members still reflect on the clan as a whole today. Brokenness in part of the clan reflects on the whole. And 'socio-moral transgressions (or, breaches of *tabu*) have ramifications in both the social and the cosmic realm in Melanesia and Polynesia'.[5]

However, there is a clear difference between the rites of reconciliation in these healing services and the traditional, communal rituals of reconciliation between Fijian kin groups, described in Chapter 2. The important element is the individual acknowledgement at an *inner* level of sin and wrong-doing, the individual taking responsibility for his or her actions and the reparation at spiritual and social levels. Speaking openly about hurt, abuse, sin, anger and so on within the family, according to Father Thomas, can free the individual to be healed. And through this freeing of the bondage of sin and the healing of an individual member of the family, the whole family is healed. This is also known within Catholic charismatic teaching as 'healing the family tree'.[6]

One part of the healing service focuses on married couples and their difficulties, hurt and anger towards one another. In what many people experienced as a both challenging and moving ritual, all couples were asked to sit together, and then to stand up and hold hands. In Fiji, neither Fijian, Pacific Islander or Indo-Fijian couples make outward expressions of affection, such as generally seen in western cultures. This rite is challenging to Fijian and Pacific Islander couples in particular because although people in towns adhere less strictly to traditional norms, and although Fiji today does not have strict gender segregation, in rural parishes women and children sit together at Mass on one side of the church, and men and young men sit together on the other.

For couples to be asked to stand up and hold each others' hands high in the air in front of the whole congregation was therefore very radical. However, they dutifully held up their their joined hands, while first the husbands and then the

---

5   Cf Koskinen 1968; Kirkpatrick 1977: 325; Leenhardt 1979; Shore 1989: 143. (Cf Becker 1995: 4 and 99)

6   See also Csordas 1997: 39-40, 43-44.

wives solemnly repeated after Fr Thomas the words of a long prayer in which they first expressed thanksgiving for their spouses and then asked them for forgiveness for all the hurt and mistakes they had made in their marriages. The prayer concluded with the couples renewing their marriage vows.

When Father Thomas later asked the couples to express in the microphone what they had felt when they held each others' hands and said those words, people appeared to answer straight from the heart. Although those who appeared to have deep troubles in their marriages clearly found this situation hard, most couples described the moment as something particularly moving, like the first time they held hands, or they described how deeply they loved their spouse, how close they felt to their spouse, or that they felt secure, close to God or at peace, or that they felt strengthened or happy. Several people I spoke to at a later stage, said that they experienced great renewal in their married and family life after experiencing this rite. Different responses included,

> '[I] thanked God for giving me a good husband';
> 'I felt fulfilled';
> 'I felt like the first time we were together';
> '[I] felt the Spirit moving me and my husband';
> 'I love him more and more';
> 'I love my God for giving me a wise wife'
> (Holy Family Church, Labasa 24 August 2003).

> 'I felt very peaceful at my husband's side';
> 'I felt the calmfulness [sic] and peacefulness of my Lord';
> 'I felt joyous and I felt a greater intimacy between us';
> 'I felt the peace and I will start loving her more';
> 'I felt much better than before';
> 'I felt very happy';
> 'It was like the first time when I said I love you';
> 'Our problems are solved';
> 'I felt so happy';
> 'Nothing can separate me from the love of my Lord'
> (St Joseph the Worker Church, Tamavua 25 August 2003).

> 'I felt the forgiveness of the Lord between us'
> (St Peter's Church, Namosi 26 August 2003).

Being healed

To be 'healed' does not necessarily mean to be 'cured'. Father Thomas emphasised on many occasions that the healing which takes place need not be the healing a person came for. A story he often told was of a man who came to Father Thomas in the hope of being healed of cancer. He died, however, before Father Thomas left Fiji. But the point of the story was that he died in peace, surrounded by his family, strengthened in his faith and reconciled to his children. This man, Father Thomas explained, had not received the physical healing he had asked for, but he had been spiritually healed.

In a predominantly Indo-Fijian parish Father Thomas encountered an old woman and her daughter in law. In the course of being prayed over the old woman's pain had not been alleviated. In a later conversation alone with the daughter in law Father Thomas asked if anyone in the family had had an abortion. He had sensed that the old woman, who had many physical ailments, was being bound in illness by this particular act. But the young woman denied this. After having prayed over the old lady a second time to no avail, Father Thomas asked to speak to the daughter in law again. In this second private talk with Father Thomas, the young woman acknowledged having had an abortion. Following this, when Father Thomas prayed over the old lady a third time, she sensed a clear change and felt that she had been released from her pain of several years.

Such confessions were not reached through any pressure and were not responded to with any indication of blame or condemnation. The point was to encourage individuals to openly acknowledge their sins and sorrows, so that through this act the bondage they or others experienced on account of what they had done would be loosened.

While this example concerns an Indo-Fijian young woman, in Fijian cultural practice considerable importance is paid on disclosing to others, i.e. not keeping to oneself, important experiences or situations. This is particularly important in relation to pregnancy. An undisclosed pregnancy can cause serious danger, even death to others. Thus my Fijian mother explained how a female relative had recently visited the household, yet had not disclosed at the time that she was pregnant. When family members subsequently fell ill and it was discovered the young visitor had been pregnant, *yet had not said so*, her failure to do so was viewed most seriously and seen as the cause of the illness in the family.[7]

The importance of disclosure in relation to pregnancy concerns the inherent importance and dangerous qualities of regenerative powers in relation to the community. My point is, however, that in a society based on the penetrative collective gaze, specifically in the context of village life, clandestine behaviour is considered a threat (cf e.g. Tuwere 2002: 161-162 re: sorcery), so the *idea* that openly acknowledging sin or traumatic events releases bondages and enables healing in others, would from this perspective be quite logical.

Father Thomas emphasised how the above case is an example of how other family members can be held in physical bondage through illness on account of the sinful actions of another member of the family. This case also emphasises the centrality of the body. The body of the daughter in law is seen as first *blocking* the health and well-being of her mother in law through the sin of having had an abortion.

7 Compare Becker on disclosure and exposure, 1995: 94-103.

When the action of abortion has been openly acknowledged by the daughter in law, her mother in law's healing is able to take place. Through acknowledgement, confession, asking God and her aborted child for forgiveness, and through the ensuing reconciliation with God, the daughter in law's body, now cleansed through reconciliation – becomes instead *the vehicle through which healing* of her mother in law's body through the power of the Holy Spirit *is achieved.*

Mere,[8] a Fijian woman, told me that her first encounter with Catholic Charismatic Renewal, had deepened her faith and made her understand connections between past and present actions and relations within her family. She realised now, she told me, that her eldest daughter Teresia's pregnancy out of wedlock some years before, that forced her to leave high school and brought shame on the family, was a consequence of the bad relations between Mere and her husband, Tomasi at the time she was carrying Teresia. When Mere was heavily pregnant Tomasi left her, and she had to return to live with her family. Not until some months after she had given birth to their daughter were the two reconciled and have since had a happy and solid marriage and are strong in their Catholic faith.

The trauma and rupture of relations between Mere and Tomasi, while she was carrying their first child had, Mere concluded, damaged their daughter spiritually and led her in turn to commit sin as a young adult. 'We have to sit down together, all three of us', she told me, 'and we, Teresia's parents, have to ask her for forgiveness for the sin we committed then, before she was born'. Only then would healing of the daughter and of the family as a whole be able to take place, she maintained. (Interview October 1998)

Lusia, a women whose son was healed of a serious ear problem he was due to be operated for, described to me a year after the healing, how Father Thomas' focus on reconciliation had led her to return home to reconcile her family before returning to a second healing service when her son was healed:

> Father Thomas kept on talking about reconciliation ... So I came home that evening, we had our prayer ... and then we had our family reconciliation ... I felt we needed to do this ... because there is no point, I mean that was how I felt, asking the Lord for healing when there is hurt in the family. Maybe ... I've hurt [the children] in some ways, because sometimes I talk to them in a way that I'm not supposed to ...
>
> So the Lord led us to come and do our reconciliation ... That's one thing about Father Thomas, he really made me realise. Sometimes we pray and pray and pray, and we don't realise that we need to reconcile first with our family members ... So I was very happy that he led me to do that, and it's sort of an on-going thing for our family [now]. (Lusia Tukidia, interview 29 October 2004)

In the first narrative, through accepting God's will in his life, a man sought a cure for his diseased body. He was not cured of his illness, yet his bodily suffering

---

8 Mere, Tomasi and Teresia are pseudonyms.

and dying became instead the channel through which wounds within the family were healed and reconciled. In the second narrative, unacknowledged bodily sin was seen as holding a family member in sickness; in the third narrative, previous sin and hurt within the family was seen as resulting in sinful bodily action one generation down. In the fourth narrative hurt was seen to block potential healing.

Healing can only take place through confession and reconciliation at both vertical and horizontal levels, with God as well as with one's neighbour. People are social creatures, enmeshed in social relations that must be restored, in order for them to be healed by God. This corresponds with Catholic understandings of reconciliation – again reflecting the Pauline text on the body (1 Corinthians 12): that in sinning against God, in causing brokenness in one's relationship to God, one sins against the whole church, causing brokenness in one's relations with brothers and sisters. It is therefore vital to reconciliation that people reach out to those they have hurt, compensate them for their hurt and reconcile with them before they can expect to be reconciled with God.

McManus notes that the Rite of Penance (1974, ICEL), now more frequently known as the Rite of Reconciliation, states: 'Penance always entails reconciliation with our brothers and sisters who remain harmed by our sins (No. 5)'. (McManus 1984: 49) It is through the individual's agency *in relation to others, especially in relation to those he or she is related to* that healing takes place.

The altar

The pivotal moment in the healing service was when people, before the start of the actual Eucharistic Mass, were invited to come up to the sanctuary and kneel round the altar. This was a radical invitation. The parish priest of St Michael's Church, Nadi, wrote of this rite in a testimony to Father Thomas just after the second healing service celebrated in his church:

> During the healing mass many parishioners were touched by the Holy Spirit and healed physically and spiritually … Many were very touched when they were asked to come up to [the] sanctuary and touch the Altar. This was the best part of [the] healing mass. I felt this healing mass was the beautiful way to praise God. (Father Marianaud, 10 August 2003)

To Catholics the altar is the most sacred object and the holiest place in a church, the second most sacred being the tabernacle, within which the consecrated host, the Body of Christ, is kept. The perpetually burning red light found in all Catholic churches near the tabernacle indicates that the tabernacle contains the consecrated host. The sanctuary area of the church, where the altar – and the tabernacle – are placed, is an area that is out of bounds during Mass to anyone other than those involved in the Mass. Although particularly during Mass, at all times the sanctuary area of a Catholic church is revered, and unless they have business to do there, people do not enter this area. In fact, at Sacred Heart Cathedral in Suva there is a notice that emphasises this sanctity of the sanctuary, forbidding anyone without authority to enter the area at any time. This rather unusual measure is probably due to the fact that with its central position in downtown Suva, many people from other churches and other faiths pass through the Cathedral at different times of the day, to light a candle, pray or sit quietly in its cool and peaceful ambience.

So this act of leaving the main body of the church and entering into the sacred space of the sanctuary is in itself radical and challenging. 'Never come empty handed to the altar', Father Thomas emphasised cheerfully after making the invitation. People were to bring all their sins, sorrows, frustrations, anger and illnesses, he said, as an offering to lay on the altar. However, many people generally still hesitated at this perceived transgression of the sacred and spatial boundaries in church, this turning upside down of their perceptions of where they belonged.

Following Fijian understandings of the head of a person's body being the 'highest' part of their body and therefore being *tabu* (cf Prologue) the sanctuary area of the church is considered the 'highest' area of the church, and only the hierarchically 'highest' or most important people should be allowed to enter the sanctuary. This gels well with Catholic understandings of the sanctity of the sanctuary area.

In Catholic churches the altar, which is placed within the sanctuary, is at one and the same time the symbol of Christ himself as the high priest offering the sacrifice to God – and the one who was offered. Every time the Eucharist is celebrated at the altar the priest becomes the instrument of the Holy Spirit in the act of transubstantiation: changing the bread and wine to the body and blood of Christ and re-enacting the sacrifice of Christ at Calvary. Time and space is collapsed in the mystery of this ritual. This explains the deep sanctity of the altar in Catholic belief. As a former seminarian described to me:

> … Like the source of his life has been pierced – the heart from which water and blood flowed for *me* … That's very powerful. In the centre of the Holy Mass we [the priest] change the bread to the body and wine to the blood of Jesus. I mean, just thinking of that. Something that happened in that time, which I too, I was there too in that moment. That moment, just imagine. And now I have been given the privilege, the right by God, through the sacrament. (Brother Mika, St Xavier's parish, Ra, interview 21 October 2004)

To place one's hands on the altar is therefore to be invited to place one's hands on the crucified Christ, the High Priest who always intercedes to God on our behalf. To ordinary people, being invited to enter the sanctuary and touch the altar is quite overwhelming.

> Normally, we don't go up to the altar. We don't have the privilege to go there, we don't have the right to go there. But once the opportunity is given … But here, the altar of sacrifice, which we offer the bread and wine reflects [the sacrifice at]

**Figure 6.4   Laying our sins and sorrows on the altar, Our Lady of the
              Immaculate Conception Church, Vatukoula, 22 August 2003**

Calvary, the blood and the flesh. On the Cross in Calvary Jesus Christ offered
himself. With nails on [his] hand[s], both feet, and then his heart was pierced.
(Brother Mika, St Xavier's parish, Ra, interview 21 October 2004)

Father Thomas sought to draw people to the power of the altar. 'Do not be afraid',
he said, 'to touch the altar'. 'Are you afraid to touch God? No! Then don't be
afraid …'. (St Joseph the Worker Church, Tamavua, 15 August 2003) On the other
hand, he also emphasised the potential and transformative power of the altar: 'The
altar is the tomb of Jesus, from where Jesus Christ was resurrected. It is a power
… When you touch the altar you are offering your sinfulness, your sincerity, as
your burnt offerings to the Lord … and he will shower his blessings on you'. (Holy
Trinity Anglican Cathedral, Suva, 8 August 2003)

   People were invited to kneel round the altar, placing the palms of their hands
on the altar. Those who could not reach the altar itself, were asked to kneel or stand
behind the first row of people who have their hands on the altar, and were asked
to put their palms on the shoulders or backs of those in front. 'If you cannot get
to touch the altar, touch the person in front of you, the Spirit of the Lord will run
through that person and cleanse you', Father Thomas told people. (St Joseph the
Worker Church, Suva, 7 August 2003)

   In this way everyone around the altar was connected physically to the altar
and to the power it represented to people, symbolic as well as real, which many

participants felt either physically or spiritually while there. At the same time people were connected to one another physically as well as vocally, and spiritually, as they repeated, line by line, almost like a mantra, a long, chanting-like prayer, a 'healing prayer', saying that they lay on this altar all their brokenness, all their mistakes, their anger, their sorrow, their pain and sins – and asking God for cleansing, forgiveness, reconciliation, healing, strength and renewal. In an entry in my Fieldwork Diary I describe one such experience:

> When people went to the altar, I went too and knelt down, put my hands on the shoulders of the small Indian who had sat in the pew opposite me. He is tiny, perhaps he had polio as a child. When we started to pray I could actually feel the words he was saying through his body. His prayers were thus being transmitted through his body to me *physically*. The chanting, repetitive nature of the prayer – with Father Thomas saying a phrase: 'Heal me Lord' and people repeating it, 'Heal me Lord', 'Touch my brokenness', 'Touch my brokenness', 'Heal my anger, Lord', 'Heal my anger, Lord', 'Cleanse my thoughts, Lord', 'Cleanse my thoughts, Lord' created a meditative rhythm that resonated through this man's body. And at the same time I too was repeating the words … and sensing that from my hands, connected as they were to his body, the prayers were physically transmitted to the rest of my body. In turn, although I was not touching the altar, I felt connected to it nevertheless. (14 August 2003)

I was reminded of the American film from the 1980s, *Children of a Lesser God*, in which the actor William Hurt plays a young, innovative teacher of deaf children. He empowers his pupils and revolutionises their lives by teaching them to learn to 'hear' music by resting their hands on enormous loud speakers, feeling the rhythm and pulse of the music physically, so that it is almost as if they could touch the music. Feeling almost physically connected to this man's prayer, I felt as if I were learning to 'hear' prayer through 'feeling' it, touching it. You could really say that here was indeed an example of the *embodiment* of faith, prayer and communion – with God and neighbour. The experience tangibly emphasised to me the sense of connectness or relationality, physical, vocal and spiritual that this rite affected and symbolised – the underlying theme of the services.[9]

As Csordas (1983: 352) argues, performance of the gesture of laying on of hands in the ritual context is 'an imitation of the healing touch of Jesus portrayed in the Bible … a metonym of the solidarity of the Christian community; the unity of the two bodies touching is the Unity of the Church as the Mystical Body of Christ'. He cites Turner's observation that 'the surface of the body seems everywhere to be treated, not only as the boundary of the individual as a biological and psychological entity but as the frontier of the social self as well'. (1980: 112) I would add to this that the surface of the body is also the frontier of the *spiritual* body.

---

9   This experience is also an example of the embodiment of cultural knowledge gained by the fieldworker's openness to using his or her own body, cf Jackson 1981.

Father Thomas emphasised the importance of people putting the *palms* of their hands flat down on the altar – or against the body of the person in front of them: '[The] palm is very important. The palm has to be open, then we will receive. That's the sign of asking. We don't ask with fists, do we?' he asked me. (Interview 21 September 2003)

This also emphasises the potential power of the stigmata, the five wounds of Christ at the Crucifixion. As Father Thomas once pointed out in a service:

> When you hit your wife you use the palm of your hand, don't you? Husbands, never hit your wives! Joseph did not hit Mary. There was no hitting in the Holy Family! Do not hit your children … unnecessarily … Bring your palms … [to the altar] Jesus had nails put through his palms …. (Holy Family Church, Labasa, 24 August 2003)

A Catholic charismatic woman, who described to me her baptism in the Holy Spirit on a different occasion, explained how she had stood in front of the Tabernacle in her local parish church during the baptism and had clearly felt an immense heat and power emanate from the tabernacle to the palms of her hands. 'Because of the nails', she told me. Feeling heat in her left palm as she later prayed over someone confirmed to her and to others that she had been granted the gift of healing.

In these two ways of referring to Christ's stigmata, a connection is made from the bodily suffering of the living Christ to the transformative power of his body through death and resurrection. So there is a sense of the collapsing of time and space between the historical event of the Crucifixion, its mystery, and the mystery of the 'now' of the present moment. A link of empowerment is made between the Body of Christ and the body of those living today: the palms of people's hands, as Father Thomas points out, containing the potential to do good and to do evil.

The woman who experienced heat in the palms of her hands during her baptism in the Holy Spirit perceived the power of the Body of Christ emanating from the Tabernacle to her hands as a spiritual empowerment from God through her body, to effectuate healing in others. When those she laid hands on similarly felt this power, she was confirmed in her understanding of the link between Christ's body, her body and the bodies of those whom she prayed for by physically laying hands on them – a link which similarly connects past, present and future, the spiritual and the physical.

The rite at the altar of offering, sacrificing at the altar one's sins, and people's ensuing sense of their being cleansed and reconciled to God through acknowledging their wrong-doings and asking God's forgiveness – clearly *symbolises* (without actually being, Father Thomas strongly emphasised) the Catholic sacrament of confession in the rite of penance (also called the rite of reconciliation).

On some occasions in villages, Father Thomas invited people to come to the altar specifically to heal their clan and forefathers, also emphasising that this rite, though it seemed like a form of confession, was not the same thing:

> Extend your hands to the altar [this is] not ... confession as in Church – when
> you do this you are bringing your forefathers [to God], ask the Lord to forgive
> them. (St Peter's Church, Namosi, 26 August 2003)

Much of the theology of the healing services was focused on generational sin and
the ways in which the actions of our forefathers or other members of our family can
bind us in spiritual or physical illness. Since this resonates with traditional Fijian and
Pacific Islander notions of the ways in which past actions are reflected in the present,
cf Chapter 2, the invitation to bring the sins of people's ancestors to the altar and
seek God's forgiveness was also particularly powerful from a cultural perspective.

Almost all those who were asked afterwards what they felt when they touched
the altar – and Father Thomas asked people before they left the sanctuary to share
their feelings with the rest of the congregation in the microphone – almost everyone
attested to having felt something extraordinary: great joy, inner peace, strength,
lightness or warmth or heat. To everyone it was a very special and moving experience
– to enter into the sanctity of the sanctuary, to physically touch the sanctity of the
altar in this way. For some it was an extremely powerful experience.

One man came back from the altar a bit frightened. He had felt such a shock
of energy there that he had withdrawn his hand immediately, thinking that there
was some electric power there and had complained to Sister Ina, who accompanied
Father Thomas, about it. 'You silly man', she replied, 'you should have kept your
hand there to be healed!' But then this man suddenly found that he could lift up his
hand and arm for the first time since he had had a stroke.

A Methodist, who came up to me after the only service held in a Methodist
church, told me that he had felt light when he touched the altar. His hands had felt
light and he had felt light inside, he said, as if something had come in (and here he
made a movement with his hand in a stroke from his breast downwards) and cleansed
him. (Wesley Church, Butt St, 14 August 2003) 'I felt my burdens are lightened';
a Hindu man said at another service, 'I felt I am leaving everything behind. I am
going to love my family and everything will be fine'. My friend Lusia from St Agnes
parish later told me:

> I felt all my guilty feelings ... the way I sometimes talk to my children, my
> impatience with them ... I felt all that just disappear there at the altar ... I felt so
> peaceful inside ... I felt I was cleansed of my sins ... I'm the kind of person that
> when I've done something wrong I'll never go back and say sorry. I don't usually
> do that. It made me completely different. Like I know if I hurt my husband, I'd
> go to him and hug him and say I'm sorry – and my children. And I don't usually
> do that. And I've taught them also to do the same; every time they've hurt us
> they must come back, always ask forgiveness. Like that experience has also
> taught me to teach my children. (Lucia Tukidia, interview October 2004)

People described both spiritual and physical sensations:

'[I felt the] spiritual tension in me relieved';
'[My] body felt lighter and [I] felt energetic and [felt] peace in my heart';
'[I felt the] pain in [my] joints gone'.
(St Peter's Anglican Church, Lautoka)

'A shock went into my hands';
'Both palms … it felt like both my hands were very hot … hot air kept coming up to my hands';
'I felt free';
'I felt strengthened';
'I feel courage';
'I felt healed of my burdens';
[Said by a child] 'I feel love';
'I feel healing in my body'.
(St Joseph the Worker Church, Tamavua, 15 August 2003)

'The people appreciated deeply to be given the golden opportunity to touch the altar. To lay at the Holy Altar of Calvary their burdens, and sorrows, all their loads, spiritually and physically … is a great renewal of faith to our Lord and Saviour who offers us and Himself to the Father on the altar', wrote Sr Ina. (30 September 2003) And Father J.J. Ryan CSS, concelebrant of the healing Mass in his church (which lasted from 4pm till 11pm, with more than 1,200 people present in and outside the church) wrote to the *Fiji Catholic* monthly newspaper of this central ritual element:

> One of the most revealing moments in the overall celebration was when people were invited and facilitated to approach the altar of The Lord, place their hands on it and openly ask Jesus for healing. The impatient eagerness of those present to be immersed in this sacred ritual of cleansing and renewal was genuinely breathtaking. The soiled condition of the altar cloth following the touch of so many wounded hands symbolically bore silent yet eloquent testimony to the depth and bredth of forgiveness and healing abundantly bestowed. (*Fiji Catholic* 3 September 2003: 1, J.J. Ryan, CSS)

The body of Christ

At the end of each Mass, connecting the symbolic sacrifice of sin and brokenness at the altar with the healing power of the Risen Christ, Father Thomas took a consecrated host, the Body of Christ, placed in what is known as a monstrance. A monstrance, from the Latin *monstrare* – to display, is a brass holder with a round, flat glass container that can be opened, into which is inserted a consecrated large host – the body of Christ. The glass 'window' is often surrounded by a circle of brass formed like a sun, perhaps studded with semi-precious stones.

Often, though not always, the monstrance is only ritually handled when a priest or deacon, wearing a humeral veil, a particular vestment used only for this purpose and worn as a cloak over the alb, holds the monstrance with his hands covered by lengths of material, so that the material and not his skin, touches the monstrance. This indicates on the one hand the holiness of the ritual gesture, the deep respect shown to Christ and the subservience and humility of the priest. On the other it indicates the potential efficacy, the potentially dangerous or overwhelming power of the Body of Christ.

Father Thomas, however, handled the monstrance with his bare hands. This did not indicate disrespect or lack of humility, but could perhaps be seen as indicating a more accessible Christ. While leading a continuous chanting of prayers, Father Thomas carried the monstrance through the church. People knelt with bowed heads, repeating the healing prayers, the Sacrament, the Body of Christ passing by everyone at one point, exuding a concentration of healing power. As the former seminarian I discussed this with emphasised:

> [Christ] is in us. We can come in contact with Jesus in this way as he passes by. When he passes by, I bow. In my whole heart I ask him to heal me, to touch me more, to heal me more. For me it's a person to person encounter. I've come in contact with Jesus in person passing by. (Brother Mika, St Xavier's parish, Ra, interview 21 October 2004)

Touching the transcendent: is healing only healing if it lasts?

At the end of the healing service people were asked to fill out a Healing Testimony Form, were given a printed 'Healing Prayer' to take home with them, and were instructed to pray this prayer daily as husband and wife or as a family in front of a lit candle for a period of nine days, as one would a *novena*.[10] Surprisingly, although the majority of people in Fiji are not generally well-versed in writing, they took very seriously the idea of filling out the Healing Testimony Form. The fact that so many of them did fill it out, indicates to me that this too was part of the whole experience of healing, expressing a sense of empowerment: to testify in writing that yes, I felt healed of such and such an ailment at such and such a moment at during this service. Several parish priests expressed their experience of the healing service on this form, or wrote in person to Father Thomas at a later stage.

I would argue that this act of writing a testimony is an extension of the ritual experience of the transcendent and of healing. Being photographed on account of having been healed and filling out the testimony forms made tangible that sense of the transcendent which might be difficult to grasp, and added, I believe, to the

---

10   A *novena* is a devotion (prayer) undertaken by an individual, a family or a group, usually over a period of nine days to pray for a particular intention, either one's own or on behalf of someone else.

sense of efficacy and potency of the healing experience. In a similar way it added to the celebratory atmosphere of 'anything' being possible in Christ.

Is healing only to be considered healing if it is lasts? Although it would be interesting to know whether the empowerment people experienced lasted, whether the healing lasted, whether the feeling lasted, the fact is that – if only for a moment – in the context of the healing services, people had *felt different*, had *felt touched* by the transcendent – perhaps even *changed* and *transformed*. From my experience of charismatic worship both within the Catholic Church and within Pentecostal churches in Fiji I believe that this is important. As Davis points out,

> Religious feeling emerges – sometimes fleetingly, sometimes lastingly, as an explicit, recognizable element in religious living. There is then an express awareness of the transcendent ... [those who experience this] have discerned and acknowledged a distinctive feeling, relating them directly to the reality with which their varied religious behaviour is concerned. That religious feeling remains as the animating element in their many religious activities and passivities. (Davis 1976: 26)

The central ritual elements of the healing services, the ritual use of the altar and of the rite of Benediction when the Body of Christ is carried through the church, are significant not merely in that they express the power of the Risen Christ, but express the journey to this empowerment through the brokenness and suffering of Christ for our sake.

In ritual and spatial terms these two rites radically transcend time; transgress and transcend liturgical and cultural boundaries between body and space, between God and people, between priest and laity. As mentioned earlier, normally, no one who is not ritually involved in a Mass is invited *into* the sanctuary area where the altar is. Those receiving Communion in a Catholic church may only go as far as where the priest and Eucharistic ministers stand to offer Communion, directly in front of the sanctuary area. To invite people *into* the sanctuary is inviting them into the holiest and most powerful part of the church space.

To furthermore invite people to kneel at the altar and place their hands on it, is to bring them into contact with the ritually and spiritually most powerful and *tabu* place in a Catholic church. This is a very tangible spiritual empowerment, experienced physically, which had a strong and powerful impact on people. Normally, the congregation of a Catholic church would experience the Eucharist either when they receive the Body and Blood of Christ in Communion in front of the sanctuary area. Or the Body of Christ, the consecrated host, would be 'exposed' on the altar in a monstrance for a period of silent prayer, ending with a Benediction in which the priest lifts up the monstrance and makes the sign of the cross.

To take the consecrated host, the Body of Christ *out* of the sanctuary area and carry it *through* the church, is symbolically and, to those experiencing it, really bringing Christ *to* people, bringing Christ *close to* people, at one and the same time emphasising his divinity, yet in bringing him close to people, also emphasising God's chosen humanity and likeness with us.

In these healing services focus was in a way deflected from the priest and healing facilitator as dramatic healer (as in the Bonnke crusade) to the celebrant as merely facilitating healing through the power of the Eucharist – a quiet, personal inner healing and transformation – yet very much based on social reconciliation, on reconciliation with one's close family. On the other hand, Father Thomas' charisma and manner drew attention to his person. And the long queues for personal, individual healing after the Mass, indicated that people attributed particular efficacy to Father Thomas' gift of facilitating healing – through the laying on of hands or his explicit prayer for them – however much he emphasised in each service that healing took place throughout the healing service.

The ways in which people in these Catholic healing services were invited to bodily transcend culturally determined spatial, hierarchical boundaries and cultural boundaries, and boundaries of the transcendent and sacred, intensified the sense of empowerment they experienced. To use their bodies in these radically different ways – to raise their hands above their heads; to speak loudly in church; to testify; and, more than anything else: to be invited to enter the sanctuary area and actually touch the altar, were spiritually transformative experiences for many people.

Especially within religious contexts the sense and understanding of community in ritual practice is central to people's experiences and central to any understanding of embodiment. People's sense of embodiment may be individual but they are not acting alone; they are acting *with* others, *in relation to* others. And it is a similar *relationality* that was stressed so many times within the healing Masses in spiritual, moral, social and temporal terms: that people's spiritual and physical health and well-being is dependent on their individual actions, yet closely connected to the actions of people's family and kin – those living as well as those of former generations.

Theologies of healing and reconciliation

The theology behind these healing Masses has many similarities with the beliefs behind traditional Fijian reconciliation rites and with Pentecostal theologies of deliverance. At the same time there are significant differences in belief and ritual practice between these forms of reconciliation.

While the doctrine expressed in the structure and liturgy of these healing services focused on the individual in relation to God and the strengthening and reconciliation of *family* relations and did not 'address the deeper problems of society'. (Father Pat Colgan SSC, interview 2005) Charismatic Catholic doctrine as I experienced it in Fiji, places the individual's relationship with God through the Holy Spirit firmly within the context of social relationships, the Church, society and the wider world.

'We can never be really growing in the Spirit', a priest said at the Catholic Charismatic Revival (CCR) Convention in Suva in July 1998, 'unless we are growing with one another'. Bearing witness, he said, should first and foremost be manifested in caring for the sick, the needy and the poor, that is, engaging with the world about us and seeking the common good for all. The 1998 CCR convention took place just before the first anniversary of the 1997 Constitution, and, expressing Catholic teachings on Social Justice, based on social responsibility and inclusivity, prayers were said for the new Constitution and for the continuing reconciliation between the different communities of Fiji.

At the 2003 CCR Convention held in Lautoka values of connectedness, communality and inclusivity were preached: 'We all need to reach out to each other ... the loving that we enter into, is a healing. I cannot heal myself ... it is Jesus who heals me ... He wants to heal broken relationships so the Church can radiate his love'. (Father Cecil Williams, 14 June 2003)

> Our spiritual life can never be fulfilled until we come together as a community to fulfil ourselves in the Eucharist. When you reach out to another person spiritually ... when we are faithful ... miracles will happen ... We look for big miracles ... but it's the small things that happen every day ... When two persons who hate each other reconcile, that's a miracle...There are many people who are hurt in this world. One of the aspects of communal spirituality is when one shares what he has ... You cannot say you love God if you fail to help others. [Through] community spirituality [we are] united in mind and soul. (Father Rokumatu, CCR Lautoko,15 June 2003)

Catholic teachings emphasise that suffering is an inevitable part of life and that following Christ may involve suffering. Yet a person's suffering is never without meaning, nor does it exist of itself; it is connected to Christ's suffering on the Cross and to others in the world. Nor is a person ever alone in their suffering, Christ is always walking with them: 'If Jesus says, "Follow me", we have to do it. How do we do it? Jesus only gives us those crosses to bear that we can carry ... And when we suffer, we are redeeming the world'. (Father Cecil Williams, 14 June 2003)

At a 'Reconciliation Workshop' during the 2003 Catholic Convention 'reconciliation' connected the spiritual level of reconciliation with God through the Sacrament of Confession to forgiveness of those who have hurt a person and to issues of social justice in society in relation to the 2000 coup. Suffering, confession, truth and justice – leading to reconciliation, were connected in relation to the coup:

> Our relationship is a bodily relationship, we have to go through pain and sorrows at times. After the coup the Ministry of Reconciliation tried to heal the wounds inflicted on our society by those perpetrators. But reconciliation cannot come about unless justice is done ... If you try to suppress the pain, our life will be like

a pressure cooker, we will never experience peace. (Father Sulio Turagakacivi
CCR, 14 June 2003)

This chapter has discussed reconciliation from personal, spiritual, experiential and
embodiment perspectives. These final quotes link to the following and concluding
chapter on reconciliation at the national level in Fiji, Christian approaches to
reconciliation, and ecumenical and interfaith dialogue.

Chapter 7
The Dignity of Difference: Paths of Dialogue in Diversity

Letter to the Colonel

sir, some people are sad
because of your words
and actions
that is why I bring you
this cup of kava
from a neighbour's soil

it contains the tears
of workers, farmers, miners
fisherfolks who go down
to the depths
of adopted seas
for food
many have lost their jobs
robbed of opportunities
to make a profit
here, take it anyway
symbol of suffering and sorrow
of women in the fields
in garment factories
at home where children
cry out their fears and frustration
take it, sir, it is yours

ah, but you see, sir
for some this cup is full
of hope
when you drink it you
will know your victory
like the kava it comes
from the roots of people's
hopes in the land
their collective confidence
will lift you up
and their new-found pride

will bloom around you
while they wait
for their duty-bound son
to bury his weapons
and liberate their souls
and by the way, sir
I hope that as you drink this
you will remember
that when the dawn breaks
no one can shut out
the light

14 May 1988 Konai Thaman[1] (1997)

---

1   For other poetry and writing by Konai Thamen, Tongan poet and academic at University of the South Pacific, see inter alia 1980, 1981, 1987, 1993, 2000. For an overview of Pacific Islander writing and publication, see Crowl 2008. Re Pacific Island poetry see Clarke 2007.

Although Konai Thaman's poem was written to Sitiveni Rabuka just over a decade after his 1987 coups, its words tragically fit just as well the suffering, destruction of everyday life and insecurity experienced by people in Fiji after the 2000 coup.

In 1994, in the atmosphere of re-building Fiji society after the 1987 coups, former Methodist President, the late Paula Niukula added two new pillars to the Three Pillars ideal of *vanua, lotu, matanitu*: 'the money economy and a pluralist society. In these areas of concern, all ethnic groups must work together. For we need each other. Our future belongs together'. (Niukula 1994: 122-123 in *Pacific Journal of Theology* 1996: 10) The Citizens' Constitutional Forum's plain language guide to the 1997 Constitution, published in English, Fijian and Hindi similarly expressed, 'Just like a chain joined together by individual rings, religious tolerance unites everybody, despite their differences'. (CCF 1998: 14)

However, as the tragedy of the 2000 coup, its chaotic and at all levels costly aftermath, and the situation since the 2006 coup, have shown, the reconciliation Reverend Niukula and so many others then and since hoped and prayed for, has now receded even further than at the time of his writing. Fiji is now more divided than it was before Cession in 1874 – and much of the division of society has taken place in the name of *vanua* and Church.

> The upheavals of May 2000 were far more divisive and traumatic than the coups in 1987. No longer was there consensus in the Fijian community. Certain of the IndoFijian were subjected to acts of violence and thuggery the likes of which one hopes never to witness again. Reconciliation and forgiveness have been vexed questions ever since. Fijians have drawn on their customs and traditions as well as their Christian heritage to initiate the process. One does not doubt the sincerity of the gesture. Neither does one question the need for some kind of healing that allows the nation to bind up its wounds. However, if reconciliation is to be meaningful, cathartic and sincere it has to be in a language everyone can speak: an engagement in which all can be involved. Anything less would be demeaning and diminishing. Unless all are part of the process, it is difficult to see how the nation can come to terms with its past hurts and pain. (Ratu Madraiwiwi, 26 October 2005)

The language of reconciliation that leads to healing, is listening, respect and dialogue. This is stated again and again from many different quarters in this final chapter. 'Without an ongoing commitment from all aspects of society to engage in dialogue, including from government and the military, the coup culture will prevail. With the right attitude, dialogue can bring people together and help reconcile Fiji with its history of political instability', Reverend Akuila Yabaki, Chief Executive Officer, Citizens' Constitutional Forum (CCF) noted in a lecture at University of Queensland, July 2009. (*Tutaka Online* 3(3) 2009: 1)

The Citizens' Constitutional Forum and ECREA are among the strongest and most vocal organisations that speak out and raise awareness of social justice issues at all levels in Fiji society. Through the media, in seminars and workshops across the islands, in DVD, CD, in plain language guides and academic publications they work to raise awareness and educate on issues of human rights, constitutional democracy, religious tolerance and freedom and equity for all people and communities of Fiji society.

Stressing the importance of listening, respect and dialogue in all areas of community and national life as a tool to bridging differences across ethnic, religious, hierarchical, gender, age, and community divides, these organisations continuously advocate the value and importance of accepting difference and diversity, and point to models for reconciliation and forgiveness.[2] In addition to this, Interfaith Search Fiji is an important voice on issues of religious freedom. In the years of my research the Catholic Church in Fiji was by far the most vocal of all the churches in speaking out against social injustice, ethnic and religious oppression.

This concluding chapter encompasses debate on a particular high-profile traditional reconciliation ceremony performed in atonement for the 2000 Coup, different Christian approaches to processes of reconciliation at inter-personal, spiritual and political levels, and inter-ethnic, ecumenical and interfaith dialogue.

Christianity – exclusive or inclusive?

> If Christians, who are supposed to be motivated by Jesus' command of love, are not able to accept, love and respect people of other races and religions, any call for Fiji to be declared a Christian state must be judged as utter hypocrisy. In fact, we have seen our Christian faith used to justify ethno-nationalism, hatred and the desecration of places of worship. This is not the way of Jesus and I am ashamed that Christianity has been used in this way. (Roman Catholic Archbishop Mataca, *Fiji Times* 1 October 2003: 7)

The above statement, from Roman Catholic Archbishop Petero Mataca, and the address of Former Vice-President, High Chief and High Court Judge Ratu Joni Madraiwiwi (a Methodist), given at a conference at the Australian National University in 2005 sum up many of the critical views presented in this and former chapters on the politicisation of the Methodist Church in Fiji and its moves with Pentecostal Churches for Fiji to be declared a Christian state:

> The Methodist Church is totally Fijianised and would be barely recognizable to the Methodist fathers in the United Kingdom. A Fijian gloss has been put on the Christian message that provides justification for the present political

---

2   See for example documentaries by Fiji playwright Larry Thomas 2001 and ECREA 2001b capturing the hate, bigotry, violence and tragedy of the 2000 coup, and discussing ways towards reconciliation, and ECREA 2004, 2009a, 2009b, Costello-Olsson 2005, ECREA and CCF 2006, CCF 2004, 2007, Barr 1990, 1998, 2004a, 2004b, 2005a, 2005b, 2007. Re multiculturalism see also Banivanua 1997, Gaunder 2007.

developments since 1987. The newer Christian Churches, which have their roots in American evangelical Christianity, have complemented the role of the Methodist church. They have made their stand on the basis of those within the foldand those outside, with the latter being considered heathens.

Such assertions leave little room for any interfaith dialogue and merely widen our differences. In this context, the concept of a Christian state is not a new theme in our history. However, it has gathered strength in recent years from the position of the Methodist Church and the stance of the newer denominations. To put this issue in perspective, the Methodist elders are more concerned with form than substance. However, any such initiative however well-intended would be divisive and dangerous. Because it would provide unscrupulous souls the means with which to impose Christianity at some time in the future. (Madraiwiwi 26 October 2005, see also *Fiji Times* 8 October 2005: 4)

Critics of the Christian state ideal emphasise that its realisation would entail Christian dominance over non-Christians, which in Fiji essentially means Fijian dominance over Indo-Fijians. Yet Christian faith was always meant to be inclusive, 'the saving power of God cannot be confined to the visible boundaries of culture, race or church', Archbishop Mataca is quoted as saying (Casimira 2002: 7):

> The spirit of God breathes where it wills and is at work outside as well as inside the church. We Christians must not be arrogant. We should respect the religious traditions of others and not condemn or insult or oppress them ... It is time for us Christians to really appropriate the message of Jesus and not be driven by narrow nationalist sentiments.

In a *Fiji Times* interview (24 May 2000 in Barr 2004a: 22) shortly after the 2000 coup, former President of the Methodist Church Josateki Koroi stated that: 'Deep down the root cause of what has been happening in Fiji since 1987 is the failure of the Church to preach the Kingdom of God ... The Methodist Church nationalist dissident group has been preaching the gospel of racism, culturalism and the superiority of the Fijian race over others, contributing to hatred'.

The language of reconciliation

In the years following the coup of 2000 before the 2006 coup, 'forgiveness' and 'reconciliation' were intensely debated topics in Fiji. Differing understandings, in particular different Christian understandings, of the concepts of forgiveness and reconciliation were debated in the media, and different high-profile reconciliation ceremonies were staged.

What was pervasive in this debate was a general lack of clarity as to what exactly forgiveness and reconciliation mean and entail. This has been pointed out many times in the past years by participants in the debate: 'Forgiveness and reconciliation are used loosely and interchangeably to describe the mending of relationships after a violation is committed'. (Concerns 2006: 3) What was also pervasive in the debate was the growing sense in many parts of Fiji society that those who purported to be seeking reconciliation paid more attention to 'form' than actual 'content' and 'substance'. Was there really a genuine desire within the government, people were asking, to actually *achieve* reconciliation? Were these ceremonies employed in part (or wholly) to side-track the judicial process of unravelling who was complicit in the 2000 coup?

> What seems to be lacking in the whole process is much evidence of genuine contrition. There has been no great and obvious conversion on the part of the coup-makers or their supporters towards the ideas of democracy or the equal rights of all Fiji's citizens. Secondly we have to ask what role the government plays. Does it see itself as the representative of the rights of all the people of Fiji who elected it? Or does it see itself as some kind of neutral body attempting to bring together two quarrelling factions? Or is it true, as many suspect, that it is merely acting as the advocate for the perpetrators of illegality? The desire to redefine certain criminal acts as political or 'associated with a political, as opposed to a purely criminal, objective' would seem to lend weight to the last of these options. (Father Kieran Moloney SSC in *Concerns* 2006: 1)

Ritualised reconciliations

In 2002 rumours abounded that the CRW (Counter Revolutionary Warfare) special unit soliders who had been arrested in November 2001 in connection with the mutinies at the Labasa barracks and at Queen Elizabeth Barracks in which Commodore Bainimarama narrowly missed an attempt on his life, were to make a public apology in the form of a traditional Fijian *isoro*. (Reverend Joni Langi, interview 2002, *Fiji Times* 12 November 2002: 1) But the media later reported that the Commander and the Chairman of the Great Council of Chiefs had refused the offer. (Cf *Fiji Times* 28 November 2002: 6, 30 November 2002: 6)

According to Reverend Langi, while in prison the soldiers had given their lives to Christ. They had become Born Again Christians and had a deep wish to seek forgiveness for what they had done. A stern Letter to the Editor from the Media Cell of the Military Forces responded to a letter in the *Fiji Times* by a reader in some consternation as to why this offer had been refused: 'We stress that the two systems [the traditional and the judicial] cannot complement each other and any reconciliation in the terms proposed by Mr Nasea can never find a lasting solution unless it is done at the conclusion of all pending cases'. (*Fiji Times* 30 November 2002: 6)

At a Women in Reconciliation workshop in 2003 University of the South Pacific lecturer Cema Bolabola expressed that the Government's use of 'Fijian

customary practices in reconciling different communities is not workable … a
farce and … unjust …because it is culturally insensitive to those whose cultures
are different from the Fijians'. (*Daily Post* 23 October 2003: 3) According to the
article Cakaudrove chief Adi Mei Kainona considered the practice of *bulubulu* to
have been 'bastardised'. 'It is all just a show and not achieving anything because
the forgiveness is not from the heart', she said. (Ibid.)

In 2004 a very costly 'Reconciliation Week' was planned to coincide with Fiji
Day on 10 October. It was framed by two high-profile reconciliation ceremonies:
a government organised *matanigasau* held in Albert Park and a 'Foot-washing
ceremony' also held in Albert Park, arranged by the ACCF. Under the heading
'President Commands Forgiveness' *The Daily Post* (5 October 2004: 1) quoted
President Ratu Iloilo at the launch of 'Reconciliation Week' as reportedly saying,
'I now call those of us, who were aggrieved, suffered losses, inflicted bodily harm,
wrongfully imprisoned during the turbulent crisis in May and November 2000, to
reconcile yourself with those who made you suffer'.

Two high chiefs, the Tui Cakau and Lands Minister Ratu Naiqama Lalabalavu led
the *matanigasau* ceremony at Albert Park, Suva, at which 20 *tabua* (whale's teeth)
were presented to seek forgiveness from the parliamentarians held hostage during
the 2000 coup. He was accompanied by Naitasiri chief Ratu Inoke Takiveikata,
Bau chief Ratu Tanoa Cakobau and Ratu Inoke Seniloli, the younger brother of
imprisoned Vice President Ratu Jope Seniloli. It was an act of contrition viewed by
many as hypocritical. Deposed Prime Minister Mahendra Chaudhry and the MPs
held hostage in 2000 were not present (Bihm 2007; Newland 2006: 332-333), and an
intense debate ensued in the English language media with much criticism levied at
the Government.[3]

> Forgiveness cannot be forced upon people and it is easier said than done for people,
> especially those hit hard by the crisis, to put the issue behind them and move on.
> More needs to be done to heal the wounds of May 2000. Justice is what Fiji's
> citizens want and justice is what the Government and the judiciary should give
> them. (*Fiji Times*, editorial 25 October 2004: 6)

Criticism concerned the ways in which the act blurred the boundaries between
traditional rites and the judicial process; that traditional reconciliation rites were
used incorrectly and politically; that high-profile traditional reconciliation acts were
put above the feelings of those wronged and emotionally wounded in the events of
2000; and that beyond the form of these reconciliation ceremonies there was little
or no attempt by the government to implement restorative justice measures and
recompensation for the victims:

---

3   *Fiji Times* 5 October 2004: 1, 3, 6 October 2004, 7 October 2004: 10, 8 October
2004: 10, 9 October 2004: 6, 10 October 2004: 2, 10, 11, 11, 11 October 2004: 6, 7, 13
October 2004, 21 October 2004: 13, 22 October 2004: 6, 23 October 2004: 7, 25 October
2004: 6, 26 October 2004: 6, *Sunday Times* 10 October 2004: 6.

An attempt to merely showcase reconciliation without any real effort to reconcile at the top political level would be futile and a waste of resources. Restorative justice will need to be a part and parcel of the national reconciliation programs. The process of forgiveness and the rule of law are two different issues and must be kept apart. Fiji Week celebrations must not be used to undermine the functions of the judiciary and the rule of law. (D. Narain, Letter to the Editor, *Fiji Times* 9 October 2004: 6)

It was pointed out by many people that the Qarase Government was rushing through a lengthy traditional process which needs full consensus from both parties before it can be conducted. Commander Bainimarama was quoted as critiquing the *matanigasau* as being premature and an empty gesture because the hostages and [Indo-Fijian] families who had been driven from their homes in several parts of the country were not present: 'They are the only ones who should be doing the forgiving … I as the military commander fully support the reconciliation exercise; this country needs reconciliation but not [by] having a matanigasau without those whose lives were affected from the political upheaval of 2000'. (*Daily Post* 5 October 2004: 1) Ratu Epeli Ganilau, former chairman of the Great Council of Chiefs, emphasised that 'such a moving ceremony loses its essence in the absence of the victims of May 2000, the very people who were wronged'. (*Daily Post* 6 October 2004: 1, see also ibid: 3, 5, 12)

Labour parliamentarian Dr Ganeshwar Chand, one of the Indo-Fijian hostages held at gunpoint during the parliamentary siege in 2000 said (*Daily Post* 6 October 2004: 1) that he 'accepts wholeheartedly the sacredness of the *matanigasau* but … it would have made more sense if those few miscreants who wronged him, his family, his Government and his nation apologised'. Pointing out that he had been invited at the last minute, on 3 October 2004, with no prior consultation, unclear as to whether the *vanua* was apologising on behalf of the few wrongdoers, which, he felt, would be quite wrong, he emphasised, 'For me, an apology would make more sense if it came without State interference. I would have thought that if there was to be any sincere repentance and atonement, there should have been a process of dialogue and discussion, leading ultimately to the ceremony'. (*Daily Post* 6 October 2004: 1)

> Reconciliation should have come after justice has been done, the court cases have taken place, those who have been proven guilty have been put into prison … they had asked for forgiveness, compensation [had been given] to those who have been affected, whether physically, economically, psychologically. Then to have reconciliation, the healing process … the reconciliation rituals which in themselves are meaningful. It's just the timing [that's wrong]. (Father George Ting, Our Lady of Fatima parish, Nadera, interview 28 October 2004)

Journalist Ema Tagicakibau (*Fiji Times* 23 October 2004: 7) described a slow and laborious process of reconciliation over several years in another country in the region, stating that performing the *matanigasau* when the victims were not ready for it and to Indo-Fijians for whom this cultural act hadn't the same meaning, 'not only trivialises custom, but also unfairly imposes on other groups to respect it the same way Fijians do. At worst, it shows the manipulation of custom to suit the Government's political agenda'. A reader in Sydney had this comment:

> It is a breath of fresh air that two women [Ema Tagicakibau in the above article and Adi Koila Nailatikau, a chief and one of the hostages, in a speech to the Senate] have stepped forward and eloquently highlighted just how meaningless the forgiveness ceremony foisted upon the Fiji public at their own cost was. (Mareko Vuli, Sydney, Letter to the Editor, *Fiji Times* 26 October 2004: 6)

Justice, forgiveness and reconciliation

'Reconciliation must be founded upon acceptance by all parties of the rule of law', a CCF press release (6 October 2004) makes clear:

> The process of reconciliation must be open to all communities in Fiji … Only a process which is inclusive of different cultural and religious traditions can bring us together … True reconciliation can only begin when wrong-doers admit what they have done and accept responsibility for the consequences of their actions … Wrongdoers must cooperate with the legal process …There can be no timetable for forgiveness. The coup and mutiny had many victims, and their healing process must be allowed to run its course … National reconciliation is a collective responsibility. (CCF Position on National Reconciliation Process, excerpt from 6 October press release in *Fiji Times*, 7 October 2004)

In a keynote speech at a Reconciliation Seminar organised by the Minister for Social Welfare and Poverty Alleviation in September 2004, Reverend Dr Russ Daye, lecturer at Pacific Theological College, stressed the slow, processual nature of 'forgiveness'. (Cf Daye 2003, 2004) Differentiating between interpersonal and political forgiveness, he emphasised that the first element in a process of political forgiveness is truth-telling. Narrative truth-telling, he explained, gives victims a public forum in which to share their stories. Although they may never be fully compensated for their suffering, 'public acknowledgment of their suffering can be like a balm on their mental wounds'. Another element of political forgiveness is justice-building, with measures oriented towards both retributive (punitive) and restorative justice. 'Only after the country has spent years seriously pursuing truth-telling, justice-building, compensation, and healing; only then would it be appropriate to expect victims to consider forgiveness', he concluded.

In 2005 the Government attempted to introduce the controversial and divisive so-called Reconciliation, Tolerance and Unity Bill which Jone Dakuvula, CCF, pointed out (Letter to the Editor, *Daily Post* 17 May 2005) 'aims to grant pardons to all persons already sentenced and in Jail and to stop all investigations and prosecutions. It will totally absolve them of any responsibility for their criminal acts through the grant of amnesty, and legally will wipe them off the Court records'. He details here the traditional meaning and protocol of *matanigasau*:

> Matanigasau, to be meaningful and effective in its objective of repairing damaged relations and righting individual and communal wrongs, must be based on prior agreement between the Parties involved, that is the appropriate process for reconciliation … usually established first through consultation between representatives of each party. This is necessary to avoid shame, rejection or aggravation of hurt feelings caused by the wrongful act. Matanigasau should not be presented unilaterally. And it has to be presented to the correct representatives of the victims. Etiquette of traditional process has to be observed if the ends of justice, forgiveness and unity is to be achieved. In the modern context, the wronged party may accept matanigasau but still want the legal process to be pursued so that the perpetrator takes personal responsibility for his act … The Reconciliation and Unity Bill … has not been the subject of prior consultation and agreement between the perpetrators and the victims. That is why the victims elected representatives have rejected the Bill from the start. Because it appears to be an imposition, indeed an insult to the principles of restorative justice. (Ibid.)

> The Government demands unconditional forgiveness from the victims [of the coup] to the perpetrators. It says this is the Fijian and Christian basis of reconciliation. Behind that is the threat that if the victims do not express forgiveness through the mechanisms of the Bill, then they are not worthy of any respect or justice. The message is you support this Bill or you are not going to get anything at all. Is that consistent with principles of Fijian reconciliation customs of *matanigasau* and *veisorosorovi*? That the party that does the wrong demands unconditional forgiveness from the victims as the price for reconciliation? Under this Bill, the perpetrators are not even required to contribute any form of recompense to the victims as in customary reconciliation. The state will pay and it is a very small sum.[4]

As discussed in Chapter 2 Fijian understandings of *ibulubulu, isoro* or *matanigasau* are that through these communal ritual processes a grievance is 'buried' – 'gone', 'over', 'finished', 'forgotten'. The wrong-doing has been confessed and acknowledged, the aggrieved clan recompensed through ritual presentations and speeches made according to given protocol. Material recompensation has been received in the form of *tabua*, kava, mats, kerosene and other valuables. There is (cf S. Niukula 2003 in Chapter 4) a sense of transformation, a sense of restoration of social and spiritual balance through the ritualised transactions.

According to several Fijians I spoke to grievances are indeed buried but, from an emotional point of view, in negative ways. In traditional rites the reconciliation

---

4   Dakuvula, *The Fiji Times* 31 August 2005: 7, see also CCF 2005, Yabaki 24 May 2005, Fiji Government 9 May 2005, Bihm 2007.

of communal relations is more important than individual feelings. The rite cleanses, reconciles and restores clan relations, but people do not at individual levels confront, acknowledge and confess their wrong-doings and seek forgiveness. The wounds of individual victims are therefore *buried*, sought forgotten, not *healed* as such. Hidden from sight the wounds continue to fester, and eventually erupt again.

The individual perpetrator of, say, a rape or murder, need not be present at a reconciliation ceremony, but is represented by a clan spokesman, who through a ritual presentation of a *tabua* and often other valuables too, asks the representative of another clan for reconciliation on behalf of his clan. As this Catholic man describes:

> In Fijian tradition, as soon as a crime is committed, the same day both sides must reconcile, they don't want to disrupt community life … There is group pressure to accept an apology … but the hurt is still there … The *mata ni vanua* represents the perpetrator, he is smart to talk … and the perpetrator might be forced to reconcile. The victim is represented by other clan members, he won't accept the apology, he accepts because of the authority of the vanua or chief … it's disrespectful to show anger … but later on they'll take revenge … the hurt inside is buried, you bury the wound within the person. ('K', interview 15 September 2005)

Conversion and reconciliation with God

2004 was declared a 'National Year of Prayer' by the ACCF in association with the Ministry of National Reconciliation and Unity. In the pamphlet for 'Season 2 of the National Year of Prayer 2004', the theme of which was 'desperation', President Iloilo wrote, 'After the dark days of 1987 and 2000, and as a result of the prayers of our people, our country is now being transformed through the process of prayer'. The pamphlet notes (emphasis as in original):

> The solution of our problem is simple! When our people, leaders, Church ministers and we who 'are called by His name humble ourselves and pray and search for Him, and turn from our wicked ways, He will hear from heaven and forgive our sins and heal our land'.
>
> Division, mistrust, and *lack of love* affect the Body of Christ in this nation, lack of love both for the Lord and for the brethren … Have we kept this Nation safe and maintained our Christian heritage? Have we defended the faith in the eyes of the world? Where is the voice of the Church? … We have turned from our Christian heritage and can no longer be called a Christian nation. We have allowed other gods to come into our Nation and because of the presence of these other gods, our right to stand for the things of God is under threat.

During a three day 'Corporate Repentance' workshop in 'Reconciliation Week' in 2004 the first speaker, then Methodist minister and principal of Davuilevu Methodist training college, Reverend Tuikilakila Waqairatu, spoke on 'Law and Grace – self-realisation and confession'. Basing his words closely on Old Testament understandings and the covenant relationship between 'Jehova God and Israel' he pointed out:

> Like Moses freed the Israelites from physical bondage, Jesus Christ will enter our hearts and transform our own spiritual bondage. When you are transformed you will love to follow the law of God. If Christ says 'love Indians', you will do that – because you want to … We are called to … recreate the constitution, *vanua*, law and business to reflect God's image, God's love, God's covenant. (7 October 2004)

Both of these quotes emphasise individual conversion and spiritual transformation as the way to reconciliation. Lack of reconciliation is seen (cf Chapter 2) in terms of spiritual bondage and, in the first text, due to not caring well enough for Fiji's Christian heritage. 'Other gods' is not a reference to ancestral gods, but to the gods of non-Christian religions. (Cf Methodist submission to the 1995 Constitution, Chapter 1)

The Corporate Repentance workshop was conducted entirely in Fijian. One Indo-Fijian man was present, but disappeared by morning tea on the first day. I asked a group of participant pastors from Christian Mission Fellowship why the focus of this 'Reconciliation Week' workshop seemed to be on reconciling intra-Fijian relations rather than on reconciliation between Fijians and Indo-Fijians. Speaking of the tremendous hurt between many Pentecostals and the Methodist Church and the *vanua* dating back many years, they explained that the first step towards reconciliation in Fiji must be reconciliation between Fijians. Once this was in place, they told me, then Fijians could address reconciliation with other communities.

I asked the pastors about the notion of a simultaneous vertical and horizontal axis of reconciliation in which the individual's reconciliation with their neighbour is necessary in order to achieve reconciliation with God. The pastors explained that the most important aspect of reconciliation is the individual's reconciliation with God (the vertical relationship). They referred to the doctrine of Justification in which God, through the sacrifice of Christ, is believed to have acquitted people once and for all of their sins, through his mercy and grace, treating them as if they were righteous. Justification, according to Luther, was granted to mankind on the basis of faith alone. (Livingstone, ed 1977) Justification, the pastors explained, means that our sins have already once and for all been forgiven on the Cross. Reconciliation between individual and neighbour and individual and God therefore does not have to happen at the same time.

Steps to reconciliation

> In the act you performed you not only hurt God, you cut your relationship
> from God, and also there is the social effect of those sins. (Archbishop Mataca,
> interview 3 November 2004)

Catholic teachings on forgiveness and reconciliation emphasise that sin hurts not
only the victim, but God, the whole Church and the perpetrator him or herself.
(Cf Chapter 6) Reconciliation therefore necessitates confession, repentance and a
conscious act of reparation by the perpetrator for the sin committed. In this doctrine
reconciliation between individual and God is only possible if there is *simultaneous*
reconciliation between individual and neighbour. In a parish talk on reconciliation
a Catholic priest emphasised the interconnectedness of these elements in relation to
the Catholic Sacraments of confession and reconciliation:

> Reconciliation to Christians is not incidental to our lives … it encompasses
> all our living. In Genesis Adam and Eve sinned, sin came into the world and
> from then on God was acting in the world as reconciliator (Genesis 6: 5) …
> Reconciliation doesn't enter into the world in bits and pieces. The Flood was the
> end of Creation, the end of the universe, the water symbolising the evil covering
> the world (Genesis 9 and 10). But (cf 2 Corinthians 5: 16) Christ died on the
> Cross to reconcile the world with God. The ministry of reconciliation invades
> every instance of the Gospels. The Sacrament of Reconciliation [achieved
> through] the Sacrament of Confession … highlights that sin is not a personal
> matter. The offender simultaneously sins against God, against the Church [the
> people of Christ] and against the victim. This is why we go to confession.
>
> Someone steals a cow in Ra, goes to confession, gets three Hail Mary's …
> *Don't* go to confession if you have not already repaired the sin … [if you haven't]
> given back the cow! Confession is not there to give an easy way out. Your
> offence is against the person and against God. I damage myself in perpetrating
> the offence, and I also damage the Church because I am part of the Church.
> I have made a wound in the Church. (Father Kieran Maloney, SSC, Pious X
> Church, Raiwaqa, 15 February 2006)

Catholic theologian Robert J. Schreiter describes (2002) three characteristics
which mark the spirituality of reconciliation: 1) an attitude of listening and waiting:
Victims of violence must tell their story over and over again in order to escape the
narrative of the lie that is expressed in the violence committed against them …
learning to wait is important, because it takes time to allow painful memories
to surface and be narrated, for deep and penetrating wounds to heal, and for
reconciliation to well up in our souls; 2) Attention and compassion: attention …
is the basis of compassion, of an ability to wait and to be with, to walk alongside
a victim at a victim's pace … and creates an environment of trust and safety;
3) A post-exilic stance: the term comes from South African theologian Charles

Villa Vicencio, who compares the post-apartheid situation in South Africa with Israel returning to Jerusalem after the Exile in Babylon. A new society has to be constructed on the ruins of the old society.[5]

A lecturer in Catholic Moral Theology explained individual reconciliation as a process of conversion:

> There is penance, then conversion [then] ... repentance ... It's about acknowledging my own helplessness ... [acknowledging] my mistake ... my own vulnerability, my own helplessness ... at the same time asking you for forgiveness is acknowledging the power you have. Even though you are the victim ... you have the power to forgive me or not to forgive me. (Reverend Father Seluini 'Akau'ola, interview 3 November 2004)

Paulo Balei, a Catholic lay missionary, working on reconciliation among prisoners, stressed this aspect of mutual powerlessness and weakness in reconciliation processes:

> It doesn't really matter whether you are the victim or ... the offender or, in terms of restorative justice you are the community that has been affected ... We are both weak, we are both powerless, we are coming from points of powerlessness. So in terms of reconciliation when the victim is not ready yet to forgive the victimiser, then that victim is coming from a point of powerlessness ... If the victimiser is not ... ready to go forward and ... apologise to the victim, he is coming from a point of powerlessness ... It is a matter of realising that you and I are both powerless human beings, that ... we need to have power coming from somewhere, from this supreme being who is a source of power for you and me, and to realise that in order to restore that relationship that has been ... harmed, we will need to come together. (Balei, interview 12 October 2004)

Concerns (2006: 3), lays out reconciliation as a conflict-handling mechanism to be attained through a process of 7 elements or steps:

1. Honest acknowledgement of harm/injury inflicted by each party on the other;
2. Sincere regret and remorse from offender;
3. Readiness from the offender to apologise;
4. Readiness of conflicting parties to 'let go' of anger and bitterness caused by conflict and injury;
5. Commitment from offender not to re-offend;

---

5 *Concerns* 2006, see also Schreiter 2003, and see Archbishop Mataca's outline of steps to reconciliation in Fiji. (Sun 6 October 2001: 20-21) For ecumenical approaches see Müller-Fahrenholtz 1996, Jacques 2000, World Council of Churches 2006. See also Kerber 2003 re restorative justice methodologies from biblical and ethical perspectives.

6. Sincere effort to redress past grievances that caused conflict and compensate the damage caused to the extent possible;
7. Entering into a mutually enriching relationship with the other party

Remembering and healing

> A lot of people say: just forgive and forget it. But we don't forgive and forget. We forgive and remember, and we'll always remember. But what happened is when it is healed I remember this but it's no longer a problem. ('Akau'ola, interview 3 November 2004)

Similar steps towards reconciliation were described by a visiting Anglican priest in Fiji in October 2005. In connection with a week's focus on Reconciliation in Fiji around the time of Fiji Day (10 October, celebrating Fiji's independence from Britain in 1970) the Ministry of Reconciliation had invited Father Michael Lapsley SSM, director of the Institute of Healing of Memories, Cape Town, to lead a seminar on reconciliation. For most of his life Father Lapsley has been involved in fighting against apartheid and it was because of his continued opposition and active engagement against apartheid that he became the victim of a letter bomb from the South African Government. On Sunday 9th October, Father Lapsley gave a sermon on the healing of memories at Holy Trinity Anglican Cathedral in Suva. His message focused on two main issues: remembering and forgiving.

Father Lapsley said, as many others who work on reconciliation in Fiji and elsewhere in the world also strongly emphasise, that we do not, cannot and should not *forget* the wrong that has been done to us, the pain that has been inflicted on us by others. *Forgiving is not about forgetting.*

Making very clear and simple, biblically based points, Father Lapsley asked 'Is it part of our calling as Christians to be a forgetting people?' He pointed out that if you type the words 'forget' into a Biblical Concordance computer programme, you will not find the word 'forget' without the two words 'DO NOT' in front of it. With regard to Old Testament understandings of *forgetting* Father Lapsley emphasised that it was because the Jews had *forgotten* where they came from that they couldn't see where they were going. Drawing on the New Testament Father Lapsley pointed to the fact that we are in fact *commanded* through the Eucharist to *remember*: 'Do this in remembrance of me', Christ tells his disciples at the Last Supper. 'Christianity, Islam and Judaism are great remembering religions. [Yet] people of faith err precisely when they forget the journey that God has travelled with them', he said.

What kind of memory does Scripture call us to have? Father Lapsley asked. We are called to have a *redemptive* memory, that is to say a memory of good that comes out of evil: the Risen Christ was also the Crucified Christ. This is so clearly exemplified in Father Lapsley's recounting of the story of Thomas, who vowed that he would not believe in the resurrection of Christ until he had 'put my finger in the mark of the nails and my hand in his side' (John 20:24-26). When Thomas did meet the Risen Lord, he did indeed put his fingers in the wounds in the Lord's hands and feet and put his hand in his side. The wounds were there to see and touch, *but they were no longer bleeding.* The scars from the crucifixion were there, *but healing had taken place.*

Just as in Father Lapsley's own experience of physical and emotional wounding: when a letter bomb blew up as he opened it, he lost both his hands, one eye and was seriously burned. How can he ever forget that? The memory not only of that moment that changed his life forever, but also the actual mutilation of his body that he lives with each day and the fact that for the rest of his life he will be dependent on others to help him – this will be a part of his life for as long as he lives.

He cannot forget, but he can actively work towards healing the memory, healing the trauma of what happened to him so that it becomes bearable to live with. Nowhere, he said, does God say or the Bible say that we are not to suffer. But what God does say is that he will never leave us, that he will be with us, even in our darkest moments to the end of time. We may walk away from God, but he will never walk away from us. And indeed, it is through his grace that we can work towards healing the memories of pain and violence inflicted on us.

We are not to ignore, to forget, Father Lapsley said – but to heal the memories: to see the good that comes out of evil, to work towards a *redemptive memory*. But how do we travel the journey from destructive memory to redemptive memory? Father Lapsley asked. It's not how we *think* about the past, it is how we *feel* about the past. If we keep the poisonous memories inside us, he said, they do not destroy our enemies, they destroy us.

The first step is an acknowledgement of the wrong that was done. Yet there is a giant step from *knowledge* of wrong-doing to actual *acknowledgement*. What of forgiveness? Christians, Father Lapsley reminded us, don't own the word 'forgiveness'; it has an important place in other religions too, including Hinduism. He emphasised that there are three parts to forgiveness: 1) Acknowledgment to myself of what I have done. I need to own what I have done. I need to express to myself that I need forgiveness; 2) Acknowledgment – if I have faith – to God; 3) To ask for forgiveness from the one I harmed.

Putting his point across very simply again, Father Lapsley explained his theory of 'bicycle theology'. 'I come here and I steal your bicycle', he announced. 'Six months later I come back and say: I'm sorry, please forgive me'. He looked out at the congregation, adjusting his glasses with the metal hook that is his artificial hand, and then added, 'But I keep the bicycle!' Several chuckles were heard in church. 'In fact', he continued, 'if I steal your bicycle I should give you back something even better – a Honda motorbike! At the very least, I should give you the bicycle back with new tyres on it and a new bell!'.

'Forgiveness is not just saying sorry', he continued, 'it involves reparation and restitution. But sometimes it is not possible to "give back the bike". Because people are dead. Nevertheless forgiveness does involve "making it up" to those who are hurt. When it does happen forgiveness, which is a choice, can bring liberation to both parties. For the person being asked to forgive, the question inevitably arises, "If I forgive, will it happen again?" Sometimes, we can even use the word forgiveness as a weapon against people. We tell them to forgive, *but they are crying out to be heard'*.

Father Lapsley pointed to this importance of *listening*: 'When I was learning to be a priest I learned how to preach – but I didn't learn how to listen'. In Fiji, he said, he had noticed how much people refer to 'us' and 'them'. For 'us' and 'them' to be transformed into '*us*' – into a true sense of sharing, he emphasised, 'I need to hear not just your words, but to hear what is in your heart'.

'When we have the opportunity to listen to each other's pain, hopes and fears in a safe space, especially those of the "other"', he said, 'we begin to be less "them" and "us". Step by step we *all* become just "us"'. (Holy Trinity Cathedral 9 October 2005)

Some days later Father Lapsley was quoted in the *Fiji Times* as saying that he 'believes the only way forward for Fiji in terms of the Reconciliation, Tolerance and Unity Bill is the total withdrawal of the amnesty-related clauses'. (*Fiji Times* 12 October 2005: 14) 'I suggest … that government deal with the Amnesty clause separately rather than having the two dealt with at the same time'. (Ibid.)

In an article by Father Lapsley, published in the *Fiji Times* on the 12th October, he added the following, 'Healing and wholeness is God's will for individuals, communities and nations. If … [we] want to live in peace … we need to accept that the future is an interfaith future in which we can remain deeply committed to our own faith whilst reverencing and respecting the faith of others. (Lapsley SSM, *Fiji Times* 12 October 2005: 10)

Talanoa

Similarly stressing the importance of respectful listening, Halapua describes a particular Pacific Island methodology of reconcilitation, *talanoa*. *Talanoa*, Halapua explains (2009: 54-55), is made up of two 'Oceanic' words: *tala*, meaning sharing stories, or 'presenting something deep within oneself or foretelling the future' and *noa*, 'space given by an individual, a group or the environment'. Such space is not empty space but cultural or sacred space, given freely for particular story telling in particular contexts, with an awareness of the sense of continuity as stories are handed on:

> *Talanoa* is then to tell stories within a community that is open and receptive …
> *talanoa* honours and celebrates belonging and diversity. (Ibid: 55-56)

Director of Pacific Island Development Programme in Hawaii Sitiveni Halapua, brother of Winston Halapua, has developed a modern democratic methodology for reconciliation and peace processes across the region, drawing on *talanoa*. This does not offer a solution to problems but a way in which to address them, through creating a culturally familiar situation, 'an extension of a traditional and time-honoured practice that recognizes … the sharing of concerns in a respectful way … *talanoa* … honours the past, brings the past to the present and enables creative change in moving to the future'. (Ibid. 58)

Successfully employed in several Pacific Island countries such as the Cook Islands and the Solomon Islands,[6] *talanoa* was also used in Fiji after the 2000 coup. Political opponents, religious leaders, former hostages and coup leaders were brought together in dialogue on the fundamental issues paralysing the country. However, the progress made 'slowed down when the leader of the Government used delaying tactics as a form of control and domination'. (Ibid. 59) And then the 2006 coup took place.

Yet *talanoa* is not only of value in Pacific Island contexts. *Talanoa* has, Halapua writes (Ibid. 64-66), four gifts to contribute to the wider world: *space, justice, listening, dialogue*:

> *Talanoa* provides a safe atmosphere for interaction. Space provided is not for some to seize or dominate … but creative space set aside to enable the welfare of all … *talanoa* honours the numinous and that which cannot yet be understood, and it gives room for interaction.
>
> *Talanoa* offers a way of securing justice. In order to realise justice, the safety of space is imperative … no one story has more space and value than others … Diversity enriches. What is good for others is also a blessing for all.
>
> *Talanoa* is about the sacredness of listening. In order for all to hear one another, talking must go hand in hand with listening … to others, to the environment and to God … when we listen we may truly hear more than we – we may hear what is deep within us … The reciprocity of the *talanoa* embraces vocal and silent interactions, respects and gives space for them all …
>
> *Talanoa* is sacred space for dialogue in which all are valued and have profound contributions to offer. There is hospitality given – hospitality that is at the very root of the formation of community. Engagement and participation are not coerced but rather offered as a privilege – as an opportunity for learning and insights, for the forging of human relationships, for the bearing of one another's burdens in times of hardship or loss.

---

6   Halapua (2008: 61-63) discusses the Anglican order of the Melanesian Brothers and their use of *talanoa* in their dangerous ministry in the Solomons, see also Brown and Nokise (2009) on storytelling and Anglican ministry in relation to the Solomons crisis.

Fusing diversity

Establishing a creative space for the musical fusion of cultural difference and diversity, blending modern and traditional Pacific Islander song and music, the immensely popular Fiji band Black Rose is an example of the potential in working together to create something that draws on and expresses roots and belonging, yet is also open to and sees the richness in that which is different. '*Valu ni Vanua*' ('war for land') is the name of a song released in 2002 on an album called *Kila...?* The track opens with Hindi-style music and chant, accompanied by traditional Indian instruments, drums and bells. The words are full of love, yet also sorrow:

> *Fiji mera desh hai*
> *Aur hamesha rehega*
> *Kahan hai mera Fiji jo mai hi janta hun*
> *Jahan azadi bahi rahti hai.*

> Fiji is my country.
> It always will be.
> Where is the Fiji that I know?
> It's where freedom rules.

As the track continues the Hindi music becomes unclear and blurred, the rhythm disturbed, the music becoming out of synch and dissonant as it is overlaid with traditional Fijian chanting, replacing the Hindi words and music

> *Ai valu ni vanua*
> *Ai valu ni qele*

> *Sekuraki ko Viti au tukuna*
> *Ni sa mai kau laivi a veiluitaki*

> *Kasura a city ko Suva*
> *Nira sa mai yavalavala ai taukei ni vanua*

> *Tei dabe mada au vakadikeva*
> *A draki ni bula i Viti nikua*
> *Sa mai sau a nodra vosa koira matua*

> *Nira vosa ko ira a vuda da tawa muria*
> *Veqaraqaravi ni oda qele a oda vanua*

> *Ai valavala ni noda vanua*
> *A veiyaloni sa yali nikua*

Tovo kei Viti me vakalotu
Me vaKalou

War in the country.
War in the land.

There has been a coup in Fiji, I say.
Leadership has been taken away.
The city of Suva has come to a standstill as the people of the land have taken the law into their own hands.
I sat down to reflect on the state of affairs of Fiji today.
The mana of the elders' words has taken effect because when our ancestors spoke they were disobeyed.
The values of our land and our country, our traditional way of life and harmony, have disappeared today.
Fiji's way of life must be made spiritual and Godly.

The words and the dissonant fusion of Hindi and Fijian chant and music, or rather the swallowing up of Hindi chant and music by traditional Fijian chant and drums on the *Valu ni Vanua* track, symbolically captures the complexity of the coup, the ways it shattered life in Fiji, and the emotional and socio-cultural cost it had to so many people across the country, in particular to Indo-Fijians. The album cover text notes, *Kila...?* in English means 'do you understand?' *Kila...?* is asking our people to look within themselves. To understand that to buil[d] a better society, we must begin with our very own selves'. (*Kila ...?* by Black Rose, produced by Mangrove, Noumea, New Caledonia 2002)

This track, Black Rose write, 'speaks about our Indo-Fijian communit[y's] cry to have back the Fiji they were first brought to work and [live] in', and seeks to provoke young people of Fiji to be self-critical about their attitudes to what is happening, to what has gone wrong in Fiji. The text raises the point that although we may not understand the complex situation, we need to at least *try* to understand what happened. It reminds Fijians that the values of *vanua* and of the Gospel, of sharing and caring for one another have been replaced by violence and division.

The song '*Nasau*' is a celebration of the group's roots to their God-given land, to the past and to the ancestors. '*Nasau* means the "mana" or blessing of our heavenly creator given to our homeland Fiji'. But while celebrating their roots in the past, Black Rose emphasise in their lyrics the need for change. There is a desperate need to address the deep divisions within Fiji society, the growing problems of poverty and corruption, and to work towards a united future. This is also the focus of other tracks on the album: '*Rogoci Viti*' (Listen Fiji), is a 'call for peace and unity'; '*Kombawa*' 'focuses on the cries of our people and on how we can build a better place individually and collectively'; '*Meda butu*' (Make a Stand) calls people in Fiji to 'make a stand and eradicate all the unnecessary divisions within our society'. (Ibid.)

Black Rose demonstrate musically and in their powerful lyrics how Fiji's different peoples and cultures, like the music of this album, can work together and blend their gifts of diversity into a new and rich creation. Emphasising how God's grace has enhanced the journey of the group, Black Rose explain that they have attempted to 'fuse the four most common musical style[s] of our communities, Fijian, Hindi, Rotuman, English', drawing on ancient chanting styles, combined 'with contemporary beats and arrangements telling stories of our journey into the new millennium. (Ibid.)

Different ways

> We have a changing society, we have to accept the others' beliefs. God Himself has created everything differently. No two creations are alike, be it two fingers, two leaves ... two waves, all are different. So if we all believe that human beings are God's creation we have to accept that we are different, that we have differences of opinion, and different faiths as well. (Hardayal Singh, interview 1998)

Hardayal Singh looked at me across the table. It was a hot afternoon. We were sitting in the cool of the Hari Krishna Ice-Cream Parlour in downtown Suva. From the window we had a view of the majestic Sacred Heart Roman Catholic Cathedral. Built on a steep hill against a backdrop of palm trees, it is a typically French style church building of light sandstone with a steep, winding stone stairway on either side. From the roof a great figure of Christ, arms outstretched to the world, reaches into the sky above.

Mr Singh, a tall, softly spoken Sikh, exuding a blend of quiet strength, deep faith, humility and patience, was the chairperson of Interfaith Search Fiji and worked for Air New Zealand. As I scribbled notes and the tape recorder whirred quietly on the table between our cups of hot, sweet, milky tea, he continued: 'A Methodist church leader once quoted this: The peak of the mountain is one, but there are many different ways of getting there. That's religion', he said, smiling. 'God is the peak of the mountain. The different paths are the different religions. None are wrong, and they all go there, but everyone follows the track he is taking. With that you'll have this understanding, this respect between different faiths'.

It was July 1998. Despite the drought, the struggles of many sugar cane farmers and dissatisfaction with the government's tardy response to their plight, there was hope and expectation for a fresh future for Fiji. The new Constitution had been ratified in 1997, a Constitution which, after the divisiveness of the military coups of 1987, offered hope of more dialogue and power-sharing between the ethnic communities in Fiji.

Ecumenical dialogue

In its submission to the Fiji Constitution Review Commission in 1995 the Roman Catholic Church in Fiji emphasised that no one group of people can claim a superior position in relation to others:

> Whilst the influence of Christianity amongst the indigenous Fijians and Rotumans cannot be doubted, in the spirit of 'ecumenism', the Roman Catholic Church [RCC] proposes a more general, less partisan acknowledgement that all men and women are created equal by God and endowed with equal dignity and fundamental rights, as being more appropriate to the multi-religious composition of Fiji and its peoples. (Roman Catholic Church, submission to Fiji Constitution Review Commission, September 1995: 4)[7]

The submission stressed the richness of cultural and religious diversity in Fiji:

> 'Equality does not mean uniformity'. For us here in Fiji who are so rich in our cultural, religious and racial diversities, it means recognising the moral and cultural differences of the other and utilizing these gifts for the welfare of the Fiji society and its citizens … The RCC also teaches that no one can boast of natural superiority or lay claim to a right to exercise discrimination that affects the basic rights of the person. This stems from the belief that 'ALL' are loved and treasured by God and therefore our mode of behaviour towards each other must be based on charitable and fraternal love. (Ibid: 1)

Ecumenical dialogue is a relatively new endeavour among Christians, first promulgated in western Protestantism in the early 20th century. Although aspirations towards ecumenism can be traced back to the New Testament, the modern ecumenical movement dates from the World Missionary Conference of 1910 in Edinburgh which, through a succession of Councils, led to the establishment of the World Council of Churches in 1948. The Roman Catholic Church entered the ecumenical scene in 1965 after the landmark document *Nostra Aetate*, the Declaration of the Relations of the Church to Non-Christian Religions, was approved in 1965 at the Second Vatican Council (1962-1965).

The Fiji Council of Churches came into being in 1965 and The Pacific Conference of Churches was formally constituted in 1966. The Roman Catholic Church became a full member of the Pacific Conference of Churches in 1975, the Pacific Island region being one of only three regions of the world where the Roman Catholic Church is a full member of a regional ecumenical body, the others being the Caribbean Conference of Churches and the Middle East Conference of Churches. (Avi 1994: 94) The Roman Catholic Church is not a member of the World Council of Churches, however it has a close working relationship with local

---

7   See also Kirata 1994, Solomone 2000, ECREA 2009.

and regional ecumenical bodies and the WCC through its national and regional Bishops' Conferences and through joint working groups.

Hope in communal prayer, dialogue and action

Suva, May 1987. In response to the ethno-religious chauvinism and divisive rhetoric of the military coup that had taken place, a number of church leaders, seeing the Church as the conscience of the nation, called for 'leaders of all religious traditions to meet and pray together for the good of Fiji and its people'. The small, white weatherboard Presbyterian church of St. Andrews in Suva played host to what became known as the 'Back to Early May' movement, a group of people of all faiths and ethnic backgrounds, headed by 25 leaders of mainstream Christian churches, including Methodist ministers Paula Niukula and Akuila Yabaki, who met once a fortnight to pray for peace in the country.

The 'Back to Early May' movement submitted a petition to the Governor General, signed by 108,000 people (with a further 12,000 signatures received from all over the country after the Governor General's deadline for submissions), denouncing the coups and calling for a return to order. (Garrett 1988: 9) By the end of 1987 the movement, having based its organisation and method of working on the Multifaith Centre in Birmingham, England (Bushell 1990: 1), had evolved to become Interfaith Search. Over the next years participants in the Back to Early May movement also continued their dialogue on constitutional issues, and in 1991 the Citizens' Constitutional Forum was formed.

The aim of the Birmingham Interfaith model was to build bridges between different people and different faiths by creating a forum in which people could discuss and dialogue about their faiths. The idea was that people, in discussing their religion for presentation to people of other faiths, gain a greater understanding of their own faith, and in listening to others present their faiths, learning more about the faiths and values of others.

Discussions of topics, such as 'Who are We?'; 'Introducing Someone of Importance in Our Tradition'; or 'The Concept of God in Our Scriptures' took place first within each religious group and were then presented to the wider forum.[8] This structure, cumbersome to maintain as more groups joined, was later simplified. This was partly due to the experience that this model of dialogue was specifically western and implicitly based on mutual understandings of equality and grass root influence. This was not a model that gelled culturally with the non-Christian organisations in Fiji. Their representatives, usually male elders, wrote and presented their pieces with little or no discussion among their members. So it

---

8   Mackenzie (2000) gives a comprehensive list of topics, including 'How do we see the task of Community and Nation building from the perspective of our own religious tradition?', 'What in our faith traditions enables us to enter into dialogue with people of other faiths?', 'What does our faith tradition say about the environment?'

was decided instead that each religious group was to present directly to the whole group.

In 1987 six religious organisations and Churches from Muslim, Hindu and Christian traditions participated in Interfaith Search Fiji; in 1988 ten; in 1995, when I started attending meetings, there were 13 groups.[9] By 1996, Interfaith Search Fiji comprised 16 different member organisations, representing, according to Chairperson Hardayal Singh in an interview on *Radio Australia's* Pacific Religion programme (7 October 1996), the majority of people in Fiji. '[Interfaith Search Fiji] is like a stone thrown into a lake; the stone itself is very small ... but the ripples are beginning to happen'. (Sister Bertha Hurley SMSM, secretary, Interfaith Search Fiji, interview 1998)

Among the things that make Interfaith Search Fiji unique, is the fact that, excepting the Methodist Church in Fiji, each religious organisation is *officially* represented; not merely interested individuals – each organisation or church has taken the responsibility for being officially represented. However, there was no official representation of the Methodist Church in Fiji, only individual members, such as those ministers who co-founded the 'Back to Early May' movement, Revds Paula Niukula and Akuila Yabaki, together with St. Andrew's Presbyterian minister, Reverend Dr Bruce Deverell.

The absence of the Methodist Church was particularly noticeable at the Thanksgiving Service for Fiji's 25th Year of Independence in 1995, 'Celebration for Life', held at the National Stadium in Suva, attended by President Ratu Mara and Prime Minister Rabuka. Especially considering the motto of the elaborate anniversary celebrations across Fiji: 'The Family: Fiji's Hope'. The address and prayers from Inter Faith Search Fiji under the heading 'Religious Unity in Diversity', expressed the movement's mission:

> We are a family of people of different faiths cherishing unity and strength in diversity. We do not want to formulate a one-world religion or even a form of prayer acceptable to all. Instead we search for ways of building bridges of respect and understanding between people of different religious traditions for the sake of the wider community. Fiji's multi-racial, multi-cultural, multi-lingual and multi-religious society is a model of oneness to God. All have contributed immensely to the development of the social, economic, spiritual and political life of Fiji. Let us today pledge to light a lamp in our hearts ... the light of love and understanding. Spread this light through our homes, villages, cities and the whole of Fiji. Let us teach our children the essence of truthful living by

---

9 The religious organisations represented in 1995 were: Shree Sanatam Dharm Pratinidhi Sabha of Fiji, Arya Pratinidhi Sabha of Fiji, Sri Sathya Sai Organisation of Fii, Fiji Hindu Society, Sikh Association of Fiji, Fiji Muslim League, Ahmadiyya Anjuman Ishaat-I-Islam (Lahore), The Methodist Church in Fiji, Roman Catholic Church, Anglican Diocese of Polynesia, Saint Andrew's Presbyterian Church, National Spiritual Assembly of the Bahai'is and the Church or Jesus Christ of Latter Day Saints.

setting examples, as we are all children of the Lord and the Lord is in all of us. (Interfaith Search Fiji 1995: 3, see Bushell 1994)

As Hardayal Singh emphasised to me, Interfaith Search Fiji wishes to be a voice which speaks out on issues in society, especially to do with poverty and injustice, such as attacks on religious faith, but also to be an educator, speaking on the principles of interfaith at schools, business organisations and public gatherings. 'You won't see a thousand people stand up and say, yes, we believe in interfaith. We prefer to see ten thousand people say their own prayers at home ... talk about God and respect members of other faiths ... It's happening in Fiji now'. (Interview 1998)

Indeed, members of Interfaith Search Fiji and an Anglican priest I interviewed described how changes were taking place in situations, such as inaugurations or meetings, where before often a Christian prayer only would be used, now organisers were requesting interfaith prayers to be said. However, almost 15 years on this has changed, and Christian prayers are now more the norm in public situations.

Listening prayerfully

All Interfaith Search Fiji discussion and prayer meetings I attended started with a moment of silent contemplation and a joint prayer, 'Prayer for Fiji', written by Interfaith Search Fiji council members. We were invited to participate if we wished, or to listen 'prayerfully', if we could not pray with those of other faiths:

> Creator God, you have entrusted these islands of Fiji to us, your people. We seek your blessing on all our hopes and all our plans for the future. Bless those who lead us and guide them with your wisdom. Bless all the people of Fiji, we come from different backgrounds, cultures and religions. Increase our understanding and our respect for each other as we strive for unity, harmony and peace. Bless our children; they are our hope for the future. Be with us all as day by day time unfolds. (*Interfaith Search Fiji*, see also *Fiji Times* 29 July 1997, *Daily Post* 23 July 1998)

Praying together with people of other faiths is a tremendous challenge to many Christians in Fiji who feel it is blasphemous to pray with non-Christians or even people of other Christian denominations. To sit 'prayerfully' while non-Christians recite prayers, is quite unacceptable to many Christians from mainstream churches as well as Pentecostal churches.

Official Interfaith prayer services started in the same way, followed by each member organisation saying a prayer, singing a chant or hymn, or quoting from their holy scriptures, and concluded by the communal singing of the National Anthem. When at Sacred Heart Roman Catholic Cathedral, these recitations took place in the sanctuary. However, such visions of Sikhs, Hindus and Muslims, standing at the pulpit or in front of the altar do not rest easily with everyone.

Figure 7.1   Muslim representatives praying at an Interfaith Search Fiji service, Sacred Heart Roman Catholic Cathedral, Suva, August 1997

Source: *Fiji Times*.

In 1998 I was invited to participate in a discussion among Anglican priests and lay-men in the Men's Group of Holy Trinity Cathedral in Suva. Although the Anglican Church in Fiji is officially represented in Interfaith Search Fiji, and the late Jabez Bryce, Bishop of Polynesia, wholeheartedly supporting the movement, as a whole it had a rather lukewarm reception among church members. In the discussion a problem raised by a Tongan priest was that as a Christian he felt called to lead others to Christ. The ideal of interfaith dialogue seemed incongruent with this important element of his calling:

> ... Interfaith Search [is] looking for common ground, well accepted ... but I still
> have to lead Muslims, Sai Baba ... whatever ... to *the* God whom I proclaim.
> And I'm aware that they will try to convert me too. If I fail to do that ... as
> a priest of the Church, then I think I am not doing justice to the word of God
> whom I am ordained to proclaim ... I am commissioned to make disciples ...

to declare that Jesus, *the* Jesus, is The Way, The Truth, Life. There is no other God.

Another problem that a Samoan priest described was the use of non-Christian symbols of worship in a Christian church, which several parishioners found problematic:

> In 1996 ... a converted parishioner from Hinduism to Anglicanism was here at an Interfaith meeting [at Holy Trinity Anglican Cathedral]. They had some sort of Hindu thing, they lit a fire here and it was broadcast on TV. And this lady was very upset and said, 'Father, if that is the way my pagan people are accepted into our Holy place, I'm going back to the Hindus'. That lady is a very committed parishioner now. But she was so offended that we invited them to do their sacred rites here.

The sacred rite referred to is the lighting of a *diya*, an oil lamp which, as symbol of the Light of God, is a central object in Hindu worship. In Interfaith meetings the *diya* was lit at the beginning of a service – as a common symbol of the Light of God, uniting the different faiths. A *diya* is also used in Catholic *misa puja* in Fiji – inculturation Masses which draw on Indian cultural elements, for example at Diwali.

The idea of cultural and interfaith dialogue remains a challenge to many people in Fiji. A lay-Anglican expresses here the difficulties he had in embracing this, difficulties that many others echo:

> In 1995 I attended an Interfaith meeting ... After the fellowship [someone asked me] How do you feel about it? I said maybe this is a long process for me to understand ... [but] Interfaith is still not on with me. She said, 'Oh, you have to sit with people of other faiths and try to bridge the gaps'. I said 'not with me, it will be ten years time before I probably come to understand the thing better'... That was my first and last time to go to Interfaith. (Member of the Anglican Men's Group, Holy Trinity Cathedral, July 1998)

Similar sentiments are expressed by Pentecostal pastor Navuniyasi:

> I respect the other churches, I know their doctrines, that my doctrine is not the same ... We ... read the same Bible, even Christians, but the preaching is different. I cannot oppose them in the face ... I don't hate them ... I really respect their individual beliefs ... all I can say is that it's better for me to stay away ... It hurts [to participate]. (Navuniyasi, interview 1998)

Sister Bertha Hurley SMSM, secretary of Interfaith Search Fiji in 1998, described an interchange that took place when Interfaith Search Fiji handed in their Submission to the Fiji Constitution Review Commission in 1995:

When we said [we didn't recommend] calling Fiji a Christian country, but we suggested calling Fiji a *God-fearing country*, the Fijian gentleman said, 'Well, which god?' And this is the attitude of a lot of people. Del Ram's response was: 'There is only one God who is Creator of us all, is the Father of us all, and who loves us all'. He said, 'look around this room, we're all different colours … nationalities … cultures … I'm of Indian background, you're of Fijian background, someone else is of Palagi [European] background – and we could call it a geographic accident … Our culture is part of this ... Whether I come to God as God or Jehovah or Allah is part of this geographical accident. And God chose my country, in the way he chose the name that I would know him by'.

Drawing on pre-Christian Fijian beliefs in ancestral deities in an effort to make a similar point, a Methodist minister expressed his thoughts on respect for religious diversity:

[Before Christianity Fijians] worshipped their own gods, but they were not denying the worship of others … they were aware of the other realities … the other *vu*. But then Christianity came and said *all* those *vu* are wrong, this is the right one … so that seemed to start off this thing about the power of the Fijians … of God …

   I come from … Moala, our *vu* is called Rovarovaevalu or … Kubunavanua … but … we know that the next island … Lau, has got another one, and the other island on the Lau side has got another one … and they are all recognised to be of divine descent … of equal status … If Fijians today are taught that there are other *vu* – if we take God to be a *vu,* eh? … and Rama to be another *vu* … and Muhammed to be another … that's how they understood their world … there were other *vu*, not just their own … if only Interfaith could link back to the early faiths of the Fijian, then I think that would greatly enhance what Interfaith is trying to do now in promoting Fiji as a place where there is this respect for each other. (Reverend Tevita Banivanua, interview 1998)

While Interfaith Search Fiji, with its dialogue based on informed understandings of people's faith, tolerance and liberal thought seems even further from the world view of Fijian villagers than are the arguments of liberal Methodists, described earlier, the ideal of interfaith prayer and dialogue represents an important voice, countering the pervasive and increasing ethno-religious nationalistic rhetoric in Fiji. This was highlighted during the Parliamentary siege in May-June 2000, when women of different faiths took the initiative to make Holy Trinity Anglican Cathedral the site for daily interfaith prayer for the release of the hostages held in the Parliamentary Complex. (See Costello-Olsson 2005)

   Bishop Reeves of the Fiji Constitution Review Commission said to members of Interfaith Search Fiji after their submission in 1995 (cf interview Sr Bertha Hurley SMSM, 1998): 'You're just one tiny candle'. To which Sister Bertha replied, 'There's more than one candle burning ... and if we have enough little candles, the light will begin to spread'.

The Churches – the conscience of the nation

The charismatic and much revered leader of the Pacific Conference of Churches for many years, Tongan Roman Catholic Bishop Patelisio Finau SM, who died suddenly in 1993, called for Church leaders to speak out against injustice and work for reconciliation. Writing of Church and State in Tonga, his words are relevant to the Christian state debate in Fiji:

> The Church and the state must be autonomous and free but ... interdependent in that they serve the common good of the nation ... Both have their rights and duties as well as their different functions and both must respect these rights, duties and special functions. There must be mutual respect between the two and no exploitation of the one by the other. The church is not a department of the government and vice versa ... The Church is the conscience of the nation. (Finau 1994: 77, see also Barr 1994)

'The rich', Brazilian Catholic Archbishop Helder Camara is said to have remarked, 'are prepared to talk about charity but woe betide those who talk of justice, rights and structural change'. (Barr 2005b: 109) 'When I give money to the poor, they call me a saint, when I ask why the poor have no food, they call me a communist'. The late Savenaca Siwatibau, former Vice Chancellor of the University of the South Pacific, used these words of Dom Camara to challenge the Churches in the Pacific to be more radical in their approach to social issues. He exhorted them not just to do charitable work but to work for justice in society:

> Should the churches stick to their role as saints and administer only to spiritual needs and the physical needs of victims? Do they ask questions about root causes and seek answers to correct these? Do they also dare to be called 'communist', following the example of Jesus?

Siwatibau went on to say,

> To ask questions about the causes is to analyse, to publicise and to work to root out the causes of exploitation, of oppression and of corruption in our countries. It is not to be afraid to question those in power. Is it possible that the churches can be accused of cowardly silence or even compliance in the face of abuse of power by those who wield it in our countries? (Siwatibau, Address to South Pacific Association of Theological Schools 2002 in Barr 2005b: 36)

Roman Cathlic Archbishop Mataca (*Fiji Sun* 12 January 2006: 7) points out that the dominant Christian voices in Fiji today, are those of fundamentalist Christians, who:

> [call] for Fiji to become a Christian state, for the gods of other nations to be driven out of our country, for homosexuals to be condemned (and even stoned to death), and for leadership positions in the country to be reserved to a list of approved good Christians … It appears that Christianity is being used by some to justify an extreme nationalist agenda … Have these fundamentalist Christian groups or group formed a comfortable alliance with the present government? I ask this question as a Christian and as an indigenous Fijian. The dominance of these legalistic and dogmatic public 'Christian' voices is disturbing and may often damage the perception of the Christian Church … Their black and white judgements on complex moral issues are offensive to those who see the message of Jesus as urging us to compassion, love and understanding … Alternative authentic Christian voices need to make themselves heard in our society today. They should speak out and represent the compassionate concern and priorities of Jesus … Moreover they should criticise and challenge any collusion between the Government and the religious right.

The dignity of difference

> Only when we realise the danger of wishing that everyone should be the same will we prevent senseless violent conflicts and loss of human lives. We will learn to live with diversity once we understand that there is dignity in difference. (Sacks 2002: 69)

Anglican Bishop Winston Halapua (2003: 200) suggests that a revaluation of *vanua* as multi-cultural relatedness could be a way forward for Fiji:

> The notion [of] *vanua*, in its unadulterated and philosophical form, once reclaimed within Fiji's multi-ethnic, multi-racial and increasingly globalising community, can provide a way forward. The understanding of *vanua* in terms of its relational interconnectedness, in contrast to the adulterated form where *vanua* is viewed as something relevant only for a particular ethnic group and taboo for others, provides a new philosophy for Fiji. The *vanua* constitutes a society in which all parts, which are distinctly different, are interconnected. It is a society where differences are honoured but cannot function in isolation. Differences contribute to the richness of the whole. Underlying all this is the spirit of reciprocity.

The Sikh chairperson of Interfaith Search Fiji describes how God made each element of Creation differently, 'be it two fingers, two leaves … two waves, all are different. So if we all believe that human beings are God's creation we have to accept that we are different, that we have differences of opinion, and different faiths as well. (Singh, interview 1998)

Rabbi Jonathan Sacks, Chief Rabbi in Britain, argues in *The Dignity of Difference* (2002) that God *created* difference and that all faiths therefore 'have the imprint of the divine image … contrary to relativism and universalism, the Jewish view is that universalism is not the end but rather the beginning'. (Yabaki 2006: 35) Methodist minister and CEO of the CCF Reverend Akuila Yabaki, drawing on arguments in Sacks' book, also sees difference as divinely ordained and therefore containing an inherent dignity. The importance of continuing to dialogue on difference is not only important between different religions, he emphasises, but also necessary in order to morally and ethically counter extreme voices within the same religion:

> Aside from the insights religions bring into the conversation on values and morals, they also need to enter into dialogue with one another for one urgent reason: the emergence of religious extremism within themselves, which can be seen as a form of seeking for certainty. When we hear politicians evoking religious sentiments or religious leaders calling for conversion crusades, we may not see the last of Bosnia, especially when poverty stricken and oppressed groups of people, often used by those who have the means and power, will respond violently. But what this means is that each of us who belong to a faith must wrestle with the sources of extremism within our own faith. This is where I believe the struggle for meaningful peace must take place. But religions must also enter into dialogue on peace for another reason … that *difference is divinely ordained and hence has dignity.* (Yabaki 2006: 11, author's emphasis)

Quoting Archbishop Mataca, Reverend Yabaki concludes that 'the test of faith is to see the divine presence in the face of the stranger, "to heed the cry of those who are disempowered; who are hungry and poor, and whose human potential is being denied the chance to be expressed'. (Mataca 2004: 5) It is this urgent issue, he points out, which the 'great religions must address and the challenge is for them to initiate a *global movement centred on the dignity of difference.* (Yabaki 2006: 14, author's emphasis)

Archbishop Mataca (2006: 79) writes that in his 'painful grappling with the issues we face in Fiji, who we are as a nation and who we are as a people belonging to distinct ethnic and religious groups', he also finds great inspiration in Rabbi Sacks' theology:

> I am convinced that at the heart of monotheism is not what has traditionally been taken to be: one God, therefore one faith, one truth, one way. Rather, it is that unity creates diversity. What is real, remarkable and ought to be the proper object of our wonder and awe is not the quintessential leaf but the 250,000 different kinds there actually are. (Ibid. 79-80)

Discussing steps to reconciliation Catholic lay-missionary Paulo Balei spoke of reconciliation taking place at *four* different levels: 'my own reconciliation with myself, reconciliation with God, with others, with nature'. (Interview 12 October 2004) This resonates with Archbishop Mataca's reflections on the interconnectedness of people in relation to Creation and how respect for the natural environment and the given boundaries and limitations of this relationship are central to peace processes:

> I believe that caring and respect for the natural environment is a teaching that is basic to most great religions, not just my own faith. This … is a key resource for peace because questions and issues concerning the environment are also fundamentally about us; who we are and our place in the universe. If we fail to understand this, we will also fail to respect the boundaries and the limits that we should not infringe. If the great religions are to enter into dialogue on the articulation and construction of an environmental ethic, they will render a very valuable and perhaps a sacred service to the world that is desperately in need of moral vision.
>
> The glory of the created world, I believe, is its astonishing diversity and multiplicity: the thousands of languages spoken by humankind; the hundreds of religious faiths; the proliferation of cultures; and the sheer variety of imaginative expressions of the human spirit. In most of these, if we listen carefully, we will hear the voice of God telling us something we need to know. It is for us to discern God's voice in the silence of our hearts and in the stillness of our minds. We must be contemplatives, and God knows we need to be today, [more] than ever before. (Mataca 2006: 79-80)

Conclusion: interconnections

This ethnography has illustrated relationality and connectedness in Fiji through the lens of contemporary relations of Christianity and tradition. The chapters have offered journeys into different facets of Christianity and tradition that each express connectedness between people, between people and the land, between people and the past, between people and God or ancestral spiritual power. I have sought to describe in detail this connectedness in ritual, rhetoric and spiritual experience, understanding the boundaries between these expressions as blurred. And I have sought to show how these interwoven practices of Christianity and tradition in Fiji are interconnected with historical regional and global processes. The chapters touch on different theoretical discussions, however I have consciously chosen to prioritise ethnographic perspectives, description and analysis, rather than engaging as fully as I otherwise might have in the relevant and important theoretical debates.

My aim has been to write a book that reflects the complexity and diversity of my ethnography and which may be of interest and use not only to anthropologists, but also to scholars of cultural and social exchange, ritual, religion and Christianity.

In particular I hope it may prove meaningful and of value to academics and non-academics in Fiji and the Pacific Islands in discussing the relations between faith, tradition and politics.

In the Introduction inculturation and contextual theology connect Christianity with Pacific Islander roots to the land and sea and to tradition. Yet from Christ-centric perspectives they also stress the prophetic voice of the Churches in speaking out against inequality and unjust social, cultural and political structures. Chapters 1 and 7 discuss ways in which Bible-based, Old Testament theologies and Fijian tradition are used politically by conservative and Pentecostal Protestants in advocating an exclusive form of Protestant Christianity to be constitutionally enshrined as a state religion.

Chapter 2 discusses traditional and Pentecostal Christian beliefs in the land as containing powerful spiritual forces. Disordered social relations, crime and infertility of the land are seen from traditional perspectives as emanating from disordered relations with ancestral spirits as part of *vanua*, and from Pentecostal perspectives as due to spiritual bondage by demonic forces – to be accordingly reconciled with or exorcised through traditional or Pentecostal rituals of transformation and healing. Chapters 3 and 4 focus on traditional ritual and relationality in the ceremonial and exchanges of a village funeral and in discussions of the socially nurturing yet at times burdensome aspects of honouring clan commitments and obligations in Fijian and Pacific Islander practices of reciprocity.

Chapter 5 discusses Pentecostal expressions of the relations between past and present, the local and the global, and how Pentecostal Fijians navigate between their faith as Pentecostals, and tradition and *vanua*. Discussing the importance of testimony in the spiritual transformation of Pentecostal Christians through the power of the Holy Spirit the chapter connects with the themes of Chapter 6, on Catholic charismatic rituals of healing and reconciliation through the power of the Holy Spirit in the sacrifice of Christ in the Eucharist.

This concluding chapter continues the theme of reconciliation, forgiveness and healing, at inter-political and inter-personal levels. Conservative Protestant and Pentecostal Christians, emphasising the vertical relationship to God as of paramount importance, espouse that if individuals lead a righteous, Born Again life in Christ, the Holy Spirit will lead them to reconcile with others and live harmoniously with their neighbour. Catholic teachings (cf Chapters 6 and 7) stress that both relationships, a person's relationship to God and to their neighbour, the vertical and the horizontal, are equally important and mutually dependent on one another. A person's relationship to God, it is stressed, cannot be deepened without relations to others simultaneously being strengthened or healed. Anglican understandings of reconciliation (cf Chapter 7) follow a similar line.

Liberal Protestant, Catholic and Anglican voices warn against the dangers of a closed, ethno-nationalist Christianity that seeks to exclude those who do not conform to its narrowly defined religious, ethnic and socio-cultural criteria, stressing, as in the examples of inculturation and contextual theology in the Introduction, the prophetic voice of the Churches as the conscience of the nation in speaking out against social injustice. Their visions are of a society that embraces and celebrates the socio-culturally dynamic nature of religious, ethnic and cultural diversity.

An Indo-Fijian Sikh, a Fijian Methodist minister, drawing on the theology of an English Jewish Rabbi, a Tongan Anglican bishop and a Fijian Roman Catholic Archbishop express in different ways their belief in a divinely ordained and interconnected profusion and richness of diversity in creation. They each point to the importance of listening and respect, of dialogue, and of learning from one another, their reflections reaching out far beyond Fiji's complex situation, addressing universal problems faced in the world today in relation to the increasing polarisation and entrenchment of fundamentalist and liberal perspectives at all levels in local, regional and global society, within and between the world religions, within politics and civil society, and between religion and an increasingly aggressive secularism and atheism.

The ocean, writes Halapua, connects all relationship in Creation. The imagery of this final epigraph sums up the themes and the spirit of this book: the innate relationality of all things – material, social, cultural, and spiritual – in time and space, the importance and necessity of acknowledging such interconnectedness and interdependence, and the enormous potential in drawing on its strengths in journeying together:

> *Moana* is a word that embraces all oceans in unity with creation. From time immemorial Oceanic people have understood the life of the *moana* as an experience of oneness. The actitivites of the *moana* are always in relationship – the currents, the rhythm of the waves, both in the depths and on the surface, interacting with heaveny bodies and the land. The *moana* with its awesome aspects, serenity, perils and turbulence cannot be *moana* without the other oceans and seas. The *moana* as ocean flowing into the lagoon of a small island is one with a life-giving interconnected world. As a metaphor, *moana* speaks of interconnectedness … all creation is interconnected. Each component in the atmosphere, in the ocean, on the land, finds its origin, definition, purpose, completion and continuity in relationship. Life in relationship is the essence of the *moana* and all its rhythm. (Halapua 2008: 10)

Bibliography

Abramson, A. 1999a. Sacred Cows of 'Development': the Ritual Incorporations of a Dairy Project in the Eastern Interior of Fiji (c.1990-1997). *Oceania* 69(4): 260-281.

Abramson, A. 1999b. Dialectics of Localisation: the Political Articulation of Land Rites and Land Rights in the Interior of Eastern Fiji (187-c.1990). *History and Anthropology* 11(4): 437-478.

Ai Vola Tabu kei na Veivuke Eso (n.d.) The Holy Bible in Fijian. Suva: The Bible Society in the South Pacific.

Albrecht, D.E. 1999. *Rites in the Spirit. A Ritual Approach to Pentecostal-Charismatic Spirituality*. Sheffield: Sheffield Academic Press.

Alexander, D. 2009. *Evolution or Creation: Do We Have to Choose?* Monarch Books.

Alexander, F.M. 1931. *The Use of Self*. London: Methuen.

Ali, A. 1980. *Plantation to Politics: Studies on Fiji Indians*. Suva: University of the South Pacific, and Fiji Times and Herald.

—— 2004. *Girmit: The Indenture Experience in Fiji* (with a new 'Preface' and two new concluding chapters). Suva: Fiji Museum and Ministry of National Reconciliation and Multiethnic Affairs.

Ali, A. (ed.) 1979. *Girmit: The Indenture Experience in Fiji*. Bulletin of the Fiji Museum No. 5, 1979.

Arendt, H. 1958. *The Human Condition*. Chicago. Chicago University Press.

Asad, T. 1993. *Genealogies of Religion: Discipline and Reasons of Power in Christianity and Islam*. Baltimore and London: The Johns Hopkins University Press.

Association of Christian Churches in Fiji (ACCF) n.d. Facilitating Reconciliation, Unity, Peace and Prosperity in Fiji. A Review: May 2001-December 2002.

—— 2004. National Year of Prayer Booklet by Association of Christian Churches in Fiji in association with the Ministry of National Reconciliation and Unity.

Austin-Broos, D. 2001. Comment to Douglas. *Current Anthropology* 42(5), December 2001: 630-631.

—— 2003. The Anthropology of Conversion: An Introduction. In *The Anthropology of Religious Conversion*. Buckster, A. and S.D. Glazier (eds). Oxford: Rowman and Littlefield.

Avi, D. 1994, Reconciling Pacific Churches to Promote Unity and Peace. *Pacific Journal of Theology* II(11): 89-96.

Ayala, F.J. 2007. *Darwin's Gift to Science and Religion*. Washington DC: Joseph Henry Press.

Babadzan, A. 1988 *Kastom* and Nation-Building in the South Pacific. In *Ethnicities and Nations: Processes of Interethnic Relations in Latin America, Southeast Asia and the Pacific*, Guidieri, R., F. Pellizzi and S. Tambiah (eds): 199-228. Houston: Rothko Chapel; Austin: University of Texas Press.

Bakker, S.W. 1986. Ceremony and Complication in an Urban Setting. In *Fijians in Town*, Griffin, C. and M. Monsell-Davis (eds): 196-209. Suva: Institute of Pacific Studies, University of the South Pacific.

Banivanua, T.N. 1997. Affirmative Pluralism: Pluralism and the Search for the Common Good. M.A. thesis in Religion, Culture and Society, Lancaster University.

Barker, J. 1990a. Introduction: Ethnographic Perspectives on Christianity in Oceanic Societies. In *Christianity in Oceania: Ethnographic Perspectives*, Barker, John (ed.). ASAO Monograph No. 12. Lanham, New York and London: University Press of America.

—— 1990b. Encounters with Evil: Christianity and the Response to Sorcery among the Maisin of Papua New Guinea. *Oceania* 61: 139-155.

—— 1992. Christianity in Western Melanesian Ethnography. In *History and Tradition in Melanesian Anthropology*, Carrier, J.G. (ed.): 144-173. Berkeley, Los Angeles: University of California Press.

—— 2001. Comment to Douglas. *Current Anthropology* 42(5) December 2001: 631-632.

—— 2007a. Introduction. In *The Anthropology of Morality in Melanesia and Beyond*, Barker, J. (ed.): 1-21. Aldershot: Ashgate.

—— 2007b. All Sides Now: the Postcolonial Triangle in Uiaku. In *The Anthropology of Morality in Melanesia and Beyond*, Barker, J. (ed.): 75-91. Aldershot: Ashgate.

—— 2007c. Comment to Robbins. *Current Anthropology* 48(1) February: 18.

—— n.d. 'Reflections on the Anthropology of Christianity in Melanesia. Presentation at the workshop, *Innovations Religieuses et Dynamiques du Changement Culturel en Océanie Contemporaine*, Paris 29-31/5/08. Sponsored by GSRL, Réseau Asie and Iris.

Barker, J. (ed.) 1990. *Christianity in Oceania: Ethnographic Perspectives*. ASAO Monograph No. 12. Lanham, New York and London: University Press of America.

Barr, K.J. 1979. *To Fulfil not to Destroy*. Nelen Yubu Missiological Series No. 2. Canberra: Chevalier Press.

—— 1990. *Poverty in Fiji*. Suva: Fiji Forum for Justice, Peace, and the Integrity of Creation.

—— 1994. Prophetic Priest or Political Activist? *The Pacific Journal of Theology* II(11): 35-48.

—— 1998. *Blessed are the Rich ... Praise the Lord ... An Examination of New Religious Groups in Fiji Today*. Suva: Fiji Council of Churches.

—— 2004a. The Church and Fijian Ethnocentrism. http://www.ecrea.org.fj/webpages/publications_files/Papers/35.doc.

—— 2004b. *Stand up and Walk: Reflections on the Theme of Empowerment.* Suva: ECREA.

—— 2005a. *Making Poverty History: Different Approaches to Addressing Issues of Poverty and Development.* Suva: ECREA.

—— 2005b. *Guidelines for Social Analysis.* Suva: ECREA.

—— 2007. *Thinking About Democracy Today.* Suva: ECREA.

Battaglia, D. 1992. The Body in the Gift: Memory and Forgetting in Sabarl Mortuary Exchange. *American Ethnologist* 19: 3-18.

Beaglehole, J.C. (ed.) 1955. *The Journals of Captain Cook Vol I The Voyage of the Endeavour, 1768-1771.* Cambridge: Cambridge University Press.

Becker, A.E. 1994. Nurturing and Negligence: Working on Others' Bodies in Fiji. In *Embodiment and Experience: The Existential Ground of Culture and Self,* Thomas J. Csordas (ed.). Cambridge: Cambridge University Press.

—— 1995 *Body, Self, and Society – the View from Fiji.* Philadelphia: University of Pennsylvania Press.

Bell, C. 1992. *Ritual Theory, Ritual Practice.* Oxford: Oxford University Press.

Belshaw, C.S. 1964. *Under the Ivi Tree: Society and Economic Growth in Rural Fiji.* London: Routledge and Kegan Paul.

Bendix, R. 1967. Tradition and Modernity Reconsidered. *Comparative Studies in Society and History* 9(3): 292-346.

Berger, P.L. 1979. *The Heretical Imperative: Contemporary Possibilities of Religious Affirmation.* New York: Anchor Press/Doubleday.

Bergin, H. and S. Smith (eds) 2004. *Land and Place: He Whenua, He Wahi*: *Spiritualities from Aoetearoa New Zealand.* Auckland: Accent Publications.

Biersack, A. (ed.) 1991. *Clio in Oceania: Toward a Historical Anthropology.* Washington and London: Smithsonian Institutional Press.

Bihm, M. 2007. The Impact of the Reconciliation, Tolerance and Unity Bill on the 2006 Election. In *From Election to Coup in Fiji: the 2006 Campaign and its Aftermath*, Fraenkel, J. and S. Firth (eds): 111-143. Canberra: IPS Publications and Asia Pacific Press, The Australian National University.

Black Rose 2002. *Kila...?* (Music CD) Noumea, New Caledonia: Mangrove.

Bloch, M. 1982. Death, Women and Power. In *Death and the Regeneration of Life*, Bloch, M. and J. Parry (eds): 211-231. Cambridge: Cambridge University Press.

Bloch, M. and J. Parry (eds) 1982. *Death and the Regeneration of Life.* Cambridge: Cambridge University Press.

Borofsky, R. 1988. *Making History: Pukapukan and Anthropological Constructions of Knowledge.* Cambridge: Cambridge University Press.

—— 2000a. An Invitation. In *Remembrance of Pacific Pasts: An Invitation to Remake History*, Borofsky, R. (ed.): 1-30. Honolulu: University of Hawaii Press.

—— 2000b. Cook, Lono, Obeyesekere, and Sahlins. In *Remembrance of Pacific Pasts: An Invitation to Remake History*, Borofsky, R. (ed.): 420-452. Honolulu: University of Hawaii Press.

Borofsky, R. (ed.). 2000. *Remembrance of Pacific Pasts: An Invitation to Remake History*. Honolulu: University of Hawaii Press.

Boseto, L. 1985. Environment and Community in Melanesia. *Melanesian Journal of Theology* 1 (1985): 91.

—— 1994. Towards a Pacific Theology of Reality: a Grassroots Response to Winds of Change. *Pacific Journal of Theology* II(12): 53-61.

Brewster, A.B. 1922. *The Hill Tribes of Fiji*. London: Seeley, Service and Co.

Brison, K.J. 2007. *Our Wealth is Loving Each Other: Self and Society in Fiji*. Lanham, MD: Lexington Books.

Brown, B., C. Nokise and R. Nokise (eds) 2009. *Mission in the Midst of Conflict: Stories from the Solomon Islands*. Suva: God's Pacific People Programme, Pacific Theological College.

Bryant, J. 1993. *Urban Poverty and the Environment in the South Pacific*. Armindale: University of New England, Department of Geography and Planning.

Bryant, J. and F. Khan 1990. Population and Housing in Fiji. In *Population of Fiji*, Chandra, R. and J. Bryant (eds). Noumea: South Pacific Commission.

Burt, B. 1982. Kastom, Christianity and the First Ancestor of the Kwara'ae of Malaita. *Mankind* 13(4): 374-399.

—— 1994. *Tradition and Christianity: the Colonial Transformation of a Solomon Islands Society*. Chur: Harwood Academic Publishers.

Bush, J.E. 1995a. Church and State in Fiji. Prepared by Joseph Bush for the seminar on the Fiji Constitutional Review sponsored by Pacific Council of Churches and Fiji Council of Churches Research Group, 26 July, ms.

—— 1995b. Statement to the Constitution Review Commission, 8 September.

—— 1995c. Submission to the Constitution Review Commission 21 September.

—— 1995d. The Vanua is the Lord's. *Pacific Journal of Theology* 2(13): 75-87.

—— 1996. Communal Methodism: Doctrinal Development in Fiji. Wesleyan Studies Group, American Academy of Religion, Annual Meeting, 24 November.

—— 1999a. Claiming a Christian State Where None Exists: Church and State in the Republic of Fiji. *Pacifica* (February 1999): 55-68.

—— 1999b. Reactionary Methodism and the Rule of Law in Fiji. In *Religion and Law in the Global Village*. Guinn, D. and C. Barriger and K.K. Young (eds): 167-179. McGill University.

—— 2000. Land and Communal Faith: Methodist Belief and Ritual in Fiji. *Studies in World Christianity* 6(1): 21-37.

Bushell, S. (ed.) 1990. *Fiji's Faiths: Who We Are and What We Believe*, Vol. 1. Suva: Interfaith Search Fiji.

—— 1994. Dialogue: The Experience of Interfaith Search Fiji. *Pacific Journal of Theology* II(12): 97-106.

Cadogan, T. 2004. A Three-Way Relationship: God, Land, People: A Maori Woman Reflects. In *Land and Place: He Whenua, He Wahi: Spiritualities from Aoetearoa New Zealand*. Bergin, H. and S. Smith (eds): 27-43. Auckland: Accent Publications.

Canberra Anthropology 1995 18(1 and 2). Special Volume, 'The Power of Kava'. Canberra: Australian National University.

Cannell, F. 2005. The Christianity of Anthropology. *JRAI* 11(2): 335-356.

—— 2006. The Anthropology of Christianity: Introduction. In *The Anthropology of Christianity*, Cannell, F. (ed.). Durham NC: Duke University Press.

—— 2007. Reply to Robbins. In *Current Anthropology* 48(1), February: 18-19.

Capell, A. 1991. (1941). The Fijian Dictionary. Second Reprint 1984. Suva: Government Printer.

Capell and Lester. 1941. Local Divisions and Movements in Fiji. *Oceania* XI(4), June: 313-341

—— 1941 and 1941, Part 2 The Nature of Fijian Totemism (cont. from Vol. XI, no. 4). *Oceania* XII.

Caplan, L. 1985. The Culture of Evil in Urban South India. In *The Anthropology of Evil*, Parkin, D. (ed.): 110-127. Oxford: Basil Blackwell.

—— 1987a. Fundamentalism as Counter-Culture: Protestants in Urban South India. In *Studies in Religious Fundamentalism*, Caplan, L. (ed.): 156-177. London: Macmillan.

—— 1987b. *Class and Culture in Urban India: Fundamentalism in a Christian Community*. Oxford: Clarendon Press.

—— 1995. Certain Knowledge: the Encounter of Global Fundamentalism and Local Christianity in Urban South India. In *The Pursuit of Certainty: Religious and Cultural Formations*, James, W. (ed.): 92-111. London: Routledge.

Carr, D. 1986. *Time, Narrative and History*. Bloomington: Indiana University Press.

Carrier, J.G. (ed.) 1992. *Tradition and History in Melanesian Anthropology*. Berkeley: University of California Press.

Casanova, J. 2001. Religion, the New Millennium, and Globalization. *Sociology of Religion* 62(2001): 415-441.

Casimira, A. 2002. A Fundamentalist Christian State, *Fiji Times* 30 November: 7.

—— 2004. The Stranger in our Midst. A Presentation to a Dialogue on Forgiveness group discussion organised by the Ministry of Women, Culture and Poverty Alleviation. Labasa, 22 September.

Chandran, R.J. (ed.) 1988. *The Cross and the Tanoa: Gospel and Culture in the Pacific*. Suva: South Pacific Association of Pacific Schools.

Christian Mission Fellowship of Fiji 2004. Healing of the Land. *Harvest Times* 33, November 2004: 12-13.

Citizens' Constitutional Forum (CCF) 1998. *Your Constitution Your Rights*: Suva: CCF, Fiji in association with Conciliation Resources, London.

—— 2005. Submission to the Sector Standing Committee on Justice, Law and Order regarding the promotion of Reconciliation, Tolerance and Unity Bill 2005. Citizens Constitutional Forum Limited.

—— 2007. *Poverty in Paradise*: *No Way to Live. Stories of Squatter Families and Those Who Work Among Them.* By ECREA staff. CCF Housing and Social Exclusion Policy Dialogue Paper No. 2, 2007.

—— 2009. *Tutaka* online. *The Quarterly Newsletter of the Citizens' Constitutional Forum Ltd.* 3(3), July.

Clammer, J. 1976. *Literacy and Social Change: A Case Study of Fiji.* Leiden: E.J. Brill.

Clarke, W.C. 1999. Poetry and Pacific Studies: Notes from the Field. *Asia Pacific Viewpoint* 40(2), August: 187-206.

—— 2007. Speaking of Home: Poetic Reflections on the Pacific Islands. Published by Division of Humanities. University of Otago.

Clifford, J. 1988. *The Predicament of Culture: Twentieth-Century Ethnography, Literature, and Art.* London: Harvard University Press.

Clifford, J. and G.E. Marcus (eds) 1986. *Writing Culture: The Poetics and Politics of Ethnography.* Berkeley: University of California Press.

Cloher, D.U. 2004. A Perspective on Early Maori Relationships with their Land. In *Land and Place: He Whenua, He Wahi: Spiritualities from Aoetearoa New Zealand.* Bergin, H. and S. Smith (ed.): 47-57. Auckland: Accent Publications.

Clunie, F. 1986. Letters from the Highlands of Vitilevu, 1877, by John Archibald Boyd. *Domodomo, Fiji Museum Quarterly* IV(I): 20-47.

Colchester, C. 2000. Bark Cloth, Reproduction and the Expansion of Endogamous Polities in Natewa. PhD thesis, University College London, University of London.

Coleman, S. 2000a. *The Globalisation of Charismatic Christianity: Spreading the Gospel of Prosperity.* Cambridge: Cambridge University Press.

—— 2000b. Moving Towards the Millenium?: Ritualized Mobility and the Cultivation of Agency among Christmatic Protestants. *Journal of Ritual Studies* 14(2): 16-27.

—— 2003. Continuous Conversion? The Rhetoric, Practice, and Rhetorical Practice of Charismatic Protestant Conversion. In *The Anthropology of Religious Conversion*, Buckster, A. and S.D. Glazier (eds). Oxford: Rowman & Littlefield.

—— 2004. The Charismatic Gift. *JRAI* (N.S.) 10: 421-442.

—— 2006a. Materializing the Self: Words and Gifts in the Construction of Charismatic Protestant Identity. In *The Anthropology of Christianity*, Cannell, F. (ed.): 163-184. Durham: Duke University Press.

—— 2006b. When Silence Isn't Golden: Charismatic Speech and the Limits of Literalism. In *The Limits of Meaning: Case Studies in the Anthropology of Christianity*, Engelke, M. and M. Tomlinson (ed.): 39-61. New York and Oxford: Berghahn Books.

—— 2007. Reply to Robbins. *Current Anthropology* 48(1), February: 19-20.

—— In Press. Voices: Presence and Prophesy in Charismatic Ritual. In *Practising the Faith: The Ritual Life of Charismatic-Pentecostal Christians.* Lindhardt, M. (ed.). New York and Oxford: Berghahn Books.

Coleman, S. and P. Collins 2000. The 'Plain' and the 'Positive': Ritual, Experience and Aesthetics in Quakerism and Charismatic Christianity. *Journal of Contemporary Religion* 15(3): 317-329.

Collingwood, R.G. 1992 [1946] *The Idea of History*. Oxford: Oxford University Press.

Collins, R. 2004. *Interaction Ritual Chains*. Princeton: Princeton University Press.

Concerns 2006. Our Nation in the Eyes of the Gospel Genuine Reconciliation – What is it really? By Father Kieran Moloney SSC. 1(1), January 2006: 1. A Justice Peace and Integrity of Creation Newsletter of the Columban Fathers, Fiji.

Costello-Olsson, K. 2003. A Prayer for Women in Conflict in Fiji. In *Weavings: Women Doing Theology in Oceania*. Suva, J., L. Alleluia Felemoni-Tofaeono and J. Alleluia Felemoni-Tofaeono (eds): 183-184. Institute of Pacific Studies, University of the South Pacific: Weavers, South Pacific Association of Theological Schools.

—— 2005. *The Journey Ahead – UN International Day of Peace – September 21st 2005*, for the Prayer Vigil at the Holy Trinity Anglican Cathedral, Suva. Suva: ECREA.

Coyne, G.S.J. 2005. God's Chance Creation. In *The Tablet* 6 August.

Crowl, L.S. 2008. Politics and Book Publishing in the Pacific Islands. PhD thesis, University of Wollongong.

Csordas, T.J. 1983 The Rhetoric of Transformation in Ritual Healing. *Culture, Medicine and Psychiatry* 1983: 333-375.

—— 1990. Embodiment as a Paradigm for Anthropology. *Ethos* 18: 5-47.

—— 1994. *The Sacred Self: A Cultural Phenomenology of Charismatic Healing*. Berkeley: University of California Press.

—— 2001. *Language, Charisma and Creativity*. New York: Palgrave.

Dakuvula, J. 1992. Chiefs and Commoners: the Indigenous Dilemma in Fiji. In *Tu Galala*, David Robbie (ed.). Annandale: Pluto Press Australia.

—— Unity Bill is Worthy??? Letter to the Editor, *Daily Post*, CCF, 17 May.

—— 2005. Bill Benefits Selected Few. Opinion. *The Fiji Times* 31 August: 7.

Damon, F.H. and R. Wagner (eds) 1989, *Death Rituals and Life in the Societies of the Kula Ring*. DeKalb: Northern Illinois University Press.

The Daily Post 1996. Temple Bandits Beasts: Rabuka condemns attacks on worship houses, by Hari Gaunder, 13 November: 1.

1998. Changing Tradition. 21 June: 7.

2003. Christian Should lead Fiji: Lagi. By Kuliniasi Ligaitamana, 18 August: 3.

—— Others Welcomed in Church State. By Joe Cava, 20 August: 3.

—— State Supports Review of Religious Laws. 20 August: 3.

—— Kaba Seeks Church Forgiveness. By Timoci Vula. 28 August: 5.

—— Miracle Healing, by Prashila Devi, 19 September: 1.

—— Chaudhry Warns on Christian State Call. By Senimili Kame, 26 September: 3.

—— Miracles, Miracles, Letter to the Editor. By Paula Rabakewa, 26 September: 6.

—— Reverend Reinhard Bonnke's Visit, 27 September: 7.

—— 250,000 ACCF Supporters are Deeply Hurt by Fiji Times Lies. Paid Advertisement by ACCF Executive Committee, 27 September: 30.

—— Apology is Significant: PM, by Epeli Tukuwasa, 15 October: 5.

—— Chiefs Apologise for Cannibalism. By Mithleshni Gurdayal. 16 October: 3.

—— 'Arsonists' Strike Temple. By Charlotte Peters, 27 October: 1.

—— Religion of Tolerance and Acceptance. Editorial, 29 October: 6.

—— Burnings Worry Chief. 29 October: 3.

—— Old Practice 'A Farce'. By Joe Cava, 29 October: 3.

2004. Military Says Fete is a Superficial One. By Mithleshni Gurdayal: 5 October: 1.

—— President Commands Forgiveness: 5 October: 1.

—— Prayers and Reconciliation. Editorial. 5 October: 6.

—— Apologise Anyway. Letter to the Editor, by Daniel Urai. 5 October: 6

—— Reconciliation Mode. By Timoci Vula. 5 October: 7.

—— Matanigasau was Meaningless. By Josephine Prasad, 6 October: 1.

—— MDF Takes Swipe at Organisers of the Reconciliation Week. 6 October: 3.

—— Ministry Rebuts Statement. By Timoci Vula. 6 October: 5.

—— It's Time to Move Forward. 6 October: 5.

—— Adding Salt to the Wound. 6 October: 5.

—— Ceremony is Premature: FDP: 6 October: 5.

—— Ceremony has no Genuine Sense: FLP: 6 October: 5.

—— Prayer Week, A Starting Point, says Beddoes: 6 October: 5.

—— Sacredness of Ceremony Comes from Heart. By Mithleshni Gurdayal: 6 October: 5.

—— Reconcile for Children. By Jone Luvenitoga, 6 October: 12.

Davis, C. 1976. *Body as Spirit: the Nature of Religious Feeling*. London: Hodder & Stoughton.

Daye, R. 2003. Finding a Model of Reconciliation. *Daily Post,* 2 September: 7.

—— 2004a. *Political Forgiveness: Lessons from South Africa*. Orbis Books.

—— 2004b. Keynote Address by Revd. Dr. Russ Daye, Pacific Theological College, at 'Dialogue on Forgiveness' workshop, arranged by Ministry for Women, Social Welfare and Poverty Alleviation, Suva, 22 October 2004. Unpublished paper.

de Coppet, D. 1981. The Life-Giving Death. In *Mortality and Immortality: the Anthropology and Archaeology of Death,* Humphreys, S.C. and Helen King (eds): 175-204. London: Academic Press.

de Marzan, J. 1987. [1907-13] Customs and Beliefs in Upland Vitilevu. Papers from Anthropos, 1907-1913, translated from the French by Nicholas Thomas. *Domodomo, Fiji Museum Quarterly 1987*, V(3 and 4) (28-62).

Dean, E. and S. Ritova 1988. *No Other Way.* Suva: The Marketing Team International Ltd.

Deane, W. 1921. *Fijian Society or the Sociology and Psychology of the Fijians.* London: Macmillan.

Dening, G. 1963. The Geographical Knowledge of the Polynesians and the Nature of Inter-island Contact. In *Polynesian Navigation: A Symposium on Andrew Sharp's Theory of Accidental Voyages*, Golsen, J. (ed.): 102-113. Polynesian Society Memoir No. 34. Wellington.

Dickhardt, M. 2000. Das Land, die Ahnen, die Dämonen, die Kirche und der Gott in der Höhe: Formen religiöser Räumlichkeit in Fiji (Land, Ancestors, Demons, the Church, and God on High: Forms of Religious Space in Fiji). In *Cartographia Religiosa – Religiöse Kartographie – Religieuse* (*Religious Cartography*) (Studia Religiosa Helvetica Series Altera 4), Pezzolo-Oligiati, D. and F. Stolz (eds): 253-288. Bern: Peter Lang.

—— 2005. Viti, the Soil from Eden: On Historical Praxis as a Mode of Connecting in Fiji. *Oceania* 75(4): 342-353.

Dobell, G. 2001. The Strange Saga of Speight's Siege in Suva. In *COUP: Reflections on the Political Crisis in Fiji*, Lal, Brij V. and Michael Pretes (eds): 126-136. Canberra: Pandanus Books, Research School of Pacific and Asian Studies, Australian National University.

Douglas, B. 2001a. Encounters with the Enemy? Academic Readings of Missionary Narratives on Melanesians. *Comparative Studies in Society and History* 43: 37-64.

—— 2001b. From Invisible Christians to Gothic Theatre: The Romance of the Millennial in Melanesian Anthropology. *Current Anthropology* 42(5), December: 615-650.

Droogers, A. 2003. The Power Dimensions of the Christian Community: an Anthropological Model. *Religion* 33: 263-280.

Durutalo, S. 1986. *The Paramountcy of Fijian Interest and the Politicization of Ethnicity*. Suva: USP Sociology Society.

ECREA 2001a. Remembering the Past for the Future. *The Pacific Journal of Theology* II(25): 3-24.

—— 2001b. *Fiji: Finding a Path Forward*. Documentary film produced by Pasifika Communications. Funded by Caritas-Aotearoa New Zealand and ECREA.

—— 2004. *Who Is My Neighbour, My Brother and Sister?* Suva: ECREA.

—— 2006. *Let's All Celebrate*. Suva: ECREA and CCF Project on multiculturalism.

—— 2009a. *Separation of Church and State*. By Father Kevin Barr MSC.

—— 2009b. *Ecumenism in Fiji 1999-2009: Crisis and Opportunities*. By Apimeleki Qihilo.

Ekolm, K. and J. Friedman 1985. Towards a Global Anthropology. *Critique of Anthropology* 5(1): 97-119.

Emberson, P. 2009a. Vi synker mens I snakker. [While You're Talking We're Sinking]. Kristeligt Dagblad, 15 May 2009: 1.

—— 2009b. Jorden og Havet er Guds Gaver til Os og Fremtidens Generationer [The Earth and the Sea are God's Gifts to Us and Future Generations]. *Kristeligt Dagblad* 15 May: 17.

Emberson-Bain, A. 1994. *Labour and Gold in Fiji*. Cambridge: Cambridge University Press.

Engelke, M. 2004. Discontinuity and the Discourse of Conversion. *Journal of Religion in Africa* 34(1-2): 82-109.

—— In Print. Past Pentecostalism: Notes on the Multi-temporal Dimensions of Rupture. *Africa* June 2010.

Eriksen, A. 2007. Comment to Robbins. *Current Anthropology* 48(1), February 2007: 20-21.

—— 2008. *Gender, Christianity and Change in Vanuatu: An Analysis of Social Movements in North Ambrym*. Aldershot: Ashgate.

Ernst, Manfred 1991. A Survey of Rapidly Growing Religious Groups and Evangelical/Fundamentalist Para-Church Organisations in the Pacific Islands. *Pacific Journal of Theology* II(6): 43-63.

—— 1994a. *Winds of Change. Rapidly Growing Religious Groups in the Pacific Islands*. Suva: Pacific Conference of Churches.

—— 1994b. The Effects of New Religious Movements on Pacific Culture. *Pacific Journal of Theology* II(12): 7-14.

—— 2006. Introduction. In *Globalization and the Re-Shaping of Christianity in the Pacific Islands*, Ernst, M. (ed.): 3-78. Suva: Pacific Theological College.

Ernst, M. (ed.) 2006. *Globalization and the Re-Shaping of Christianity in the Pacific Islands*. Suva: Pacific Theological College.

Errington, Frederick K. and Deborah B. Gewertz 1995. *Articulating Change in the 'Last Unknown'*. Boulder: Westview Press.

Ete-Lima, M. 2003. A Theology of the Feagaiga: A Samoan Theology of God. In *Weavings: Women Doing Theology in Oceania*. Suva, J., L. Alleluia Felemoni-Tofaeono and J. Alleluia Felemoni-Tofaeono (eds): 24-31. Institute of Pacific Studies, University of the South Pacific: Weavers, South Pacific Association of Theological Schools.

Eves, R. 1996. Colonialism, Corporeality and Character: Methodist Missions and the Refashioning of Bodies in the Pacific. *History and Anthropology* 10(1): 85-138.

—— 2000. Waiting for the Day: Globalisation and Apocalypticism in Central New Ireland, Papua New Guinea. *Oceania* 71(2) December: 73-91.

—— 2003. Money, Mayhem and the Beast: Narratives of the World's End from New Ireland (Papua New Guinea). In *JRAI* 2003, 9.

Ewing, K.P. 1994. Dreams from a Saint: Anthropological Atheism and the Temptation to Believe. *American Anthropologist* 96(3): 571-583.

Ewins, R. 1982. Fijian Artefacts. In *The Tasmanian Museum and Art Gallery*: 5-21. Hobart: Tasmanian Museum and Art Gallery.

Fa'asi, U. 1993. Gospel and Culture in the Ava Ceremony. *Pacific Journal of Theology* 10: 61-63.

Fabian, J. 1983. *Time and the Other: How Anthropology Makes its Object*. New York: Colombia University Press.

—— 2001. Comment to Douglas. *Current Anthropology* 42(5), 2001: 633-634.

Fer, G. 2007. *Les femmes dans L'Église Protestante ma'ohi: Religion, Genre et Pouvoir en Polynésie Francaise*. Paris: Karthala.

Fer, Y. 2005a. *Pentecôtisme en Polynésie Francaise*. Geneva: Labor et Fides.

—— 2005b. Genèse des émotions au sein des Assemblées de Dieu polynésiennes. *Archives de Sciences Sociales des Religions* 131-132 (Juillet-Decémbre 2005): 143-163.

—— 2005c. The Growth of Pentecostalism in French Polynesia: a Hakka History. *China Perspectives* 57, January, February 2005: 50-57.

—— 2006. La pentecôtisme en Polynésie Francaise: Une religion efficace pour des temps d'incertitude? *Pacific Journal of Theology* II(35): 18-47.

—— n.d. Beyond the Local Church: Evangelical Networks and Polynesian Cultures on the Move. Paper presented at the workshop, *Innovations Religieuses et Dynamiques du Changement Culturel en Océanie Contemporaine*, Paris 29 31 May. Sponsored by GSRL, Réseau Asie & Iris.

Field, M. 2007. The Media and the Spectre of the 2000 Coup. In *From Election to Coup in Fiji: the 2006 Campaign and its Aftermath*, Fraenkel, J. and S. Firth (eds): 174-184. Canberra: IPS Publications and Asia Pacific Press. The Australian National University.

Fiji Catholic 2003. Healing Mass at Holy Family, Labasa. By Fr. J.J. Ryan, CSS. 3 September: 1.

Fiji Council of Churches 1995. Statement to the Constitution Review Commission.

Fiji Council of Churches Research Group n.d. Constitution Review Commission Report Guideline (draft paper).

Fiji Islands Bureau of Statistics 2007 Census. September 2008.

Fiji Islands Population Profile 1999 Based on the 1996 Census – a Guide for Planners and Policy-makers. Published with financial assistance from AusAID. Noumea, New Caledonia: Secretariat of the Pacific Community.

Fiji Government 2005. Statement on the Reconciliation, Tolerance and Unity Bill. In *Fiji Times* 9 May: 19-21.

Fiji Museum n.d. Site 1/2001 Site records of Jean Charlot Murals and Church of Saint Francis Xavier. Master copy, Fiji Museum Archives.

Fiji Sun 2003. Curse Broken. By Ana Tudrau, 27 August: 1.

—— Lifting the Curse, Comment, 10 November: 4.

—— Cannibal Victim's Relatives to Visit Fiji, 13 November: 10.

—— Rev Baker's Family Forgive, Accept Apology. By Atunaisa Sokomuri and Otilly Rabuku, 14 November: 1 and 5 (photos).

—— Navatusila Ceremony Historic for Fiji – Qarase, 15 November: 5.

—— Is Natvatusila Cursed? By Swadesh Singh, Letter to the Editor, 18 November: 4.

—— Lifting the Curse. By Sanaila Ravia, Letter to the Editor, 27 November: 4.

2006. In The Name Of All That's Holy. By Archbishop Mataca, 12 January: 7.

Fiji Times 1996. Maintaining our Dear Relations: Weighing the Cost of Keeping Fijian Custom Against Competing Demands. By Mere Momoivalu, 8 November: 7.

—— 1997. Coup was the best option. By Sitiveni Rabuka, 14 May: 1-2.

—— Methodists oppose Christian State plan. By Margaret Wise, 28 June: 1

—— Recognising True Christianity. Editorial Comment, 28 June: 6.

—— Five Thugs Desecrate Family Temple, 30 June: 3.

—— Religious Tolerance Is Vital, Editorial Comment, 30 June: 6.

—— Men Deny Insult to Religion Charge, 30 October: 2.

—— Adi Kuini Launches Book, 18 December.

—— 1998. Politics is Not On, Says Church, 20 February.

—— Beware of New Sects: Priest, 5 March: 5.

—— Pastors Want to be MPs. By Margaret Wise, 10 March: 1.

—— Expressing a Basic Right. Editorial, 10 March: 6.

—— Who'll be Party to This? By Netani Rika, 'On the Bright Side', 14 March.

—— Spreading God's Word. By Ernest Heatley, 15 March: 10.

—— Methodists Back Political Party, 17 March.

—— Church Denies Claim, 18 March: 5.

—— Keeping the Church Separate, Editorial 24 March: 6.

—— Church Maintains Stand on Political Party, 27 March: 5.

—— For the Love of God and Country. Ruby Taylor-Newton, 28 March: 2-3.

—— We Win 7s Cup, 30 March 98: 1

—— God Helped Us, 30 March: 36

—— Temple Vandals Set Free. By Dharmend Prasad, 31 March: 5.

—— Desecration Case Appeal Likely: DPP Studies Sawani Temple Attack File, 1 April: 2.

—— Temple Desecration. Sanatan Dharm Pratinidhi Sabha of Fiji, Letters 15 April: 5.

—— Christian Sects Hit Over Politics, 7 April: 5.

—— Church in Politics. Josua Mudreilagi, Suva. Letters, 14 April: 6.

—— Moving Tribute to Dr Bavadra. By Seona Smiles, 7 May: 7.

—— Interfaith Group Prays for Fiji. By Leba Harrison, 29 July.

—— Church Must be Neutral: Chief, 22 August.

—— 1999. Leave Church Alone: Tuwere, 22 February: 1.

—— 2001. Role of the Church. Editorial, 28 August: 6.

—— Methodist Church Media Release, 19 September: 47.

—— 2002. The Need to Reconcile. By Archbishop Mataca, 20 September: 7.

—— Rebel Troopers to Seek Forgiveness. By Reijeli Kikau, 12 November: 1.

—— New Church 'Sect' Divides Villagers. By Vasemaca Rarabici, 20 November: 3.

—— Blessings for Sale. Editorial, 21 November: 6.

—— Only by Love. By R.T. Nasea, Letter to the Editor, 28 November: 6.

—— Forgive and Forget. By Vasiti Dealinadogo, Letter to the Editor, 30 November: 6.

—— Lasting Solution. N. Leweni, Media Cell, RFMF, Letter to the Editor, 30 November: 6.

—— Villagers Burn House, Hall. By Elenoa Masi Baselala, 4 December: 1.

—— Un-Christian Acts. Editorial, 4 December: 6.

—— Police Watch Religious Situation, 5 December: 3.

—— Church Supports Cleansing Exercise. By Elenoa Masi Baselala, 6 December: 2.

2003. Thieves Steal Temple Statue. By Timothy Naivaluwaqa, 10 June: 4.

—— Too Many Churches, 12 August: 1

—— Too Many Churches, Editorial, 13 August: 6.

—— Confused by History. By Neelesh Gounder, Letter to the Editor, 13 August: 6.

—— Review of Churches a Must: A-G, 14 August: 3.

—— 'Christian State a Must': Methodist Takes Cue from Pakistan, 16 August: 3.

—— Religious Freedom. By Interfaith Search Fiji: Letter to the Editor, 16 August: 6.

—— Christian Dominance. By George Samisoni. Letter to the Editor, 18 August: 6.

—— Christian State. By Henry Rigamoto, Interfaith Search Fiji. Letter to the Editor, 22 August: 6.

—— Christian State. By Aisake Verebasaga, Letter to the Editor, 23 August: 6.

—— Party Backs Christian state, 23 August: 16.

—— Chiefs Made a Covenant with God. By Vani Catanasiga, 29 August: 5.

—— Religious Freedom. By Suruj Pal, Letter to the Editor, 30 August: 6.

—— Love thy Neighbour. By Ashneel Sudhakar, Letter to the Editor, 3 September: 6.

—— Deed of Cession. By Isireli Vuibau, Letter to the Editor, 3 September: 6.

—— Religious Tolerance. Editorial, 7 September: 6.

—— Christian State. By Prue Rouse, Letter to the Editor, 11 September: 6.

—— Christian Common Sense. Editorial, 17 September: 6.

—— Police deny Bonnke Claims. By Imran Ali, 20 September: 1.

—— Beware of Miracles. Editorial, 20 September: 6.

—— Bonnke: Miracle Man or Heretic? By Esita Cakau, 20 September: 9.

—— A Man of God. By Tomasi Kolinitoga. Letter to the Editor, 23 September: 6.

—— A World of Miracles. By Sanaila Ravia, Letter to the Editor, 24 September: 6.

—— Warning on Evangelists. By Aida Whippy. Letter to the Editor, 25 September: 6.

—— A Genuine Man of God. By Kalisito Tunaulu. Letter to the Editor, 25 September: 6.

—— Salvation and Miracles. By Jeremaia N. Soko. Letter to the Editor, 25 September: 6.

—— Chaudhry Warns On Christian State Call. By Senimili Kame, 26 September: 3.

—— Miracles, Miracles. By Paul Rabakewa Letter to the Editor, 27 September: 6.

—— False Prophets. By Manasa Daunakamakama, Letter to the Editor, 27 September: 6.

—— VIP Welcome for Preacher. By Erwin Karl Skiba, Letter to the Editor, 27 September: 6.

—— Bonnke's Fiji Escort Unofficial: Police Chief, by Imran Ali, 30 September: 2.

—— Are Those who Merely ask Questions now Agents of the Devil? Full page advertisement, written and authorized by Tony Yianni on behalf of *Fiji Times* Ltd, 1 October: 50.

—— Faith Healing. By Peter Johnston, Letter to the Editor, 2 October: 6.

—— Wrong Attitude. By Talei Burness, Letter to the Editor, 23 October: 6.

—— Science vs Christianity. By Atish Chand, Letter to the Editor, 23 October: 6.

—— Temple Icons Lost in Fire. By Imran Ali, 27 October: 3

—— Chief calls for Church Control. By Reijeli Kikau, 3 November: 3.

—— Koroi Condemns Baker Plan. By Reijeli Kikau, 5 November: 3.

—— Villagers Prepare to Seek Forgiveness. By Reijeli Kikau, 10 November: 2.

—— Group Blasts Church [temple] Attacks. 3 November: 5.

—— Navatusila Curse. By Swadesh Singh, Letter to the Editor, 17 November: 6.

—— Thomas Baker. By Dr Andrew Thornley. Letter to the Editor, 23 November: 6.

—— Thomas Baker. By Aida J. Whippy, Letter to the Editor, 29 November: 6.

2004. Christian state. By N.D. Mishra, Letter to the Editor, 17 September: 6.

—— Forgive us – Chief: Tears Flow at Ceremony. By Reijeli Kikau, 5 October: 1.

—— Iloilo Calls for Forgiveness. By Reijeli Kikau, 5 October: 3.

—— Beddoes urges Leaders to Lead by Example. By Katonivualiku, 5 October: 3.

—— Parties Prefer Fiji Islander Identity. By Unaisi Ratubalavu, 5 October: 3.

—— CCF Position on National Reconciliation Process, press release of 6 October, 7 October: 10

—— Traditional Apology. By Eunice Singh, Letter to the Editor, 8 October: 10.

—— Genuine Reconciliation. By D. Naran, Letter to the Editor, 9 October: 6.

—— Indian Leader. By Praneet Singh, Sacramento, CA, Letter to the Editor, 9 October: 6.

—— Chief Wants Coup Backers to Own Up, 10 October: 2.

—— Reconciliation: Is it Really our Way Forward? 10 October: 10 and 11.

—— National Apologies. By S. Kabarokoro. Letter to the Editor, 11 October: 6.

—— A Need to Reconcile. By Serafina Qalo, 11 October: 7.

—— Call for Genuine Reconciliation. By Sudesh Kissun, 13 October.

—— Christian State. By Sue Cauty, Letter to the Editor, 21 October: 6.

—— Reconcile or Leave: Senator. By Reijeli Kikau, 21 October: 13.

—— Unity for Fiji. By Wame Nabete. Letter to the Editor, 22 October: 6.

—— The Politics of Forgiving. By Ema Tagicakibau, 23 October: 7.

—— Time for the Truth, leader, 25 October: 6.

—— Politics of Forgiveness. By Mareko Vuli, Sydney, Letter to the Editor, 26 October: 6.

—— Vinaka Adi Koila. Bruce Rounds, Letter to the Editor, 26 October: 6.

—— Christian State. By W. Sausau. Letter to the Editor, 2 November: 10.

2005 Churches Must Preach Unity. By Archbishop Mataca, 9 February: 7.

—— Do not Politicise Religion: Casimira. By Vani Catanisaiga, 16 March.

—— Tradition and Democracy. By J.B. Raiova, Letter to the Editor, 13 September: 6.

—— Christian State. By Peni Tuibusa, Letter to the Editor, 1 September: 10.

—— Jail a Must for Temple Raids. By Mereseini Marau, 26 September: 5.

—— Ratu Jone Talks of Unity. By Amelia Vunileba, 8 October: 4

—— Christians Must be in Politics: Church. By Brenda Ragg, 11 October: 3.

—— Healing and Remembering. By Father Michael Lapsley, SSM, 12 October: 10.

—— Lapsley Urges Review of Bill, 12 October: 14.

—— Fijian Origin. Paul Geraghty, Letter to the Editor, 2 November: 6.

Finau, Bishop P.S.M. 1994. Church, the Conscience of a Nation. *Pacific Journal of Theology* II(11): 77-78.

Fison, L. 1888. Notes on Fijian Burial Customs. *The Australasian and Centennial* p.9, ms, Mitchell Library, Sydney. Photocopied by kind permission from Dr Paul Geraghty.

Forman, C.W. 1990. Some Next Steps in the Study of Pacific Island Christianity. In *Christianity in Oceania: Ethnographic Perspectives.* ASAO Monograph No. 12, Barker, J. (ed.): 25-31. Lanham, New York and London: University Press of America.

—— 1996. Methodism in the Pacific and Fiji Context. In *Mai Kea Ki Vei? Stories of Methodism in Fiji and Rotuma,* Proceedings of the Fiji Methodist History Conference, Davuilevu 10-13 October 1995, Thornley, A. and T. Vulaono (eds): 1-16. Suva: Fiji Methodist Church.

—— 2005. Finding our Own Voice: The Reinterpreting of Christianity by Oceanian Theologians. *International Bulletin of Missionary Research* 29(3): 115-122.

Foster, R.J. 1990. Nurture and Force-Feeding: Mortuary Feasting and the Construction of Collective Identities in a New Ireland Society. *American Ethnologist* 17: 431-148.

—— (ed.) 1995a. *Social Reproduction and History in Melanesia: Mortuary Ritual, Gift Exchange, and Custom in the Tanga Islands.* Cambridge: Cambridge University Press.

—— 1995b. *Nation-Making: Emergent Identities in Postcolonial Melanesia.* Ann Arbor: Michigan University Press.

Frankel, S. 1986. *The Huli Response to Illness.* Cambridge: Cambridge University Press.

Fraenkel, J. and S. Firth (eds) 2007. *From Election to Coup in Fiji: the 2006 Campaign and its Aftermath.* Canberra: ANU E PRESS, IPS Publications; University of the South Pacific; Asia Pacific Press, The Australian National University.

Fraenkel, J., S. Firth and B. Lal (eds) 2009. *The 2006 Military Takeover in Fiji: A Coup to end all Coups?* Canberra: Australian National University Press.

France, P. 1966. The Kaunitoni Migration: Notes on the Genesis of a Fijian Tradition. *Journal of Pacific History* 1: 107-113.

—— 1969. *The Charter of the Land: Custom and Colonization in Fiji.* Melbourne: Oxford University Press.

Freeth, M. 1990. Modern Maori Image 'Invented'. *New Zealand Herald*, 24 February.

Friedman, J. 1992. The Past in the Future: History and the Politics of Identity. *American Anthropologist* 94(4) December: 837-859.

—— 1996. Introduction. In Melanesian Modernities. Friedman, Jonathan and James G. Carrier (eds): 1-9. Lund: Lund University Press.

Fry, G. 1996. Framing the Islands: Knowledge and Power in Changing Australian Images of 'The South Pacific'. Working Paper No. 1996/5. Department of International Relations. Research School of Pacific and Asian Studies. The Australian National University. Also published in *The Contemporary Pacific* 9, 1997.

—— 2000. When a Big Brother Crumbles. *The Australian* 22 May: 15.

Garma, C. Reply to Robbins. *Current Anthropology* 48(1) February 2007: 21-22.

Garrett, J. 1982. *To Live Among the Stars: Christian Origins in Oceania.* Suva and Geneva: World Council of Churches in association with the Institute of Pacific Studies, University of the South Pacific.

—— 1988. The Coups in Fiji: A Preliminary Social Analysis. *Catalyst* 18: 1-15.

—— 1990. Uncertain Sequel: The Social and Religious Scene in Fiji Since the Coups. *Contemporary Pacific* 2(1): 87-111. Spring 1990.

—— 1992. *Footsteps in the Sea: Christianity in Oceania to World War II.* Suva and Geneva: World Council of Churches in association with the Institute of Pacific Studies, University of the South Pacific.

—— 1995. The State and Religions in Fiji. Paper submitted to the FCRC.

—— 1996. Methodism in Fiji Since 1964. In *Mai Kea Ki Vei? Stories of Methodism in Fiji and Rotuma.* Proceedings of the Fiji Methodist History Conference, Davuilevu 10-13 October 1995, Thornley, A. and T. Vulaono (eds): 193-202. Suva: Fiji Methodist Church.

—— 1997 *Where Nets were Cast: Christianity in Oceania since World War II.* Suva and Geneva: World Council of Churches in association with the Institute of Pacific Studies, University of the South Pacific.

Gaunder, P. 2007. *An Elusive Dream: Multiracial Harmony in Fiji 1970-2000.* Saarbrucken: VDM Verlag Dr Muller Aktiengesellschaft & Co.

Geddes, W.R. 1945. Deuba: A Study of a Fijian Village. *Memoirs of the Polynesian Society* 22.

Geraghty, P. 1977. Geraghty, Paul 1977. How a Myth is Born – the Story of the Kaunitoni Story. *MANA* 2(1): 25-29.

—— 1983. *The History of the Fijian Languages.* Honolulu: University of Hawaii Press.

—— 1997. The Ethnic Basis of Society in Fiji. In *Fiji in Transition: Research Papers of the Fiji Constitution Review Commission* Vol. 1, Lal, B.V. and Tomasi R. Vakatora (eds): 1-23. Suva: School of Social and Economic Development, University of the South Pacific.

—— 2005 Fijian Origin. Letter to the Editor, *Fiji Times* 2 November: 6.

—— n.d. Nadrogā Fijian. Unpublished manuscript (copied with kind permission from the author).

—— n.d. The Kaunitoni Myth (with kind permission from the author).

Gewertz, D.B. and F.K. Errington 1991. *Twisted Histories, Altered Contexts: Representing the Chambri in a World System.* Cambridge: Cambridge University Press.

Gifford, P. 1992. Reinhard Bonnke's Mission to Africa and his 1991 Nairobi Project. In *New Dimensions of African Christianity*, Gifford, P. (ed.): 157-182. Nairobi: AACC (All African Council of Churches).

Gillion, K.L. 1962. *Fiji's Indian Migrants: a History to the End of Indenture in 1920.* Melbourne: Oxford University Press.

Godelier, M. 1999. *The Enigma of the Gift.* Chicago: Chicago University Press.

Gordon, A.J. 1879. *Story of a Little War* Vols. I and II. Privately published. Held at the National Archives, Suva.

—— 1986. An Account of Mr Walter Carew's Tour of the Island of Na Viti Levu on Behalf of the Government – 1875. *Domodomo*, Fiji Museum Quarterly IV(2): 55-82.

Gounis, C. and H.J. Rutz 1986. Urban Fijians and the Problem of Unemployment. In *Fijians in Town*. Griffin C. and M. Monsell-Davis (eds): 50-88. Suva: Institute of Pacific Studies, University of the South Pacific.

Green, R.H. Rev. n.d. My Story [Memoirs]. Ms, Pacific Theological College, Suva and Dept. of Pacific History, Australian National University.

Gregory, C. 1980. Gifts to Men and Gifts to God: Gift Exchange and Capital Accumulation in Contemporary Papua. *MAN* 15(4) (Dec 1980): 626-652.

—— 1982. *Gifts and Commodities.* London: Academic Press.

—— Forthcoming. Exchange. In *Handbook of Sociocultural Anthropology*, Carrier, J.G. and D.B. Gewertz (eds). Oxford: Berg.

Griffen, A. (ed.) 1997. *With Heart and Nerve and Sinew: Post-coup Writing from Fiji.* Suva: Christmas Club.

Gunson, N. 1978. *Messengers of Grace: Evangelical Missionaries in the South Seas, 1797-1860.* Melbourne: Oxford University Press.

Halapua, W. 1998. Fakakakato: Symbols in a Pacific Context. In *Pacific Journal of Theology* 20(1998): 26.

—— 2001. *Living on the Fringe: Melanesians in Fiji.* Suva: Institute of Pacific Studies, University of the South Pacific.

—— 2003. *Tradition, Lotu and Militarism in Fiji.* Lautoka: Fiji Institute of Applied Studies.

—— 2008. *Waves of God's Embrace: Sacred Perspectives from the Ocean.* Norwich: Canterbury Press.

Handler, R. and J. Linnekin 1984. Tradition, Genuine or Spurious. *Journal of American Folklore* 97: 273-290.

Hanlon, D.L. and G.M. White 2000. Introduction. In *Voyaging through the Contemporary Pacific*, Hanlon, D.L. and G.M. White (eds): 1-24. Lanham: Rowan and Littlefield.

Hanlon, D.L. and G.M. White (eds) 2000. *Voyaging through the Contemporary Pacific*. Lanham: Rowan and Littlefield.

Hanson, Allan 1989. The Making of the Maori: Culture Invention and its Logic. *American Anthropologist* 91: 890-902.

Harding, S.F. 1987. Convicted by the Holy Spirit: the Rhetoric of Fundamental Baptist Conversion. *American Ethnologist* 14(1), February: 167-181.

—— 1991. Representing Fundamentalism: The Problem of the Repugnant Cultural Other. *Social Research* 58: 373-393.

Harris, O. 2007. Comment to Robbins. *Current Anthropology* 48(1) February: 22.

Hastrup, K. 1995. *A Passage to Anthropology: Between Experience and Theory*. London: Routledge.

Hau'ofa, E. 1993. *Our Sea of Islands. In A New Oceania: Rediscovering Our Sea of Islands*: 2-16. Suva: SSED, University of the South Pacific.

—— 1997. The Ocean in Us. In *Dreadlocks in Oceania* Vol. 1. S. Mishra and Elizabeth G. (eds): 124-148. Dept. of Literature and Language, University of the South Pacific.

—— 2000. Epilogue: Pasts to Remember. In *Remembrance of Pacific Pasts: An Invitation to Remake History*, Borofsky, R. (ed.). Honolulu: Hawaii University Press.

Havea, J. 1993. A Reconsideration of *Pacificness* in a Search for a South Pacific Theology. *Pacific Journal of Theology* II(10): 5-16.

Hereniko, V. 1994. Representations of Cultural Identity. In *Tides of History: the Pacific Islands in the Twentieth Century*, Howe, K.R., R.C. Kiste and B.V. Lal (eds): 406-434. Honolulu: University of Hawaii Press.

—— 2000. Mapping the Territory: Emerging Writers of the Pacific. In *Conversations, Occasional Writing from the Research School of Pacific and Asian Studies*, Australian National University 1(2) December: 27.

—— 2003. Interdisciplinary Approaches in Pacific Studies: Understanding the Fiji Coup of 19 May 2000. *Contemporary Pacific* 15(1): 75-90.

—— 2004. *The Land Has Eyes, Pear ta ma' on maf*. A feature film written and directed by Vilsoni Hereniko. Te Maka productions. Distributed by Ronin Films. www.thelandhaseyes.com.

Hereniko, V. and R. Wilson (eds) 1999. *Inside Out: Literature, Cultural Politics and Identity in the New Pacific*. Lanham, MD: Rowman & Littlefield.

Hexham, I. and K. Poewe 1997. New Religions as Global Cultures: Making the Human Sacred. Boulder: Westview Press.

Hezel, F.X. 1994. When the Winds Blow, the Islands Will Rock. *Pacific Journal of Theology* II(12): 33-40.

Hobsbawm, E. and T. Ranger 1983. *The Invention of Tradition*. Cambridge: Cambridge University Press.

Hocart, A.M. 1912. On the Meaning of Kalou and the Origin of Fijian Temples. *JRAI* XLII: 437-449.

—— 1914. Mana. *MAN* 1914: 97-101.

—— 1915a. Chieftainship and the Sister's Son in the Pacific. *American Anthropologist* 17: 631-646.

—— 1915b. Rotuman Conceptions of Death. *MAN* 15: 10-12.

—— 1923. The Uterine Nephew. *MAN* 23: 11-13.

—— 1926. Limitations of the Sister's Son's Right in Fiji. *MAN* 26: 205-206.

—— 1929. The Lau Islands, Fiji. Bulletin 62. Bernice P. Bishop Museum.

Hoiore, C. 2003. A Maohi Perspective on Birth and Belonging. In *Weavings: Women Doing Theology in Oceania*, Suva. Johnson, L. and J. Alleluia Felemoni-Tofaeono (eds): 43-48. Suva: Weavers, South Pacific Association of Theological Schools and Institute of Pacific Studies, University of the South Pacific.

Hoiore, J. 1995. Elements of an Ethic of Pacific/Oceanic Theologising. *Pacific Journal of Theology* 13(1995): 51-52.

The Holy Bible. The New Revised Standard Version: Catholic Edition 1993 and 1989.

Hooper, S.J.P. 1982. *A Study of Valuables in the Chiefdom of Lau.* PhD Thesis, University of Cambridge.

Hooper, S. and J. Roth (eds) 1990. *The Fiji Journals of Baron Anatole von Hügel 1875-1877.* Suva: Fiji Museum in association with Cambridge University Museum of Archaeology and Anthropology.

Howard, A. 2006. Presenting Rotuma to the World: the Making of the Film The Land Has Eyes. *Visual Anthropology Review* 22(1): 74-96.

Howell, B.M. 2007. Comment to Robbins. *Current Anthropology* 48(1) February: 22-23.

Im Thurn, Everard and L.C. Wharton (eds) 1982. *The Journal of William Lockerby, Sandalwood Trader in the Fijian Islands During the Years 1808-1809.* Suva: Fiji Times and Herald Ltd.

Interfaith Search Fiji 1995. Address by Hardayal Singh, Chairperson Interfaith Search Fiji, at Thanksgiving Service for Fiji's 25th Anniversary of Independence, National Stadium, 8 October.

Interfaith Search Fiji 2005. Submission to the Constitution Review Commission. 23 August.

Islands Business. We Say. *Islands Business* January 2006: 7, 8.

Jackson, M. 1981. Knowledge of the Body. In *MAN* 18: 327-345.

—— 1998. Minema Ethnographica: Intersubjectivity and the Anthropological Project. Chicago: Chicago University Press.

—— 2002. *The Politics of Storytelling: Violence, Transgression and Intersubjectivity.* Copenhagen: Museum Tusculanum Press.

Jacques, G. 2004. *Beyond Impunity: An Ecumenical Approach to Truth, Justice and Reconciliation.* Second Printing. Geneva: WCC Publications.

Pope John Paul II 2001. *Ecclesia in Oceania.* Post-Synodal Apostolic Exhortation. Rome 22 November.

Johnson, M. 1987. *The Body in the Mind: the Bodily Basis of Meaning, Imagination and Reason.* Chicago: Chicago University Press.

Johnson, L. and J. Alleluia Filemoni-Tofaeono (eds) 2003. *Weavings: Women Doing Theology in Oceania*. Suva: Weavers, South Pacific Association of Theological Schools and Institute of Pacific Studies, University of the South Pacific.

Jolly, M. 1992a. Spectres of Inauthenticity. *The Contemporary Pacific* 4, Spring 1992: 46-63.

—— 1992b. Custom and the Way of the Land: Past and Present in Vanuatu and Fiji. Special Issue of *Oceania* 62(4), M. Jolly and N. Thomas (eds).

Jolly, M. and N. Thomas (eds) 1992. Introduction. The Politics of Tradition in the Pacific. Special Issue of *Oceania* 62(4), M. Jolly and N. Thomas (eds): 241-248.

Jorgensen, D. 2001. Comment to Douglas. *Current Anthropology* 42(5) December 2001: 635-636.

—— 2005. Third Wave Evangelism and the Politics of the Global in Papua New Guinea: Spiritual Warfare and the Recreation of Place in Telefomin. *Oceania* 75(4): 444-461.

Jourdan, C. 1996. Where Have All the Cultures Gone? Sociocultural Creolisation in the Solomon Islands. In *Melanesian Modernities*. Friedman, J. and J.G. Carrier (eds): 34-52. Lund: Lund University Press.

—— (ed.) 1997. Essays in Honour of Roger Keesing. *Canberra Anthropology*, Special Volume 20(1 and 2).

Kaeppler, A.L. 1978a. *Me'a faka'eiki*: Tongan Funerals in a Changing Society. In *The Changing Pacific: Essays in Honour of H.E. Maude*, Gunson, Niel (ed.): 174-202. Melbourne: Oxford University Press.

—— 1978b. Exchange Patterns in Goods and Spouses: Fiji, Tonga and Samoa. *Mankind* 11: 246-252.

Kame'eleihiwa, L. 1992. *Native Land, Foreign Desires*. Honolulu: Bishop Museum Press.

Kamikamica, J.N. 1996. Fiji Native Land: Issues and Challenges. *Fiji in Transition. Research Papers of the Fiji Constitution Review Commission* Vol.1, Lal, B.V. and Tomasi R. Vakatora (eds): 259-290. Suva: School of Social and Economic Development, University of the South Pacific.

Kamu, L. 1996. *The Samoan Culture and the Christian Gospel*. Suva: Donna Lou Kamu.

Kanongata'a, Sr. K.A. 1992. A Pacific Women's Theology of Birthing and Liberation. *Pacific Journal of Theology* 7(1992): 4-7.

—— 1996. Domestic Theology. *Pacific Journal of Theology* 15(1996): 73-74.

—— 2002. Why Contextual? *Pacific Journal of Theology* II(27): 21-40.

Kaplan, M. 1988. The Coups in Fiji: Colonial Contradictions and the Postcolonial Crisis. *Critique of Anthropology* 8(3): 93-116.

—— 1989a. Luve ni Wai as the British saw it: Constructions of Custom and Disorder in Colonial Fiji. *Ethnohistory* 36: 349-371.

—— 1989b. The 'Dangerous and Disaffected Native' in Fiji: British Colonial Constructions of the Tuka Movement. *Social Analysis* 26: 22-45.

—— 1990a. Meaning, Agency and Colonial History: Navosavakadua and the Tuka Movement in Fiji. *American Ethnologist* 17(1): 91-110.

—— 1990b. Christianity, People of the Land, and Chiefs in Fiji. In *Christianity in Oceania: Ethnographic Perspectives*. Association of Anthropologists in Oceania Monograph 12, Barker, J. (ed.): 124-147. Lanham: University Press of America.

—— 1995a. *Neither Cargo Nor Cult: Ritual Politics and the Colonial Imagination in Fiji*. Durham and London: Duke University Press.

—— 1995b. Blood on the Grass and Dogs will Speak: Ritual Politics and the Nation in Independent Fiji. In *Nation Making: Emergent Identities in Postcolonial Melanesia*, Foster, R.J. (ed.): 95-123. Ann Arbor: University of Michigan.

Katz, R. 1993. *The Straight Path: a Story of Healing and Transformation in Fiji*. Reading, Massachusetts: Addison-Wesley Publishing Company.

Keane, W. 1997. Religious Language. *Annual Review of Anthropology* 26: 47-71.

Keesing, R.M. 1982. Kastam in Melanesia: An Overview. In *Reinventing Traditional Culture* Special Issue of *Mankind* 13(4): 297-301.

—— 1989. Creating the Past: Custom and Identity in the Contemporary Pacific. *Contemporary Pacific* 1(1 and 2): 19-42.

—— 1990. New Lessons from Old Shells: Changing Perspectives on the *Kula*. In *Culture and History in the Pacific*, Siikala, J. (ed.): 139-163. Helsinki: Finnish Anthropology Society.

—— 1991. Reply to Trask. In *The Contemporary Pacific*. Dialogue. Spring: 168-171.

—— 1992a. *Custom and Confrontation: The Kwaio Struggle for Cultural Autonomy*. Chicago: Chicago University Press.

—— 1992b. The Past in the Present: Contested Representations of Culture and History. In *Other Sites: Social Anthropology and the Politics of Interpretation*, Goldsmith, M. and K. Barber (eds). Palmerston North: Massey University.

—— 1996. Class, Culture, Custom. In *Melanesian Modernities*, Friedman, J. and J.G. Carrier (eds): 162-182. Lund Monographs in Social Anthropology 3. Lund: Lund University Press.

Keesing, R.M. and R. Tonkinson (eds) 1982. Reinventing Traditional Culture: The Politics of Kastom in Island Melanesia. Special issue of *Mankind* 13(4).

Keller, E. 2007. Comment to Robbins. *Current Anthropology* 48(1), February: 23-24.

Kelly, J.D. and M. Kaplan 2001. *Represented Communities: Fiji and World Decolonization*. Chicago: Chicago University Press.

Kerber, G. 2003. Overcoming Violence and Pursuing Justice. An Introduction to Restorative Justice Procedures. *The Ecumenical Review* 55(2) April: 151-157.

Khan, C.A. and K.J. Barr MSC 2003. *Christianity, Poverty and Wealth at the Start of the 21st Century. Fiji Country Case Study*. Suva: ECREA.

Kirata, B. 1994. An Ecumenical Response to Winds of Change. *Pacific Journal of Theology* II(12): 17-21.

Kirkpatrick, J.T. 1977. Person, Hierarchy, and Autonomy in Traditional Yapese Theory. In *Symbolic Anthropology: A Reader in the Study of Symbols and Meanings*. Dolgin, Janet, Davis S. Kemnitzer, and David M. Schneider (eds) New York: Columbia University Press.

Klarr, C. 2005. Painting Paradise for a Post-Colonial Pacific: the Fijian Frescoes of Jean Charlot. PhD thesis. The Florida State University School of Visual Arts and Dance (Tallahasser).

Kurulo, S. 2004. Restoring Broken Relationships. In *Harvest Times* 28 March 2004: 4-8.

Knauft, B. M. 2001. Comment to Douglas. *Current Anthropology* 42(5) December 2001: 636-637.

Knox, M. 1997. *Voyage of Faith: The Story of the First 100 Years of Catholic Missionary Endeavour in Fiji and Rotuma*. Suva: Archdiocese of Suva.

Knox-Mawer, J. 1965. *A Gift of Islands*. London: John Murray.

Koroi, J. n.d. Education for the Defence and Promotion of Human Rights and Other Rights. Keynote Address to the 62nd Annual Conference of the Fiji Teacher's Union, 29 April 1992.

Koskinen, A.A. 1968 **kite: Polynesian Insights into Knowledge*. Helsinki: Finnish Society for Missiology and Ecumenics.

Lal, B.V. 1988. *Power and Prejudice: The Making of the Fiji Crisis*. Wellington: New Zealand Institute of International Affairs.

—— 1999. A Time to Change: The Fiji General Elections of 1999. Regime Change and Regime Maintenance in Asia and the Pacific, Discussion Paper No. 23. Canberra: Dept. of Political and Social Change, Research School of Pacific and Asian Studies, Australian National University.

—— 2000a. Fiji: Damaged Democracy. Rspas.anu.edu.au/ccp/fijidd.htm.

—— 2000b. Fiji: Wandering Between Two Worlds. *Fijilive* online 1 June and *The Australian* 1 June: 13.

—— 2004. *Girmitiyas: the Origins of the Fiji Indians*. (Reprint from 1983 with a Foreword by Clem Seecharan). Lautoka: Fiji Institute of Applied Studies.

—— 2007. This Process of Political Readjustment: Aftermath of the 2006 Fiji Coup. Discussion Paper 2007/2. State, Society and Governance in Melanesia. The Australian National University.

Lal, B.V. (ed.) 1990. As the Dust Settles: Impact and Implications of the Fiji Coups. *Contemporary Pacific* 2(1), Special Issue, Spring 1990.

—— 2000. *Fiji Before the Storm: Elections and Politics of Development*. Canberra: Asia Pacific Press, Australian National University.

Lal, B.V. and T. Vakatora 1997. *Fiji in Transition: Research Papers of the Fiji Constitution Review Commission*. Suva: School of Social and Economic Development, University of the South Pacific.

Lal, B.V. and K. Fortune (eds) 2000. *The Pacific Islands: An Encyclopedia*. Honolulu: University of Hawaii Press.

Lal, B.V. and M. Pretes 2001. *Coup: Reflections on the Political Crisis in Fiji*. Canberra: Pandanus Books, RSPAS, Australian National University.

Lal, V. 1990. *Fiji: Coups in Paradise: Race, Politics and Military Intervention.* New Jersey: Zed Books.

Lawson, S. 1991. *The Failure of Democratic Politcs in Fiji.* Oxford: Clarendon Press.

—— 1997. Chiefs, Politics, and the Power of Tradition in Contemporary Fiji. In *Chiefs Today: Traditional Pacific Leadership and the Postcolonial State,* White, Geoffrey M. and Lamont Lindstrom (eds) Stanford: Stanford University Press: 108-118.

Lebot, V., M. Merlin and L. Lindstrom 1992. *Kava: The Pacific Drug.* New Haven: Yale University Press.

Lester, R.H. 1953. A Few Customs Observed by Fijians in Connection with Birth, Betrothal and Marriage and Death. *Transactions of the Fiji Society 1945-1947* 3(1-3) December: 113-129.

Levison, M., R. Gerard Ward and J.W. Webb 1973. *The Settlement of Polynesia – A Computer Simulation.* Canberra: Australian National University Press.

Lieber, M.D. 1990. Lamarckian Definitions of Identity on Kapingamarangi and Pohnpei. In *Cultural Identity and Ethnicity in the Pacific*, Linnekin, J. and L. Poyer (eds) Honolulu: University of Hawaii Press.

Liep, J. 1989. The Day of Reckoning on Rossel Island. In *Death Rituals and Life in the Societies of the Kula Ring*, Damon, F.H. and Roy W. (eds) DeKalb: Northern Illinois University Press.

—— 2009. *Papuan Plutocracy, Ranked Exchange on Rossel Island.* Aarhus: Aarhus University Press.

Lindhardt, M. 2004. Power in Powerlessness: a Study of Pentecostal Life Worlds and Symbolic Resistance in Urban Chile. PhD thesis, Aarhus University, Denmark.

—— 2009a. The Ambivalence of Power: Charismatic Christianity and Occult Forces in Urban Tanzania. In *Nordic Journal of Religion and Society* 1(22): 37-54.

—— 2009b. Narrating Religious Realities: Conversion and Testimonies in Chilean Pentecostalism. *Suomen Antropologi: Journal of the Finnish Anthropological Society* 34(3): 25-43.

—— 2009c. More Than Just Money: The Faith Gospel and Occult Economies in Contemporary Tanzania. *Nova Religio – The Journal of Alternative and Emergent Religions* 13(1): 41-67.

—— In Press. Introduction. In *Practicing the Faith: the Ritual Life of Charismatic-Pentecostal Christians*, Lindhardt, M. (ed.). New York and Oxford: Berghahn Books.

Lindstrom, L. and G.M. White 1997. Introduction. Chiefs Today. In *Chiefs Today: Traditional Pacific Leadership and the Postcolonial State*, White, G.M. and L. Lindstrom (eds): 108-118. Stanford: Stanford University Press.

Linnekin, J. 1983. Defining Tradition: Variations on the Hawaiian Identity. In *American Ethnologist* (10): 241-252.

—— 1991. Text Bites and the R-Word: The Politics of Representing Scholarship. In *The Contemporary Pacific*. Dialogue. Spring: 172-177.

—— 1992. On the Theory and Politics of Cultural Construction in the Pacific. *Oceania* 62: 249-263.

Linnekin, J. and L. Poyer 1990. *Cultural Identity and Ethnicity in the Pacific*. Honolulu: Hawaii University Press.

Livingstone, E.A. (ed.) 1977. *Concise Dictionary of the Christian Church*. Oxford: Oxford University Press.

Lock, M. 1993. Cultivating the Body: Anthropology and Epistemologies of Bodily Practice and Knowledge. In *Annual Review in Anthropology* 22: 133-155.

Longgar, W.K. 2009 *Kaugu Gunan Ma Kaugu Pia: My Village and My Land. A Theological Significance of Land in the New Guinea Islands of Papua New Guinea*. Goroka: Melanesian Institute.

Luhrmann, T. 2007. Reply to Robbins. *Current Anthropology* 48(1) February: 24.

MacCormack, S. 2007. Comment to Robbins. *Current Anthropology* 48(1) February: 25.

Mackenzie, T. 2000. The Situation in the South Pacific Islands. http://www.wcc-coe-org/wcc/what/interreligious/cd35-20html. Accessed 4 November 2009.

Macnaught, T. 1982. *The Fijian Colonial Experience*: *A Study of the Neotraditional Order Under British Colonial Rule prior to World War II*. Pacific Research Monograph No. 7. Australian National University.

Madraiwiwi, R.J. n.d. Governance in Fiji: The Interplay between Indigenous Culture, Tradition and Politics. Keynote remarks delivered by Vice President Ratu Joni Madraiwiwi at Conference on the Pacific, Globalisation and Governance, Australian National University, Canberra 26 October, 2005.

Malogne-Fer, G. 2006. L'émergence d'une theologie de la libération au sein de l'église évagelique de Polynésie Francaise. *Pacific Journal of Theology* II(35): 84-108.

—— 2007. *Les Femmes dans L'Église Protestante Ma'ohi: Religion, Genre et Pouvoir en Polynésie Francaise*. Paris: Éditions KARTHALA.

Mansale, R. 2003. Partnership: a Value of Church and Culture in Vanuatu. In *Weavings: Women Doing Theology in Oceania*. Suva. Johnson, Lydia and Joan Alleluia Felemoni-Tofaeono (eds): 172-174. Weavers, South Pacific Association of Theological Schools and Institute of Pacific Studies, University of the South Pacific.

Marcus, G. and M.M.J. Fischer 1986. *Anthropology as Cultural Critique: An Experimental Moment in the Human Sciences*. Chicago and London: Chicago University Press.

Marshall-Fratani, R. 1998. Mediating the Global and the Local in Nigerian Pentecostalism. *Journal of Religion in Africa* 28(3): 278-315.

Martin, D. 2002. *Pentecostalism: The World, Their Parish*. Oxford: Blackwell.

Mataca, P. 2003. Dry the tears of misery. *Fiji Times*, 1 October: 7.

—— 2004. Implications of the Vice-President's trial and sentencing on forgiveness and the role of the BLV [Great Council of Chiefs]. Unpublished paper.

—— 2006. The Natural Environment: its Key Resources for Peace. *Pacific Journal of Theology.* Series II, No.35: 66-83.

Maude, H.E. 1968. *Of Islands and Men: Studies in Pacific History.* Melbourne: Oxford University Press.

Mauss, M. 1990. *The Gift: the Form and Reason for Exchange in Archaic Societies.* London: Routledge.

Maxwell, D. 2007. Comment to Robbins. *Current Anthropology* 48(1), February 2007: 25-26.

Mayer, A.C. 1983. *Indians in Fiji.* London: Oxford University Press.

McDonald, H. 2001. *Blood, Bones and Spirit: Aboriginal Christianity in an East Kimberley Town.* Melbourne: Melbourne University Press.

McManus, J. CSsR 1984. *The Healing Power of the Sacraments.* Ave Maria Press. Notre Dame. Indiana.

McMullen, E. 2009. Unruly Passions, Saving Grace. Review of Denis, A. *Evolution or Creation? Do we have to Choose? The Tablet* 24 January: 21.

Meo, J. 2002. How Do We Do Contextual Theology? *Pacific Journal of Theology* II(27): 41-60.

Meo, I. 1994. A Woman's Response to Winds of Change: a Critical Analysis of a Culture-Oriented Church. *Journal of Pacific Theology* II(12): 63-67.

—— 2003. Assering Women's Dignity in a Patriarchal World. In *Weavings: Women Doing Theology in Oceania.* Suva. Johnson, Lydia and Joan Alleluia Felemoni-Tofaeono (eds): 150-160. Suva: Weavers, South Pacific Association of Theological Schools and Institute of Pacific Studies, University of the South Pacific.

Methodist Church in Fiji 1995. Submission of the Methodist Church throughout Fiji and Rotuma to the Constitution Review Commission.

Meyer, B. 1992. 'If You are a Devil, You are a Witch and, if You are a Witch, You are a Devil'. The Integration of 'Pagan' Ideas into the Conceptual Universe of Ewe Christians in Southeastern Ghana. *Journal of Religion in Africa* 22(2): 98-132.

—— 1995. 'Delivered from the Powers of Darkness': Confessions of Satanic Riches in Christian Ghana. *Africa* 65: 236-255.

—— 1998a. 'Make a Complete Break with the Past': Memory and Post-Colonial Modernity in Ghanaian Pentecostalist Discourse. *Journal of Religion in Africa* 28(3): 316-349.

—— 1998b. The Power of Money: Politics and Cult Forces and Pentecostalism in Ghana. *African Studies Review* 3: 15-37.

Miyazaki, H. 1997. Artefacts of Truth. PhD thesis, Australian National University.

—— 2000. Faith and its Fulfillment: Agency, Exchange, and the Fijian Aesthetics of Competition. *American Ethnologist* 27(1) (Feb. 2000): 31-51.

Monsell-Davis, M. 1993. Urban Exchange: Safety-net or Disincentive? Wantoks and relatives in the urban Pacific. *Canberra Anthropology* 16(2): 45-66.

—— 2000. Social Change, Contradictions, Youth and Violence. In *Reflections on Violence in Melanesia*. Dinnen, S and A. Ley (eds): 209-222. Canberra: Hawkins Press/Asia Pacific Press.

—— n.d. Youth and Social Change in the Pacific. Unpublished paper, 1998 (cited with kind permission from the author).

Moore, C., J. Leckie and D. Munro 1990. *Labour in the South Pacific*. Townsville: James Cook University of North Queensland.

Müller-Fahrenholz, G. 1996. *The Art of Forgiveness: Theological Reflections on Healing and Reconciliation*. Geneva: WCC Publications.

Munn, N.D. 1988. *The Fame of Gawa, a Symbolic Study of Value Transformation in a Massim (Papua New Guinea) Society*. Cambridge: Cambridge University Press.

Munro, D. 2005. In the Wake of the Leonidas: Reflections on Indo-Fijian Indenture Historiography. Review Article. *The Journal of Pacific Studies* 28(1) 2005: 93-117.

Munro, D. and A. Thornley (eds) 1996. *The Covenant Makers: Islander Missionaries in the Pacific*. Suva: Pacific Theological College and Institute of Pacific Studies.

Nacanaitaba, S. 1995. The Christian State Debate: Crusading or Crucified Church? An Exploratory Paper.

Naidu, V. 1980. *The Violence of Indenture in Fiji*. Suva: World University Service in association with the School of Social and Economic Development, University of the South Pacific.

—— 2004. *The Violence of Indenture in Fiji*. Reprint from 1980, with new 'Preface' and 'Epilogue'. Lautoka: Fiji Institute of Applied Studies.

Nai Lalakai 1998. Saqata na Lotu Wesele na Festival of Praise. Ivakamacala, Talatala Doketa Ilaitia Tuwere, *Nai Lalakai* 19 March: 2.

Narsey, W. 2006. *Just Living Wages for Fiji: Lifting Workers out of Poverty*. Suva: ECREA.

Nayacakalou, R. 1957. The Fijian System of Kinship and Marriage. *Journal of the Polynesian Society* 66(1).

—— 1975. *Leadership in Fiji*. Suva: University of the South Pacific in association with Oxford University Press.

Neich, R. and M. Pendergrast 1997. *Traditional Tapa Textiles of the Pacific*. London: Thames and Hudson.

Neumann, K. 1992. *Not the Way It Really Was: Constructing the Tolai Past*. Pacific Islands Monograph Series, No. 10. Honolulu: University of Hawaii Press.

Newland, L. 2004. Turning the Spirits into Witchcraft: Pentecostalism in Fijian Villages. *Oceania* 75(1): 1-18.

—— 2006. Fiji. In *Globalization and the Re-Shaping of Christianity in the Pacific Islands*, Ernst, M. (ed.): 317-389. Suva: Pacific Theological College.

—— 2007. The Role of the Assembly of Christian Churches in Fiji in the 2006 Elections. In *From Election to Coup in Fiji: the 2006 Campaign and its Aftermath*, Fraenkel, J. and S. Firth (eds): 300-314.

Nissen, W. 1990. Academics to Stand Up for Maoritanga. In *New Zealand Herald* 1 March: 20.

Niukula, P. 1991. *O Keda na Lotu* (We the people of the church). Suva: Lotu Pasifika Productions.

—— 1992a. *O Keda na Vanua* (We the people of the land). Suva: Lotu Pasifika Productions.

—— 1992b. *O Keda na Matanitu* (We the people of the state). Suva: Lotu Pasifika Productions.

—— 1994. *The Three Pillars: the Triple Aspect of Fijian Society*. Suva: Christian Writing Project.

—— 1997. Religion and the State. In *Fiji in Transition. Research Papers of the Fiji Constitution Review Commission* Vol. 1. Lal, B.V. and Tomasi R. Vakatora (eds): 53-79. Suva: School of Social and Economic Development, University of the South Pacific.

Niukula, S. 2003. A Fijian Woman's Faith Journey at the Interface of Gospel and Culture. In *Weavings: Women Doing Theology in Oceania*. Johnson, L. and J. Alleluia Felemoni-Tofaeono (eds): 204-213. Suva: Weavers, South Pacific Association of Theological Schools and Institute of Pacific Studies, University of the South Pacific.

Norris, R.S. 2003. Converting to What? Embodied Culture and the Adoption of New Beliefs. In *The Anthropology of Religious Conversion*. Buckster, A. and S.D. Glazier (eds). Oxford: Rowman & Littlefield.

Norton, R. 1990. *Race and Politics in Fiji*. 2nd Edition. St. Lucia: University of Queensland Press.

—— 1993. Culture and Identity in the South Pacific: a Comparative Analysis. *MAN* 28: 741-759.

—— 2000a. Reconciling Ethnicity and Nation: Contending Discourses in Fiji's Constitutional Reform. *The Contemporary Pacific* 12(1) Spring: 83-122.

—— 2000b. Understanding the Results of the 1999 Fiji Elections. In *Fiji Before the Storm: Elections and Politics of Development*, Lal, Brij V. (ed.): 49-72. Canberra: Asia Pacific Press, Australian National University.

—— 2007a. Epilogue. Understanding Fiji's Political Paradox. In *From Election to Coup in Fiji: the 2006 Campaign and its Aftermath*. Fraenkel, J. and S. Firth (eds): 403-419. Canberra: IPS Publications and Asia Pacific Press, The Australian National University.

—— 2008. The Great Council of Chiefs in Fiji's Era of Crisis and Reform. In *1987 – Twenty Years On*. Chand, Ganesh and Brij Lal (eds) Lautoka: Institute of Applied Studies, University of Fiji.

—— 2009. The Historical Trajectory of Fijian Power. State, Society and Governance in Melanesia, RSPAS, Australian National University. http://rspas.anu.edu.au/melanesia/dplist.php?searchterm=2009.

O'Hanlon, M. 1989. *Reading the Skin: Adornment, Display and Society Among the Wahgi*. London: British Museum.

Obeyesekere, G. 1992. *The Apotheosis of Captain Cook: European Mythmaking in the Pacific*. New Jersey: Princeton University Press.

Ogan, G. 1997. Review of Martha Kaplan, Neither Cargo nor Cult: Ritual Politics and the Colonial Imagination in Fiji. *The Contemporary Pacific* Spring: 270-272.

Oh, E.F. 2003. The Dream as Metaphor for a New Vision of Church in the Pacific. *Weavings: Women Doing Theology in Oceania*. Suva. J., L. Alleluia Felemoni-Tofaeono and J. Alleluia Felemoni-Tofaeono (eds): 141-149. Weavers, South Pacific Association of Theological Schools and Institute of Pacific Studies, University of the South Pacific.

Oliver, D.L. 1989. *Oceania: the Native Cultures of Australia and the Pacific Islands*. Honolulu: University of Hawaii Press.

Orta, A. 2001. 2001. Comment to Douglas. *Current Anthropology* 42(5) December 2001: 637-638.

Otto, T. 1992. The Ways of Kastam: Tradition as Category and Practice in a Manus Village. *Oceania* 62(4): 264-283.

Otto, T. and P. Pedersen (eds) 2000. Tradition Between Continuity and Invention: An Introduction. *Folk: Journal of the Danish Ethnographic Society* 42: 3-17.

Otto, T. and N. Thomas (eds) 1997. *Narratives of Nation in the South Pacific*. Amsterdam. Harwood Academic Publishers.

Pacific Islands Monthly 1997. 10 Years Later ... , March: 18-24.

—— 1998. 'Food and Body Shape, a Polynesian Issue – but Now the Talk is Shifting to Diet and Exercise' by Michael Feld. May.

The Pacific Journal of Theology 1994. Responses to New Religious Groups in the Pacific 2(12).

—— 1996. 'Touched by the Hand of God': The Reverend Paula Niukula 1937-1996 II(15): 3-10.

Palu, V. 2003. Tapa Making in Tonga: a Metaphor for God's Care. In *Weavings: Women Doing Theology in Oceania*. Suva. Johnson, Lydia and Joan Alleluia Felemoni-Tofaeono (eds): 62-71. Weavers, South Pacific Association of Theological Schools and Institute of Pacific Studies, University of the South Pacific.

Parkin, D. 1985. Evil and Morality, Introduction. In *The Anthropology of Evil*, Parkin, D. (ed.): 1-25. Oxford: Blackwell.

Parry, J. 1986. THE GIFT, The Indian Gift and the 'Indian Gift'. *MAN* (21): 453-473.

Paunga, M. 2005. 'Sharing on the Journey'. Community Eucharist Homily, Pacific Regional Seminary, 16 September.

Pawley, A. 1999. Language. In *The Pacific Islands: Environment and Society* Rapaport, M. (ed.). Honolulu: Bess Press.

Peel, J.D.Y. 1995. For Who Hath Despised the Day of Small Things? Missionary Narratives and Historical Anthropology. *Comparative Studies in Society and History* 37(3): 581-607.

——— 2000. *Religious Encounter and the Making of the Yoruba*. Bloomington and Indianapolis: Indiana University Press.

——— 2001. Comment to Douglas. *Current Anthropology* 42(5) December: 639.

——— 2007. Comment to Robbins. *Current Anthropology* 48(1) February: 26-27.

Pich, R. 1993. Theology at the Cross (Cultural) Roads. *Pacific Journal of Theology* II(10): 77-88.

Poewe, K. (ed.) 1994. *Charismatic Christianity as a Global Culture*. Columbia: University of South Carolina Press.

Power Magazine 1998. Think Serevi, think (and thank) God. Cover story, 1998 May: 15-20.

——— Freed from Idolatry to Find a Life in Jesus, Testimony, 1998 May: 46-47.

——— From gangs to God, Testimony, 1998 June-July: 42.

Prior, R. 1993. I am the Coconut of Life: an Evaluation of Coconut Theology. *Pacific Journal of Theology* II(10): 31-40.

Puloka, M. 1987. An Attempt at Contextualizing Theology for the Tongan Church. In *South Pacific Theology: Papers from the Consultation on Pacific Theology, Papua New Guinea 1986*. Oxford: Regnum Books.

Quain, B. 1948. *Fijian Village*. Chicago: University of Chicago Press.

Rabuka, S.L. 1999. The Fiji Islands in Transition: A Personal Reflection. Unpublished paper given at Australian National University, July 1999.

Raitiqa, L. 2003. Ruth, Redeemer of the Land. In *Weavings: Women Doing Theology in Oceania*, Johnson, L. and J. Alleluia Felemoni-Tofaeono (eds): 99-107. Suva: Weavers, South Pacific Association of Theological Schools and Institute of Pacific Studies, University of the South Pacific.

Rakoto, A. 1986. Can Custom be Custom-Built?: Cultural Obstacles to Fijian Commercial Enterprise. In *Fijians in Town*, Griffin, C. and M. Monsell-Davis (eds): 180-185. Suva: Institute of Pacific Studies, University of the South Pacific.

Raku, F. 1988. Wholeness of Life (Perspective from Life in the Island). In *The Cross and the Tanoa: Gospel and Culture in the Pacific*, Chandran, R. (ed.): 97-98. Suva: South Pacific Association of Theological Schools.

Rakuita, T. 2007. *Living by Bread Alone: Contemporary Challenges associated with Identity and Belongingness in Fiji*. Suva: ECREA.

Ratuvili, S. 1979. *Spiritual Bases for Rural Development in the Pacific*. Suva: Lotu Pasifika.

Ravuvu, A.D. 1983. *Vaka i Taukei: the Fijian Way of Life*. Suva: University of the South Pacific, Institute of Pacific Studies.

——— 1987. *The Fijian Ethos*. Suva: University of the South Pacific, Institute of Pacific Studies.

——— 1988. *Development or Dependence: the Pattern of Change in a Fijian Village*. Suva: University of the South Pacific.

——— 1991. *The Façade of Democracy: Fijian Struggles for Political Control 1830-1987*. Suva: Reader Publishing House.

Reeves, Sir P., T. Rayalu Vakatora, B.Vilash Lal 1996. *The Fiji Islands – Towards a United Future. Report of the Fiji Constitution Review Committee.* Parliament of Fiji. Parliamentary Paper No. 34 of 1996. Suva: Government Printer.

The Review 1995a. Hope of the Church. October: 14-16.

—— 1995b. Back to the Drawing-Board, interview with Ilaitia Tuwere, By Jo Nata. October: 16-22.

—— 1997a. 1987-97: The Lost Decade. May: 12-27.

—— 1997b. Miracles of Faith. By Shailendra Singh. November: 56-61.

Rika, N. 1986. Is Kinship Costly? In *Fijians in Town*. Griffin, C. and M. Monsell-Davis (eds): 189-196. Suva, Institute of Pacific Studies, University of the South Pacific.

Rimon, M. 1988. The Land of Bouru: Understanding the Kingdom of God as Self-Realizing Eschatology. In *The Cross and the Tanoa: Gospel and Culture in the Pacific*. Chandran (ed.): 99-105. Suva: South Pacific Association of Theological Schools.

Robbins, J. 1995. Dispossessing the Spirits: Christian Transformations of desire and Ecology among the Urapmin of Papua New Guinea. *Ethnology* 34(3): 211-224.

—— 2001. Introduction: Global Religions, Pacific Island Transformations. *Journal of Ritual Studies* 15(2) 2001: 7-12.

—— 2003a. What is a Christian? Notes towards and anthropology of Christianity. Introduction to the Symposium. *Religion* 33(2003): 191-199.

—— 2003b. On the Paradoxes of Global Pentecostalism and the Peril of Continuity Thinking. *Religion* 33(3), July 2003: 221-231.

—— 2004a. *Becoming Sinners: Christianity and Moral Torment in a Papua New Guinean Society*. Berkeley: University of California Press.

—— 2004b. The Globalization of Pentecostal and Charismatic Christianity. *Annual Review of Anthropology* 2004 (33): 117-143.

—— 2007. Continuity Thinking and the Problem of Christian Culture: Belief, Time, and the Anthropology of Christianity. *Current Anthropology* 48(1) February 2007: 5-38.

—— 2009. History, Cosmology and Gener: Christianity and Cultural Change among the Urapmin of Papua New Guinea. In *Religious and Ritual Change —— Cosmologies and Histories*, Stewart, P.J. and A. Strathern (eds): 109-132. Durham, North Carolina: Carolina Academic Press.

—— In Press. Pentecostal Networks and the Spirit of Globalization: On the Social Productivity of Ritual Forms. In *Practicing the Faith: the Ritual Life of Charismatic-Pentecostal Christians*, Lindhardt, M. (ed.). New York and Oxford: Berghahn Books.

Robertson, R.T. and Tamanisau 1988. *Fiji: Shattered Coups*. Leichardt: Pluto Press.

Robertson, R. 2007. Elections and Nation-building: the Long Road since 1970. In *From Election to Coup in Fiji: the 2006 Campaign and its Aftermath*, Fraenkel,

J. and S. Firth (eds): 250-260. Canberra: IPS Publications & Asia Pacific Press, The Australian National University.

Robertson, R. and W. Sutherland 2001. *Government by the Gun: The Unfinished Business of Fiji's 2000 Coup.* Annandale: Pluto Press Australia.

Roman Catholic Church in Fiji 1995. Submission of the Roman Catholic Church to the Constitutional Review Commission.

Rosaldo, M. 1984. Toward an Anthropology of Self and Feeling. In *Culture Theory*, Shweder, R. and R. LeVine; 137-1554. Cambridge: Cambridge University Press.

Roth, G.K. 1954. *The Fijian Way of Life.* Melbourne: Oxford University Press.

Routledge, D. 1985. *Matanitu: The Struggle for Power in Early Fiji.* Suva: Institute of Pacific Studies, University of the South Pacific.

Rumsey, A. 2008. Confession, Anger and Cross Cultural Articulation in Papua New Guinea. *Anthropological Quarterly* 81(2) Spring: 455-472.

Rutz, H. 1987. Capitalizing on Culture: Moral Ironies in Urban Fiji. *Society for Comparative Study of Society and History* 29: 532-257.

—— 1995. Occupying the Headwaters of Tradition: Rhetorical Strategies of Nation Making in Fiji. In *Nation Making: Emergent Identities in Postcolonial Melanesia*, Foster, R.J. (ed.): 71-93. Ann Arbor: University of Michigan.

Rutz, H.J. and C. Gounis 1986. Urban Fijians and the Problem of Unemployment. In *Fijians in Town*, Griffin, C.M. and M. Monsell-Davis (eds): 50-88. Suva: Institute of Pacific Studies, University of the South Pacific.

Ryle, J. 1996. Jilli Binna: To Look and Listen: Creating a Cultural Past. In *Melanesian Modernities*, Friedman, J. and J.G. Carrier (eds): 10-33. Lund Monographs in Social Anthropology 3. Lund: Lund University Press.

—— 2001a. My God, My Land: Interwoven Paths of Christianity and Tradition in Fiji. PhD thesis, School of Oriental and African Studies, University of London.

—— 2001b. Na Sala ni Ibe: a Path of Mats – a Village Funeral in Nadrogā. *Domodomo: A Scholarly Journal of the Fiji Museum* 13(1): 7-19.

—— 2004. Religion: Tro, Tradition, Politik [Religion: Belief, Tradition, Politics]. In *Viden om Verden: en Grundbog i Antropologisk Analyse*, Hastrup, K. (ed.). Copenhagen: Hans Reitzel.

—— 2005. Roots of Land and Church: The Christian State Debate in Fiji. *International Journal for the Study of the Christian Church* 5(1): 58-78.

—— 2009. Les Chemins de la Foi et du Pouvoir: Christianisme, Tradition et Politique à Fidji [Paths of Faith and Power: Christianity, Tradition and Politics in Fiji]. In *Anthropologie du Christianisme en Océanie.* Fer, Y. and G. Malogne-Fer (eds): 73-101. Cahiers du Pacifique Contemporain (no. 4). Paris: L'Harmattan.

—— In press. Laying our Sins and Sorrows on the Altar: Ritualising Charismatic Catholic Reconciliation and Healing in Fiji. In *Practicing the Faith: the Ritual Life of Charismatic-Pentecostal Christians*, Lindhardt, M. (ed.). New York and Oxford: Berghahn Books.

Sacks, J. 2002. *The Dignity of Difference*. London and New York: Continuum.

Sahlins, M. 1962. *Moala: Culture and Nature on a Fijian Island*. Ann Arbor: University of Michigan Press.

—— 1985. *Islands of History*. London and New York: Tavistock.

—— 1993. Cery Cery fuckabede. *American Ethnologist* 20(4): 848-867.

Said, E. 1978. *Orientalism*. London: Routledge and Kegan Paul.

Scarr, D. 1984 *Fiji: a Short History*. Sydney: George Allen & Unwin.

—— 1988. *Fiji: The Politics of Illusion: The Military Coups in Fiji*. Kensington: New South Wales University Press.

Schade, A. 1999. *Armut und Statuswünsche: Fijianische Frauen als Haushaltsvorstände in der Hauptstadt des südpazifischen Inselstaates Fiji*. Spektrum. Berliner Reihe zu Gesellschaft, Wirtschaft und Politik in Entwicklungsländern, Band 55. Münster: LIT Verlag.

Schieffelin, B. 2007. Comment to Robbins. *Current Anthropology* 48(1) February: 27-28.

Schieffelin, E. and R. Crittenden 2000. Remembering First Contact: Realities and Romance. In *Remembrance of Pacific Pasts: An Invitation to Remake History*, Borofsky, R (ed.): 133-151. Honolulu: University of Hawaii Press.

Schreiter, R.J. 2002. *Reconciliation, Mission and Ministry in a Changing Social Order*. New York: Orbis.

—— 2003. *The Ministry of Reconciliation: Spirituality and Strategies*. New York: Orbis.

Scott, M.W. 2007. *The Severed Snake: Matrilineages, Making Place, and a Melanesian Christianity in Southeast Solomon Islands*. Durham N.C.: Carolina Academic Press.

Seremetakis, N. (ed.) 1994. *The Senses Still: Perception and Memory as Material Culture in Modernity*. New York: Westview Press.

Shameem, N. 2007. Anomie. In *With Heart and Nerve and Sinew: Post Coup Writing from Fiji*, Griffen, A. (ed.): 180-181. Suva: Christmas Club.

Shils, E. 1981. *Tradition*. Chicago: University of Chicago Press.

Shoaps, R.A. 2002. 'Pray Earnestly': The Textual Construction of Personal Involvement in Pentecostal Prayer and Song. *Journal of Linguistic Anthropology* 12(1): 34-71.

Sinha, I. 2002. *The Death of Mr Love*. London: Scribner.

Siwatibau, S. 2002. Some Issues for Consideration by the Churches and Theological Schools in the South Pacific. *The Pacific Journal of Theology* 11(28).

Sjørslev, I. 1992. Når Guder Blinker. Tanker om Ritualets Væsen [When Gods Blink: Reflections on the Nature of Ritual]. *Tidsskriftet Antropologi* 25: 5-19.

Shore, B. 1989. Mana and Tapu. In *Developments in Polynesian Ethnology*, Howard, Alan and Robert Borofsky (eds). Honolulu: University of Hawaii Press.

Smidt, D. et al 1995. *Pacific Material Culture: Essays in honour of Dr. Simon Koojiman on the Occasion of his 80th Birthday*. Leiden: Rijksmuseum voor Volkenkunde.

Smith, B. 1985. *European Vision and the South Pacific*. Second Edition. New Haven: Yale University Press.

—— 1992. *Imagining the Pacific: In the Wake of the Cook Voyages*. Victoria: Melbourne University Press.

—— 2000. Constructing 'Pacific' Peoples. In *Remembrance of Pacific Pasts: an Invitation to Remake History*, Borofsky, R. (ed.): 152-168. Hawaii: University of Hawaii Press.

Solomone, K. 1997. One Gospel: Contextually Inclusive and/or Exclusive. *Pacific Journal of Theology* 17(1997): 7-23.

Soronakadavu 2003. The Traditional Role of Fijian Women With Reference to Christian Justice. In *Weavings: Women Doing Theology in Oceania*. Johnson, L. and J. Alleluia Felemoni-Tofaeono (eds): 161-164. Suva: Weavers, South Pacific Association of Theological Schools and Institute of Pacific Studies, University of the South Pacific.

—— 2000. Ecumenism in Oceania. *Pacific Journal of Theology* II(24): 88-106.

Sovaki, M. 2003. Paradise: Turmoil and Rebirth. In *Weavings: Women Doing Theology in Oceania*. Johnson, L. and J. Alleluia Felemoni-Tofaeono (eds): 181-182. Suva: Weavers, South Pacific Association of Theological Schools and Institute of Pacific Studies, University of the South Pacific.

Spate, O.H.K. 1959. *The Fijian People: Economic Problems and Prospects*. Legislative Council of Fiji, Council paper no. 13 of 1959. Suva: Government Press.

Spencer, D.M. 1941. *Disease, Religion and Society in the Fiji Islands.* Monographs of the American Ethnological Society 2. Seattle and London: University of Washington Press.

Spencer, N. 2009. *Darwin and God*. London: SPCK.

St John's Training Centre 1988. *The Love of God Among Us: The Easter Story.* Illustrations by Robert Park, Volunteers for Mission, Episcopal Church USA. Suva: The Anglican Diocese of Polynesia.

—— 1989. *MANA: The Resurrection and Pentecost*. Illustrations by Robert Park, Volunteers for Mission, Episcopal Church USA. Suva: The Anglican Diocese of Polynesia.

Stewart, P.J. and A. Strathern 2000. Religious Change in the Highlands of Papua New Guinea. *Journal of Ritual Studies* 14(2): 28-33.

—— 2001. Comment to Douglas. *Current Anthropology* 42(5) December: 640.

—— 2002. *Remaking the World: Myth, Mining, and Ritual Change among the Duna of Papua New Guinea*. Washington and London: Smithsonian Institution Press.

Stewart, P.J. and A. Strathern (eds) 2000. *Identity Work: Constructing Pacific Lives*. Pittsburgh: University of Pittsburgh Press.

—— 2001. Charismatic and Pentecostal Christianity in Oceania. *Journal of Ritual Studies* 15(2).

—— 2008. *Exchange and Sacrifice*. Carolina Academic Press.

Strathern, A. 1971. *The Rope of Moka: Big-Men and Ceremonial Exchange in Mount Hagen, New Guinea*. Cambridge: Cambridge University Press.

—— 1981. Death as Exchange: Two Melanesian Cases. In *Mortality and Immortality: the Anthropology and Archaeology of Death*, Humphreys, S.C. and H. King (eds): 205-223. London: Academic Press.

—— 1996. *Body Thoughts*. Ann Arbor: University of Michigan Press.

Strathern, A. and P.J. Stewart 2000. *Arrow Talk: Transaction, Transition, and Contradiction in New Guinea Highlands History*. Kent, Ohio and London: The Kent State University Press.

—— 2004. *Empowering the Past, Confronting the Future: the Duna People of Papua New Guinea*. New York: Palgrave Macmillan.

—— 2009. History, Conversion and Politics. In *Religious and Ritual Change – Cosmologies and Histories*, Stewart, P.J. and A. Strathern (eds): 309-328. Durham, North Carolina: Carolina Academic Press.

Strathern, M. 1988. *The Gender of the Gift: Problems with Women and Problems with Society in Melanesia*. Berkeley: University of California Press.

Stritecky, J.M. 2001. Israel, America, and the Ancestors: Narratives of Spiritual Warfare in a Pentecostal Denomination in Solomon Islands. *Journal of Ritual Studies* 15(2): 62-77.

Subramani 1995. *Altering Imagination*. Suva: Fiji Writer's Assocation, University of the South Pacific.

Suguta, A. 1986. The Dilemma of Tradition. In *Fijians in Town*, Griffin, C. and M. Monsell–Davis (eds): 185-189. Suva: Institute of Pacific Studies, University of the South Pacific.

Sukuna, Ratu Sir Lala 1983. *Fiji: The Three Legged Stool*, Deryck Scarr (ed.). London: Macmillan Education.

Sun 2001. Reconciliation – A Conversion Of Mind and Heart. By Dolores Prasad, 6 October: 20-21.

—— And Justice For All. By Archbishop Petero Mataca, RC Church, 4 November: 8.

The Sunday Post 2003. One for Bonnke, 21 September: 3.

—— Bonnke Wields Healing Power and Glory, 21 September: 2.

—— Bonnke's Fiery Crusade, by Eliki Nukutabu, 21 September: 4.

—— The Bonnke Crusade, 28 September: 6.

—— The Bonnke Crusade. By Laisa Levula Letter to the Editor, 28 September: 6.

—— Navatusila – An Apology. By Niko Rabuku. 23 November: 10-13.

The Sunday Times 2003. Call for Religious State under Fire. By Ana Niumataiwalu, 24 August: 2

—— Love thy Neighbour. By Ashneel Sudhakar. Letter to the Editor, 31 August: 6.

—— Thomas Baker. By Reverend Dr Andrew Thornley, Letter to the Editor, 23 November: 6.

—— That 'Common' Something. Editorial. 10 October: 6.

Swain, T. and G. Trompf 1995. *The Religions of Oceania*. London and New York: Routledge.

Talapusi, F. 1995. The Future of Theology in the Pacific. *Pacific Journal of Theology* 13(1995): 44.

Tapu-Qilio, F. 2003. Singing the Lord's Song in a Strange Land: The Theological Quest of Young Exiles of the Pacific. In *Weavings: Women Doing Theology in Oceania*, Suva. Johnson, L. and J. Alleluia Felemoni-Tofaeono (eds): 175-180. Weavers, South Pacific Association of Theological Schools and Institute of Pacific Studies, University of the South Pacific.

Taylor, D. 1985. Theological Thoughts about Evil. In *The Anthropology of Evil*. Parkin, D. (ed): 26-41. Oxford: Basil Blackwell.

Teaiwa, T. 2000. An Analysis of the Current Political Crisis in Fiji. 22/5/2000. *Fijilive* online (http://fijilive.net/coup/news).

Telban, B. 2009. A Struggle with Spirits: Hierarchy, rituals and charismatic Movement in a Sepik Community. In *Religious and Ritual Change – Cosmologies and Histories*. Stewart, P.J. and A. Strathern (eds): 133-158. Durham, North Carolina: Carolina Academic Press.

Thamen, K.H. 1980. *You, the Choice of my Parents: Poems by Konai Helu Thaman*. Suva: Mana Publications.

—— 1981. *Langakali: Poems by Konai Helu Thamen*. Suva: Mana Publications.

—— 1987. *Hingano: Selected Poems 1966-1986*. Suva: Mana Publications.

—— 1993. *Kakala*. Suva: Mana Publications.

—— 1997. Letter to the Colonel. In *With Heart and Nerve and Sinew: Post-Coup Writing from Fiji*, Griffen, A. (ed.): 227-228. Suva: Christmas Club.

—— 2000. Of Daffodils and Heilala: Understanding (Cultural) Context in Pacific Literature. In *Navigating Islands and Continents: Conversations and Contestations in and Around the Pacific*. C. Franklin (ed). Honolulu: University of Hawaii and East-West Center.

The Holy Bible. The New Revised Standard Version: Catholic Edition. 1993 and 1989.

Theology and Science. 2008. Darwin's Gift to Science and Religion: Commentaries and Responses. 6(2): 179-196.

Thomas, L. 2001. *A Race for Rights*. A documentary film directed by Larry Thomas.

Thomas, N. 1989a. The Force of Ethnology: Origins and Significance of the Melanesia/Polynesia Division. *Current Anthropology* 30(1): 27-41.

—— 1989b. On the Melanesia/Polynesia Division: Reply to Comments. *Current Anthropology* 30(2): 211-213.

—— 1990a. Sanitation and Seeing: The Creation of State Power in Early Colonial Fiji. *Comparative Studies in Society and History* 32(1): 149-217

—— 1990b. Regional Politics, Ethnicity, and Custom in Fiji. *The Contemporary Pacific* 2(1) Spring: 131-146.

—— 1991. *Entangled Objects: Exchange, Material Culture, and Colonialism in the Pacific*. Cambridge Massachusetts and London: Harvard University Press.

—— 1992a. Substantivization and Anthropological Discourse: the Transformation of Practices into Institutions in Neotraditional Pacific Societies. In *History and*

Tradition in Melanesian Anthropology. Carrier, J.G. (ed): 64-85. Berkley: University of California Press.

—— 1992b. The Inversion of Tradition. *American Ethnologist* 19: 213-232.

—— 1992c. Contrasts in Marriage and Identity in Western Fiji. *Oceania* 62: 317-329.

—— 1993. Beggars can be Choosers. *American Ethnologist* 20(4): 868-876.

—— 1995. *Oceanic Art.* London: Thames and Hudson.

Thomas, N., H. Guest and M. Dettelbach 1996. *Observations Made During a Voyage Round the World: Johann Reinhold Forster.* Honolulu: University of Hawaii Press.

Thomson, B. 1895 The Kalou-vu (ancestor gods) of the Fijians. *JRAI* XXIV: 340-359.

—— 1968 [1908]. *Fijians: A Study of the Decay of Custom.* London: Dawsons of Pall Mall.

Thompson, L. 1940. *Fijian Frontier: Studies of the Pacific no. 4.* San Franscisco, New York, Honolulu: American Council, Institute of Pacific Relations.

Thornley, A.W. 1979. Fijian Methodism, 1874-1945: the Emergence of a National Church. PhD thesis, Australian National University.

—— 1996a. Fijians in the Methodist Ministry: the First Hundred Years, 1848-1945. In *Mai kea ki vei? Stories of Methodism in Fiji and Rotuma.* Thornley, A. and Tauga Vualono (eds): 33-49. Proceedings of the Fiji Methodist History Conference, Davuilevu 10-13 October 1995. Suva: Fiji Methodist Church.

—— 1996b. Cross over the Islands: Historical articles on Methodism and other Christian Denominations in Fiji. A compilation of articles written for the Fiji Times, 1994-96. Photocopied by kind permission of the author.

—— 2000a. *The Inheritance of Hope – John Hunt: Apostle of Fiji. Nai Votavota Ni nuinui – Ko Joni Oniti: Na Apostolo Ki Na Kawa Taukei.* Translated into Fijian by Tauga Vulaono. Suva: Institute of Pacific Studies, USP.

—— 2000b. Conveying Text in Context: Bilingual History. Paper presented at Pacific History Association Millennium conference, Australian National University, June 2000.

—— 2002. *Exodus of the I Taukei: The Wesleyan Church in Fiji 1848-74. Na Lako Yani ni Kawa I Taukei.* Suva: Institute of Pacific Studies.

—— 2005a. *A Shaking of the Land: William Cross and the Origins of Christianity in Fiji. Ko Wiliame Korosi kei na I Tekitekivu ni Lotu Vakarisito e Viti.* Suva: Institute of Pacific Studies.

—— 2005b. Through a Glass Darkly: Ownership of Fijian Methodism, 1850-80. In *Vision and Reality in Pacific Religion. Essays in Honour of Neil Gunson,* Herda, P., M. Reilly and D. Hilliard (eds): 132-153. Christchurch: Macmillan Brown Centre for Pacific Studies, University of Canterbury New Zealand and Canberra Pandanus Books, Research School of Pacific and Asian Studies, The Australian National University.

——Thornley, A. and T. Vulaono (eds) 1996. *Mai kea ki vei? Stories of Methodism in Fiji and Rotuma.* Proceedings of the Fiji Methodist History Conference, Davuilevu 10-13 October 1995. Suva: Fiji Methodist Church.

Tippett, A.R. 1955. Anthropological Research and the Fijian People. *International Review of Missions* 44: 212-219.

—— 1968. *Fijian Material Culture: A Study of Cultural Context, Function, and Change.* Honolulu: Bishop Museum Press.

—— 1980. *Oral Tradition and Ethnohistory: The Transmission of Information and Social Values in Early Christian Fiji 1835-1905.* Canberra: St Marks.

Tischner, H. (ed)1984. Theodor Kleinschmidt's Notes on the Hill Tribes of Viti Levu, 1877-1878. Translated by Stefanie Waine. In *Domodomo, Fiji Museum Quarterly* II(4) December: 146-191.

Tofaeono, A. 2000. *Eco-theology: Aiga – the Household of a Life: aœ Perspective from the Living Myths of Samoa.* Erlangen: Erlangen Verlag für Mission und Ökumene.

Toganivalu, D. 1917. Ai Yau kei nai Yaya Vakaviti (Fijian Property and Gear). *Transactions of the Fijian Society*: 1-24.

Tomlinson, M. 2002 . Sacred Soil in Kadavu, Fiji. *Oceania* 72(4): 237-257.

—— 2004. Perpetual Lament: Kava-drinking, Christianity and Sensations of Historical Decline in Fiji. *Journal of the Royal Anthropological Institute* 10(3): 653-673.

—— 2006. The Limits of Meaning in Fijian Methodist Sermons. In *The Limits of Meaning: Case Studies in the Anthropology of Christianity.* Engelke, Matthew and M. Tomlinson (eds): 129-146. New York and Oxford: Berghahn Books.

—— 2009 *In God's Image: the Metaculture of Christianity in Fiji.* Berkeley: University of California Press.

Tomlinson, M. and M. Engelke 2006. Meaning, Anthropology, Christianity. *The Limits of Meaning: Case Studies in the Anthropology of Christianity.* Engelke, Matthew and Matt Tomlinson (eds): 1-37. New York and Oxford: Berghahn Books.

Tonkinson, R. 2000. 'Tradition' in Oceania, and Its Relevance in a Fourth World Context (Australia). *Folk: Journal of the Danish Ethnographic Society* 42: 169-195.

Toren, C. 1988. Making the Present, Revealing the Past : the Mutability and Continuity of Tradition as Process 23(4): 696-717.

—— 1990. Making Sense of Hierarchy: Cognition as Social Process in Fiji. London: London School of Economics.

—— 1994. The Drinker as Chief or Rebel: Kava and Alcohol in Fiji. In McDonald M. (ed) *Gender, Drink and Drugs*: 153-173. Oxford: Berg.

—— 1995a. Seeing the Ancestral Sites: Transformations in Fijian Notions of Land. In Hirsch, E. and M. O'Hanlon (eds) *The Anthropology of Landscape*: 163-183. Oxford: Oxford University Press.

—— 1995b. Cosmogenic Aspects of Desire and Compassion in Fiji. In *Cosmology and Society in Oceania.* de Coppet, D. and A. Iteanu (eds). Oxford: Berg.

—— 2004. Becoming a Christian in Fiji: an Ethnographic Study of Ontogeny. *JRAI* 10(1): 221-240.

—— 2006. The Effectiveness of Ritual. In *The Anthropology of Christianity.* Cannell, F. (ed): 185-210. Durham NC: Duke University Press.

Trask, H.K. 1991. Natives and Anthropologists: The Colonial Struggle. Dialogue. *The Contemporary Pacific* Spring: 159-167.

Trompf, G. 1991. *Melanesian Religion.* Cambridge: Cambridge University Press.

——1994. *Payback: The Logic of Retribution in Melanesian Religions.* Cambridge: Cambridge University Press.

—— 1995. Oceania. In *The Religions of Oceania*, T. Swain and G. Trompf. London and New York: Routledge.

—— 2001. Comment to Douglas. In *Current Anthropology* 42(5) December: 640.

Trnka, S. (ed) 2002. Ethnographies of the May 2000 Fiji Coup. In Special Issue of *Pacific Studies* 25(4).

Trnka, S. 2008. *State of Suffering: Political Violence and Community Survival in Fiji.* New York: Cornell University Press.

Tugaue, A. 1994. Dust of the Ground and the Breath of God: A Theological Exploration into the Relation of the Land and the Spirit of God. MTh thesis, Pacific Theological College 1994.

Turner, J.W. 1995. Substance, Symbol and Practice: the Power of Kava in Fijian Society. *Canberra Anthropology* 18(1 and 2). Special Volume, 'The Power of Kava'. Canberra: Australian National University.

Turner, T. 1980. The Social Skin. In *Not Work Alone: A Cross-Cultural View of Acitivites Superfluous to Survival.* Jeremy Cherfas and Roger Lewin (eds) Beverley Hills, CA: Sage.

Tutaka Online 2009. Breaking the Cycle of Coups in Fiji. In *The Quarterly Newsletter of the Citizens' Constitutional Forum Ltd* 3(3) July: 1. www.ccf. org.fj.

Tuwere, I.S. 1992. Making Sense of Vanua (land) in the Fijian Context: a Theological Exploration. Doctor of Theology thesis. Melbourne School of Divinity.

—— 1994. Mana and the Fijian Sense of Place: A Theological Reflection. *South Pacific Journal of Mission Studies* July 1994: 3-15.

——1997a. The Christian Community Within the Human Community. ChristianState Question. Unpublished draft statement proposed to the Standing Committee of the Methodist Church in Fiji and Rotuma. Christian State Working Committee, Suva, 18 June 1997.

—— 1997b. The Church-State Relation in Fiji. In *Fiji in Transition, Research Papers of the Fiji Constitution Review Commission Vol.1.* Lal, B.V. and Tomasi R. Vakatora: 43-52. Suva: School of Social and Economic Development, University of the South Pacific.

—— 1998. *Na Were-Kalou kei na Tamata.* Suva: Methodist Church in Fiji and Rotuma.

—— 2001. Statement of the Methodist Church in Fiji and Rotuma on the Armed Seizure of Government. In *COUP: Reflections on the Political Crisis in Fiji*. Lal, Brij V. and Michael Pretes (eds): 168-173. Canberra: Pandanus Books, RSPAS, University of Australia.

—— 2002a. *Vanua: Towards a Fijian Theology of Place*. Suva: Institute of Pacific Studies, University of the South Pacific and Auckland: College of St John the Evangelist.

—— 2002b. What is Contextual Theology – A View from Oceania. *Journal of Pacific Theology* II(27): 7-20.

Uriam, K. 1999. Theology and Practice in the Islands: Christianity and Island Communities in the New Pacific, 1947-1997. PhD thesis, Australian National University.

—— 2005. Doing Theology in the New Pacific. In *Vision and Reality in Pacific Religion. Essays in Honour of Neil Gunson*. Herda, P., M. Reilly and D. Hilliard (eds): 287-311. Christchuch: Macmillan Brown Centre for Pacific Studies, University of Canterbury New Zealand and Canberra: Pandanus Books, Research School of Pacific and Asian Studies, The Australian National University.

Valjavec, F. 1989. Reply to Thomas. *Current Anthropology* 30(1): 38.

Varea, S. n.d. The Vision of Jean Charlot: the murals of Naiserelagi, Ra-Fiji Islands. How successfully have these murals embraced the concept of reconciliation in Fiji? Essay, Fiji Museum archive.

Veitokani ni Lewe ni Vanua Vakarisito n.d. Manifesto of the Veitokani ni Lewe ni Vanua Vakarisito. The Constitution of the Veitokani ni Lewe ni Vanua Vakarisito Party.

Vidal, G. n.d. La Contextualisation de la Théologie Protestante dans le Pacifique depuis Années 60. Paper presented at the workshop, Innovations Religieuses et Dynamiques du Changement Culturel en Océanie Contemporaine, Paris 29-31 May 2008. Sponsored by GSRL, Réseau Asie and Iris.

Vusoniwailala, L. 1986. Communication, Social Identity and the Rising Cost of Fijian Communalism. In *Fijians in Town*, Griffin, C. and M. Monsell-Davis (eds): 166-180. Suva: Institute of Pacific Studies, University of the South Pacific.

Wagner, R. 1975. *The Invention of Culture*. Chicago: Chicago University Press.

Ward, R.G. 1969. Land Use and Land Alienation in Fiji to 1885. *Journal of Pacific History* 4: 3-25.

—— 1995a. Land, Law and Custom: Diverging Realities in Fiji. In *Land, Custom and Practice in the South Pacific*. Ward, R.G. and E. Kingdon (eds). Cambridge: Cambridge University Press.

—— 1995b. Land in Fiji. A Paper Prepared for the Fiji Constitutional Review Commission, 1995. Ms.

—— 1997. Land Tenure: the Gap between Law, Customs and Practice. In Sociocultural Issues and Economic Development in the Pacific Islands. *Pacific*

Studies Series II: 39-69. Roundtable Proceedings 19-20 November 1996, Suva, Fiji.

—— 1999. Widening Worlds, Shrinking Worlds? The Reshaping of Oceania. Pacific Distinguished Lecture 1999, Centre for the Contemporary Pacific, RSPAS, Australian National University.

Waterhourse, J. 1997 [1866]. *The King and People of Fiji*. Reprint. Auckland: Pasifika Press.

Weiner, A. 1976. *Women of Value, Men of Renown: New Perspectives in Trobriand Exchange*. Austin and London: University of Texas Press.

—— 1980. Reproduction: a Replacement for Reciprocity. *American Anthropologist* 7(1): 71-85.

—— 1985. Inalienable Wealth. In *American Ethnologist* 12: 210-227.

—— 1992. *Inalienable Possessions: The Paradox of Keeping-While-Giving*. Berkeley and Los Angeles: University of California Press.

Weir, C. 2000a. 'The Gospel Came ... Fighting is Ceasing Amongst Us': Methodist Representations of Violence in Fiji and New Britain, 1830-1930. In *Reflections on Violence in Melanesia*. Dinnen, S. and A. Ley (eds), Canberra: Hawkins Press and Asia Pacific Press.

—— 2000b. The Churches in Solomon Islands and Fiji: Responses to the Crises of 2000. *Development Bulletin*, November 2000: 49-53.

Wendt, A. 1976. *Inside Us the Dead: Poems 1961 to 1974*. Auckland: Longman Paul.

White, G.M. 1991. *Identity Through History: Living Stories in a Solomon Islands Society*. Cambridge: Cambridge University Press.

Wilde, C. 1998. Review of Martha Kaplan, Neither Cargo nor Cult: Ritual Politics and the Colonial Imagination in Fiji. *Oceania* 69: 133-134.

Wilford, J.N. 1990. Anthropology Seen as Father of Maori Lore. *The New York Times*, 20 February: B5 and B8.

Williams, T. 1982 [1858]. *Fiji and the Fijians Vol. 1: The Islands and their Inhabitants*. Stringer Rowe, G. (ed) Reprint. Suva: Fiji Museum.

Wolf, E. 1982. *Europe and the People Without History*. Berkeley: University of California Press.

World Council of Churches 2006. *Participating in God's Mission of Reconciliation: A Resource for Churches in Situations of Conflict*. Faith and Order Paper 201. Geneva: World Council of Churches.

Yabaki, A. 2004. Religion in the Public Sphere: Challenges and Opportunities. Presentation at an International Academy for Freedom of Religion and Belief symposium on 'Internal Law and Religion', Brigham Young University 3-6 October.

—— 2005. Fiji Needs National Reconciliation, but not this Bill. Press Release, NGO Coalition on Human Rights, 24 May.

—— 2006. Religion in the Public Sphere: Challenges and Opportunities. *Pacific Journal of Theology* II(35): 5-16.

Young, M. 1995. Commemorating Missionary Heroes: Local Christianity and Narratives of Nationalism. In *Narratives of Nation in the South Pacific.* Otto, T. and N. Thomas (eds). Amsterdam: Harwood Academic Publishers.

Zehner, E. 2007. Comment to Robbins. *Current Anthropology* 48(1) February 2007: 28-29.

Appendix I
Fiji

Fiji is an archipelago of some 300 islands, located in the south-west Pacific Ocean. Scattered over an area of 709,660 square kilometres, 97 per cent of which is water, the Fiji islands comprise a total land area of 18,272 square kilometres. Only about 100 of the islands are inhabited, and approximately 70 per cent of the population lives on the main island of Vitilevu, an area of 10,388 square kilometres. Fiji's population is 837,271 (*2007 Census*, Fiji Islands Bureau of Statistics: 2008). Indigenous Fijians comprise 51 per cent of the population, owning 83 per cent of the land (recent transfers of Crown/state land to Fijian ownership probably bring this figure to 90 per cent). Indo-Fijians make up 44 per cent and 'Others' 5 per cent of the population (Part Europeans, Rotumans and Other Pacific Islanders make up three-quarters of this percentage).

The Fijian language is one of the languages within the Oceanic subgroup of the vast Austronesian family (formerly called 'Malayo-Polynesian'), which stretches two-thirds of the way around the tropical world from Madagascar through south-east Asia across the Pacific to Easter Island (cf Pawley 1999: 181-194). Standard Fijian is the official language, also known as Bauan, the language of the paramount chiefly power base of Bau during the 19th Century. It became the standardised language for communication on account of missionary and colonial government acceptance of Bauan political supremacy at the time (France 1969: 7; and Clammer 1976). It is the official dialect used in the media, in church and in literature. The Indo-Fijian community primarily speaks Fiji Hindi, but children are taught English from their first year at school.

Doing research in rural Nadrogā gave me certain methodological problems, as although most villagers had some understanding of Standard Fijian, no one outside Nadrogā understands the Nadrogā language. Finding someone from Nadrogā in Suva, who was able to translate and transcribe the tapes of church services I had recorded proved quite difficult. The language is spoken by relatively few people – approximately 5,000 people in some 20 villages, including Indo-Fijians in the area, as well as about 5,000 Nadrogā emigrants (Geraghty 1983: 278-287 and 290-291 in Geraghty n.d.). There is no literature in the Nadrogā language.

Tables: Population and Religious Affiliation

Population distribution by ethnic group

Ethnic Groups	1986	1996		2007
		Numbers	**Percentage**	
Total	715,375	775,077	100%	837,271
Fijian	329,305	393,575	50.8%	475,739
Indian	348,704	338,818	43.7%	313,798
Part European	10,297	11,685	1.5%	10,771
Rotuman*	8,652	9,727	1.2%	Categorised within
Other Pacific Islanders*	8,627	10,463	1.3%	All others
Chinese	4,784	4,939	0.6%	4,704
European	4,196	3,103	0.4%	2,953
All Others	810	2,767	0.4%	29,306

Note: *The Fiji Islands Population Profile of 1999 differentiates in figures from the 1986 and 1987 census between 'Rotumans', 'Other Pacific Islanders' and 'All Others'. In the figures from the 2007 census published by the Fiji Islands Bureau of Statistics in 2009 'Rotumans' and 'Other Pacific Islanders' are classified within the group 'All Others'.

Religious affiliation

Religious Groups	1996 Numbers	1996 Percentage	2007 Numbers
Total	**775,077**	**100%**	**837,271**
Christians	449,482	58%	539,553
Anglicans	6,325	0.8%	6,319
Assemblies of God	31,072	4.0%	47,791
Catholic	69,320	8.9%	76,465
Methodist	280,628	36.2%	289,900
7th Day Adventist	22,187	2.9%	32,316
Other Christian	39,950	5.2%	86,672
Hindu	261,097	33.7%	233,414
Sikh	3,076	0.4%	2,540
Muslim	54,323	7.0%	52,505
Other Religion	1,967	0.2%	2,181
No Religion	5,132	0.7%	7,078

Source: Fiji Islands Population Profile 1999: 65, Fiji Islands Bureau of Statistics 2009.

Appendix III
Glossary

Entries in *italics* are in Standard Fijian, entries in <u>*underlined italics*</u> are in Nadrogā, entries in *ITALIC CAPITALS* are in other Pacific Island languages.

bili ni mua	final *tabua* presentation in a Nadrogā funeral, acknowledging the finalisation of exchanges
bilo	drinking vessel; polished half shell of a coconut, used to stir and serve yaqona.
<u>*bito*</u>, *tokatoka*	lineage group
bogitini	Tenth Night [after the death],
bogidrau	Hundredth Night [after the death],
bogiva	Fourth Night [after the death],
bogilima	Fifth Night [after the death], in Nadrogā replaces the Eastern Fijian *bogiva*
bula	life, health; also meaning 'hello'
bula vakavuravura	worldly life/living, as opposed to spiritual
ibulubulu	burial place, that which buries it; the rite through which people or clans can reconcile (bury) an injury
bure, were	traditional house with woven walls and thatched roof, in pre-Christian times the term for men's house
bure kalou	pre-Christian god-house
burua	Eastern Fijian post-burial feast and redistribution of valuables
<u>*cālevu*</u>	path, pathway, route (sala); also the term for particular relations of allegiance between villages in western Vitilevu
<u>*cālevu ni veiluveni*</u>	lit. paths of parent/children relations, term for particular relations between families in different villages in western Vitilevu
icibaciba	jumping off point at a river or in the sea for the dead on the path to the afterworld
cobo	ritual, resonant clap made with cupped hands prior to accepting a *bilo* of kava
icōcō	large, thickly woven plain mat
<u>*covacova*</u>	shelter
<u>*idarodaro*</u> (*idavodavo, SF*)	'sleeping mat', also edged with coloured fringe
<u>*drakwata*</u>	mortuary compensation to maternal kin
<u>*hila na hēhē, dua na sāsā*</u>	measuring entity of ten mats

icake	above, also used in terms of hierarchically classifying space and place, such as in houses or villages
iō, ibe	mat
ira	below, also used in terms of hierarchically classifying space and place, such as in houses or villages
ivāvivi, ivīvivi	a roll of mats
holi ni lewa	give authority to
juberi ni ulu, tuberi ni ulu	the post-burial exchange and redistribution of valuables given during the *vura*
juvavatu ni bulubulu,	
tuvavatu ni bulubulu	to put stones round the grave
kalouca	lit. evil spirit
kalou vu	lit- root gods, deified ancestors
kava	see *yaqona*
kava kavanua, vakavanua	the way of the land
kerekere	to ask, make a request
koi cālevu	lit. paths of relations
kōvana, vasu	clan of the mother, the most honoured guests of a Nadrogā funeral, who receive almost all valuables presented
lobi ni iō	to fold the mats, rite at the end of a funeral in Nadrogā in which the women of the *kōvana* remove and take home with them the mats presented and laid one on top of each other in the 'house of death' during the funeral.
loloma	love, loving trust, compassion; God's grace
loma ni vale	centre of the house
loqi	hierarchically 'highest' or most private part of a Fijian house; location of sleeping quarters
loqi tabu	sanctuary of a church
lotu	church, Christianity, religion, to convert, faith'
lotu tagitagi	lit. Church of tears, of crying, Pentecostal Church
lotu qiriqiri	lit. Church of the guitar, Pentecostal Church
madua	ashamed, shy, embarrassed, shame
magimagi	plaited coconut fibre string (tied to *tānoa* with cowrie shell at the end)
magisi	feast
mana	spiritual power or efficacy
masi	barkcloth
matakarawa ni yau	welcoming round of kava to 'welcome the valuables'
matanigasau	rite of reconciliation
matanitu	chiefly governance, state
mataqwali, mataqali	clan

matau ni lolovo	tabua presentation by the 'owners of the dead' to formerly request the *kōvana* to dig the grave.
māzi ni vavi, madi ni vavi	When the kovana have left the 'owners of the dead' prepare a feast of food and *yaqona* called *mazi ni vavi* to distribute the valuables brought by the *kōvana*
MOANA	the sea in Tongan and other Polynesian languages
mōmō	mother's brother
NGATU	large tapa (Tongan)
niju, vu	a spirit
PALAGI	in Samoan and other Polynesian languages, foreigner, outsider, *valagi* in Standard Fijian
qwele, qele	soil
ravuniqweleqwele	lit. something you put on the ground – the mats that would line the grave, brought by members of the *kōvana*
ruku	lit. to walk under, a rite in which mourners ritually pass twice under the coffin
sala ni yalo	soul paths which the dead travel along to the afterworld
sautu	prosperity and abundance
sevusevu	presentation given by a visitor and ceremonial drinking of kava to welcome a visitor
sili i wai	presentation of *sulu, waiwai* (oil) and sweets from the
weka ni mase	women of the village to the women of the *kōvana* after the burial.
sisi, *salusalu*	garland
isoro	atonement /reconciliation
sulu	ankle-length wrap-around length of material
sulu vakataga	formal, tailor-made *sulu* for men
tabu	lit. forbidden; also meaning sacred or holy, such as in *na Vola Tabu*, the Holy Bible (lit. the forbidden book)
tabua	whale's tooth
tabua icegu	lit. breath, the name of particular tabua used in Nadrogā funerals
tabua kali	lit. pillow, name of particular *tabua* used in Nadrogā funerals
talanoa	stories, storytelling
talatala	Methodist minister
tānoa	kava mixing bowl, usually made of wood, in Nadrogā often made of clay
TA'OVALA	Tongan formal attire, worn by both women and men, is a soft, very finely woven mat worn round the waist and tied round the middle with a string of plaited pandanus.

tapa	Tongan term for barkcloth, used in esp. Eastern Fiji
tatau	leave-taking of a person in mortuary rites in Nadrogā: 5 *tabua* presentations the *tarai ni yaqona*, made by the family of the departed to the *kōvana*, to give the body to them.

- the *tatau ni loju*, made by the family to the minister after the church service, to request the deceased's taking leave of the church and its responsibilities.
- the *tatau ni vanua*, made by the family to the elders of the *vanua*, to request the deceased's taking leaving of the clan.
- the *tatau ni were*, made by Tai's household to the *kōvana* to request future protection or acknowledgement of the deceased's children and grandchildren by the *kōvana*. (Although considered an integral part of a Nadrogā funeral, this presentation was not made on this occasion).
- the *vadaroi ni yago*, made by the lineage group to the *kōvana*, giving their consent for the body to be buried – whale's tooth mortuary presentation used in Nadrogā nowadays but is clearly a borrowed concept from Eastern Fiji (Geraghty pers comm. 2010)

itaukei ni mase	lit. 'owners of death'
itaukei ni vanua	lit. joint owners of the land who share a common descent
tevoro	devil, spirit
itovo vaviti, *vakavanua*	lit. the way of the land; Fijian tradition and custom
ulu	*headstone of a grave (in Eastern Fiji)*
ulu	head (of a person)
ulu	portion of wealth allotted to the kin of the mother of the deceased, kin of mother's mother etc. Different *vanua* have different *juva ulu*
imatai ni **ulu**	the first, *ulu* meaning first or top, but also, in Nadrogā, head, and in other places in Fiji, headstone. Before the relatively recent adoption of the term *kōvana* into the Nadrogā language, it may possibly have been referred to as *matai ni ulu* (lit. creator of head, or first head).
itaukei ni **ulu**	(lit. owners of the head) – the maternal relatives of the dead
kōvana	*matai ni* **ulu**, first *ulu*, *ulu* being the name of the pile of yams which will be presented. This group belongs to the clan (*mataqwali*) of the mother (M) of the departed and are the direct descendants of the mother's brother.
Karua ni **ulu** (second *ulu*)	the clan of the father's mother (FM) of the departed.

*Katolu ni **ulu*** (third *ulu*)	this is the clan of the father's father's mother (FFM) of the departed.
uro	(slang) handsome, sweet, sexy
vābasi	mat (slightly smaller, fringed mat)
vajukolo, *vatukolo*	partitioning curtain, usually of *masi*
vakarokoroko	respect
vakataraisulu	ceremony of 'lifting of the mourning' 100 nights after a death, involving the presentation of enormous lengths of *tapa* and material, tied together, wound round members of the mother's side and ritually removed and presented to the *vasu,* together with other valuables.
vakatawa	catechist
vakatevoro	lit. the way of the devil; sorcery
vabasi mats	medium-sized fringed mats
vāvinavinā, *vavinavinaka*	presentation of kava roots to thank for hospitality
vakaviti	lit. the way of Fiji (Viti)
valagi	foreigner, outsider
vanua	land, chiefdom, custom, traditional practice
vanua tabu	lit. forbidden land
vasu	relationship between the children, especially the sons, of a woman and her brother.
veitokoni	caring and sharing
veiwekani	kin relations
vikila (*mōmō*)	more generally, all males one generation older on the mother's side, and *mōmō* in parts of eastern Fiji, of the deceased and in his stead, his direct male descendants
na ivahobu	lit. the taking down of the body. *Tabua* mortuary presentation. This is used in Nadrogā nowadays but is clearly a borrowed concept from Eastern Fiji (Geraghty pers comm. 2010).
vunisipi	large embroidered and fringed mat
vura (*reguregu*)	'a present of [and the presentation of] *tabua* made to male friends of a deceased person, on which occasion the visitors kiss the corpse; to the woman a presentation of mats, cloth etc. is made, and their personal attendance at the house where the body awaits burial is required (Capell 1991: 172)
werenimase, *valenimate*	house of death
iyatoyato, ilakolako	group of mourners
yaqona	kava, piper methysticum plant.
iyau ni vanua	valuables of the land, i.e. exchange valuables such as whales teeth, mats, barkcloth

yavu	foundation, house mound
yavusa	confederation of chiefdoms

Appendix IV

Acronyms

ACCF	Association of Christian Churches in Fiji
ALTA	Agricultural Landowner and Tenants Act
AOG	Assemblies of God
ANU	Australian National University
BLV	*Bose Levu Vakaturaga*, Great Council of Chiefs
CCF	Citizens' Constitutional Forum
CM	Society of St Vincent
CMF	Christian Mission Fellowship
CSsR	Redemptorist order
COG	Church of God
DP	Daily Post
ECREA	Ecumenical Centre for Research, Education and Advocacy
FCC	Fiji Council of Churches
FCRC	Fiji Constitution Review Commission
FT	Fiji Times
GCC	Great Council of Chiefs
IB	Islands Business
IFSF	Interfaith Search Fiji
JPSC	Joint Parliamentary Selection Committee
LDS	The Church of Jesus Christ of Latter Day Saints (the Mormon Church)
MCF	The Methodist Church in Fiji and Rotuma
MSC	Missionary of the Sacred Heart (Missionaire Sacre Coeur)
NRSV	New Revised Standard Version (Bible translation)
OSA	Order of St Augustin
PCC	Pacific Conference of Churches
PRS	Pacific Regional Seminary
PTC	Pacific Theological College
RC	Roman Catholic
RCC	Roman Catholic Church
SDA	Seventh Day Adventist Church
SJ	Society of Jesus
SM	Society of Mary
SMSM	Missionary Sisters of the Society of Mary
SOLN	Society of our Lady of Nazareth
SPATS	South Pacific Association of Theological Schools
SSC	Society of Saint Columban

SSM	Society of the Sacred Mission (Anglican Order)
SVT	*Soqosoqo ni Vakavulewa ni Taukei* (lit. Group of Decision Makers for the Indigenous People)
USP	University of the South Pacific
VLV	*Veitokani ni Lewe ni Vanua Vakarisito* – Christian Democratic Alliance Party
WHC	World Harvest Centre

Appendix V
Funeral Exchanges
as Described in Chapter 3

Record of valuables (*iyau*) presented to the 'owners of death' by the *vanua* at *vura* for Tai:

whales teeth (*tabua*):	19
drums of kerosene (*karisini*)	63
kava (*yaqona*)	16.5 kg
barkcloth (*kumi*, large Tongan style)	5
cows (*bulumakau*)	7
pigs (*vuaka*)	1
baskets of cooked taro (*magisi dalo*)	6
rice (*raisi*)	1 x 50kg bag
bread (*madrai*)	12 cartons
flour (*falawa*)	1/2 x 25 kg bag
sugar (*suka*)	1 x 50kg bag

Record of valuables presented to the women of the *kōvana* at *vura* for Tai:

10 large, thickly woven plain mats (*icōcō*)
15 smaller, fringed mats (*vabasi*)
46 finely woven, fringed sleeping mats (*idarodaro*)
8 pieces of brown patterned Tongan-style barkcloth (*kumi*)

In all, 71 mats and 8 pieces of barkcloth plus several lengths of material.

Appendix VI
Interviews Conducted in Suva 1997-2005, Written Testimonies

1997

Adi Kuini Speed	November

1998

Tauga Vulaono	March
Reverend Dr Iliatia Tuwere, President of the Methodist Church	6/4
Reverend Sereima Lomaloma, Holy Trinity Anglican Cathedral	1/6
Pastor Ratu Meli Navuniyasi, Apostolic Churches of Fiji	29/5; 5/6;
	12/6; 23/6;
	26/6/
Father Fereima Cama, Dean, Holy Trinity Anglican Cathedral	19/6; 24/6
Bishop Bryce, Anglican Diocese of Polynesia	22/6
Sister Bertha Hurley SMSM, Interfaith Search Fiji	25/6
Reverend Tevita Banivanua, SPATS	3/7; 23/7
Hardayal Singh, Interfaith Search Fiji	3/7
Reverend Suliasi Kurulo, Every Home for Christ	7/7
Reverend Josateki Koroi, former president of Methodist Church	11/7
Dale Tonawai	16/7
Reverend Jovili Meo, Principal, Pacific Theological College	17/7
Meli Waqa	21/7
Sainimere Niukula	22/7
Sister Emi Oh, Fiji Council of Churches	July
Reverend Mesake Tuima, Methodist Church Chaplain,	
Royal Fiji MilitaryForces	23/7

2002

Pastor Aloete Suguta, AOG	October
Reverend Tevita Banivanua, SPATS	October
Bishop Bryce, Anglican Diocese of Polynesia	1/10

Father John Rae, Lamb of God Christian Covenant Community,
New Zealand Aotearoa 8/10
Roman Catholic Archbishop Petero Mataca 15/10
Reverend Jone Langi, General Secretary MCF 24/10
Pastor Ralph Dunn, First Church, AOG 6/11
Reverend Suliasi Kurulo, Christian Mission Fellowship 13/11
Reverend Dr John Bonato, SM, University of the South Pacific November
Reverend Akuila Yabaki, CCF (no date)

2003

Bruce Yocum, Sword of the Spirit, Ann Arbor, USA 8/7
Father Thomas Mathew Nechikat, OSA 12/8, 21/9
Father Sulio Turagakacivi, Our Lady of Fatima Parish, Nadera 15/8
Reverend Suliasi Kurulo, CMF 22/10

2004

Reverend Suliasi Kurulo, CMF 28/9
Paulo Balei, Columban Mission 29/9
Father Iosefo Tuvere, Sacred Heart RC Cathedral 30/9
Very Reverend Veremo Dovarua, Pacific Regional Seminary 1/10
Paulo Balei, Columban Mission 12/10
Anaseini and Aselemo, Raiwaqa RC parish 14/10
Aisake Casimira, ECREA 15/10
Brother Mika, St Xaviar's RC parish, Ra 21/10
Father John Rae, Lamb of God Christian Covenant Community,
New Zealand Aotearoa 24/10
Clancy, Trinity Broadcasting Network 27/10
Father Beniamino Kaloudau, Vicar-General, RC Diocese of Suva 28/10
Reverend Dr Koru Tiko, PRS 28/10
Father George Ting, Our Lady of Fatima RC parish 28/10
Lusia Tukida, St Agnes RC parish 29/10
Fiona Vamarasi, Assemblies of God Bible School 29/10
Father Seluini 'Akau'ola SM, Marist College 1/11
Reverend Ledua Kacimaiwai, Wesley Church, ACCF 1/11
RC Archbishop Petero Mataca 3/11
Father Seluini 'Akau'ola SM, Marist College 3/11
Sereana Nasome, Wesley Church 4/11
Reverend Poate Mata, Gospel Apostolic Outreach 9/11
Reverend Dr John Bonato SM, University of the South Pacific November

2005

Father Pat Colgan SSC, Pacific Regional Seminary   24/9

Written testimonies

Sent by e-mail in response to questions
Kasanita Seruvatu, Christian Mission Fellowship, 2008 and 2009
Fiona Vamarasi, Assemblies of God, 2009 and 2010

Appendix VII
Main Catholic Charismatic Events Attended 1998-2004

1998

Fiji Catholic Charismatic Renewal Convention, Suva   June

2002

Charismatic Healing Rally, Pius X Church, Raiwaqa   October
Led by Father John Rae, Lamb of God Christian Covenant Community,
New Zealand Aotearoa.

2003

Fiji Catholic Charismatic Renewal Convention, Lautoka   June

Healing Services led by Father Thomas Mathew Nechikat OSA

Sacred Heart Catholic Cathedral, Suva	6 August
St Joseph the Worker Church, Suva	7 August
Holy Trinity Anglican Cathedral, Suva	8 August
St Matthew's Anglican Church, Suva	13 August
Wesley Church, Butt St. (Methodist Church), Suva	14 August
St Joseph the Worker Church, Suva	15 August
St Michael's Church, Nadi	20 August
Tavua Catholic Chapel	21 August
Our Lady of the Immaculate Heart Church, Vatukoula	22 August
Christ the King Church, Ba	22 August
St Peter's Anglican Church, Lautoka	23 August
Misa Puja, St Agnes Church, Suva	23 August
Holy Family Church, Labasa	24 August
St Joseph the Worker Church, Suva	25 August
St Peter's Church, Nakavika, Namosi	26 August
St Peter's Anglican Church, Lautoka	30 August
St Joseph the Worker Church, Suva	2 September
St Joseph the Worker Church, Suva	14 September
St Joseph's Church, Naililili	14 September

Pius X Catholic Church, Raiwaqa, Suva   15 September
Mary of the Immaculate Conception Church, Solevu   22 September

2004

Charismatic Healing Rally, Wesley Church, Butt St.   1 October
Led by Father John Rae,
Lamb of God Christian Covenant Community, New Zealand Aotearoa.

Holy Spirit Workshop, Wesley Church, Butt St.   2 October
Led by Father John Rae, Lamb of God Christian Covenant Community.

Appendix VIII
Interfaith Search Fiji Meetings and Services Attended, Suva 1995-1997

Celebration for Life, National Stadium, Fiji's 25th Anniversary	8/10/95
Sacred Heart Roman Catholic Cathedral, meeting	31/10/95
St. Andrew's Presbyterian Church, meeting	15/11/95
Arya Pratinidhi Sabha Hall, meeting	25/9/96
Senior Citizens' Prayers, Holy Trinity Anglican Cathedral	6/10/96
St. Andrew's Presbyterian Church, meeting	19/3/97
Prayers, 10th commemoration of military coups, Ratu Sukuna Park (cancelled on the day, as Police permission to hold meeting was not granted)	14/5/97
Prayers for the People of Fiji, Sacred Heart Cathedral	13/6/97
Prayers for Constitution Day, Sacred Heart Cathedral	28/7/97
Memorial Service for Princess Diana and Mother Teresa, Sacred Heart Roman Catholic Cathedral	Sept 97

Appendix IX
Seeing and Believing

When I first visited Fiji in 1993 and travelled round the islands, every Fijian I met asked me which Church I belonged to. I had at that time little sense of my own faith and found it somewhat disconcerting to have to answer, time and time again what I felt to be a rather invasive question from strangers I met on buses, at market places and anywhere else. I was baptised and brought up an Anglican, attended Church of England schools, and had a strong faith as a child, although for years I had been a non-communicant, nominal Anglican. However, given the insistence of people enquiring into my faith and the impossibility of evading the question, I decided that in all fairness I could honestly say that I was Anglican, *Lotu Jaji*, even though the degree of my faith could have been described as tepid, and my practice of it as, at best, rusty.

When Catholics heard that I was *Lotu Jaji* their faces broke into warm smiles. They held up the index fingers of their hands close together and explained that our churches were then very close; we had much in common in terms of our faith. While enjoying this sense of familiarity and inclusiveness, these sentiments puzzled me somewhat. Brought up in England in the 1960s I had no sense at all of any closeness between Anglicans and Catholics – indeed quite the contrary. In those days, and up until the cautious warming of relations in recent years, there was still a deep chasm between the two Churches, and little or no co-operation between them.

I later understood these comments in the context of Catholics' belonging to a minority Church (some 9 percent of the population of Fiji are Catholic). By comparison with the Methodist Church in Fiji, Catholics and Anglicans (who make up less than 1 percent of the population) indeed had a much greater mutual affinity – doctrinally and liturgically, and not least also in terms of a marginal position in relation to the dominant Christian discourse. Although I was not aware of it at the time, given the sense of difference between the two Churches that I had grown up with, Anglican liturgy and a good deal of its ritual, depending on how High Church or Anglo-Catholic a parish might be, is very close to that of the Catholic Church.

For two years of my childhood I had attended a Methodist girl's boarding school. I therefore assumed I would easily find myself at home in the Methodist Church in Fiji. The Wesleyan hymns I had loved singing as a child at school and in Church of England services, although sung in Fijian were delightfully familiar. But, to my surprise, apart from this the Methodism I found in Fiji bore little resemblance to the Methodism I had known as a school girl in England.

These early fieldwork experiences and the subsequent reflections they engendered emphasise the points I discuss in the Introduction of the imperative of historical contextuality in studies of Christianity. Christianity is of course never incorporated wholesale into another culture. The ways in which different forms of Christianity develop, and people's experience of particular forms of Christianity, depend on numerous interrelated factors concerning the development of Church missions within particular shifting cultural and historical contexts and, not least, the different characters and approaches of the Christians who influence the course of those histories – clergy as well as lay-people. Although there will obviously always be some enduring qualities, and in some churches these may be more easily discernable than in others, we can never assume that because a particular version of Christianity takes on one form in one culture, it will automatically be the same in another.

During the course of my fieldwork the ritually more expressive Pacific Islands High Church worship practices than I knew from the rural Anglicanism of my childhood drew me back from the margin to the centre of the Anglican fold. While inspired by the Catholic teachings on social justice that were strongly advocated among Catholics in Fiji, by the end of my doctoral research in 1998 I had become a regular church-goer at Holy Trinity Anglican Cathedral in Suva. From then on my faith became central to my life. I returned to Fiji in 2002 to conduct postdoctoral research on Protestant and Catholic charismatic Christianity and on processes of reconciliation and forgiveness. In the course of my research the spirituality and ritual I experienced within Catholicism and its focus on social justice issues eventually resulted in my decision to become a Catholic. I was received into the Catholic Church in Copenhagen in 2005 – half way through my year of teaching anthropology at Pacific Regional Seminary.

That fieldwork will always somehow shape and change the fieldworker goes without saying. And it is logical that my personal spiritual journey, taking place in conjunction with and strongly inspired by my research into Christianity, necessarily seriously influenced the way that research developed and the relations I as a researcher had to those with whom I worked. I view this as an asset, something that has added considerable depth to my research. My relations in the field were strengthened by the mutual ground I shared with Christians, a mutual ground that is difficult to define, yet which clearly gave us a shared framework for communication at a different level than we otherwise would have had. And my personal experience of Christian faith, worship and spirituality has given me a more nuanced and better understanding of other people's faith and worship practices – whether I shared all their particular beliefs and experiences or not.

Index